Perspectives on

Indian History, Historiography, and Philosophy of History

Perspectives on

Indian History, Historiography, and Philosophy of History

G.P. Singh

D.K. Printworld (P) Ltd.
New Delhi

Cataloging in Publication Data — DK

Courtsey: D.K. Agencies (P) Ltd. <docinfo@dkagencies.com>

Singh, G.P. (Girish Prasad), 1942-
Perspectives on Indian history, historiography, and philosophy of history / G.P. Singh.
p. cm.
Articles; previously published.
Includes bibliographical references.
Includes index.
ISBN 13: 9788124604878
ISBN 10: 8124604878

1. India — History. 2. India — Antiquities. 3. India — Historiography. 4. History — Philosophy. I. Title.

DDC 954 22

ISBN 13: 978-81-246-0487-8
ISBN 10: 81-246-0487-8
First published in India in 2009

Published and printed by:
D.K. Printworld (P) Ltd.
Regd. Office: 'Srikunj', F-52, Bali Nagar
Ramesh Nagar Metro Station
New Delhi-110 015
Phones: (011) 2545 3975; 2546 6019; *Fax*: (011) 2546 5926
E-mail: dkprintworld@vsnl.net
Website: www.dkprintworld.com

Preface

INDIA'S is the longest literary tradition in mankind's history that began with *Ṛgveda* composed in the second millennium BCE. These hymns, carefully handed down by word of mouth for generations, were collected and arranged after a millennium. Equal in antiquity are the Purāṇas which, some say, are 108 in number, but 18 are regarded as the principal ones. Its antiquity apart, Indian literary tradition is immense with endless possibilities for research and re-interpretations. Though this vast literature cannot be called historiography by contemporary yardsticks, these time-honoured sources — Vedic Saṁhitās, epics, Purāṇas, etc. — have greatly helped historiographers in building up India's ancient past.

Together with the Hindu scriptures, the Buddhist and Jaina texts as well tell us fascinating stories of development of these religions and their impact on India's history in the first two millennia CE.

This volume is a collection of some of my papers, written during the past three decades on certain aspects of Indian history, historiography, and philosophy of history, and which have appeared in reputed journals and publications. Most of these papers relate to ancient Indian history and culture which has been the main field of my study and research, and these are put together in one volume with the object of making all the material embodied in it easily accessible to the readers.

The papers contained in this book cover varied subjects such as ancient India as depicted in Greek and Assyrian literature; the role of brāhmaṇas in anti-Alexander movement (*c.* 325 BCE); the cultural expansion of the Aryans outside India; a comparative study of the national philosophy of Veda Vyāsa, Manu and Kauṭilya; concepts of *varṇa* and *jāti* in Jaina and Buddhist traditions; national integration, trade and commerce in ancient India; invasions and conquest of north-east India by Indian kings; politico-cultural relations of Tibet and Myanmar (Burma) with Bihar; tribal-Mughal conflicts in north-east India; and medieval Indian society and culture. A paper of topical interest — antiquity of Ayodhyā and historicity of Rāma — is also included in this volume.

G.P. Singh

Contents

Acknowledgements

THIS volume is a collection of some of my papers written during the past three decades on certain aspects of Indian history, historiography, and philosophy of history published in journals, books, etc. Most of the papers included in the volume relate to ancient Indian history and culture which has been the main field of my study and research. I have put them together in one volume with the object of making all the material embodied in it easily accessible to the readers. I believe they will be useful to them.

I crave the readers' indulgence for all the errors that may be discernible to their eyes.

The author and the publisher would like to thank the editors and publishers of the journals and books for permission granted for inclusion in this volume of the papers published in them as shown below:

"Was Herodotus of Greece the Father of History?", *Adhyayana*, Journal of the Bhāratiya Itihāsa Adhyayan Saṁsthān, Allahabad, 1993.

"A New Approach to the Study of Historical Data in the Epic and Purāṇic Literature on Ancient India", Proceedings of the UGC-sponsored National Seminar on History and Literature, 9-11 February, 1991, Sardar Patel University, Vallabh Vidyanagar (Gujarat).

"The Purāṇic Tradition of Historiography in India", *The Indian Historical Review*, Published by the Indian Council of Historical Research, New Delhi, in 2004. (The paper has also been published in *Proceedings of the 17th Conference of the International Association of Historians of Asia*, 18-22 December, 2002, University of Dhaka, Published in 2004.)

"The Fundamental Aspects of Ancient Indian Culture and Civilization", *An Introduction to General Foundation Course*, ed. I.R. Babu Singh, Published by Manipur University (MU), Imphal, in 1999.

"Sources of the History of Uttar Pradesh (Ancient Period)", *Sources of the History of India*, vol. II, ed. S.P Sen, Institute of Historical Studies, Calcutta, 1979.

"The Dionysiaka: A Classical (Greek) Source of History of Ancient India", *Shodhak*, A Journal of Historical Research, Jaipur, Published in 1999.

"The Colonial and Cultural Expansion of the Aryans Outside India as Gleaned from the Vedic Literature", *Journal of the Department of History*, MU, Imphal, 1987.

"Antiquity of Ayodhyā and Historicity of Rāma: Literary, Archaeological and Scientific Perspectives", *Krishna-abhinandana* (*B. Krishna Shastri Felicitation Volume*): *History, Culture and Archaeological Studies*, ed. P. Chenna Reddy, New Delhi, 2008.

"Veda Vyāsa, Manu and Kauṭilya: A Comparative Study of their National Philosophy in Historical Perspective", *Journal of the Department of History*, MU, Imphal, 1986.

"The Concepts of Varṇa and Jāti in the Jaina and Buddhist Traditions", *Adhyayana*, Journal of the Bhāratiya Itihāsa Adhyayan Saṁsthān, Allahabad, 1997.

"The Role of the Brāhmaṇas in Anti-Alexander Movement in North-West India *c.* 326-325 BC", *Studies in History and Culture*, Journal of the PG Deptt. of History, Berhampur University, Berhampur (Orissa), 1995.

"The Concept of National Integration in Ancient India", *Dimensions of National Integration: The Experiences and Lessons of Indian History*, ed. N.R. Ray, Punthi-Pustak and the Institute of Historical Studies, Calcutta, 1993.

"North-west India as Described by the Greek and Assyrian Travellers of the First Century", *Journal of the Asiatic Society of Mumbai* (New series), Pub. by The Asiatic Society of Mumbai in 2004. (The paper is in a little modified form of the earlier one "Early History of North-West India as Described by the Greek and Assyrian Travellers", *Journal of Indian History*, Trivandrum, Platinum Jubilee Volume, 2001).

"Trade and Commerce in Ancient India in the Light of Jaina and Buddhist Traditions Bearing on its Economic and Cultural Contacts with the Asian Countdries", *Studies in History and Culture*, Journal of the PG Deptt. of History, Berhampur University, Berhampur, 1996.

"Traditional and Historical Accounts of Politico-Cultural Relations of Tibet and Burma with Bihar and their Impact: Ancient and Early Medieval Period", *The Thinker*, Journal of the Thinkers Forum, Kohima, 1981.

"Historical Interpretations of Kālidāsa's Description of Raghu's Conquest of Prāgjyotiṣa", *Proceedings of North-East India History Association*, X[th] Session, Shillong, 1989.

"Historicity of Bilhaṇa's Account of Vikramāditya's Invasion of Kāmarūpa in the Eleventh Century AD", *Shodhak*, A Journal of Historical Research, Jaipur, 1997.

"Medieval Indian Society and Culture", *An Introduction to General Foundation Course,* ed. I.R. Babu Singh, MU, Imphal, 1999.

"Development of Trade and Commerce in Southern India (13th to 15th Centuries): Travellers Accounts (Persian, Arabic, Russian and Italian Sources)", *Shodhak,* A Journal of Historical Research, Jaipur 1997.

"Development of Trade and Commerce in Northern and Eastern India in the 16th and 17th Centuries from the Narratives of the Travellers", *Shodhak,* A Journal of Historical Research, Jaipur, 1998.

"The Annals of Tribal-Mughal Conflicts in North-East India during the Reign of Jehangir (1605–1627)", *Journal of Indian History,* Trivandrum, 1981.

Transliteration Chart

VOWELS

अ *a*	आ *ā*	इ *i*	ई *ī*	उ *u*	ऊ *ū*	ऋ *ṛ*	ॠ *ṝ*[1]
(Roman)	(palm)	(it)	(police)	(put)	(rule)	(rig)	
ऌ *ḷ*	ॡ *ḹ*[1]	ए *e*	ऐ *ai*	ओ *o*	औ *au*		
(able)		(there)	(aisle)	(no)	(loud)		

CONSONANTS

Guttural	क *ka* (skate)	ख *kha*[2] (blockhead)	ग *ga* (gate)	घ *gha*[2] (ghost)	ङ *ṅa* (sing)
Palatal	च *ca* (chunk)	छ *cha*[2] (catch him)	ज *ja* (john)	झ *jha*[2] (hedgehog)	ञ *ña* (bunch)
Cerebral	ट *ṭa* (start)	ठ *ṭha*[2] (anthill)	ड *ḍa* (dart)	ढ *ḍha*[2] (godhead)	ण *ṇa* (under)
Dental	त *ta* (path)	थ *tha*[2] (thunder)	द *da* (that)	ध *dha*[2] (this)	न *na* (numb)
Labial	प *pa* (spin)	फ *pha*[2] (philosophy)	ब *ba* (bin)	भ *bha*[2] (abhor)	म *ma* (much)
Semi-vowels	य *ya* (young)	र *ra* (drama)	ल *la*[3] (luck)	व *va*[4] (vile)	
Sibilants	श *śa*[5] (shove)	ष *ṣa*[5] (bushel)	स *sa* (so)	ह *ha* (hum)	
Others	क्ष *kṣa* (*kṣatriya*)	त्र *tra* (*triśūla*)	ज्ञ *jña* (*jñānī*)		

अं (ं) *ṁ* *anusvāra* is a nasal off-glide that immediately follows the pronunciation of a vowel as in *saṁskṛti*.

अः *visarga* = *ḥ* consists in abrupt release of breath after a vowel as in *prātaḥ*.

ऽ *Avagraha* shows non-pronunciation, that is, deletion of "a" after "e" or "o" as in *ime 'vasthitāḥ*. In Vedic Sanskrit, it can also show word division.

HINDI LETTERS (extras)

ँ = *m̐*	ं = ṅ	ड़ = *ṛa*	ढ़ = *ṛha*
(*candrabindu*)	(*anusvāra*)		

---

1 Longer form of the preceding vowel.

2 Aspirated forms of the preceding consonants. The compound words given as examples should be pronounced without a syllabic break at the underlined places. "tha" and "pha" should not be pronounced as fricatives.

3 retroflexed and written as "L *la*" in certain phonetic contexts.

4 Pronounced like "w," without aspiration.

5 "śa" is palatal; "ṣa" cerebral or retroflex.

1

Was Herodotus of Greece the Father of History?*

THE present paper aims at re-examining the historical validity of the conventional view that Herodotus, a native of Halicarnassus, a Greek city on the south-west coast of Asia Minor, was the "Father of History." Actually, it was the Roman prose writer-cum-historian, Cicero (*c.* 106-43 BCE), who first called him the "Father of History" the reasons for which are not far to discover. Perhaps taking Herodotus as a pioneer in the field of historiography or judging by his own standard of historiography as a branch of rhetoric, Cicero accorded this recognition to him. But, Cicero was far in advance of the age for pronouncing such historic judgement. Moreover, in those days there was no accepted principle or law of historiography, except some rhetorical precepts and rules, to give such a kind of verdict. However, his fanciful notion gradually assumed the character of a historical reality, which eventually resulted in the universal recognition of Herodotus as the "Father of History" which can be questioned. The obsession on the part of the scholars, in general, with this conventional phraseology went on creating an impression that he was the first to produce history. But, this impression can reasonably be dispelled on the basis of some rare sources at our disposal. One of the basic questions, which follows here, is was he worthy of the

---

* From *Adhyayana: Journal of the Bhāratīya Itihāsa Adhyayana Saṁsthāna*, vol. III, nos. 1 and 2, 1993, pp. 1-10.

honour bestowed on him by the Roman scholar concerned? This is one of the controversial questions in the history of historical writing. The finding of a suitable answer to this question calls for an intensive enquiry into the subject.

II

The historical writing in Greece (so-called birthplace of history) itself began much before the appearance of Herodotus on its historical stage in the middle of the fifth century BCE. In ancient Greece, history developed as a branch of literature, first in the form of poetic compositions and then through prose writings, and historical works were judged as much on their dramatic and stylistic merit as on their accuracy and precision. The poetical works of considerable historical importance quoted by Herodotus in his *Historiai* are those of Homer (*c.* 900 BCE), Hesiod, Archilochus, Aristeas, Aeschylus, Bachylides, Olen, Pindar and Simonides.[1]

III

It was the sixth century BCE which really marked the beginnings of Greek historiography. It was an epoch of transition from myth to history. In fact, the historical composition in the form of prose writing had begun from the middle of the sixth century BCE. Those twenty historians from different parts of Greece, who preceded Herodotus as authors of different books on different historical subjects, belonged to the sixth and first half of the fifth century BCE. They were all fellow countrymen of Herodotus and wrote annals and local history or chronicles

1. W.W. How and J. Wells, *A Commentary on Herodotus*, vol. I, Bks. I-IV (Oxford, 1914), pp. 20-21; Stephen Usher, *The Historians of Greece and Rome* (London, 1969), pp. 1-2, 8; J.T. Shotwell, *Introduction to the History of History* (Columbia, 1939), vol. 1, pp. 163-65; J. Talboys Wheeler, *The Geography of Herodotus* (Lodon, 1854) p. 4; Arnold Toynbee, *Greek Historical Thought from Homer to the Age of Heraclius* (London, 1924), pp. 2-10.

without rhetorical adornment before or about the time of Herodotus, when he commenced his historical writings. Their narrative histories, which were based on civic records, palace records and temple records — all factual records held by princes and kings — oral traditions, their travels and eyewitness accounts and dealt with the origins of peoples, the emergence and growth of great and small cities, contemporary events, etc., constituted the historical literature. The origin of the Greek historiography actually lies in the Ionian thoughts of the sixth centuary BCE. Those early Ionian historians from the Greek settlements in the South-West Asia Minor (to which Herodotus himself belonged) or the islands in its immediate vicinity, who learnt the art of writing real history before Herodotus, were Cadmus of Miletus (*c.* 550 BCE), Hecataeus of Miletus (*c.* 550–478 BCE, or 549–486 BCE), Dionysius of Miletus (a contemporary of Hecataeus), Hellanicus of Lesbos (*c.* 482–397 BCE), Charon of Lampasacu (*c.* 470 BCE), Pherecydes of Leros (*c.* 450 BCE), Eugaeon of Samos, Bion and Deiochus of Proeonnesus, Eudemus of Paros, Ameleragoras of Chalcedon, Democles of Phygela, Damastes of Sigeum, Xanthus of Sardis or Lydus, and Scylax of Caryanda (*c.* 522–436 BCE). The others of considerable reputation in more distant parts of Greece were Anthiochus of Syracuse, Acusilaus of Argos (*c.* 500 BCE), Theagenes and Hippys of Rhegium and Polyselus of Messenia. They were the originators of history in the real sense of the term. They laid the foundation of the Greek tradition of historical writings on which Herodotus later erected the superstructure or an edifice of his history. Herodotus drew the historical material mostly from the *Periegesis* (divided into two books and based on travels of Western Asia particularly Persia and Europe with cartographic illustration, eyewitness account of the Persian invasion, etc.) and the *Genealogies* of Hecataeus, the *Persica* (History of Persia in five books) dealing with the progress of the nation from the time of Cyrus (*c.* 558–530 BCE) to a period of Xerxes (486–465 BCE) of Dionysius of Miletus, the *Hellenica* (History of Greece in 4 books), the *Persica* (History of Persia in two books dealing with Persian wars) and the *Prytanes* (or Chief Rulers of Sparta with chronological details) of Charon of Lampsacus (a contemporary of Herodotus), the *History of the People of Greece* of Hellanicus of Lesbos (who travelled like his contemporary Herodotus and introduced a system of definite chronology in local history) and Anthiochus of Syracuse, the *Lydian History* of Xanthus of Lydus and the historical work (based on voyages) of Scylax of Caryanda, who was *sent* in 518-17 BCE by the Persian king, Darius I (*c.* 522–486 BCE) to explore the course of the Indus.[2] But he did not maintain the courtesy and honesty of acknowledging the works of his predecessors (except quoting once Scylax in Bk. IV, 44 and Hecataeus in Bk. VI, 137.1) as Kauṭilya and Kalhaṇa did in ancient India. Many historians passed into oblivion and the loss of the fragments of their historical works proved to be one of the calamities of history to the posterity despite the adverse comments on their reliability.

---

2. G. Rawlinson, "On the sources from which Herodotus Compiled his account," in *History of Herodotus* (London, 1862), vol. I, Ch. II, pp 30-58; J.W. Thompson, *A History of Historical Writing from the Earliest Times to the End of the Seventeenth Century* (Berkeley, 1967), vol. 1, pp. 22-24, 29; L. Pearson, *Early Ionian Historians* (Oxford, 1939), pp. 3ff; Stephen Usher, op. cit., pp. 2-3; W.W. How and J. Wells, op. cit., pp. 22-35; J. Talboys Wheeler, op. cit., p. 4: J.T. Shotwell, op. cit., pp. 167-68; J.B. Bury, *The Ancient Greek Historians* (London, 1909), pp. 5ff; A Review in *The Nation*, LXXXVIII, 1909, cf. Thompson, op. cit., p. 22; E.H. Bunbury, *A History cf Ancient Geography among the Greeks and Romans from the Earliest Age till the fall of the Roman Empire* (New York, 1959), vol. 1, p. 134; *The New Encyclopedia Britannica* (hereinafter abbrev. as *EB*) 15th edn., 1980, vol. 8, p. 946.

Herodotus was held in high esteem by all the Greek citizens and considered "as one of the fathers of the colony."[3]

IV

Hecataeus of Miletus, the most prominent among the Ionian historians and immediate predecessor and one of the forerunners of Herodotus was the first to formulate the basic principles of historiography with due emphasis on-trustworthiness of the accounts, fidelity to truth and critical examination of the conventional evidence. He was, in fact, the first to record the historical traditions of several Greek and Persian cities by undertaking travels and to present a scientific history embracing genealogies of the reigning families within a chronological framework, ethnology of the people of Greece and Persia, contemporary events, etc. He was the first to adopt a rationalistic approach to the study of the subject and to make a sincere attempt at presentation of factual accounts marking a departure from the earlier literary tradition. He reconciled mythology with history in his *Genealogies*. He was the first to link his geographic enquiries with true history. As a historian he had all the qualities, which Herodotus was endowed with. That is why, he has been considered as the "first historian of Greece."[4] J.W. Thompson has judiciously called him the "Father of History."[5] Herodotus used the fragments of the historical writings of Hecatacus in his work, but did not acknowledge him to an extent he ought to have done, rather tried to discredit him by casting his doubt on his credibility probably with the

3. J. Talboys Wheeler, op. cit., p. 4.
4. W.W. How and J. Wells, op. cit., pp. 25, 46, see also 27-35; Stephen Usher, op. cit., pp. 2-3; E.H. Bunbury, op. cit., p. 134; *EB*, vol. 8, pp. 946-47; E.H. Benbury, op. cit., vol. 11 (1768), pp. 442-45; J.T. Shotwell, op. cit., pp. 167ff.
5. Op. cit., pp. 22, 24.

intention of pushing him into the background and bringing his own name into the limelight for being recognized as the first historian in the world.

V

Herodotus not only consulted the historical works of the Greeks, but also that of the Egyptians, Assyrians, Babylonians and Persians. Like the ancient Greeks they also had the distinction of producing historical literature comprising the annals of the political events with chronological sequence maintained by the kings, and royal Chronicles, and the archival records, inscriptional records, etc. in pre-Herodotus period. Herodotus in course of his travels to Egypt, Babylonia, Persia, etc. during the exile period collected the information for history from various sources. He found in Egypt the annals kept by Pharaohs from the remotest antiquity and the literature composed between 2000 and 1300 BCE. The Babylonian tradition of historical writings began much before 747 BCE and further continued. The *Babyloniaca* or the History of Babylonia written in Greek by a Chaldaean priest named Berossus, either before Herodotus or in the third century BCE was a very important work. Herodotus is believed to have derived his knowledge of Assyrian and Babylonian civilization from this source. The Assyrian historiography began about *c.* 1100 BCE and reached the height of progress during the reign of Ashurbanipal (626–608 BCE).

Some Assyrian historical works were destroyed by Esarhaddon (745–728 BCE) as some of the older annals were destroyed by Nabonassor of Babylonia during the period, *c.* 647–561 BCE. Two important historical works of the Assyrians were known as Synchronous History (which contained an account of Assyrio–Babylonian relations from 1600 to 800 BCE) and the Assyrian chronicle. The Persian historical tradition virtually began in 538 BCE and further continued. Herodotus obtained a lot of valuable information from the Persian historical records.[6]

VI

Deriving his authority from the different historical works and on the basis of his travels Herodotus completed his work, *Historia* (which was later divided into nine books by his successor), dealing mainly with the Graeco–Persian war culminating into the Greek Victory in "Xerxes" invasion of 410–79 BCE. The merit of Herodotus as a historian and the value of his history as a work of utility should not only be judged by the copiousness and authenticity of the material used, but also by the style of their presentation. His presentation of facts is more artistic than scientific. Nor was he a critical historian. As a consummate artist and narrator of events as well as legends he has not been surpassed by others. The written and oral traditions of the preceding age, myths, legends, anecdotes, popular religious beliefs and historical facts all were skilfully combined into one and woven together into the texture of his history. He failed to detach history from the common literary traditions of the past ages. His history is artistic masterpiece. He could not produce the scientific history because of his blind faith in mythology and tradition. The most remarkable fact is that his method and

6. J.W. Thompson, op. cit., pp. 3-17; Joseph Reither (ed.), *Masterworks of History* (London, 1973), vol. L, pp. 3-5; A.H.L. Hecren, *Historical Researches into the Politics, Intercourse and Trade of the Principal Nations of Antiquity* (Oxford, 1833) vol. 1, *Asiatic Nations*, p. 282; A.T. Olmstead, *Assyrian Historiography* (Columbia, Missouri, 1916, 1, pp. 1-4; J.H. Breasted, *Ancient Records of Egypt: Historical Documents from the Earliest Times to the Persian Conquest* (New York, 1909), p. 109; E.G. Browne, *A Literary History of Persia from the Earliest Times until Firdausi* (New York, 1902), pp. 7f; *EB*, vol. 8, pp. 946-47; Issac Cory, *Ancient Fragments of the Phoenician, Chaldaean, Egyptian, Carthagian, Indian, Persian, etc.* (London, 1832), pp. 19-43.

style of narrating the story is very much simliar to that of Homer. He has presented his accounts more in a story-teller's fashion than in a historian's manner. That is why their authenticity is often doubted. Morever, the accounts are not in a proper order from chronological point of view. He has narrated the stories without examining their relevance. The stories and legends have not been properly historified. His history is full of amusing stories. He was perhaps guided by the belief that a historian is a great poet whose purpose is to amuse the public by magnifying the events and glorifying the deeds of heroes of history.[7]

VII

Among the ancient critics of Herodotus mention may specifically be made of Strabo (*c.* 64 BCE – CE 19 or 21), who was well known among the Greek geographers and historians for his critical faculty of judgement. He was in a much better position to assess the degree of his originality. Strabo treated the work of Herodotus with altogether contempt, passed some disparaging remarks about him and classed him with the Greek historiographer Ctesias (*c.* 416–398 BCE), who was a compiler of fables, on whom heavy accusations of mendacity have been heaped by the classical writers and whose statements are mostly unworthy of credence.[8]

It is said that Herodotus was "a poet as well as a historian." He has been mentioned both as the "Father of History" and

7. G. Rawlinson, op. cit., pp. 58ff; J.E. Powell's tr. of *History of Herodotus* (Oxford 1939), pp. XXI, 51; G.C. Macaulay's tr. of *History of Herodotus* (London, 1904), pp. 10 f; Stephen Usher, op. cit., pp. 4-22; A.H. Sayce, *Herodotus* 1-111 (1883); VII-IX (1908); M. Rennell, *The Geographical System of Herodotus* (London, 1830) pp. 6f; F.H. Bunbury, op. cit.; vol. 1, pp. 156-222; *EB*, vol. 11, pp. 442-45.
8. E.H. Bunbury, op. cit., vol. 11, p. 215.

the "Father of prose composition."[9] Stephen Usher, one of the renowned authorities on the Classical Historiograhy has clearly stated that an attempt has been made to project him as the first historian, but he was "a mature literary artist. . . . To talk of relevance in Herodotus is thus itself an irrelevancy."[10] A.L. Rowse, while defending the role of a historian as an artist, poet or novelist placed Herodotus, Thucydides, Tacitus, Livy, etc. in the rank of an artist, tut did not call anyone of them either as a father or as a son.[11]

However it cannot be denied that Herodotus was gifted with all the qualities of a great historian. He was the idol of the Greek historians of all ages. He was the author of the earliest comprehensive historical work. As the first constructive artist historian he reconstructed the history of whole past life of man.[12] The contribution of this celebrated historian to the evolution of historiography will, of course, be acknowledged for ages to come. But to say that he was the "Father of History" is not justified and it can fairly be contested. J.L. Myres' arguments in support of the view that he was the "Father of History"[13] are not very convincing.

VIII

Thucydides (*c.* 460–404 BCE or 456–396 BCE), an authority on the *History of the Peloponnesian War* (431–404 BCE), made equally significant contributions to Greek historiography. He was rather the first to lay down the principles of scientific historiography and formulate the canons of criticism. He

9. J.W. Thompson, op. cit., pp. 25-26, also 3; Stephen Usher, op. cit., p. 22.
10. Op. cit., pp. 4-5.
11. *The Use of History* (London, 1947), pp. 112-13.
12. H.E. Barnes, *A History of Historical writing* (New-York. 1963), pp 29-30; J.T. Shotwell, op. cit., pp. 185-86.
13. Herodotus, *Father of History* (Oxford, 1953), pp. 11ff.

throughout maintained a clear distinction between history and fiction. But, Prof. Shotwell[14] and Prof. Barnes,[15] the two great noted admirers of Herodotus, have criticized him mainly because of the fact the he was essentially a political historian and as such he neglected the social, economic and cultural factors in history. But according to some other authorities, he was the greatest of all the historians which the ancient Asian and European nations had.[16] Actually, it was Thucydides' style of writing and not that of Herodotus, which influenced the Classical (Graeco-Roman) Historiography of the subsequent periods, as it appears from the writings of the Greek historians, Xenophon (*c.* 430–354 or 350 BCE), Polybius (*c.* 204–122 BCE), Diodorus Siculus (*c.* 80–29 BCE) and Timaeus (*c.* 329–289 BCE) and the Roman historians, Fabius Pictor (the first historian of the third century BCE), Claudius (second century BCE), Sallust (*c.* 86–34 BCE), Livy (*c.* 59 BCE – CE I7). Tacitus (*c.* 55–120 CE), Arrian (second century CE) and Ammianus Marcellinus (*c.* CE 380–400). They judged Thucydides a better historian than Herodotus because of the former's meticulous regard for truth and objective outlook.

IX

It is noteworthy that like ancient Greece, Rome, Egypt, Babylonia, Assyria, Persia, India and China also maintained the literary traditions of historiography in the ancient past. The ancient historians of all these countries influenced each

14. Op. cit., pp. 195-97, 201.
15. Op. cit., p. 31.
16. Joseph Reither, op. cit., pp. 79-81; F.E. Acock, *Thucydides and His History* (Cambridge, 1963), pp. 58-59, 107-9; G.B. Grundy, *Thucydides and the History of his Age* (London. 1911) p. 480; S. Usher, op. cit., pp. 24-25; Thompson, op. cit., pp. 29-33; J.H. Finley, *The Origins of Thucydides' Style* (Harvard, 1930), 1, pp. 35ff; J.B. Bury, *The Ancient Greek* Historians, pp. 15f.

other in the cultivation of this tradition. The historiograhical traditions evolved there contemporaneously. Different styles and methods were followed by them for presenting their histories. In India it was Vyāsa and his disciples who initiated this tradition in the Vedic age, which can also be confirmed by the statements of some authorities on ancient Indian historiography.[17] F. Max Müller, has referred to the Veda as the earliest historical record in the world. Both India and Greece, according to him, made contributions to the development of historical traditions in ancient times.[18] In China, though the beginnings of historiography date back to *c.* 753 BCE it was the second century BCE which really saw the production of real history *Shih-Chi* (*c.* 100 BCE) attributed to su-ma-Chien (*c.* 145-85 BCE).[19] How can only Herodotus represent all the different families of producers of histories of different ancient nations as the "Father of History?" He did not possess any such exceptional qualities which entitle him to this honour. Evea in his own country he was not accepted as the father of history by the historians posterior to him. The whole concept of a common father of discipline like history is misleading. There is none, who can be accepted as the father of history in global context. E.H. Carr has observed that "Like the ancient civilization of Asia, the Classical civilization of Greece and Rome was basically unhistorical. . . . Herodotus as the father of history had few children. . . ."[20]

---

17. U.N. Ghoshal, *The Beginnings of Indian Historiography* (Calcutta, 1944), pp. 21-23, 50-52; A.K. Warder, *An Introduction to Indian Historiography* (Bombay, 1972), pp. 15-25; V.S. Pathak, *Ancient Historians of India* (Bombay, 1966), pp. 15-22.
18. *A History of Ancient Sanskrit Literature* (Varanasi, 1968), pp. 11-16, 57-59.
19. W.G. Beasley and B.G. Pulleybland (ed.), *Historians of China and Japan* (London, 1961), pp. 24-26.
20. *What is History?* (Middlessex, 1977), p. 109.

X

On the basis of the results obtained from our inquiries into the subject it is very difficult to ascertain as to who is the father and who is the child of history. The validity of the conventional view concerned is questionable. Herodotus was actually one of the fathers of history and not the "Father of History." We hope the present line of inquiry will open a new avenue for further research into the subject.

2

History and Philosophy

HISTORY and philosophy, two important branches of knowledge, are closely related to each other. History is part of philosophy and philosophy part of history particularly regarding study of religio-cultural life of the people. Historical explanations generally go with philosophical thoughts in the realm of religion and culture. In fact, religion, morality and art are constituents of both history and philosophy. Philosophy remained intimately connected with history till the latter was regarded as an art with Clio as one of the Muses. Philosophical ideas were applied in artistic explanation of a historical subject in socio-cultural milieu. Philosophical ideals can very well be tested on the touchstone of history.

There is functional similarity between a historian and a philosopher to a considerable extent. There is not much difference between the tasks or functions of both. The only difference between the two is that of degree of emphasis on the course of historical events relating to social transformation, religious movements and cultural growth. Both historians and philosophers are concerned with history, culture and civilization of mankind.

The classical historian Dionysius, who belonged to second half of the first century BCE and early first century CE, was the first to identify history with philosophy. He categorically stated that history is philosophy which could be taught by way of illustration for better perception of the subject.

It is striking to note that philosophy of history has developed with the development of history itself. The philosophy of history elucidates the nature of historical thinking and historical knowledge, explains the significance and relevance of historical statement and importance of making historical disquisition into causation, and deals with truth and objectivity in historical explanation. A philosopher who is not inclined to consider history is not a real philosopher. Likewise, a historian is not a historian if he refuses to accept philosophy of history. "The history of philosophy is no more philosophy than the philosophy of history is history." (R.F. Atkinson, *Knowledge and Explanation in History*, 1978, p. 8.) For writing history in a broader perspective sometimes philosophers approach to history is to be adopted, that is, to discover some formula to narrate the past events with analyses of the causes thereof.

It was the Italian philosopher and historian G. Vico (1668–1744) who laid the foundation of modern philosophy of history. He evolved a historical method and took up the study of the history of remote antiquity wrapped in obscurity with very scanty and dubious sources. He did not accept myths and legends as facts. He successfully debunked myth from reality. He expressed the view that each historian can contribute to the building up of historical knowledge by interpreting the data the past has left behind. He enumerates a number of prejudices against which a historian is supposed to guard himself. He has rightly pointed out that "the feeling of nationalism tends to prejudice the view of a historian while painting a picture of his country's past in most favourable colours." Here we may add that a historian has to forget his caste or class, creed or religion, and national feeling for presenting an objective and scientific history.

It is believed that the term "philosophy of history" was invented in modern times by Voltaire (eighteenth century), one of the intellectuals, political philosophers and thinkers of France. In fact, he used the term more in the sense of an artistic history than in the sense of a scientific or critical history. The philosophy of history developed in France especially in the eighteenth century. Turgot (1727-81), Condorcet (1743-94) and others explained philosophy of history. All emphasized the need of making a systematic enquiry into the history of progress of mankind with special reference to society and culture.

We cannot deny the fact that philosophers also made some contributions to the evolution of history as a scientific discipline. Philosophers of history propounded different theories of history, expounded epistemology of history, and interpreted the rules of history which provided the key to the understanding and writing of history in the correct perspective.

There were two broad schools of philosophical thought — Idealist and Positivist. The former stood for the autonomy of history and the latter for its assimilation to science.

B. Croce (1866–1952), the great philosopher of history of the Idealist School, belonged to Italy. He aptly remarked: "History cannot be disentangled from philosophy." He asserted that like science history must be based on facts, observation and experiments. (*Theory and History of Historiography*, 1921, pp. 7ff.) But later he changed his opinion. He strongly advocated free historical enquiry. He held that historians are at liberty to follow their method of enquiry be it artistic or scientific. (*History as the Story of Liberty*, originally written in 1938, Eng. tr., 1941, p. 47.)

With the publication of the first part of Herder's *Ideas for a Philosophical History of Mankind* (1784) the philosophy of history got recognition as a separate subject. He did not support the idea of judging past ages only from a cultural standpoint. He laid emphasis on the study of history and culture of each race.

The philosophical interpretation of history by one of the noted German philosophers, Immanuel Kant (1724–1804), is of unique value. He insisted on going deep into the gradual progress of the mankind in the perspective of culture. He said that the study of universal history is feasible but it demands a union of historical and philosophical thought.

It was Hegel (1770–1831) who raised history to a great height. He added a new dimension to the study of world history. He thought that each nation contributes to the making of world history. Every nation, according to him, has its own characteristic which is reflected in its religion, its political institutions, its legal system and its science, art, etc. He realized the importance of the past for the understanding of the present. He firmly believed that a philosopher who has knowledge of an idea could have deeper insight into the facts. He was an upholder of idealistic system of knowledge. He used the term "philosophy of history" in a dialectical sense, that is, about application of rules and modes of reasoning or of distinguishing truth from error, and of exposing fallacies of arguments advanced in support of or against any view.

Marx (1818-83) presented to the historians a new method of explaining history. His economic interpretation of history, that economic factors are fundamental for the understanding of all historical situations (M.M. Bober, *Karl Marx's Interpretation of History*, 1948), finds adumbration in the writings of historians of the so-called Marxist School. Marx's philosophy of history is easily distinguishable from that of others.

Spengler (1880–1936), one of the most prominent among German philosophers of history, maintained that each culture passes through three different stages — rise, growth, and decline. His idea greatly inspired the historians of the succeeding period interested in the study of rise and fall of cultures or civilizations.

The famous British historian A. Toynbee in his *magnum opus, A Study of History* (10 vol., 1934-54; abridgement of vols. I-VI and VII-X by D.C. Somervell, 1946, 1957), emphasized the need of making a comparative study of all great civilizations of the past.

R.G. Collingwood, who belonged to England, was an eminent historian and philosopher of the Idealist School. He held that though science, philosophy, and history are independent disciplines, history is nearer to philosophy than science. He took past worthy of study, and suggested that the entire history of mankind should be studied from the primitive age to the growth of civilized society. (*The Idea of History*, 1946, rpt., 1973, pp. 87-88.) His historical thought centres round the fact that history is the re-enactment of past experience or past thought in the historian's mind. (Ibid., pp. 228, 282.) He explicitly states that the historian's business is to discover what the past was. His philosophical interpretation of history is contained in his *Essays in the Philosophy of History* (1965).

Supporting the view of Collingwood, E.H. Carr wrote, "The past which a historian studies is not a dead past, but a past which in some sense is still living in the present." (*What is History*? p. 22.) He has correctly stated that "The function of the historian is neither to love the past nor to emancipate himself from the past, but to master and understand it as the key to understanding of the present." (Ibid., p. 26) He further adds that "The past is intelligible to us only in the light of the present; and we can fully understand the present only in the light of the past. To enable man to understand the society of the past, and to increase his mastery over the society of the present, is the dual function of history." (Ibid., p. 55.)

In contradistinction to the view of Carr, M. Oakeshott, a historian of the Idealist School, says that history studies the past for the sake of the past and not for the sake of the present.

His contention is that it never seeks to justify present policies by reference to the past nor does it take back the concerns of the present into the past. He suggests that the historian should explain his viewpoints by giving complete details thereof and not by means of generalization. ("The Activity of Being an Historian," in his *Rationalism and Politics*, 1962, pp. 140ff.)

W.H. Walsh, one of the English philosophers of history, perspicuously states that historians should not present a mere chronicle of catalogue in which the events are set down within chronological framework but are otherwise unrelated. They should rather provide a narrative of past events in a chronological order showing their connections and bearing on one another. He further opines that speculative philosophy of history in its classic form need not be employed in an enquiry into the laws governing historical change which could be conducted in a strictly scientific spirit. (*An Introduction to the Philosophy of History*, 1951, rpt. 1967, pp. 13ff.)

The positivists also made their contributions towards the development of the philosophy of history. As a result of the thought they upheld, historical studies received great impetus and steps were taken to collect rich source material which proved of immense value to the subsequent historians.

The two noted philosophers of the positivist school were Karl Popper and C.J. Hempel. The former in his *The Open Society and its Enemies* (vol. II, 1945) and the latter in his "The Function of General Laws in History," 1942 (rpt. in *Theories of History*, ed. by P. Gardiner, 1959) argued in favour of assimilation of history to science. Gardiner (*The Nature of Historical Explanation*, 1952; *The Philosophy of History*, ed. 1974) was for both scientific and philosophical treatment of history.

Some of the philosophers of history, notably, W.B. Gallic (*Philosophy and the Historical Understanding*, 1964), A.C. Danto (*Analytical Philosophy of History*, 1965), H. Fain (*Between*

Philosophy and History, 1970) and G.J. Renier (*History : Its Purpose and Method,* 1950) rejected the assimilationists' conceptions of history and gave prominence to narration of events in history.

Chronology is the soul of history. Some of the historical events are, of course, datable. The sequence of events may be arranged in a proper order and explained without any ambiguity so as to do a fair justice to history. This aspect of history received the serious attention of G.R. Elton (*The Practice of History,* 1969).

Both the historians and philosophers of modern age laid down some basic rules of investigation into the history, culture and civilization of the past ages.

3

History of History: From Vedic Antiquity to Modern Times

An Introduction

THE history of history is a systematic record of evolution of different ideas, thoughts, perceptions, principles, laws, forms, kinds, constituents, theories and schools of history. J.T. Shotwell puts it in a different way: "The history of the history is the story of that deepening memory and scientific curiosity which is the measure of our social consciousness and of our intellectual life" (*Introduction to the History of History*).

The earliest allusion to *itihāsa*, the nearest equivalent Sanskrit word for history (derivative of the Greek word *Historia*), occurs in the later Vedic text *Atharvaveda*. It literally means "thus it happened" or "so indeed it was." *Itihāsa* (past events), *purāṇa* (any old tale or ancient lore) and *ākhyāna* (narratives) constitute the three rudimentary specimens of history. They contained the seeds of history. Both *itihāsa* and *purāṇa* signify record of the past. They provide traditional account of past events. They have been mentioned conjointly in the Vedic, Epic and Purāṇic literature. The traditional history of India has been presented in *itihāsa-purāṇa* tradition. The three legitimate constituents of this tradition were myth, genealogy and historical narrative. This tradition profoundly influenced the historical thoughts and writings in ancient India. Toynbee, a well-known British historian, in his monumental work, *A Study of History* (in 12 vols.), has correctly stated that history grew out of myth, fiction, stories, legends and tradition. The emergence of six constituents of *itihāsa* or history, viz. *purāṇa*, *itivṛtta* (an account of past events, a narrative or story), *ākhyāyikā* (biography of a historical personage), *udāharaṇa* (an illustration), the *Dharmaśāstra* (law) and the *Arthaśāstra* (science of polity or state and government) in the fourth century BCE is attributed to Kauṭilya. The importance of dynastic history, genealogies and chronology was first realized by the ancient *purāṇakāra*s of India. The composition of historical biographies and chronicles in India between the seventh and eighteenth centuries gave fillip to biographical study as well as historical studies in chronicles. Kalhaṇa (twelfth century CE), a chronicler of Kashmir and the best of all ancient historians of India, first emphasized the need of a thorough critical examination of all past records for producing a historical work. His historical principles and laws were further followed by the Kashmiri chroniclers of the medieval age. He was the forerunner of many Indian historians in the realm of debunking the truth from falsehood. He is often compared with Herodotus of Greece. The historians of three prominent schools, Gujarat, Rajasthan and Kashmir, left indelible imprints of their historical genius on the thoughts and writings of the succeeding generations of Indian historians. The Buddhist and Jaina historians of India also gave impetus to the writings of biographies and preservation of dynastic genealogies and chronology. The Buddhists presented history mainly in the form of an *Avadāna* and the Jains in the forms of *Paṭṭāvali*s (political succession lists), *Rājāvali*s (chronicles of kings), *Prabandha*s (historical narratives), etc. Their works virtually made the earlier history of ancient India richer. The traditional Indian concept of history went on changing with developing historical sense, prevailing historical tradition in a contemporary age and events of the time.

Historiography became by and large regional in character in medieval India. Regional histories gradually started assuming significance. They are to a considerable extent complementary to national history.

The writing of local chronicles in Rajasthan and Kashmir in the north; Sindh, Gujarat and Maharashtra in the west; and in Orissa, Assam, Manipur and Tripura in the east in different forms during the medieval period, and of historical biographies in almost all parts of India including the south during all the three periods of history were the two significant stages in the evolution of Indian historiography. Though the Chinese historian Ssu-ma Chien (*c.* 145–85 BCE) was the first to initiate the tradition of biographical writing by dealing with the lives of a number of eminent personalities (all his contemporaries) in his *magnum opus*, the *Shih-Chi*, it is the Greek Plutarch (*c.* CE 50–125), the author of the *Lives of the Noble Grecians and Romans*, who got universal recognition as a "father of biography." The Roman Tacitus (*c.* CE 55–120) also produced a work, *Life of Agricola*. The different traditions of biographical writing which evolved in China, Greece, Rome and India in different ages went a long way in according the biographical history a place it deserves.

The establishment of certain basic principles and laws of history in the classical tradition also deserves our notice. Hecataeus (*c.* 549–486 BCE) was the first among the early Greek historians to lay emphasis on two fundamental principles of historiography, viz. truthfulness and critical examination of the conventional myths which find reflection in one of his works: *Book of Local Genealogies*. Nearly twenty Greek historians including predecessors and contemporaries of Herodotus (*c.* 484–425 BCE), the so-called "Father of History," concentrated their attention mainly on political histories of Greece and Persia. It is the political history which received the highest attention of Herodotus as evidenced by the description of the

Graeco-Persian war and other political events in his *Historia* (in nine volumes). He presented history combining in himself the qualities of a historian and skills of a literary artist and story-teller. Thucydides (*c.* 456–396 BCE) laid stress on objectivity in the presentation of political history as reflected in his *The History of the Peloponnesian War*. The later Greek writers of the early period produced histories of mixed nature dealing with society, economy, polity, etc. of different countries including India. In fact, the ancient Greeks wrote history of all characters, literary, social, economic, political, biographical, universal, annals, local chronicles and memoirs. They were the originators of the history in the modern sense of the term. They first learnt the art of writing real history, and perceived its purpose, meaning and laws. The two distinguished Roman historians, Livy (*c.* 59 BCE – CE 17) and Tacitus (*c.* CE 55–120), emphatically asserted that a historian has to present history by keeping himself free from bias and pride and prejudice. It is noteworthy that the art of writing a biography developed in Greece and Rome in the first and second centuries of the Christian era. *The Lives of the Noble Grecians and Romans* by the Greek Plutarch and the *Life of Agricola* by the Roman Tacitus mentioned before, are "the best specimens of historical biography that the ancient world produced."

As in ancient India so in Greece and Rome history developed as a branch of literature. To the Greeks and Romans also history was an art and not a critical science, as stated by J.W. Thompson (*A History of Historical Writing*), J.B. Bury (*The Ancient Greek Historians*), Stephen Usher (*The Historians of Greece and Rome*) and A.L. Rowse (*The Use of History*). However, it cannot be denied that history attained a new status and high dignity at their hands.

The development of history as art and science has also a history. The treatment of history as an art at the hands of historians at global level continued till the end of the seventeenth century CE, as stated by Thompson. In fact, history retained its artistic value in the following two centuries also. Voltaire of France, and Hume (1711-76), Gibbon (1737-94), the author of *History of the Decline and Fall of the Roman Empire*, Macaulay (1800-58), the author of *History of England*, and Carlyle (1795–1881), the author of *French Revolution*, of England have been called both historians and "literary artists." J.R. Seeley (1834-95) and J.B. Bury (1861–1927), the two noted historians of Cambridge School, persistently went on saying that "history is a science, no less and no more" from the standpoint of truth, exactness, accuracy and objectivity. G.M. Trevelyan (1876–1962), the famous British historian and author of a unique work, *Clio: A Muse*, consistently opposed their view and firmly stood for history both as a science and as an art, arguing that if the former discovers the truth the latter deals with social and cultural factors in human life. He further contended that literary history is not unscientific. G.J. Renier (*History: Its Purpose and Method*) repeatedly told that "history is a story, no more and no less." Rowse also pleaded for an artistic history in the sense that a historian needs to be an artist to narrate the events. Toybee has aptly remarked: ". . . no historian can be great if he is not also a great artist." Actor, Renan and others were for both scientific and literary history. As a matter of fact, Bury's and Seeley's persistency of the treatment of history only as a science and Trevelyan's and others' advocacy of history as a science and art resulted in legitimization of both scientific and literary interpretation of facts. The presentation of history both ways depending on the themes, context and time still holds good. R.G. Collingwood is absolutely justified in holding that "Instead of the historians choosing the subject, the subject chooses the historian" (*The Idea of History*). The prevailing attitudes in any age are the most important factors in guiding the historian in the treatment of his subject. This is what H.E. Barnes has highlighted again and again in his *A History of Historical Writing*.

The different branches of history sprang forth in different ages from different philosophical and historical thoughts and assumed relative importance.

Ibn Khaldun (1332–1406), one of the greatest Muslim historians, saw a unity and continuity in historical development. He maintained that like the individual organism the history undergoes constant changes. He advocated that history is concerned with the whole range of socio-cultural development of the people.

The idealists and positivists represent two broad schools of historical thought. B. Croce (1866–1952) of Italy, an idealist philosopher and a historian, in his *History as the Story of Liberty* pointed out that the historian's task is not only to chronicle the past events but also to deal with socio-cultural problems, and as an artist he is to apply his imagination and freedom. The idealists stood for autonomy of history. The historians of positivist school emphasized the importance of only political history ignoring the history of religion, culture and art. Karl Popper of that school propounded the theory that history is concerned with what people did and not what they failed to do. The historians of romantic school laid emphasis on the entire history of man as a single process of development. The two German philosophers, Kant (1724–1804) and Hegel (1770–1831), made a rational analysis of historiography as the logical development of human civilization. Karl Marx (1818-83) viewed history in the light of socio-economic transformation in the lives of men. The economic factors got prominence over other factors involved in the socio-economic development of the people. The economic history developed only in the nineteenth century. It is worthy of remark that without social history economic history is barren and without both the cultural history is unintelligible.

For the beginning of a new era of critical historiography in modern times the credit goes to the renowned German historian Ranke (1814-36).

G.R. Elton in his *The Practice of History* put emphasis on the study of the individual history with datable events. Those who popularized the study and writing of intellectual history include Karl Lamprecht (1856–1915) of Leipzig and J.H. Robinson (1863–1936).

All kinds of history, social, economic, political, religious, cultural, biographical and intellectual received the attention of different historians in different countries. Each of them has its own value. L. Gottschalk in his *Understanding History — A Premier of Historical Method*, has rightly pointed out that history whether large (about the very earliest civilization) or small (about knowledge of the early man) has its value.

The history we have today has its own history. It is not the product of one age or one brain. There are successive stages of its development. It has had an organic development. Its constituents, ramifications, etc. are the legacies of the past experiences of several centuries. Its body has been shaped by the historians of different schools that flourished in different ages in different countries and by the thoughts of historical schools of the period ranging from the Vedic age to modern times. "... History is what the historian makes" (E.H. Carr, *What is History*?). P. Smith in his *The Historians and History* has also expressed more or less the same view.

4

A New Approach to the Study of Historical Data in the Epic and Purāṇic Literature on Ancient India*

THE study of historical data available in the epic and Purāṇic literature as a whole relating to the pre- and post-Bhārata war dynasties and kingdoms of both Solar and Lunar races, traditional genealogy, dynastic chronology and genealogy of early historical period, dynasties of post-Sātavāhana and post-Gupta period, *janapada*s or territorial units, *mahājanapada*s or territorial states, towns and cities, various other urban centres, evolution of kingship, state formation, polity and administration, origin and expansion of Aryans and non-Aryan social groups, etc. can scientifically as well as profitably be made with the help of those Buddhist and Jaina traditions which fairly attest and corroborate them in certain respects, those archaeological evidences, which are consistent with the epic and Purāṇic traditions and those data brought to light by oriental and occidental historians and Indologists on the basis of their researches which are useful in supplementing them to a considerable degree.

* From proceedings of the National Seminar on History and Literature, 9-11 February, 1991, Sardar Patel University, Vallabh Vidyanagar (Gujarat), pp. 1-14.

The historical reliability of the Purāṇic accounts of the dynasties and kingdoms and genealogies of the Ikṣvāku rulers of Kosala with its capital at Ayodhyā[1] and those of rulers of Videha with its capital at Janakapur,[2] Vaiśālī of both Mālwā region and northern Bihar and of Ānartta (Gujarat) of Śaryāti line with its capital at Kuśasthalī,[3] all belonging to Solar race, is beyond doubt. Likewise, the details provided in some of the Purāṇas of the dynasties, kingdoms and genealogies of the descendants of Pururavas, the progenitor of the Lunar race are of great historical value. The Purāṇic description of Purus of Madhyadeśa or Gaṅgā–Yamunā doab; the Yādavas including the Haihayas of northern, western, central and southern India; Āṇavas of north; Druhyus of north; west and Turvasus of south-west, all five branches, which sprang up from Yayāti; of Kāśī and Kānyakubja dynasties; of Kurus with two principal kingdoms, Hastināpura and Indraprastha; of Pāñcālas with Ahicchatra and Kāmpilya, their northern and southern capitals respectively; of five kingdoms, notably, Magadha with capital at Giribraja founded by Bṛhadratha and Kośāmbī founded by Kośāmba — two of the five descendants of Vasu-Uparicara of Cedi-deśa in Kuru's line, etc.[4] are historically and archaeologically well-tested

---

1. *Vāyu Purāṇa* (Allahabad, 1987), 88, 3-212; *Matsya* (Gorakhpur, 1985), Ch. 12; *Viṣṇu* (Gorakhpur, 9th edn. Saṁ. 2041), iv, 2, 637; IV 3, 40f; *Brahmāṇḍa* (Bombay, 1906), 3, 60, 63; *Brahma*, ch. 8.

2. *Vāyu*, Ch. 89; *Viṣṇu*, iv, 5; *Brahmāṇḍa*, 3, 64; *Bhāgavata* (Gorakhpur, 8th edn., Saṁ. 2040), ix, 13.

3. *Vāyu*, 86, 22-28; *Viṣṇu*, IV, 1, 62-65, 91-94; *Matsya*, 12, 21-24.

4. *Vāyu* Ch. 94; *Matsya*, Ch. 43; *Viṣṇu*, IV.11; *Bhāgavata*, ch. ix; *Brahmāṇḍa*; 3, 65-70; *Agni* (Prayāga, 1986) Ch. 275.

The information provided in the *Mahābhārata*[5] about the genealogies and kingdoms and capital cities of the rulers of Lunar dynasties, particularly of Puru's line are supplementary to that obtainable from the Purāṇas. It is significant to note that in order to make an accurate historical study of the various branches of the Yādava tribes like confederate republican tribes, Andhaka-Vṛṣṇis, Bhojas, Kukuras, etc. their expansion in various directions, the reasons behind the shifting of their capital from Mathurā in the north to Dvārakā in the west, of Dvārakā as a city of Kṛṣṇa's time, the destruction of the Yādavas in the fratricidal war thereafter, the submerging of the said city under the seawater, re-settlements'of the Yādava tribes, etc. reliance can be placed on the combined testimony of the *Mahābhārata*,[6] the Purāṇas,[7] and the archaeological finds of S.R. Rao from Bet-Dvārakā between 1982 and 1988. It is worthy of remark that the political importance of the seals of Dvārakā made out of shells with lotus engraved on them and their economic value in the market have also been highlighted

5. Ed. Damodar Satavalekar with Hindi tr. *Ādi Parva* (Paradi, Gujarat, 1968), 1, 44-45 138; 57, 2-9, 27-30; 70, 11-45; Ch. 71; 80, 26; 82, 5; Chs. 88-89; 89, 5-43; Ch. 90, 1-50; *Anuśāsana Parva* (1978), Ch. 31, 6-26; *Sabhā Parva* (1981-82), 13, 3-51; 18, 21-30; 19, 1-22; see also Vasudeva Sharan Agrawala, *Bhārata Sāvitrī* (Delhi, 1977), vol. 1, pp. 83-87, 150-72.

6. *Ādi Parva*, 210, 15-20; 213, 23-55; *Sabhā Parva*, 13, 5-55; *Āraṇyaka Parva* (1969), 16, 5-23; 17, 1-33; *Mausala Parva* (1977), 2, 1-20; 4, 32-41; 6, 1-15; 7-9-22; 8, 4-10, 47-74; *Mahāprasthānika Parva* (1977), 1, 43; *Śānti Parva* (1979-80) 82, 8-17, 25-29; see also V.S. Agrawala, *Bhārata Sāvitrī*, vol. 1, pp. 206-7; vol. 3 (Delhi; 1st edn. 1968), pp. 221-23, 259-60 and K.P. Jayaswal, *Hindu Polity* (Bangalore, 1981) App-A, p. 355.

7. *Harivaṁśa* (Gorakhpur, 4th edn. Saṁ. 2044) 34 , 1-22; 35, 1-111, 36, 1-40; 39, 10-32; 56, 7-35; 58, 3-36; *Bhāgavata*, X, 50, 7-19, 21-23, 34-57; X, 52, 5 f; X, 53, 5-22; X, 58, 12; X, 80, 8-12; XI, 30, 4-48; *Viṣṇu*, V, 23, 9-1 5; V, 24, 5-7; V, 37, 22-39; 42-63; V, 38, 34-35, *Brahma*, 14,

→

in "the Āraṇyaka Parva[8] of the *Mahābhārata* and the *Harivaṁśa*[9] respectively. The archaeological discovery of Kṛṣṇa's Dvārakā city by Rao along with the said seals and other remains go to prove the historicity of the details provided in the epic and the Purāṇas about the subject matter concerned. The epic and Purāṇic evidences regarding the said two dynasties of pre-Bhārata war period can also be confirmed by the researches of S.N. Pradhan,[10] F.E. Pargiter,[11] H.C. Raychaudhuri,[12] H.D. Sankalia,[13] A.D. Pusalker,[14] Romila Thapar,[15] H.H. Wilson,[16]

→ 53-56; 196, 5-15; 210, 56-58; *Vāyu*, 95, 14-47; 96, 46, 87-112; *Viṣṇu* IV, 12, 2-45; *Matsya*, 44, 14-47; *Brahmāṇḍa*, 3, 70, 14-48; *Brahmavaivartta* (Prayāga, 1985), 103, 7-33 & 80.

8. 16, 19, 80, 83.

9. Viṣṇu Parva, 58, 57-66; G.P. Singh, "A Fresh Literary Discovery of the Seals of Dvārakā in the Epic Age as a supplement to Archaeological Discovery by S.R. Rao," a paper presented in Ancient India section of Indian Hist. Cong. held at Calcutta, 28-30 December 1990.

10. *Chronology of Ancicnt India* (Varanasi, 1979), pp. 61-153.

11. *Ancient Indian Historical Tradition* (Delhi, 1972), pp. 90-119; 253-86.

12. *Political History of Ancient India* (6th edn. Calcutta, 1953), pp. 48-84.

13. "Prehistoric Colonization in India; Archaeological and Literary Evidence," in *Aspects of Indian History and Archaeology* (Delhi, 1977), pp. 298-312.

14. "Traditional History from the Earliest Times to the Accession of Parikshit," in the *Vedic Age* (ed. R.C. Majumdar, Bombay, 1965), pp. 271-304.

15. "Purāṇic Lineages and Archaeological Cultures," in *Ancient Indian Social History* (Hyderabad, 1984), pp. 242 ff; "The Tradition of Historical Writing in Early India," in op. cit., pp. 272ff; "Origins Myths and the Early Indian Historical Tradition," in op. cit., pp. 294ff; "Genealogy as a Source of Social History," in op. cit., pp. 326ff. 339.

16. Tr. *Viṣṇu Purāṇa* (Calcutta, 1961), pp. 338-41, 68.

and B. Morton Smith.[17] Some Sanskrit Buddhist texts like *Lalitavistara* (p. 406) *Bodhisattvāvadāna Kalpalatā* (3rd Pallava, 116; 64 Pallava), *Divyāvadāna* (p. 435) and *Mahāvastu* (vol. 11, pp. 2f, 94-95; vol. III, pp. 57, 361) and other Buddhist sources[18] and Jaina texts[19] also help us in supplementing the epic and Purāṇic accounts of pre-war dynasties, kingdoms, towns and cities, etc.

The first phase of Pauravas settlement in Sarasvatī and upper doab archaeologically associated with ochre-coloured pottery (OCP) of late Haṛappan period (*c.* 2200–1700 BCE) and Yādavas settlements in Narmadā, Mālwā, Gujarat and Gaṅgā–Yamunā doab associated with chalcolithic Black and Red Ware (BRW) ascribed to *c.* 2000 BCE are also worthy of our attention from archaeological point of view.

The existence of urban centres like Hastināpura, Indraprastha, Kośāmbī, Ahicchatra, etc. in the Gangetic valley as described in the epic-Purāṇic literature has been archaeologically proved and associated with Painted Grey Ware (PGW) and Northern Black Polished Ware (NBPW) cultures. On the basis of Radio-Carbon (14) dating the archaeologists have placed them in the first millennium BCE which is not beyond dispute. However, H.D. Sankalia, while placing his reliance on both tradition and archaeology, has reasonably concluded that the antiquity of towns and cities as

---

17. *Dates and Dynasties in Earliest India* (Delhi, 1973), pp. 38-44.

18. See B.C. Law, "Countries and Peoples of India; Epic and Purāṇic Sources," in *Geographical Essays Relating to Ancient Geography of India* (Varanasi, 1976), pp. 119ff, also pp. 14-31; B.C. Law, *India as Described in Early Texts of Buddhism and Jainism* (Delhi, 1980), pp. 38-103; *Ghata Jātaka*, IV, pp. 79-89.

19. See J.C. Jain, *Life in Ancient India as Depicted in Jaina Canon and Commentaries* (Delhi, 1984), pp. 350-349, 458-59; See also Jaina text *Vasudevhiṇḍi* (Bhavanagar, 1930-31), pp. 77f, 110f, 357f (for Andhaka-Vṛṣṇis).

occurring in the *Mahābhārata* and Purāṇas can also be proved by archaeological evidences. He has aptly remarked, "Traditions, whether epic or Purāṇic, Jaina or Buddhist or purely local have an important role to play in helping unravel our past cultures and civilization."[20]

A. Altekar has categorically stated that pre-Bhārata war history can be reconstructed with the help of epic-Purāṇic evidences.[21] The credibility of traditional history from the earliest times to the accession of Parīkṣit II (36 years after the War) as recorded in the *Mahābhārata* and Purāṇas thus need to be carefully examined with the help of all available sources.

The dynasties and kingdoms of post-war period extending from the beginning of Kaliyuga down to the sixth century BCE, notably the Kurus of Hastināpura of post-Parīkṣit period, Ikṣvākus of Kosala, Bṛhadrathas (32 kings who ruled for 1000 years) of Magadha, Pradyotas (5 kings who ruled for 52 years) of Avantī, and the kingdom of Kāśī and the shifting of capital from Hastināpura to Kauśāmbī by eight successors of Parīkṣit, the rule of Udayana over Kauśāmbī, the progeny of Buddha belonging to Śākya clan, etc. are vividly portrayed in the Purāṇic records.[22] The genealogical accounts of the rulers concerned are also historically important.

20. "Archaeology and Tradition," in op. cit., pp. 277-78 and 281, also p. 308.

21. "Can we Reconstruct pre-Bhārata War History," in *Journal of Banaras Hindu University* (*JBHU*), vol. IV, pp. 183-223.

22. See *Matsya*, 50, 58-79; 271, 4-30; 272, 1-5; *Vāyu* 99, 249-314; *Viṣṇu*, IV, 21, 2-18, IV, 22, 1-13; IV, 23, 2-13; IV, 24, 1-8, *Bhaviṣya Purāṇa* (Bareilly 1978), vol. 1, pp. 309-34. See also S.N. Pradhan, op. cit., pp. 61, 118 f, 169 f, 232 f; F.E. Pargiter, *Ancient Indian Historical Tradition*, pp. 285-87; *The Purāṇa Text of the Dynasties of the Kali Age* (hereafter as *DKA*), London 1913, pp. 7-66; Rapson (ed.), *The Cambridge History of India* (*CHI*), vol. 1, *Ancient India*, pp. 165-66. H.C. Raychaudhary, op. cit., pp. 36-47; A.D. Pusalker, op. cit., pp. 323-32; H.H. Wilson, op cit., pp. 369-72.

The details provided in the *Mahābhārata* about the Kuru Kingdom of Hastināpura, ruled by the successors of Parīkṣit II are also of considerable historical importance.[23] The Buddhist and Jaina sources[24] also throw some light on the subject concerned to a considerable extent.

The Purāṇic accounts of the dynasties of early historical period are of exceptional value. It is the Purāṇic literature from which it appears that ten Śiśunāga kings comprising Bimbisāra (*c.* 558–491 BCE), Ajātaśatru (*c.* 491–459 BCE) both contemporary of Buddha (*c.* 563–483 BCE) and others ruled roughly for 165 to 200 years between 642 BCE and 402 BCE.[25] The Purāṇic length of years varying from 360 to 321 years are inflated. The nine Nandas (Mahāpadmananda and his eight successors) ruled for about 8 years between (402 BCE and 322 BCE.[26] Ten Mauryan kings (Candragupta Maurya and his successors) ruled for about 137 years between fourth and second centuries BCE.[27] Ten rulers of the Śuṅga dynasty (second–first century BCE) ruled for about 112 years.[28] The Kaṇvas (first century BCE ruled exactly for 45 years.[29] About 30 rulers of the Sātavāhana dynasty ruled over the Deccan for about 460 years between the third century BCE and second

23. Ādi Parva, 111, 18, 144-80; 31, 5-18, 40, 6-8; 45, 13f; 52, 5-19.
24. See B.C. Law, *India as Described in the early texts of Buddhism and Jainism*, p. 94; J.C. Jain, op. cit., pp. 460-73.
25. See *Matsya*, 272, 5-11; *Vāyu*, 99, 314-20, *Viṣṇu*, 24, 9-19; *Bhaviṣya*, vol. 1, p. 332.
26. *Matsya*, 272, 12-13; *Vāyu*, 99, 322-30; *Viṣṇu*, IV, 24, 25-26; *Bhaviṣya*, vol. 1, p. 333.
27. *Matsya*, 272, 21-26; *Vāyu*, 99, 331-36; *Viṣṇu*, IV, 24, 29-32; *Bhaviṣya*, vol. 1, p. 333-35.
28. *Matsya*, 272, 26-28; *Vāyu*, 99, 339-43; *Viṣṇu*, IV, 24, 33-37.
29. *Matsya*, 272, 28-33; *Vāyu*, 99, 343-47, *Viṣṇu*, IV, 24, 38-42.

century CE.[30] The evidences furnished by some authorities[31] on the subject concerned are also helpful in substantiating the Purāṇic accounts of the dynasties concerned.

The Purāṇic records also testify to the fact that in the post-Sātavāhana period the seven dynasties comprising that of Gaddavila, Muruṇḍa, Abhira, Yavanas, Śūdras, Magas and Vikramāditya Śālivāhana of Ujjain with total 76 princes reigned for more than five centuries over different parts of India.[32]

The Purāṇic literature slightly deals with the history of the Gupta period but it does not go beyond the time of Candragupta (fourth century CE).[33]

The *Bhaviṣya Purāṇa* in particular also deals with the histories of Bhojas Paramāra dynasty of Mālwā (with its capital at Dhār 60 km from Indore) belonging to the tenth and eleventh centuries CE, of Pratihāras and Gāhaḍavālas of Kannauj (ninth to twelfth century CE), of Jayacanda period (1170-91 CE) and of Cauhāna rulers like Pṛthvīrāja Cauhāna.[34]

---

30. *Matsya*, 273, 1-17; *Vāyu*, 99, 348-58; *Viṣṇu*, IV, 24, 43-50; *Brahmāṇḍa*, 3, 74, 160-70.

31. S.N. Pradhan, op. cit., pp. 21I f; Pargiter, *Anct. Ind. Historical Tradition*, pp. 286-87. *DKA*; pp. 18-25, 67-69; also his "Ancient Indian Genealogies and Chronology;" in *JRAS* (London, 1910), pp. 56 f. B.C. Law, *The Magadhas in Ancient India* (Varanasi, 1976), pp. 6-15; V.A. Smith, *Early History of India* (London, 1924) pp. 41-45; E.J. Rapson (ed.), *CHI*, vol.1, pp. 168 f; 467 f; R.S. Tripathi, *History of Ancient India* (Delhi, 1935), pp. 113-14; H.C. Raychaudhury, op. cit., pp. 225-29; H.H. Wilson, op. cit., pp. 373-82; R.M. Smith, op. cit., pp. 346-78.

32. *Matsya*, 273, 18-28; *Vāyu*, 99, 359-83.

33. *Vāyu*, 99, 383-84.

34. Vol. 1, pp. 313-31, 335-37, 416-24; 429-35; vol. 2, pp. 9, 30, 160, 172, 96; 339, 416-20, 425-44.

It is worthy of remark that the genealogies of the said dynasties of early historical period (Śiśunāga, Nanda, Maurya Śuṅga, Kaṇva and Sātavāhana) are chronologically arranged in the Purāṇas. Many of the dynasties are historically authenticated. Regnal years and the time-span of rulers are given with slight variations in the Purāṇas, which can be verified with the help of other faithful historical records. The Purāṇic data concerned are extremely important for genealogical and chronological reconstruction of ancient history of the periods concerned.[35]

The data provided by F. Wilford,[36] William Jones,[37] and John Bentley[38] are very very important for making a research-oriented study of the Purāṇic genealogies and chronology of the above-mentioned historical dynasties.

The data provided in two important Ceylonese Buddhist Chronicles, *Dīpavaṁsa* (an ancient Buddhist historical record)[39] and *Mahāvaṁsa* (fifth century CE)[40] and other Buddhist texts

---

35. See Romila Thapar, *Ancient Indian Social History*, pp. 326-28, 352.

36. "An Essay on the Sacred Isles in the West . . .", "Kings and their Chronology," in *As. Res.* (Delhi, 1979), vol. 9, pp. 84-116; "Chronology of the Hindus," in *As. Res.*, vol. 5, pp. 241 f.

37. "On the chronology of the Hindus" written in 1788, pub. in *As Res.*, 1st in 1799 and then in *As. Res.* (Delhi, 1979), vol. 2, pp. 167-113; also the works of William Jones (in 13 vols.), vol. IV, ed. Lord Teignmoth (London 1807), pp. 36-40.

38. "On the Hindu System of Astronomy and their connection with History in Ancient and modern times," in *As. Res.* (Delhi, 1979), vol. 8, pp. 225 ff; "On the Principal Eras and Dates of the Ancient Hindus," in *As. Res.* (Delhi, 1979), vol. 5, pp. 318-43.

39. Ed. & tr. H. Oldenberg (London, 1879), 111, 50-60; vol. 97.

40. Ed. W. Geiger (Palitext Society, PTS, London, 1908) and tr. him (P.T.S. London, (912), 11, 28-31; IV. 1-3.

like *Dīgha Nikāya*,[41] *Sumaṅgala-Vilāsinī* (commentary on above Nikāya),[42] *Saṁyutta Nikāya*,[43] and *Vinaya Piṭaka*[44] are also important for the purpose of filling up gaps in the Purāṇic accounts of the Śiśunāga dynasty of Magadha of both Buddhist and post-Buddhist period.

There are some rare Jaina texts like *Tiloyapaññati* of Yativr̥ṣabha ascribed to *c.* CE 176 (ed. A.N. Upadhye and H.L. Jain, Solapur, 1951, IV, vv. 95-99), *Harivaṁśa Purāṇa* by Jinasena ascribed to CE 783 (Bombay 1930), *Trilokasāra* of Nemicandra; *Uttarapurāṇa* of Guṇabhadra (Benares, 1952), *Paṭṭāvali Samuccaya* (A collection of Śvetāmbara Paṭṭāvalis by Muni Darśana Vijaya (in 2 vols.), 1933), *Vicāraśreṇī* by Merutuṅga (CE 130), *Prabhāvakacarita* (CE 1277) ed. Jinavijaya (Bombay, 1940) and *Vividha-Tīrtha-Kalpa* of Jina Prabhās Sūri (ed. Jinavijaya, Bombay, 1934)[45] which also deal with Nanda, Maurya, Śuṅga and post-Sātavāhana dynasties and Guptas. They are helpful for the purpose of supplementing the Purāṇic accounts of the dynastic chronology of the rulers concerned.

For making a thorough study of the evolution of kingship, origin, nature, formation and seven constituent elements of the state (popularly known as *saptāṅga* theory) its aims and functions, and decline and its various forms including the *gaṇarājya* and polity and administration in ancient India, the

41. Ed. T.W. Rhys Davids and J.E. Carpenter (PTS, London, 1890-1911), 1, p. 86.
42. Ed. T.W. Rhys Davids J.E. Carpenter (3 vols. PTS, London, 1886-1932), 11., pp. 516-17.
43. Ed. Rhys Davids (PTS, London 1884-1904) 1, 82-5.
44. Ed. H. Oldenberg (London, 1879-82), 1, p. 179; *Vinaya*, 11, p. 490.
45. See *The Jaina Sources of the History of Ancient India (100 BCE – CE 900)* (Delhi, 1964), pp. 255-60.

epic[46] and Purāṇic[47] data are to be combined together and strictly scrutinized and analysed.

The same approach is to be adopted to the study of ancient Indian *janapadas* (countries and peoples, both Aryan and non-Aryan) of Madhyadeśa, North-Western, South-Eastern, Eastern, Dakṣiṇāpatha, Vindhya region, and mountain regions and sixteen *mahājanapadas*, like Kuru, Pañcāla, Kāśī, Kosala, Aṅga, Magadha, Cedi, Avantī, Gandhāra, Kāmboja, etc. of the sixth century BCE.[48]

The original settlements of the Aryans in the region extending from the western coast of the Yamunā to Kurukṣetra on the bank of Sarasvatī, (also known as Sārasvata region) as described in the Āraṇyaka Parva[49] of the *Mahābhārata* and

---

46. See Śānti Parva (1979-80), 56, 2-36; 57, 4-5, 10-42; 58, 1-24; 59, 13-18, Chs. 67, 91-95, 97; 104, 11-30; 108, 8-31; see also V.S. Agrawala, *Bhārata Sāvitrī* (Delhi, 1977), vol. 1, pp. 139-41, 144-45, 150-72; vol. 3 (Delhi, 1968), pp. 23, 41-58, 67-69, 89-95.

47. *Matsya*, chs. 215-17; 220, 9-20, Chs. 225-27; *Agni*, Chs. 218-27; 233, 11-23; Ch. 235; 239, 11-45; *The Svargakhaṇḍa of the Padma Purāṇa* (by A. Chatterjee Shastri, Varanasi, 1972), 36, 2-8; Ch. 37; Ch. 38, vv. 1-40, 59-60, 61-65; See also B.B. Mishra, *Polity in the Agni Purāṇa* (Calcutta, 1965) pp. 27-81.

48. See *Mahābharata*, Bhīṣma Parva (1972), 10; 37-68; 12, 33-35; Droṇa Parva (1975), 4, 4-5; 6, 2-7; 10, 15-16. Chs. 17-19 and 22-23; Karṇa Parva (1973), 27, 71-91; 30, 9-81; Udyoga Parva (1969), 19, 7-32; Sabhā Parva, 23, 13-22; 24, 1-27; 26, 1-16; 27, 1-22, 28, 1- 49; 29, 1-25; 35, 6-25; 47, 10-26; 48, 3-13; V.S. Agrawala, *Bhārata Sāvitrī* (Delhi, 1977) vol. 2, pp. 121-47, 247-76; Purāṇas: *Matsya*, 114, 15-57; *Vāyu*, 45, 108-37; *Viṣṇu*, 2, 3, 15-17; *Agni*, 118-8; *Mārkaṇḍeya* (Meerut, 1983) 54, 35-57; 55, 6-52; see also D.C. Sircar, *Studies in the Geography of Ancient and Medieval India* (Delhi, 1971), pp. 26-73; S.M. Ali, *The Geography of the Purāṇas* (Delhi, 1983), pp. 133-69; B.C. Law, *Geography of Early Buddhism* (Varanasi, 1973) pp. 1-55.

49. 81, 1-7.

supported by V.S. Agrawala[50] and also their expansion from their original homeland in Pratiṣṭhāna (Prayāga) as depicted in the Purāṇas[51] and corroborated by H.D. Sankalia[52] provide some clues about their indigenous origin in contradistinction to their foreign origin.

The historical value of the details provided in the *Mahābhārata* can be judged from different angles. The Ādi Parva[53] and the Svargārohaṇa Parva[54] themselves refer to the text concerned as a part of history, what can be supported by the statements of V.S. Agrawala[55] and C.V. Vaidya.[56] However, the text suffers from the deficiency of the chronological sequence of the events.

Likewise, the value of *Itihāsa-Purāṇa* tradition is also fairly illustrated in some of the Purāṇic texts.[57] The historical authenticity of the Purāṇic data from the dynastic, genealogical and chronological points of view have also been acknowledged by Pargiter,[58] A.K. Warder,[59] H.H. Wilson,[60]

---

50. *Bhārata Sāvitrī*, vol. 1, pp. 255-56.
51. See Pargiter, *Ancient Indian Historical Tradition*, pp. 295-300.
52. *Prehistory of India* (Bombay, 1973), p. 179; *Aspects of Indian History and Archaeology*, p. 308.
53. 1, 24-25, 28-52; 11, 31-33; 56, 15-27.
54. Svargārohaṇa Parva (1977), 5, 39; 5, 43.
55. *Bhārata Sāvitrī*, vol. 3, p. 229.
56. *The Mahābharata: A Criticism* (Delhi, 1966), pp. 50 ff.
57. See *Kūrma Purāṇa* (Varanasi, 1972), Pūrva Kāṇḍa, 1.1.3; 1.1.5; 1.112; *Brahmavaivartta Purāṇa* (Allah. 1985), Uttara Ḳāṇḍa, 133, 5-6.
58. *Ancient Indian Historical Tradition*, pp. 2, 9-12, 61-63; "Ancient Indian Genealogies and Chronology," *JRAS*, 1910, p. 56.
59. *An Introduction to Indian Historiography* (Bombay, 1972), pp. 17-25.
60. Op. cit., pp. 1-10.

R. Morton Smith,[61] A.D. Pusalker,[62] U.N. Ghoshal,[63] Romila Thapar,[64] A. Banerjee Shastri,[65] V.R. Ramachandra Dikshit,[66] A. Altekar,[67] D.R. Mankad,[68] Kota Venkatachalam,[69] and others.

Keeping in view the facts stated above it can be observed that for making an accurate historical study of the subject-matter concerned reliance should be placed on the combined testimonies of the epic, Purāṇic, Jaina and Buddhist traditions and archaeology.

V.A. Smith, while attesting high value to the traditional history as embodied in literature has also admitted that dependence must be placed wholly upon ancient literary tradition of India, but unfortunately he like Elphinstone has

---

61. *Dates and Dynasties in Earliest India*, Intro.; also his two papers on the "Ancient Chronology of India" pub. in *Jour. of American Oriental Society*, vol. 77, no. 2, April – June 1957 and no. 4, December 1957.

62. *Studies in Epics and Purāṇas* (Bombay, 1955); "Conception of History in Ancient Indian Literature," in *Our Heritage* (1964), vol. 12, Pt. 2 pp. 35-52; also *Historians and Historiography on Modern India* (ed. S.P. Sen, Calcutta, 1973), pp. 32-34.

63. *The Beginnings of Indian Historiography and other Essays* (Calcutta, 1944), pp. 21 f, and 51.

64. *Ancient Indian Social History*, pp. 272-73, 326-28, 331 f, 352.

65. "On Ancient Indian Historical Tradition," in *JBORI*: vol. XIII, pp. 62-79.

66. "The Purāṇa: A Study," in *IHQ*, vol. VIII, pp. 747-67.

67. See *JBHU*, vol. IV, pp. 183-223.

68. "Studies in the Purāṇic History, Genealogies and Chronology in Modern Times," in *Purāṇa*, vol. 4, 1962, no. 1, pp. 3-22; See also his *Purāṇic Chronology* (Vallabh Vidyanagar, 1951).

69. *The Plot in Indian Chronology* (Vijayavada, 1953), pp. 80-100; *Chronology of Ancient Hindu History*, in 2 parts (Vijayawada, 1957), pt. 1, pp. 90-100.

not acknowledged the importance of early historical tradition of India anterior to the sixth or fourth century BCE.[70]

A.B. Keith[71] and Maurice Winternitz[72] while affirming the historical sense of ancient Indians and the historical writing in early India clearly state that ancient Indian literary tradition had great value.

U.N. Ghoshal, on the basis of his study of the historical traditions preserved in the Vedic Saṁhitās, brāhmaṇas, epics and the Purāṇas, has also accepted that "the historical sense had dawned upon the Indians at the beginning of their history."[73] A.D. Pusalker in one of his research papers: "Conception of History in Ancient Indian Literature,"[74] has strongly advocated the historical validity of the epic and Purāṇic data about various aspects of ancient Indian history and culture. Romila Thapar has also stated that the ancient Indians did maintain records of their history which they felt significant. The Purāṇas constitute very faithful records from the dynastic, genealogical and chronological points of view and not from the political point of view. But paradoxically she mentions that the Indian literature prior to the dawn of the seventh century cannot be considered as historical writing.[75] Thus, we find some contradictions in her statements. M.

---

70. *See Early History of India* (rev. 4th edn. by S.M. Edward, London 1967), pp. 4f and 10 and Elphinstone's *History of India* (London, 1911), p. 11.
71. *A History of Sanskrit Literature* (1st pub. Oxford, 1920, Delhi, 1973), pp. 144-45.
72. *History of Indian Literature* (1st pub. Calcutta, 1927, rpt. Delhi, 1977), pp. 29-30.
73. Op. cit., pp. 21-23, 50-52.
74. Pub. in *Our Heritage* vol. 12 (1964), Pt. 2, pp. 35-52.
75. *Ancient Indian Social History*, pp. 268-69, 272-73, 326 f. 352. *The Past and Prejudice* (Delhi, 1975), pp. 2-3.

Krishnamachariar[76] strongly supports the historical value of the Purāṇic data concerned.

But on the other hand, we find that some foreign and Indian scholars like J. Allan, Wolseley Haig and H.H. Dodwell,[77] A.A. Macdonell,[78] J.W. McCrindle,[79] Alberni,[80] R.S. Tripathi,[81] H.C. Raychaudhari,[82] and D.D. Kośāmbī[83] have tried to prove that ancient Indians (the brāhmaṇas, Jains and Buddhists) had no sense of history and chronology; their works cannot be compared with the historical writings of ancient Greece and Rome and ancient Indian literature is destitute of historical material. Their views can be disposed of on the basis of the richness of the historical data which we find in ancient Indian literature including epic and Purāṇic.

E.J. Rapson has reasonably maintained that the large and varied literature of the brāhmaṇas, Jains and Buddhists cannot be compared with the works of ancient historians of Greece and Rome, but the dynastic list and genealogies preserved in

---

76. *History of Classical Sanskrit Literature* (Delhi, 3rd edn., 1974), pp. 1 ff, 10 ff, 50 f.

77. *Cambridge Shorter History of India* (Delhi, 1964), p. 1.

78. *A History of Sanskrit Literature* (1st pub. Oxford, 1899, 3rd edn. Delhi, 1972), pp. 10-11.

79. *Ancient India as Described in Classical Literature* (Westminster, 1901), p. XII.

80. See E.G. Sachau, *Alberani's India* (2 vols., London, 1910, rpt. Delhi, 1964), vol. 11, Ch. XLIX, pp. 10-11; See also Alberani's *Chrcnology of Ancient Nations* tr. E. Sachau (London, 1879), pp. 6, note 368.

81. *History of Ancient India* (Delhi 1985), p. 1.

82. Op. cit., p. 1.

83. *The Culture and Civilization of Ancient India in Historical Outline* (Delhi, 1972), pp. 9-10; *An Introduction to the Study of Indian History* (Bombay 1975), p. 1.

ancient Indian literature marks the beginnings of history in ancient India and its development was carried beyond this rudimentary stage. He also refers to the historical material in literature and its deficiency from the standpoint of political events.[84]

84. *CHI* (Delhi, 1962), vol. 1; *Ancient India*, pp. 51-52.

5

The Purāṇic Tradition of Historiography in India*

ONE of the most important traditions of historiography in ancient India was the Purāṇic one. The Purāṇic historiography is important from dynastic, genealogical and chronological points of view.

The Purāṇa, originally a single text (divided into eighteen parts) and called both *Purāṇa Saṁhitā* and *Itihāsa Saṁhitā*, was composed by Veda Vyāsa in the Dvāpara age (some time before the Great Bhārata battle began) which can irrefutably be proved on the combined testimony of the Purāṇas themselves.[1]

---

* From *Indian Historical Review*, vol. XXXI, nos. 1 & 2, 2004, pp. 1-17. This is a revised version of the paper presented at the 17th conference of the International Association of Historians of Asia held at the University of Dhaka, 18-22 December, 2002.

1. *Matsya* (text with Hindi tr., Gorakhpur, 1985), 53, 3-11, 68-69; *Vāyu* (text with Hindi tr. R.P. Tripathi Sastri, Prayāga, 1987), 103, 48-51, 55-58; *Viṣṇu* (text with Hindi tr. M.L. Gupta, Gorakhpur, Saṁvat 2041), III, 3, 2-21; III, 4, 1-10; III, 6, 15; *Brahmāṇḍa* (text, Bombay, 1913), I, 1, 173; IV, 4, 47-50, 54-58; *Bhāgavata* (text with Hindi tr. and annotation, Gorakhpur, Saṁvat 2040) ed. with English tr. by C.L. Goswami (Gorakhpur, 1982), I, 4, 20; III, 12, 39; *Kūrma* (ed. with Hindi tr. of Shree Chaudhari Shree Narayana Singh by A.S. Gupta, Varanasi, 1972), I, 1, 3 and 5; I, 50, 10-14 and 20-21; also II, 44, 145; *Brahmavaivartta*, ed. with Hindi tr. T. Jha (Allahabad, 1985), 133, 5; *Vāmana* (ed. with Hindi tr. G.C. Vedanta Sastri, Shree Chaudhari Shree Narayana Singh and G.S. Rai by →

Vyāsa, the original author *of Bhārata Saṁhitā* or *Bhārata Itihāsa* (later called *Mahābhārata*) and Purāṇa, has been called by Uma Shankar Dikshit *Itihāsakarttā* (composer of historical works) and "a great historian"[2] which can be corroborated by the statements of A.K. Warder,[3] a noted authority on Indian historiography, and N.S. Rajaram.[4] The original Purāṇa (like *Bhārata Saṁhitā,* or *Bhārata Itihāsa)* contained the dynastic history of only pre-Bhārata war period. It saw several recensions with additions between the sixth century BCE and the fifth century CE. The *purāṇakāra*s applying their historical sense from time to time incorporated the historical events of the past along with other subjects in it not only during this period but also the later.

The Purāṇas in general are partly legendary and partly historic! Of the eighteen main Purāṇas, the six — *Matsya, Vāyu, Viṣṇu, Brahmāṇḍa, Bhāgavata* and *Bhaviṣya* — are very important from a historical point of view. The first two have been called by their composers *Purātana Itihāsa* (ancient history)[5] in support of their historicity as they (like the other four Purāṇas) deal with historical subjects. These six Purāṇas really constitute very faithful historical records. A. Weber has also admitted that some of the old Purāṇas contain historical portions with

---

→ A.S. Gupta, Varanasi, 1968), 12, 3; *Padma,* ed. V.N. Mandalika (Poona, 1893-94), V, 2, 53; *Viṣṇudharmottara* (text, Bombay, 1912), III, 15, 1.

2. *Maharṣi Veda Vyāsa: A Historical and Cultural Biography* (Varanasi, 1968), p. 13.

3. *An Introduction to Indian Historiography* (hereafter *IIH*) (Bombay, 1972), pp. 116-17.

4. "Distortions of Indian History from Haṛappā to Ayodhyā", in *The Astrological Magazine,* ed. B.V. Raman, Bangalore, vol. 87, no. 1, January 1998, p. 75.

5. *Matsya,* 72, 6; *Vdyu,* 103, 48.

kings, dynasties, genealogies and chronology.[6] Of the six Purāṇas mentioned here, in the first four additions to the original contents were made up to the fourth or fifth century CE, in the fifth up to the eight or ninth century CE, and in the sixth up to the twelfth century CE. Thus, the Purāṇas are not the productions of one age or of one brain. Besides these six, some other Purāṇas are also important for historical purposes.

The two very important historical subjects the Purāṇas deal with are *vaṁśa* (genealogies) and *vaṁśānucarita* (accounts of the dynasties of kings mentioned in the genealogies).[7] The dynastic genealogies, in fact, constitute the nucleus of the political history in the Purāṇas. V.A. Smith observes:

> . . . the most systematic record of the Indian historical tradition is that preserved in the dynastic lists of the Purāṇas. . . . Modern European writers have been inclined to disparage unduly the authority of the Purāṇic lists, but closer study finds in them much genuine and valuable historial tradition.[8]

The Purāṇic accounts of the kingdoms and dynasties with genealogies of the Ikṣvāku rulers of Kosala with its capital at Ayodhyā[9] and that of the rulers of Videha with its capital at

---

6. *History of Indian Literature*, English tr. from the 2nd German edn. by J. Mann and Th Zachariae (London, 1882, Delhi rpt. 1981), pp. 213-15.

7. *Matsya*, 53, 64; *Viṣṇu*, III, 6, 25 and 27; *Bhāgavata*, XII, 7, 9-10; *Brahmavaivartta*, 133, 6; *Kūrma*, I, 1, 12.

8. *Early History of India* (hereafter *EHI*), revised by S.M. Edwards, 4th edn. (London, 1967), p. 11.

9. *Matsya*, 12, 34-35, 42-57; *Vāyu*, 88, 3-212; *Viṣṇu*, IV, 2, 34-70; IV, 3, 1-28; IV, 4, 5-40, 75-112; *Brahmāṇḍa*, III, 63, 115, 120-41, 186-91; *Bhāgavata*, IX, 6, 20-39; IX, 8, 17-19; IX, 13, 1-16; RE. Pargiter, *Ancient Indian Historical Tradition* (hereafter *AIHT*) (London, 1922, Delhi rpt., 1972), pp. 90-94.

Mithilā (Janakpura),[10] of Vaiśālī[11] and of Ānartta (later called Gujarat) with its capital at Kuśasthalī (Dvāravatī or Dvārakā)[12] of the Solar family of pre-Bhārata a war period are historically reliable. Likewise, the details provided in some of the Purāṇas of the kingdoms and dynasties with genealogies of the lineal descendants of Purūravā, the progenitor of the Lunar family and ruler of Pratiṣṭhānapura on the bank of the Gaṅgā in Prayāga of the same period are of great historical value. The Purāṇic descriptions of Purus of Madhyadeśa or Gaṅgā–Yamunā doab, the Yādavas in Yadu's line, including the Haihayas of northern, western, central and southern India, the Āṇavas of the north, Druhyus of the north-west and Turavasus of the south-east — all five branches that sprang up from Yayāti — and that of Kāśī and Kānyakubja dynasties, of Kurus in the main Paurava line, of Pañcālas, and of five kingdoms, notably, Magadha founded by Bṛhadratha (who was succeeded by another nine rulers during the period) and Kauśāmbī founded by Kośāmba — two of the five descendants of Vasu Uparicara of Cedideśa in Kuru's line[13] — are historically and archaeologically well tested.

---

10. *Vāyu,* 89, 1-23; *Viṣṇu,* IV, 5, 1-34; *Brahmāṇḍa,* III, 64, 1-19; *Bhāgavata,* IX, 13, 1, 11-27; *AIHT,* pp. 95-96.

11. *Vāyu,* 86, 14-22; *Viṣṇu,* IV, I, 43-61; *Brahmāṇḍa,* III, 61, 12-17; *Bhāgavata,* IX, 2, 33-36; *AIHT,* pp. 96-97; R.P. Sharma, *Paurāṇika Kośa* (hereafter *PK*) (Varanasi, Saṁvat 2028), p. 481.

12. *Matsya,* 12, 21-24; *Vāyu,* 86, 22-28; *Viṣṇu,* IV, 1, 62-64; *Brahmāṇḍa,* III, 61, 18-24; *Bhāgavata,* IX, 3, 1-2, 27-36; *Agni* (text with Hindi tr. T. Jha and G.S. Tripathi, Prayāga, 1986), 273, 12-16; *Brahma* (text with Hindi tr. T. Jha, Prayāga, 1976), 7, 27-29; *AIHT,* pp. 97-98.

13. *Matsya,* 43, 7-52; 44, 14-36, 45-85; 45, 1-34; 46, 1-29; 48, 6-9, 22-29; 49, 1-59; 50, 26-33; *Vāyu,* 91, 1-103; 92, 1-75; 93, 26-27, 87-92; 94, 1-54; 95, 14-47; 96, 1-160; 99, 6-12, 25-28, 167-70, 194-249; D.R. Patil, *Cultural History from the Vāyu Purāṇa* (Poona, 1946, Delhi rpt. 1973), pp. 8-13; *Viṣṇu,* IV, 8, 1-21; IV, 10, 1-32; IV, 11, 1-30; IV, 12, 2-45; IV, 13, 1-20, 35-70, 108-61; IV, 14, 1-45; IV, 17, 1-

→

It is significant to note that the first phase of Paurava's settlements in the Sārasvata region and upper doab and Yādavas' settlements in Narmadā, Mālawā, Gujarat and Gaṅgā–Yamunā doab are archaeologically associated with Ochre-Coloured Pottery (OCP) of late Haṛappan period (*c.* 2200–1700 BCE) and Chalcolithic Black and Red Ware (BRW) ascribed to *c.* 2000 BCE respectively.[14]

The Purāṇic history of the early Aryans has its own importance. The Purāṇic data about their origin and expansion is really valuable. According to some Purāṇas, their original homeland was Pratiṣṭhāna from where they expanded all over the Gangetic doab.[15] The Purāṇic evidence goes to prove their indigenous origin in contradistinction to their foreign origin.

→ 5; IV, 18, 1-30; IV, 19, 1-85; IV, 20, 1-53; *Brahmāṇḍa*, III, 65, 45-46; III, 66, 1-75; III, 67, 1-79; III, 68, 27, 90-92; III, 69, 3-55; III, 70, 14-48; III, 71, 1-144; III, 74, 7-12; *Bhāgavata*, IX, 14, 1 ff.; IX, 15, 1-36; IX, 17, 2-10; IX, 20, 1-39; IX, 21, 1-35; IX, 22, 1-18; IX, 23, 1-39; IX, 24, 6-45; *Brahma*, 10, 13-68; 12, 18-19; 13, 154-207; 14, 14-25; 15, 30-45; 16, 9-49; *Agni*, 274, 1-23; 275, 1-51; 277, 4-14; 278, 27-41; *AIHT*, pp. 99-119 and Ch. XXIV ("Ancient History from Tradition"), pp. 258-84; also see A.D. Pusalker, "Traditional History from the Earliest Time to the Accession of Parikshit", in R.C. Majumdar, ed., *The Vedic Age* (Bombay, 1965), pp. 277 ff; G.P. Singh, *Early Indian Historical Tradition and Archaeology* (hereafter *EIHTA*) (Delhi, 1994), pp. 50-98.

14. See Romila Thapar, "Purāṇic Lineages and Archaeological Cultures", in idem, *Ancient Indian Social History* (hereafter *AISH*) (Hyderabad, 1984), pp. 242 ff. and Genealogical Table facing p. 262.

15. For details, see *Vāyu*, 91, 5-8 and 51; 92, 1-7; *Viṣṇu*, IV, 1, 16-17; *Brahma*, chapters 10-12; *AIHT*, pp. 296-302; *EIHTA*, p. 50 ff.; H.D. Sankalia, "Prehistoric Colonization in India: Archaeological and Literary Evidences", in *Aspects of Indian History and Archaeology* (hereafter *AIHA*), ed. by S.P. Gupta and K.S. Ramachandran (Delhi, 1977), pp. 308-10; J. Kennedy, "The Purāṇic Histories of the Early Aryas", *Journal of the Royal Asiatic Society* (hereafter *JRAS*) (London, 1915).

> The Purāṇas profess to give us the ancient history of Aryan India. In doing so they begin from the earliest Ṛgvedic period describing genealogies of kings who established kingdoms and principalities and thus parcelled out and ruled ancient India. . . .[16]

William Jone's statement, that the traditions of pre-Kaliyuga periods are purely mythological and that of the Kali age historical,[17] is not a balanced one. A.S. Altekar has rightly pointed out that the pre-Bhārata war dynasties mentioned in the Purāṇas are as historical as the dynasties of the post-war period or the Kali age. He further adds that the history of India of pre-Bhārata war period can be reconstructed with the help of epic and Purāṇic evidence.[18]

The traditional history of India from the earliest times to the accession of Parīkṣit II (thirty-six years after the war) is well recorded in the Purāṇas.

The kingdoms and dynasties of the post-Bhārata war period extending from the accession of Parīkṣit or the beginning of Kali age down to the sixth or fifth century BCE have also been covered in the Purāṇa records. Twenty-nine kings of Puru dynasty called the Pauravas of the Lunar family who ruled over Hastināpura, Indraprastha and Vatsa (Kauśāmbī),[19] thirty kings of Ikṣvāku dynasty of Kosala of the

---

16. S.N. Pradhan, *Chronology of Ancient India* (Delhi, 1979), Preface, p. xi.
17. "On the Chronology of the Hindus", *Asiatic Researches* (hereafter *AS*) (Delhi, 1979), vol. 2, p. 111.
18. "Can we reconstruct pre-Bhārata war History", *Journal of the Benares Hindu University*, Benares, vol. IV, pp. 183-223; also his Presidential Address, Section 1: Archaic and Early Cultural History, Indian History Congress, Third Session, Calcutta, 15-17 December, 1939.
19. *Matsya*, 50, 57-89; *Vāyu*, 99, 249-79; *Viṣṇu*, IV, 21, 1-18; *Bhāgavata*, IX, 22, 33-44; Pargiter, *Purāṇa Text of the Dynasties of the Kali Age* (hereafter *PDKA*) (Oxford, 1913), pp. 4-5, fn. 16.

Solar family including the predecessors and successors of Prasenajīt[20] and twenty-two kings of the Bṛhadratha dynasty of Magadha (with their regnal years)[21] have all been incorporated in the dynastic lists of kings. The genealogical lists containing the names of kings of the said dynasties have also been furnished. The information supplied in the Purāṇas about the rule of the famous king Udayana over Kauśāmbī, the pedigree and progeny of the Buddha of the Śākya clan and the kingdoms of Pañcāla, Śūrasena, Videha, Aṅga and Kāśī have historical credibility.

The five kings of Pradyota dynasty who ruled the kingdom of Avantī are mentioned in the Purāṇas with their regnal years and total duration of their rule. They are said to have ruled for 138 years.[22] But, in fact, they ruled for 102 years (*c.* 513–411 BCE).

The Purāṇic accounts of the major dynasties of early historical period are of exceptional value. Ten kings of Bimbisārian and Śaiśunāga dynasties including Bimbisāra (*c.* 558–491 BCE) and Ajātaśatru (*c.* 491–459 BCE), both contemporaries of the Buddha (*c.* 563–483 BCE), Udayin, Śiśunāga and others are said to have ruled for 360 or 362

---

20. *Matsya*, 271, 4-18; *Vāyu*, 99, 280-93; *Viṣṇu*, IV, 22, 1-13; *Brahmāṇḍa*, III, 74, 104-07; *PDKA*, pp. 10-11; 66-67.

21. *Matsya*, 271, 18-30; *Vāyu*, 99, 294-308; *Viṣṇu*, IV, 23, 1-13; *Brahmāṇḍa*, III, 74, 107-21; *Bhāgavata*, IX, 22, 46-49; *Harivaṁśa* (text with Hindi tr. and commentary, Gorakhpur, Saṁvat 2044), I, 32, 63-78; *PDKA*, pp. 13-22; *PK*, p. 356; *AIHT*, pp. 285-87; see also Pusalker, "Traditional History from the Accession of Parīkṣit to the End of the Brahadratha Dynasty", in *The Vedic Age*, op. cit., pp. 323-33; *EIHTA*, pp. 141-54.

22. *Matsya*, 272, 1-5; *Vāyu*, 99, 308-14; *Viṣṇu*, IV, 24, 1-8; *Brahmāṇḍa*, III, 74, 121-25; *Bhāgavata*, XII, 1, 2-4; *PDKA*, pp. 18-21; 68-69; *Viṣṇu*, English tr. H.H. Wilson (Calcutta, 1961), p. 372; *PK*, p. 333.

years.[23] They actually ruled for 200 years (*c.* 543–343 BCE). The nine Nandas are said to have ruled for 28, 40 or 100 years.[24] In reality, only two of them, the first (Mahāpadmananda, the founder of the dynasty) and the last (Dhanānanda, identical with Agrammes or Xandrammas of classical [Greek and Roman] writers, and contemporary of Alexander) were the reigning kings who altogether ruled for 22 years (*c.* 343–321 BCE). We are also informed that a period of 1050 years had elapsed between the birth of Parīkṣit and the coronation of Mahāpadmananda.[25] It is also clearly stated in some of the Purāṇas that it was Cāṇakya (Kauṭilya) who uprooted the Nandas and installed Candragupta Maurya on the throne of Magadha (in 321 BCE),[26] which is a historical fact. Ten kings of the Maurya dynasty including Candragupta, Aśoka and his successors are said to have ruled for 137 years (*c.* 321–184 BCE),[27] which is perfectly accurate. In one of the Purāṇas, it is also mentioned that Candragupta Maurya was married to the daughter of Sulūva[28] (Seleucus, a general of Alexander called

23. *Matsya*, 272, 5-13; *Vāyu*, 99, 314-21; *Viṣṇu*, IV, 24, 9-19; *Viṣṇu*, English tr. Wilson, pp. 372-75; *Brahmāṇḍa*, III, 74, 127-33; *Bhāgavata*, XII, 1, 5-7; *PDKA*, pp. 21-26, 67-69; *PK*, p. 496; see also Max Müller, *History of Ancient Sanskrit Literature* (hereafter *HASL*) (Varanasi, 1968), pp. 265-66.

24. *Matsya*, 272, 14-21; *Vāyu*, 99, 321-28; *Viṣṇu*, IV, 24, 20-24; *Viṣṇu*, English tr. Wilson, p. 374; *Brahmāṇḍa*, III, 74, 139-44; *Bhāgavata*, XII, 1, 8-11; *PDKA*, pp. 23-24, 69; *PK*, pp. 257 and 407; also *HASL*, p. 266.

25. *Matsya*, 273, 36; *Vāyu*, 99, 415; *Viṣṇu*, IV, 24, 104; *Viṣṇu*, English tr. Wilson, p. 389.

26. *Matsya*, 272, 21-22; *Vāyu*, 99, 329-31; *Viṣṇu*, IV, 24, 25-28.

27. *Matsya*, 272, 22-26; *Vāyu*, 99, 331-36; *Viṣṇu*, IV, 24, 29-32, *Viṣṇu*, English tr. Wilson, pp. 374-76; *Brahmāṇḍa*, III, 74, 145-49; *Bhāgavata*, XII, I, 12-15; *PDKA*, pp. 28-30; *PK*, p. 434; also *HASL*, p. 266.

28. *Bhaviṣya* (ed. with Hindi tr. Ram Sharma Acarya, 2 vols., Bareilly, 1978), 1, v. 43, pp. 334-35; see also v. 44 for two other Maurya rulers, Bindusāra and Aśoka.

"Paurasādhipati," one who subdued King Poros) following the peace treaty concluded between the two in 303 or 302 BCE. Ten rulers of the Śuṅga dynasty from Puṣyamitra to Devabhūti are said to have ruled for 112 years (*c.* 184–72 BCE),[29] which is absolutely correct. Four kings of the Kaṇva dynasty from Vasudeva to Suśarman ruled exactly for 45 years (*c.* 72–27 BCE).[30] These six dynasties ruled successively Magadha and other kingdoms on the whole from the sixth to the first century BCE. The Purāṇas also contain some information about the rise and fall of these dynasties. Thirty rulers of the Sātavāhana dynasty from its founder Śimuka to Pulumāvi IV are said to have ruled for 456 or 460 years.[31] The Purāṇas also supply the information that a period of 836 years intervened between Mahāpadmananda and the last Sātavāhana king, Pulumāvi.[32]

---

29. *Matsya*, 272, 26-33; *Vāyu*, 99, 336-42; *Viṣṇu*, IV, 24, 33-37; *Viṣṇu*, English tr. Wilson, pp. 376-77; *Brahmāṇḍa*, III, 74, 150-55; *Bhāgavata*, XII, 1, 16-18; *PDKA*, pp: 30-32, 70.

30. *Matsya*, 272, 32-37; *Vāyu*, 99, 343-47; *Viṣṇu*, IV, 24, 38-42; *Viṣṇu*, English tr. Wilson, p. 377; *Brahmāṇḍa*, III, 74, 155-60; *Bhāgavata*, XII, I, 19-21; *PDKA*, pp. 33-38, 71.

31. *Matsya*, 273, 1-17; *Vāyu*, 99, 348-58; *Viṣṇu*, IV, 24, 43-50; *Viṣṇu*, English tr. Wilson, pp. 378-80; *Brahmāṇḍa*, III, 74, 160-70; *Bhāgavata*, XII, 1, 22-28; *PDKA*, pp. 38-43, 71; *AIHT*, pp. 286-87; see also V.A. Smith, *EHI*, pp. 216-17, 220; R.G. Bhandarkar, *Early History of the Dekkan* (Delhi, 1979), pp. 15-23; *A Peep into the Early History of India* (Delhi, 1978), pp. 36-37; S.P. Sen, ed., *Historians and Historiography in Modern India* (Calcutta, 1973), pp. 32-34.

    For details of pre- and post-Maurya dynasties upto Sātavāhana, as recorded in the Purāṇas, see G.P. Singh, *EIHTA*, pp. 161-89; "A New Approach to the Study of Historical Data in the Epic and Purāṇic Literature Regarding Ancient India", *Proceedings of the UGC sponsored National Seminar on History and Literature* (Sardar Patel University, Vallabh Vidyanagar, Gujarat, February 9-11, 1991), p. 4.

32. *Vāyu*, 99, 416-17; *Matsya*, 273, 37.

According to this chronological data, the Sātavāhanas' rule began 376 years after the Nanda and lasted for 460 years. According to our chronological calculation and computation, they reigned (in Maharashtra and Andhra Pradesh) for not more than 252 years (*c.* 27 BCE – CE 225). There is some epigraphic and numismatic evidence[33] to partly confirm the historicity of Purāṇic genealogy of this dynasty. The genealogical list of the dynasty contains the names of many actual rulers like Śrī Śātakarṇi I, Śātakarṇi II, Gautamīputra Śātakarṇi, Pulumāvi and Yajñaśrī Śātakarṇi. The political achievements of some kings of some of the aforesaid dynasties have also been highlighted in the Purāṇas.

It is worthy of note that the above-mentioned seven dynasties that ruled different kingdoms are historically authenticated. Their genealogies are chronologically arranged. Most of the kings mentioned in the genealogical lists are real. The length of reign of each individual king as well as the total duration of the rule of each dynasty are given. Some figures are, of course, inflated but some are accurate. The total duration of reigns of the Mauryas, Śuṅgas and Kaṇvas given in the Purāṇas has been accepted by almost all the historians of ancient India. The Purāṇic data are extremely useful for genealogical and chronological reconstruction of ancient Indian history of the period concerned.

---

33. D.C. Sircar, ed., *Select Inscriptions Bearing on Indian History and Civilization* (Calcutta, 1965), vol. I, pp. 176-80, 197-201; *Epigraphia Indica* (hereafter *EI*), vol. VIII, No. 5, pp. 36-49, 60-61 (1, 5, 7), 73-74; *EI*, vol. X, 1910, p. 160 (nos. 1113, 1114, 1144); *Journal of Indian History* (hereafter *JIH*), vol. LVI, no. I, 1978, pp. 48-49, 52-53; E.J. Rapson, *Catalogue of Coins in the British Museum, the Andhra Dynasty, etc.* (1908), p. XXX; K.P. Jayaswal, *Journal of the Bihar and Orissa Research Society* (hereafter *JBORS*), vol. XVI, Nos 3&4, pp. 265-66; also *Journal of the Numismatic Society of India*, vol. III, no. 1, June 1941, pp. 43-45.

The historical value of the Purāṇic data from dynastic, genealogical and chronological points of view has been acknowledged by some noted authorities on the Purāṇa and some other scholars.[34] Acknowledging the historical value of the Purāṇic genealogies of the royal dynasties, F.E. Pargiter wrote: "Though historical works about ancient India are wanting, yet tradition has handed down fairly copious genealogies of the ancient dynasties. These state the succession of kings, and in the way are historical. . . ."[35] Further, "Genealogies are essentially chronological; and the old tales, especially those narrated in the course of the best versions of the genealogies, have also an historical character. Royal genealogies certainly do not lack the historical sense. . . ."[36]

---

34. D.R. Mankad, "Studies in Purāṇic History, Genealogies and Chronology in Modern Times", *Purāṇa* (Half-yearly Bulletin of the Purāṇa Department, All India Kasiraj Trust, Ramnagar, Varanasi), vol. IV, no. I, 1962, pp. 3-22; A. Banerji Sastri, "On Ancient Indian Historical Tradition", *JBORS*, vol. XIII, pp. 62-79; V.R.R. Dikshitar, "The Purāṇa: A Study", *Indian Historical Quarterly* (hereafter *IHQ*), vol. VIII, pp. 747-67; R. Morton Smith, *Dates and Dynasties in Earliest India* (hereafter *DDEI*), ed. J.L. Sastri (Delhi, 1973), pp. 38ff; "The Early Chronology of India", *Journal of the American Oriental Society*, vol. 77, no. 2, April-June 1957 and no. 4, December 1957; Pargiter, *PDKA*, pp. 4ff.; "Ancient Indian Genealogies and Chronology", *JRAS*, 1910, pp. 26-56; "Earliest Indian Traditional History", *JRAS*, 1914, pp. 267f.; Max Müller, *HASL*, pp. 265-68; K. Venkatachalam, *The Plot in Indian Chronology* (Vijayawada, 1953), pp. 23ff, 38ff, 80-100; *Chronology of Ancient Hindu History*, 2 Parts (Vijayawada, 1957), Part I, pp. 34ff.; F. Wilford, "Chronology of the Hindus", *AS*, vol. V (Delhi, 1979), pp. 241-92. J. Bentley, "On the Principal Eras and Dates of the Ancient Hindus", *AS*, vol. V, pp. 315-43 (for different dynasties of the post war period as given in the Purāṇas).
35. *AIHT*, p. 11.
36. Ibid., pp. 60-61.

James Todd has also observed that the Purāṇas afford materials for the history of ancient India. They "contain many facts that serve as beacons to direct the research of the historian."[37] The "traditional genealogies are rarely faithful records of times past."[38] And the traditional chronology is partly reliable.

The later Sātavāhana or the successors of the Sātavāhana of the Deccan have been referred to in the Purāṇas as Āndhravṛtyas. They belonged to the lineage of the feudatories of the Āndhras. There were seven kings in this line. The Śrīparvatīya-Āndhras (of Teliṅgānā) have been assigned a reign-period of 52 years. One of the five minor dynasties that came into being after the dismemberment of the Sātavāhana empire was that of the Ābhiras of western India (Maharashtra). The ten Ābhira kings are said to have ruled for over a period of 67 years. The total length of the reigns of the seven kings of Gardabhilla dynasty (of Ujjayinī, the capital of Avantī, western Mālawā) is also mentioned in the Purāṇas. There are incidental references in the Purāṇas to some of the foreign powers like the Yavanas (Greek Princes of Bactria), the Śakas, the Tuṣāras, Muruṇḍas (a branch or kinsmen of the Śakas), and the Hūṇas with length of rule of each.[39]

---

37. *Annals and Antiquities of Rajas than* (Delhi, 1971), vol. I, Introduction, p. xv.

38. Thapar, "Genealogy as a source of Social History", in idem, *AISH*, p. 326.

39. *Matsya*, 273, 18-24; *Matsya* (ed. with Eng tr. and notes of various oriental scholars by J.D. Akhtar, *Sacred Books of the Aryan Series*, Delhi, 1972), vol. I, pp. 339-41; *Vāyu*, 99, 359-64; *Viṣṇu*, IV, 24, 51-54 and 58; *Viṣṇu*, English tr. Wilson, pp. 380-82; *Brahmāṇḍa*, III, 74, 170-77; *Bhāgavata*, XII, 1, 27-32; *PDKA*, pp. 42-48, 50-51; R.K. Arora, *Historical and Cultural Data from the Bhaviṣya Purāṇa* (Delhi, 1972), pp. 37f.; Patil, op. cit., p. 262; also see *AS*, vol. VI, p. 35; IX, p. 147; *JASB*, December 1835, p. 688; *JRAS*, vol. III, p. 385.

The details of Vikramāditya (son of Mahendrāditya) of Ujjayinī and his dynasty have been provided in the Pratisarga Parvan of the *Bhaviṣya Purāṇa*.[40] The total length of the reigns of Vikramāditya and his four successors is also given. The former is said to have reigned for 60 years (commencing from 57 BCE) and the latter, including his son Śālivāhana, for 75 years[41] which comes to a total of 135 years, which is absolutely correct. The Jaina historical tradition also affirms it.

We come across some inaccuracies and discrepancies in the Purāṇas with regard to the number of kings of some of the dynasties of foreign origins and total duration of their rule. The trustworthiness of some reign periods is also doubtful. There are, of course, some fabrications, interpolations and distortions in the Purāṇas, but we cannot deny that there are also some facts which have been jumbled up with myths. The Purāṇic details of the subjects cannot be put aside as wholly unworthy of credence.

The Purāṇas do contain some useful information about the rule of the Nāga dynasties at Vidiśā (the capital of eastern Mālawā), Padmāvatī (modern Padam Pawaya near Narwar in the Gwalior state), Kāntipurī (modern Kotwar, about 25 miles north of Gwalior) and Mathurā (UP) between the second century BCE and the fourth century CE.

The historicity of most of the kings of Vidiśā mentioned in the Purāṇas[42] has been proved and they have been chronologically arranged by K.P. Jayaswal.[43] Nine Nāga kings

---

40. *Bhaviṣya*, I, vv. 8-26, pp. 337-40; II, vv. 13-21, pp. 161-64.
41. Ibid., I, vv. 17-19, 33, pp. 416-19; vv. 1-4, pp. 419-20; vv. 1-2, p. 425; II, vv. 22-23, pp. 163-64; vv. 24-42, pp. 164-67.
42. *Vāyu*, 99, 366-70; *Viṣṇu*, IV, 24, 56; *Viṣṇu*, English tr. Wilson, pp. 382-83.
43. *History of India (CE 150–350)* (Lahore, 1933), pp. 3-15.

of Padmāvatī referred to in the Purāṇas[44] are known from coins and inscriptions.[45] The archaeological excavation carried out at Kotwar in the recent past has proved the settlements of the Nāgas at Kāntipurī. The rule of seven Nāga kings of Mathurā can also be confirmed on the testimony of the Purāṇas.[46] The coins discovered from Mathurā bear the names of the said seven kings.[47] It is on the authority of the Purāṇas that Pargiter has stated that the Nāga families ruled from more than one place, Vidiśā, Padmāvatī and Mathurā.[48]

The information available in some Purāṇas regarding the earliest phase of the Gupta rule (*c.* CE 275–300) is very valuable. It is fairly stated in the Purāṇas that the Guptas set up their rule over Anugaṅgā (the middle Gangetic basin), Prayāga (Allahabad), Sāketa (adjoining Ayodhyā) and Magadha (south Bihar).[49] It is historically a proven fact that the kingdom of the Guptas originally comprised only some parts of Uttar Pradesh and Bihar at the end of the third century CE. They gradually expanded from Prayāga over the neighbouring regions and

---

44. *Vāyu*, 99, 382-83; *Viṣṇu*, IV 24, 63; *Viṣṇu*, English tr. Wilson, p. 385; *Brahmāṇḍa*, 111, 74, 194, 197; *PK*, p. 267.
45. E.J. Rapson, *Indian Coins* (Varanasi, 1969), p. 28 and Plate V; V.A. Smith, *Catalogue of the Coins in the Indian Museum, Calcutta, Coins of Ancient India* (hereafter *CCIM*), (Oxford, 1906, rpt. Varanasi, 1972), vol. I, pp. 176-77; *JRAS*, 1897, p. 643; *JASB*, 1865, p. 115; J.F. Fleet, *Corpus Inscriptionum Indicarum* (Calcutta, 1888), vol. III, no. I, lines 20-21.
46. *Vāyu*, 99, 382-83, 453, *Viṣṇu*, English tr. Wilson, p. 385; *Brahmāṇḍa*, III, 74, 194-95, 267; *PK*, pp. 267, 393.
47. *CCIM*, vol. I, pp. 176-77.
48. *PDKA*, p. 49.
49. *Vāyu*, 99, 383; *Viṣṇu*, IV, 24, 63; *Viṣṇu*, English tr. Wilson, p. 385; see also D.R. Patil, "Gupta Inscriptions and Purāṇic Tradition", *Bulletin of the Deccan College Research Institute*, vol. II, pp. 2-58; V.A. Smith's Views of *Indian Antiquary*, 1902, p. 258, fn.

the whole of Magadha. The Purāṇic passage shows the extent of the Gupta dominions of pre-Candragupta period and not of his time (*c.* CE 319-35) as held by Pargiter.[50] The *Bhaviṣya Purāṇa* in particular informs us that the seven kings of the Gupta dynasty ruled for 245 years.[51] But we find that in the imperial Gupta line there were twelve or thirteen kings (from Śrīgupta to Bhānugupta) who ruled for 235 years (*c.* CE 275–510).

H.H. Wilson has clearly stated that the dynastic lists of kings of the post-war period (Kali age) have been preserved in the Purāṇic historical records with greater precision which offer political and chronological particulars. Their general accuracy has been controvertibly established. Some Āndhra and Gupta rulers mentioned in the Purāṇas find confirmation in the inscriptions on columns of stones or rocks and on coins deciphered by archaeologists and others.[52]

The information contained in the Purāṇas about the Vākāṭakas of the Deccan (third to sixth century CE) is very meagre but authentic. The founder of the Vākāṭaka dynasty, Vindhyaśakti (who flourished about the middle of the third century CE), figures in the Purāṇas. The length of his reign and that of his son and successor, Pravīra, are also given therein.[53] There are some inscriptional and other reliable evidences to partly prove the historical authenticity of the information supplied by the Purāṇas about the Vākāṭakas,

---

50. *PDKA*, Introduction, vol. XII and p. 20.
51. See M. Krishnamachariar, *History of Classical Sanskrit Literature* (Delhi, 1974), Introduction, pp. XLVIII-XLIX.
52. *Viṣṇu Purāṇa*, English tr. Wilson, Preface, pp. LXVIII-LXX.
53. *Vāyu*, 99, 365, 370-72; *Viṣṇu*, IV, 24, 56; *Viṣṇu*, English tr. Wilson, pp. 382-83, *Brahmāṇḍa*, III, 74, 184-86; *PDKA*, p. 44.

particularly about their genealogy and chronology.[54] This dynasty ceased to exist in the second quarter of the sixth century CE.

A.K. Warder opines that the Purāṇas provide a comprehensive view of ancient Indian history from the earliest recorded kings and the ancient dynasties down to the early fourth century CE. They mention Guptas and throw some light on the history of early Vākāṭakas.[55]

The Purāṇic history of the post-Harṣa period (CE 650–1200) also deserves our notice. The information contained especially in the *Bhaviṣya Purāṇa* (Pratisarga Parvan) about the Pratihāras of Kannauj, the Paramāras of Mālawā, the Cāhamānas of Ajmer and Delhi and the Cāḷukyas (called Solaṅkīs) of Ānartta (Gujarat) the four Rājpūt families of the Agnivaṁśa are of considerable historical importance.

A notable ruler of Pratihāra dynasty named Vatsarāja (identified with the father of Nāgabhaṭṭa II, CE 805-33) figures in the Purāṇa as a king of Avantī.[56] It is a well-known fact that prior to the conquest of Kannauj the Pratihāras established their rule in Avantī with its capital at Ujjayinī. Vatsarāja ascended the throne in about CE 778. Bhoja I (CE 836-85) and Bhoja II (CE 910-12) were the Pratihāra rulers of Kannauj. We

54. V.V. Mirashi, "Some Purāṇic passages corroborated by Inscriptional and Numismatic Evidence", *Purāṇa,* vol. I, no. 1, pp. 31-38; "The Vākāṭaka Chronology", *IRQ,* vol. XXIV, pp. 148-55; M. Govinda Rai, "Genealogy and Chronology of the Vākāṭakas", *JIH,* vol. XIV, 1935, pp. 1-26; 165-204; R.C. Majumdar, "Note on the Genealogy and Chronology of the Vākāṭakas", *Journal of the Royal Asiatic Society of Bengal (Letters),* vol. XII, p. 150; S.K. Aiyangar, "The Vākāṭakas and their place in the History of India", *Annals of the Bhandarkar Oriental Research Institute* (hereinafter *ABORI*), vol. V, pp. 31-54.

55. *IIH,* p. 157.

56. *Bhaviṣya,* II, v. 32, p. 165.

find the description of the Bhojas in the Purāṇa[57] but neither their periods nor the details of their achievements are given therein. However, the Pratihāras continued to exercise their sway over Kannauj. The last king of this dynasty, Rājyapāla (CE 991–1018), also figures in the Purāṇa.[58] His capital Kannauj was invaded by Mahmud of Ghazni in CE 1018, but he could not defend it and fled away out of fear.

The Candellas, who established their sway over the kingdom of Bundelkhaṇḍ in the tenth century CE, are vividly portrayed in the Purāṇa. They were the feudatories of the great Pratihāra emperors of Kannauj. The Purāṇic tradition confirms it that Kāliñjar was under their rule. The name of its founder with period of his rule and the names of all those who ruled over it are given in the Purāṇa.[59] One of them called Karvarman can be identified with Kīrtivarman who ruled some time between CE 1100 and CE 1129.

The Paramāras of Mālawā, according to the Purāṇa, were the descendants of King Paramāra of Avantī. He is said to have ruled over Avantīpura (Ujjayinī, which had an extent of four *yojanas*) for six years.[60] Muñja or Muñjavarman (CE 974-98), who was the seventh king of this dynasty, also finds mention in the Purāṇa. The details about Sindhurāja are also given therein.[61] The most famous king of this dynasty was Bhoja (son of Sindhurāja) who ruled for about forty-two years from CE 1018 to CE 1060. The Purāṇa explicitly mentions his name as a king of this dynasty.[62] The later Paramāra kings of

---

57. Ibid. I, pp. 419-20, 425; II, p. 165.
58. Ibid., II, v. 35, pp. 165-66.
59. Ibid., I, vv. 1-2, p. 366; II, vv. 1-37, pp. 184-90.
60. Ibid., I, v. 49, p. 335; v. 8, p. 337; II, vv. 13-15, pp. 161-62.
61. Ibid., II, vv. 25-30, pp. 175-77.
62. *PK*, p. 385; see also Wilford, *AS*, vol. IX, pp. 176-77.

Mālawā are also mentioned in the Purāṇa.[63] But the historicity of only two of them, Naravarman and Udayāditya, has been established. The copper plate of the former (nephew of Bhojarāja) preserved in Archaeological Museum of Indore proves that the latter (CE 1059-94) was brother of Bhoja. According to the Purāṇa, Udayāditya was the founder of Udayapur[64] which can be confirmed by "Udepur" inscription[65] in which he has been described as the successor of Bhoja.

The Purāṇic accounts of the Tomaṛas of Delhi and the Cauhānas of Ajmer and Delhi are of paramount historical importance. It is clearly stated in the Purāṇa that the Tomaṛa dynasty founded by Anaṅgapāla I ruled at Indraprastha (Delhi).[66] His descendants also figure therein.[67] Ajayarāja, called Ajayapāla, was one of the Cauhāna rulers of Ajmer. He is credited with having founded that city. One of the famous rulers of this dynasty was Viśāladeva or Vigraharāja IV (CE 1152-64) who captured Delhi about CE 1158 from the Tomaṛas. In the Purāṇic genealogy of the Cauhāna rulers, his name figures as Viśāla. His descendants and other noted rulers are also mentioned in the Purāṇa.[68] The most famous and illustrious king of the Cauhāna family, Pṛthvīrāja (CE 1179-92), figures in the Purāṇa as a ruler of Delhi. It is clearly stated therein that after the death of Anaṅgapāla II, the last king of the Tomaṛa dynasty, he became a full-fledged ruler of Delhi. He made it a fortified city. It became an extensive and magnificent city during his time.[69]

63. *Bhaviṣya,* II, vv. 31-35, pp. 176-77.

64. Ibid., v. 34, p. 176.

65. *EI,* I, pp. 232-38.

66. *Bhaviṣya,* I, v. 5, p. 424; vv. 1-14, pp. 429-32.

67. Ibid., II, vv. 1-6, pp. 168-69.

68. Ibid., vv. 15-22, pp. 170-71 (the pedigree and progeny of king Viśāladeva are given); also I, v. 4, p. 430.

69. Ibid., vv. 22-25, p. 171; I, vv. 1-15, 22-28, pp. 430-34.

Further historical narratives of the subject in the Purāṇa show that Pṛthvīrāja's overlordship of northern India was disputed by Jayacandra of Kannauj, the most famous king of Gāhaḍavāla dynasty who ruled from CE 1170 to CE 1194. It is said that the former turned the latter into an enemy by forcibly carrying off his beautiful daughter Saṁyogitā from her *svayaṁvara*. The rivalry between the two resulted in a battle which was fought at Sukar. In this battle, soldiers of both the sides were killed. The hostility between the two potentates proved to be disastrous for the Agnivaṁśa[70] and a blessing for Muhammad Ghori. The Purāṇa even records the death of Pṛthvīrāja at the hands of Sahoddin (Sihabuddin Ghori)[71] which is indicative of the fact that the latter after having defeated the former in the second battle of Tarāin (about fourteen miles from Thāneśvara) fought in CE 1192 put him to death. And thereafter he occupied Delhi and Ajmer. It is also narrated in the Purāṇa that after his death a large number of women of the Cauhāna family fell into the hands of the Muslims.[72]

The Purāṇa makes a brief mention of the Cāḷukyas of Ānartta (Gujarat). The regnal years of some rulers are, of course, given in the Purāṇa,[73] but it is very difficult to establish their identities and to determine their reign-periods.

The Purāṇic accounts of the dynasties of Rājpūt princes are neither systematic nor complete. There are some gaps in the dynastic accounts as well as in the genealogical lists. However, the historical validity of the information contained in the Purāṇa regarding the important events cannot be

70. Ibid., I, vv. 17-21, 29-38, pp. 432-35; vv. 1-63, pp. 435-45; also v. 4, pp. 424-25.

71. Ibid., II, v. 25, p. 171.

72. Ibid., vv. 26-28, pp. 171-72.

73. Ibid., I, v. 4, p. 336; II, vv. 1-28, pp. 172-76.

doubted. Some of the details are in full accord with the facts recorded in ancient and early medieval history of India.

While critically judging the value of Purāṇas, E.J. Rapson observed:

> The descriptions of ancient monarchs and of their realms (therein) are essentially historical. They may be compared to the sagas and the medieval chronicles of Europe. They are the products of an imaginative and uncritical age in which men were not careful to distinguish fact from legend. It is the task of modern criticism to disentangle the two elements. . . .[74]

The historical material available in the Purāṇas regarding kingdoms and dynasties covers the period from primaeval king Manu Vaivasvata down to the times of Pṛthvīrāja Cauhāna and not only up to the early fourth century CE as held by some scholars. It will not be correct to say that the Purāṇas provide dynastic history only up to the beginning of the Gupta rule.

There are some other aspects of ancient Indian history like towns and cities, *janapadas* (territories and peoples), kingdoms, state and government, polity and administration, society, religion and culture which are also recorded in the Purāṇas.

The Purāṇic data about the foundations, naming, planning, antiquity, growth and decay of towns and cities are extremely important for the study of history of urbanization in ancient India. This is one of the aspects of judging the historical value of the Purāṇas. The Purāṇa records also throw light on the nature and patterns of urban settlements. The archaeological discoveries of the remains of most of the towns described in the Purāṇas not only confirm their existence but also prove

74. "The Purāṇas", in *Cambridge History of India,* vol. I, *Ancient India,* ed. E.J. Rapson (Delhi, 1962), p. 267.

the historicity of Purāṇic accounts of the subject. The towns of especially the Gaṅgā Valley are archaeologically associated with Painted Grey Ware (PGW) and Northern Black Polished Ware (NBPW) phases of culture. Archaeologists on the basis of Carbon-14 dates place them in the first millennium BCE. H.D. Sankalia, while placing his reliance on both tradition and archaeology has reasonably maintained that the antiquity of towns and cities as occurring in the *Mahābhārata* and Purāṇas can also be proved by archaeological evidence.[75] The Purāṇas contain genuine historical tradition which also finds corroboration in archaeology. R. Morton Smith is perfectly correct in stating that ". . . the Purāṇa makes a good historical sense, consistent with the idea of archaeology."[76]

The *janapadas* mentioned in the Purāṇas include Kuru, Pañcāla, Kāśī, Kosala and Śūrasena of Madhyadeśa; Bāhlīka, Gāndhāra, Kāmboja, Sindh and Kashmir of Uttarāpatha (north-western region); Aṅga, Baṅga, Puṇḍra, Prāgjyotiṣa, Videha and Magadha of Prācyadeśa (eastern region); Sārasvata, Saurāṣṭra, Ānartta and Bharukaccha of Aparānta (western region); the Pāṇḍyas, Keralas, Coḷas, Muṣikas, Māhiṣaka (Mysore) and Kaliṅga of Dakṣiṇāpatha (southern region); and Avantī, Vidiśā, Tripurī of Vindhyan region, and the Kirātas, Khasas, Dārdas and Trigarttas of mountain region.[77]

---

75. *AIHA*, pp. 277-78 and 280.

76. *DDEI*, Preface, also see pp. 1-3.

77. *Matsya*, 114, 34-57; *Vāyu*, 45, 108-37; 47, 42-62; *Viṣṇu*, II, 3, 15-17; *Brahma*, 19, 15-18; 27, 41-64; *Vāmana*, 13, 35-57; *Kūrma*, I, 45, 39-42; *Mārkaṇḍeya* (ed. with Hindi tr. D.N. Sastri, Meerut, 1983), 54, 32-57; 55, 6-32, 49-52; *Padma* (Svargakhaṇḍa), ed. A.C. Sastri (Varanasi, 1972), 15, 41-59; *Garuḍa* (English tr. M.N. Dutta, Delhi, 1908, rpt. 1983), vol. I, Chapter LV, p. 146; also see S.M. Ali, *The Geography of the Purāṇas* (Delhi, 1983), pp. 133-76; D.C. Sircar, *Studies in the Geography of Ancient and Medieval India* (Delhi, 1971), pp. 26-74; B.C. Law, "Countries and Peoples of India" (Epic and →

The Purāṇas throw a good deal of light on the evolution of kingship, emergence of the state and its seven constituents, inter-state relations, administrative organization, revenue system, etc.[78] The data concerned have their own value in the realm of study of political thought or political ideas and institutions in ancient India.

The Purāṇic description of socio-religious life of the people with references to the *varṇāśrama dharma* (fourfold stages of life), class and caste, Śaiva, Śakti and Vaiṣṇava cults of Hinduism, etc. have considerable historical value.

The present author is not in perfect agreement with Romila Thapar with the following statements of hers: "The Indian tradition until the seventh century CE lacks any literature which can be specifically described as historical writing,"[79] and ". . . The Indian historical tradition, particularly in the period prior to the seventh century CE, was not concerned primarily with keeping a record of essential political events, since they were not always believed to be the most relevant by those who

---

→ Pauranic Sources), *ABORI*, vol. XVII, no. 3, 1936, pp. 225 ff; *Geographical Essays* (Delhi, 1976). pp. 119-71; M.R. Singh, *A Critical Study of the Geographical Data in the Early Purāṇas* (Calcutta, 1972), pp. 59 ff.

78. For details, see *Matsya*, chapters 215-220, 225-227; *Agni*, chapters 218-27; 233, 11-23; 234, 1-25; chapters 235-36; 239, 1-45; 240, 1-32; chapters 242-43, 251-52; B.B. Mishra, *Polity in the Agni Purāṇa* (Calcutta, 1965), pp. 27f., *Padma* (Svargakhaṇḍa), op. cit., chapters 36-37, 38, 1-40, 59-65; *Viṣṇudharmottara*, II, 65, 2-70; also II, chapters 6, 18, 68, 150, 177-181; Patil, *Cultural History from the Vāyu Purāṇa*, pp. 47-54; J.L. Sastri, *Political Thought in the Purāṇas* (Lahore, 1944); Om Prakash, *Political Ideas in the Purāṇas* (Allahabad, 1977); G.P. Singh, *Political Thought in Ancient India* (Delhi, 1993), pp. 21ff.

79. "The Tradition of Historical Writing in Early India", in *AISH*, p. 268.

were responsible for maintaining the historical tradition."[80] We find that the Purāṇic literature of pre-seventh century CE contains a lot of historical writing. Even prior to the seventh century CE the *purāṇakāras* maintaining historical tradition kept a record of all important historical events in the form of a Purāṇa.

The *purāṇakāras*, no doubt, made significant and substantial contributions to the evolution of historiographical tradition in ancient India. The observation made by J.F. Fleet is worth-quoting here:

> . . . the ancient Hindus could write short historical compositions concise and to the point but limited in extent. The historical chapters of the Purāṇas do certainly indicate a desire on the part of the ancient Hindus not to ignore general history altogether and are clearly based on ancient archives which had survived in a more or less complete shape and were somehow accessible to the composers of those works. . . .[81]

The historical data contained in the Purāṇas constitute one of the evidences to disprove the opinion expressed by some Indian and foreign scholars that the ancient Indians (mainly the Hindus) had no sense of history and chronology.

80. Ibid., p. 269.

81. *Imperial Gazetter of India* (new edition), vol. II, p. 17.

6

Fundamental Aspects of Ancient Indian Culture and Civilization*

Foundation of Indian Culture and its Evolution

THE Indian culture is not the creation of any particular racial group. The Aryans and non-Aryans are the joint builders of Indian culture and civilization. As a matter of fact, the foundation of Indian culture was laid by the non-Aryans in the prehistoric age. This age marks the formative stages of Indian culture and civilization.

In fact, it was the Neolithic age, the most blooming phase of prehistoric cultures, which heralded the beginning of Indian civilization. The rudiments of culture were first provided by the Neolithic tribes who were the pre-Aryans and pre-Draviḍians. The settlement of the people in the village which was the earliest stage of social formation, the primitive system of agriculture (which we call today *jhūma* cultivation) and domestication of animals first began in this very age. This age also saw the emergence of the concept of religion based on animism which was the earliest form of religion. The animistic cult was fundamentally based on the worship of stones, trees, animals and other inanimate and supernatural objects which were supposed to be the abodes of malevolent and benevolent spirits. The religious beliefs of the Indus Valley

---

* From *An Introduction to General Foundation Course* (Manipur University, Imphal, 1999), pp. 33-51.

people and the Vedism, Brāhmanism or the early phase of Hinduism were largely based on the tribal concept of animism. The primitive religious beliefs based on superstition, polytheistical and eschatalogical beliefs, ancestor worship, doctrine of *kārma* and transmigration of soul profoundly influenced the religio-philosophical thoughts of the subsequent period. These were later aissimilated into Hinduism.

The Aryans and later the Hindus borrowed some elements of their culture from the tribal people after having come into contact with them. This cultural fusion was the logical culmination of their socio-cultural fellowship. The Neolithic men also learnt the art of pottery. They acquired some skill and attained proficiency in the field of painting and decorating the earthen pots. They also cultivated the art of sculpture. Some sections of them were acquainted with the art of woodcarving. They also knew the art of spinning and weaving cloth. One of the monumental legacies of the Neolithic age is the Megalithic culture which still survives in our country. The Megalithic monuments comprising dolmens, menhirs, cromlechs, cairns and other sepulchural objects were created by the tribal people in memory of the dead. This was based on their age-old socio-religious tradition. Such monuments were usually created by the Khāsīs and Jaintias of present-day Meghalaya, some Nāgā tribes of present-day Nagaland and Manipur, the tribes of south Bihar, south India, Deccan, Orissa, M.P., Gujarat, etc. Their stone memorials are believed to have influenced the religious structures of the Hindus and the Buddhists. The art of painting the walls of the caves also developed in the prehistoric age. This art was learnt by those tribes who lived in the caves. They used to paint the walls with the scenes of hunting and dancing and with figures of various wild and domesticated animals. The rock shelters containing hundreds of wall paintings have been found at Bhīmbeṭkā in M.P. The recent archaeological discovery of about

42 rock shelters and caves containing prehistoric painting depicting the lifestyles of primitive man and his environment dating from the lower palaeolithic period to the Neolithic period in the tribal belts of Nawadah and Giridih districts of central Bihar is also worth mentioning. The primitive paintings not only contain figures of animals but also human activities hunting, gathering, dancing, etc. This folk art further developed and found expression in various forms of painting. The prehistoric culture was basically the tribal culture. The prehistoric age in general and its Neolithic phase in particular gave birth to several cultural and artistic traditions which continued to survive.

The ancient Aryans and the non-Aryans jointly contributed to the building up of the fabric of Indian culture and civilization. The Indian culture is the creation of different racial groups. The Negritos (the tribes of the Andaman Island), the proto-Australoids (especially the Muṇḍas of Chhotanagpur of south Bihar and the Mon-Khmer Khāsīs of present-day Meghalaya), the Mongoloids (the hill tribes of north-east and those living on the slopes of the Himalayas in Bhutan, Sikkim, Nepal, Almora and Garhwal), the aborigines or primitive tribes (the Kols and the Santhals of Chhotanagpur region and Orissa, the Bhils of Rajasthan, the Vindhya hills and M.P. and Goṇḍs in some parts of M.P.), the indigenous Kirātas (the tribes living in the hills and forests of India who are often confounded with the Mongoloids), the Draviḍians (the people of Ceylon, south India, M.P. and Chhotanagpur), the Mongolo-Draviḍians (those people of Bengal and Orissa who have mixture of Draviḍian and Mongoloid elements), the Aryo-Draviḍians (found in the Gangetic plains and in some parts of the Punjab, Rajasthan and Bihar) and the Aryans (who occupied Afghanistan, Punjab, Rajasthan, Kashmir and the upper Gangetic basin), and the religious groups like the Hindus, the Jains and the Buddhists have contributed their share to the evolution of Indian culture and civilization. Each group possessed some elements of culture which saw their amalgamation in the due course of time.

The Negritos' contribution to the Indian civilization is not of much importance. Only some of their words found place in the altered form in the Bengali and Oriya vocabularies. The proto-Australoids made notable contributions to the Indian culture. Some Sanskrit words have been derived from the Austric family of languages. Many myths and legends current in India have an Austric origin. The incorporation of a fertility cult into Hinduism paved the way for the Tāntric form of worship. The Mongoloids and other primitive tribes have also left indelible imprints of their culture in the fields of totemism, superstitious beliefs, etc. The Kirātas popularized the worship of both Śiva and Śakti (female energy or Mother-Goddess like Kālī and Caṇḍī or Durgā). The Draviḍians made substantial contributions to the Indian culture. Hinduism by and large has its root in the Draviḍian concept of religion. The worship of an image or a symbol of divinity, offering of flowers, fruits and water to the deities during the *pūjā* ceremony, symbols of gods and goddesses like the lion or bull, the Śaiva cult, the worship of Śiva-liṅga, or phallic worship, the conception of Mother-Goddess or Śakti cult, the institution of *yoga*, the worship of *grāma devatā*s or village divinities in the form of heaps of stones, etc. are the lagacies of the Draviḍians. These are all of pre-Aryan origin. They were gradually absorbed into Hinduism. The Draviḍians are also credited with having evolved the urban culture. The Aryans had borrowed from them the art of constructing forts and cities. It is a proven fact that the elements of the Draviḍian language have been incorporated in the Sanskrit language. The Aryans consciously or unconsciously had borrowed in course of time some elements of the Draviḍian religion and culture. It is believed that some of the social system and traditions of today are of Draviḍian origin. The Aryan contributions to Indian culture include their philosophical doctrines, religious and spiritual conceptions and Sanskrit language and literature. The Jains and the Buddhists also made significant contributions to the development of Indian culture. Their ethical codes, the doctrine of *ahiṁsā* (non-violence), image worship, concept of intellectual freedom, social equality, tolerance, etc. became part and parcel of Indian cultural system. The growth of Prākr̥t language and Jaina literature and that of Pāli language and literature are also worth mentioning. They developed a new style of architecture, sculpture and painting which became an integral part of Indian art and culture. Thus we find that the Indian culture evolved as a composite culture because of fusion or synthesis of various racial and cultural elements.

Society

Ancient Indian social set-up frequently underwent changes. From the earliest ages to the end of the early Vedic age ancient India had classless and casteless society. The formation of class and caste began from the later Vedic age (*c.* 1000–600 BCE) onwards. The division of society into four classes, viz. the brāhmaṇa, the kṣatriya, the vaiśya and the śūdra first took place in the later Vedic period. The status and privileges, the functions and duties and occupation and obligations of the four classes were differentiated. The brāhmaṇas were supposed to learn and teach the Vedas and to perform the religious ceremonies. The kṣatriyas were warriors *par excellence* and protectors, represented nobility and belonged to ruling or aristocratic class. The vaiśyas were engaged in the economic pursuits, trade, agriculture and industry. The śūdras, the tillers or the cultivators, represented the lowest social order. It was their bounden duty to render services to the three upper classes. The supremacy or superiority of the brāhmaṇas over the three other classes was firmly established. These developments resulted in the social distinctions, which gradually paved the way for the origin of the caste system. In the age of the Sūtras and Dharmaśāstras (Smṛtis or law books), the caste distinctions because of the Brāhmanical orthodoxy became rigid. The fourfold division of the society based on the Brāhmanical tradition continued to exist till the dawn of the sixth century BCE. The Buddha and Mahāvīra (sixth and fifth centuries BCE) denounced the caste system, and in order to challenge the supremacy of the brāhmaṇas slightly changed the existing social order. The kṣatriyas occupied the first place and the brāhmaṇas were placed next to them. The position of other classes remained unaltered. The basic structure of society remained the same. There is no doubt about the fact that till both of them remained alive the social equality was maintained to some extent. Each class was free to choose its own profession. There was hardly any taboo on intermarriages. But suddenly after their death the caste distinctions were followed. But it was free from the rigidity of the Brāhmanical age. Considerable amount of flexibility was enjoyed by the people. The formation of several castes and sub-castes including the despised and degraded classes within the caste began to take place. The same social scenario more or less began to prevail up to the fourth century CE. This caste system continued to exist up to CE 1200. The brāhmaṇas again occupied the highest position and enjoyed more privileges than the other three classes.

The position of women in ancient Indian society changed from time to time. In the early Vedic age (*c.* 1500–1000 BCE) they were held in high esteem. They enjoyed full freedom. They were allowed to take part in all social and political activities. But, unfortunately, their position started deteriorating from the later Vedic age. However, during the Rājpūt period (CE 650–1200) their position considerably improved. They once again enjoyed a position of honour. They were mostly well-educated and took active part in public life.

The system of both endogamy and exogamy were followed in ancient times in respect of marriages. Both monogamy and polygamy were in vogue. Polygamy was generally resorted to by the ruling class.

The institution of slavery also existed between the sixth century BCE and the eleventh century CE. There were various kinds of slaves. The war prisoners or persons whose death sentences were commuted became slaves. Those who failed to pay their debts were also made slaves. Slaves could be given as gifts. They were also sold. They were sometimes beaten or treated harshly but generally treated with kindness. A slave could get freedom either by pleasing his master or by making a payment of money to him. In some cases the slaves were required to cultivate the lands of the priests. Female slaves were employed for household work. Some of them were also used for sexual enjoyment by their masters.

Economy

Agriculture has been the backbone of Indian economy since time immemorial. The Indus Valley people were the first to practise agriculture in the real sense of the term. The art of cultivation was known to them. They probably used wooden ploughshare. It was mainly the occupation of the village folk. The dwellers of the towns and cities mainly depended on the surplus production. The early Vedic Aryans also used plough cultivation. It was the later Vedic age which saw the transition from the primitive economy to agrarian economy. The later Vedic Aryans knowledge of iron technology resulted in the introduction of iron-tipped cultivation which is still in use in our country. The application of new technology in the field of cultivation paved the way for higher production. This system of agriculture continued to be one of the principal occupation of the Indian people. Various kinds of crops including wheat, rice and maize were grown in ancient times, which were the means of subsistence of the people. Cotton was produced in large quantity.

Ancient India also witnessed the growth of various arts, crafts and indigenous industries. There were different occupational or professional groups who were actively engaged in various works. They include weavers, potters, basket makers, chariot makers, stone cutters, leather workers, dyers, jewellers, blacksmiths, ivory workers, carpenters, masons, etc. Spinning and weaving of cotton and woollen cloth were common. Dyeing and embroidery developed as subsidiary industries.

One of the distinctive features of ancient Indian economic life was the formation of a guild (a kind of economic institution, corporation or league) in the sixth century BCE. There were various kinds of guilds. The artisans, merchants, traders and various other professional classes formed their respective guilds to protect their economic rights. The guilds continued to exist till the end of the Gupta period.

Internal and external trade flourished side by side in ancient India. The former was carried on by land routes and river routes and the latter also by both land routes and sea routes. The former was entirely based on barter system and latter on the exchange of products between the traders of two countries. The two types of trade were carried on simultaneously for the first time by the Indus Valley people. The people of Moheṅjo-Dāṛo and Haṛappā traded with different parts of India. The small-sized seals were most probably used in connection with trade. They had commercial links with Afghanistan and Iran. The sea-borne trade was also carried on. Boat was used for navigation purpose. Moheṅjo-Dāṛo was a great land port which was used for carrying on trade with Mesopotamia, Sumeria and Egypt. The archaeological discovery of Lothal in Gujarat has brought to light the fact that this city was not a seaport but dock yard which was used in the late phase of the Haṛappan culture for unloading the ships coming form outside India laden with merchandise. The Indus Valley people used to export mainly cotton to outside world and in exchange they secured tin, copper, precious stones, etc. In the early Vedic age commerce was largely controlled by a class of traders called *paṇi*. There are abundant references in the *Ṛgveda* to navigation, sea voyages, etc. It is believed that the Paṇis entered into commercial intercourse with Babylonia and other distant countries.

The period extending from the sixth century BCE to the sixth century CE is very important from the point of view of the growth of internal and external trade in India. During this period the famous trade emporiums were Campā, Mithilā, Varanasi, Ujjain and Taxila. These centres were used mainly for carrying internal trade. The Tāmralipti (in the Midnāpur district of West Bengal), Bhroach (in Gujarat), and Sopārā (in Thane district of Maharashtra) were famous sea ports which were used for carrying on maritime trade with outside world. This trade was carried on through the Bay of Bengal and the Arabian sea. In ancient Indian trade relation was not only established with the neighbouring South Asian country, i.e. Ceylon, but also with South-East Asian countries including Burma (Brahmadeśa), Campā along the eastern coast of Indo-China (now known as Annam), Kambuja and Suvarṇadvīpa comprising Malay peninsula, Sumatra, Java, Bali, Borneo and other islands of the East Indies. As a matter of fact both the land routes and sea routes were followed for trade with South-East Asian countries. The Hindu and Buddhist traders settled in different countries and islands of South-East Asia and introduced Indian religion, language and literature, art and culture at different periods of history. Trade was also one of the means for expansion of Indian culture in South-East Asia. The external trade relation was also established with China in east Asia, Persia in south-west Asia and also with Central Asia. The commercial contacts of India which started in the first century CE, nourished in the Gupta period and continued up to the Coḷa period. The principal articles which India used to export to different countries outside include cotton, woollen and silk cloths, ivory works, precious gems, perfumes, etc. Articles which India imported from outside include spices from Suvarṇadvīpa, silk from China, etc.

The well-developed agricultural system, various arts, crafts and indigenous industries and flourishing trade and commerce paved the way for the economic prosperity of the country.

Polity

The state and government formed important parts of ancient Indian polity. The emergence of state was preceded by the evolution of the institution of kingship. In the beginning there was neither king nor state. In the absence of both, the people felt their life insecured. For some time the golden age prevailed which is characterized by peaceful and happy life. But in absence of any legal guardian and law enforcing political institution, chaos and confusion set in the society which was followed by the political instability. The growth of political consciousness enabled them to realize the presence of both the king and the state. The people in the society reached an understanding and consequently they decided to appoint the king as their legal guardian. This is compatible with the social contract theory of Rousseau. The first king was Manu. The king as the head of the state got both social and political recognition. According to ancient Indian political thinkers, no state was recognized as a full-fledged state until and unless it possessed its seven constituents, viz. king, ministers, territory, treasury, army, forts and fortifications, and allies. There were various types of state. The states with extensive territories were ruled by sovereign rulers. Two states jointly ruled (e.g. Kuru-Pañcāla) by the kings were called *dvirājya*. The independent states were called *svarājya*. The power of the king started increasing from the sixth century BCE onwards with the emergence of large territorial states.

The two popular forms of government which existed side by side in ancient India are monarchical and republican. The earliest form of government was monarchical which was later replaced by republican. Both the forms of governments have their own history. The form of government that existed in the Vedic age was neither monarchical nor republican. It was rather a combination of aristocracy and democracy which can be amply substantiated by the powers of the king and style of functioning of two political bodies called *sabhā* and *samiti*. The former (a village assembly) was not a fully representative institution as it was not represented by the common people. It was dominated by the king and his advisers. The will of the king was the law. This body was more aristocratic than democratic in nature. On the other hand the latter (a national parliament) was a real democratic body since everything was decided by two-third majority. The king was elected by the members of this body. However, the election was rot the rule but the exception. The king was guided by his ministers or advisers who belonged to the priestly class. There was considerable influence of religion over politics. The king continued to dominate the political scene.

The monarchical form of government became deeply rooted or embedded in ancient Indian political system from the age of the Mauryas onwards. Under this form of government the king concentrated enormous powers in his hands. He was at the helm of affairs. He was the head of the executive, legislature and judiciary. The king strongly favoured the idea of centralization of power. There was hierarchy of subordinate officials to assist the king in running the government. The centralized bureaucracy constituted the nucleus of this form of government. By the dawn of the fourth century CE, the divine theory of kingship got recognition. The Gupta kings being influenced by this theory considered themselves as the representatives of God. The monarchy was the prevailing form of governments in the post-Gupta times too.

Ancient India had a very rich republican tradition. The republics actually flourished in the post-Vedic times. There were various types of republic. There were some republican states in which powers were vested either in the whole community or their elected representatives. In some states powers were centred in a small body or council consisting of a few selected members or nobles. The states in which powers were vested in kṣatriya chiefs of artistocratic family come under the category of aristocratic republic, aristocratic oligarchy or aristocratic democracy. There were some confederate states in which the powers were jointly shared by two different communities or chiefs.

On the whole, about seventy-five republics flourished in ancient India between the sixth century BCE and the fourth century CE. Only at the time of the Buddha (*c.* 563–483 BCE) ten republics flourished which include the Licchavis of Vaiśālī and the Videhas of Mithilā in north Bihar the Śākyas of Kapilavastu in Nepal and seven others in eastern U.P. These republics belonged to the Buddhist kṣatriya tribes. In northern or north-western India, Afghanistan, Punjab and Sindh had numerous republics. Punjab and Sindh were the two important seats of republics at the time of Alexander (*c.* 327–325 BCE). These republics belonged to only the brāhmaṇas and kṣatriyas. The famous republican communities in the Punjab were the Kaṭhas, Adhr̥ṣṭhas, Śibis, Kṣudraka-Mallavas, Ambasthas and Yaudheyas and in the lower Indus Valley the brāhmaṇas maintained their republican states and there was one state of Pattala managed by two chiefs belonging to two different families. The states were just like the small city states of Greece. The other famous republican communities were the Arjunāyans of Agra-Jaipur tract, Kunindas of the hilly areas of Punjab, the Madras of central Punjab, etc.

Each republican state was governed by its own constitution. The large state had both General Assembly and Executive Council. The smaller states had only Assembly. The strength of the members of General Assembly varied from state to state. The Licchavis of Vaiśālī had the highest members, i.e. 7,707. Next to it Yaudheyas had 5,000 members. The number of members of Executive council varied from 4 to 20. All important matters were unanimously decided at the Supreme Assembly.

There were various factors which led to the decline and disappearance of republics in ancient India. There was a general tendency on the part of the rulers of monarchical states to conquer the neighbouring republican tribes and absorb their states. The Licchavis of Vaiśālī were conquered by Ajātaśatru of Magadha and their state was annexed to the Magadhan empire. The Sākyas of Kapilavastu met the same tragic end at the hands of king Prasenajīt of Kosala. Porus the Elder of Punjab absorbed fifteen republics which were within the territorial limits of his kingdom. Many republics fell prey to Mauryan imperialism. Alexander and his army destroyed many republican states in course of his invasion of north-west India. The final blow to republics was struck by Samudragupta. Most of the republics disappeared from the pages of ancient Indian history by the end of the fourth century CE.

Religion

The animism of the prehistoric age continued to hold its ground for a considerable period of time. It had its impact to a certain extent on the religious system of the protohistoric age. The Indus Valley people also adopted the animistic cult which is evidenced by their worship of trees, stones, waters and various other inanimate objects. This cult existed side by side with various other religious cults. There are some archaeological evidences to show that one of the popular cults was directly associated with the worship of the mother-goddess. Numerous terracotta figurines of women have been found at Haṛappā in the Montgomery district of Punjab. The bronze image of a female goddess has been found at Moheṅjo-Dāṛo in the Larkānā district of Sindh. The discovery of various seals at both the places depicting the scene bearing the semblance of sacrifice of goats and buffaloes gives us the impression that the worship of Śakti (female energy), which is manifestation of mother-goddess, had taken its root there. The sacrifice of animals constitutes the most characteristic feature of the mother-goddess or Śakti cult. The seal of the male god called Paśupati (identified with the traditional image of Paśupati Mahādeva or Śiva) flanked by subsidiary gods has been found at Moheṅjo-Dāṛo. The prevalence of the phallus worship (of non-Aryan origin) which later became intimately connected with Śiva, can be testified by the discovery of numerous symbols of the phallus and female genital organs made of stone at Haṛappā. Many pointed conical and cylindrical stone pieces have also been discovered which look exactly like a Śivaliṅga, the form in which Śiva worship is still prevalent in different parts of the country. It goes without saying that the Śaivism associated with the phallus worship and Śāktism — the two important sects of Hinduism are of pre-Aryan origin.

The religious beliefs and conceptions of the Vedic Aryans were largely based on polytheism. They used to worship their gods represented by Indra, Varuṇa, Mitra, Rudra, Viṣṇu, etc. by offering prayers and sacrifices. The sacrifices and *yajñas* involving the slaughter of animals were performed by the brāhmaṇas or priestly class. The rituals were elaborate, expensive and cumbersome. The mode of worship followed by the rituals concerned became the part and parcel of Brāhmanical religion. A large number of people came within the fold of Brāhmaṇism before the advent of Buddhism and Jainism (the two reformed forms of Hinduism) in the sixth century BCE.

The sixth century BCE was the landmark in the religious history of ancient India. Actually this was the period of socio-religious reform movements as well as cultural renaissance. With the advent of two new religious sects, Jainism and Buddhism, founded by Mahāvīra and Gautama Buddha respectively, the whole socio-religious structure of ancient India underwent significant changes. The social inequality, the caste distinction, the supremacy of the brāhmaṇas, sacrifices, burden of ritualism, etc. became things of the past. The doctrines of these new sects attracted a large number of people. Many of them came out of the fold of Hinduism and embraced these two new religions. Between the sixth century BCE and the tenth century CE both Jainism and Buddhism spread in different parts of the country. The latter, in particular, spread in different parts of the world including Ceylon, Burma, Tibet, Thailand, China, Japan and Korea. The division of the Buddhists initially into two groups, the Mahāyānists and the Hīnayānists and later into eighteen groups, and likewise the division of the Jains into the Śvetāmbars and Digambars and various other evil practices which had crept in both gradually led to their decline.

Brāhmaṇism suffered a great setback due to the religious reform movements of the sixth and fifth centuries BCE Hinduism was pushed into the background for some time. However, Brāhmaṇism was revived in the post-Maurya age (second century BCE to the third century CE). The Śuṅgas and Kaṇvas of Magadha and the Sātavāhanas of the Deccan restored the Brāhmanical faith. Hinduism was further revived in the Gupta period. Many temples and images of Hindu gods and goddesses were built, the temples were dedicated to Śiva, Viṣṇu, Durgā, Pārvatī, etc. The number of their votaries went on increasing. The Śaivism, Śāktism and Tantrism — the three sects of Hinduism, evolved in the sixth century CE and continued to flourish in the post-Gupta period (CE 650–1000). Śiva was worshipped in both human and phallic form by those who had faith in the Śaiva cult. The female goddesses like Durgā, Caṇḍī, Ambā, Kālī, etc. were propitiated by the followers of the Śakti cult. The Tāntric form of religion developed as an offshoot of Śāktism. This was based on magic, sorcery, witch crafts, charms, elements of sexo-yogic practice, etc. The emergence of the Tāntric Buddhism in the post-Harṣa period was another religious development. Its followers condemned the practice of austere penance, difficult vows, fasting, going on pilgrimage, etc. They held that for the attainment of the highest spiritual experience men and women must be united together in body, mind, and spirit.

Vaiṣṇavism, one of the popular sects of Hinduism, has its own history. The devotees of Viṣṇu were called Vaiṣṇavas. There were two important schools of Vaiṣṇavism represented by the Bhāgavatas and the Pañcarātras. The former developed a sect called Bhāgavatism. They had unflinching faith in the supremacy of Vāsudeva. The latter school upheld fivefold manifestations of Vāsudeva, namely Para, Vyūha, Vibhava, Antaryāmin and Ārca forms. The Vāsudeva cult developed as Vāsudeva-Kṛṣṇa cult. These sects or cults have very high antiquity. In the post-Gupta period Vaiṣṇavism was a very popular form of religion in northern India. Bhakti cult (the worship of a personal god through love and devotion) first spread in the eighth century CE and saw its efflorescence in the fourteenth and fifteenth centuries CE.

The Śaiva, Śakti, Tāntric and Vaiṣṇava cults of Hindu religion existed side by side with Buddhism and Jainism. One of the distinguishing hallmarks of the religio-cultural history of ancient India is that Hinduism, Buddhism and Jainism, the three of the six principal schools of religion, co-existed despite their perpetual conflicts and contests. The populace and potentates had faith in the fundamental unity of these three religions.

Art and Culture

The Indian culture and civilization find reflection also in the artistic heritage. The art in the broader sense of the term finds expression in its three different forms, viz. architecture, sculpture and painting. In all the three branches of art, India has had the distinction of maintaining very rich traditions.

In fact, the history of the Indian art begins with the advent of the Mauryas. The Mauryan emperors erected several magnificent buildings and other monuments of great artistic merit. They patronized arts and consequently architecture and sculpture attained a very high level of excellence. The buildings, palaces and monuments built by Candragupta Maurya (321–298 BCE) have perished as they were mostly made of wood. The monuments of Aśoka's period (273–232 BCE) were made of hard grey sandstone. They were nicely chiselled and polished. They are the expression of a sophisticated and fully developed art. A city was protected by walls, built of baked bricks. The large and imposing buildings in the city consisted of several storeys. Their grandeur, beauty, decorative richness and ornamentation are amply testified not only by the relief carvings of early Indian art but also the extensive and elaborate cave façades. Excavations at Bulandī Bāgh and Kumrahār near Patna have brought to light the city walls and multi-pillared hall of the royal palace of Pāṭaliputra. In order to enshrine the relics of Buddha or of his chief disciples the *stūpa*s were erected. A *stūpa* is a solid domical structure of brick or stone on a round base. Aśoka is traditionally believed to have built more than eighty thousand *stūpa*s all over the country. The most glaring example is the big *stūpa* at Sāñcī near Bhopal, not far away from Vidiśā in Madhya Pradesh. Several *caitya* halls were also constructed. The monolithic pillars set up by Aśoka at various places are the characteristic specimens of the remains of art of his period. These pillars have been discovered at Topra, Meerut, Allahabad, Lauriya Nandangarh, Rāmpurvā, Sāñcī, etc. The rock-cut architecture also developed during the Maurya period. Caves were cut out of hard and refractory rocks. Caves were not only the dwelling places of monks but they also served the purpose of assembly halls. Aśoka and his grandson Daśaraśa got several such caves built. Many such caves are found on the Barābar Hills near Gayā in Bihar and the Nāgārjuna Hills in the south. A very large number of rock-cut monasteries were also made. The majestic figures of lions, bulls, etc. on the Aśokan pillars represent examples of the sculptural art of the Maurya period. It is far-fetched imagination that the Mauryan rulers borrowed some elements of the Greek and Persian arts.

The Śuṅga period (185–75 BCE) ushered in a new era in the field of the art of building. The wooden railing of the Buddhist *stūpa*s of the Maurya period were replaced by stone railings and magnificent long stone gateways. The remains of the Bharhut *stūpa* are notable examples of these changes. The sculpture-reliefs on the gateways, pillars and crossbars on the railings give beautiful, vivid and pictorial representations of the nature of the art of this period. A group of rock-cut *stūpa*s and a large excavated *caitya* hall near the old *vihāra* at Bhaja near Poona, *caitya* halls at Nasik and Ajantā, *stūpa*s at Amrāvatī, the beautiful railings at Bodh-Gayā, the Garuḍa pillar at Besnagar (M.P.) are among the well-known examples of Śuṅga monuments and sculpture. The period extending from the first century BCE to the third century CE is also important from the point of view of many changes in the forms of arts. A large number of *stūpas*, rock-cut *vihāras* and *caitya* halls were built. The influence of the Greek ideas on the Indian art in the north-west gave rise to a new school of art which is generally known as the Gāndhāra school of art.

The earliest extant examples of painting are in the Jogimare cave in the Rāmgaṛh hills in the Surgujā district of M.P. There appears a few rows of human figures and representation of large aquatic animals, etc. in yellow and other colours. These figures on walls are lively, rhythmical and well-balanced in alignments. These paintings are assigned to about the middle of the first century BCE. The next important phase of paintings began a century-and-a-half later. Its finest specimens are the mural paintings in some of the Ajantā caves (cave nos. 9 and 10). These are the earliest paintings of Ajantā. The tradition of painting continued to flourish.

The Jains and Buddhists made significant contributions in almost all the fields of art. It is worthy of note that they utilized art for the propagation of their respective faiths. In the early centuries of the Christian era the Jains erected *stūpas* like those of the Buddhists in honour of their saints adorned with stone-railings, decorated gateways, elaborated carved pillars and abundant statues. Many of these have been found at Mathurā.

The Jaina tradition of icon-worship or the worship of the images of *tīrthaṁkaras* and other divinities, which may be traced back to the Maurya-Śuṅga period gave fillip to the growth of the art of sculpture. The Khaṇḍagiri and Udayagiri caves of Orissa contain some early Jaina reliefs. The image worship was prevalent among the Jains of Mathurā region also. Many well-carved Jaina images of exquisite beauty and several Jaina votive tablets with the figures of Jaina *tīrthaṁkaras* have been discovered at Mathurā. They belong to the centuries immediately preceding and following the Christian era. Many remarkable Jaina images belonging to the period extending from the tenth to the twelfth centuries CE have been discovered at various places in our country.

The rock-cut architecture of the Jains is worth mentioning. The Jaina caves with their relief works and statues near Vidiśā in M.P. and at Ellorā in Maharashtra are excellent examples of both architectural and sculptural art. The Jains have also constructed cave temples cut out of the rocks, the earliest example of which is Hāthīgumphā caves in Orissa which belong to the second century BCE or later. Such temples were also built at Ellorā.

The Jains maintained their own style of temple architecture. The Jains have erected a number of magnificent temples and other architectural monuments belonging to different ages. The temples at Kundapur in M.P., Muktagiri in Andhra Pradesh, Ranakpur near Jodhpur in Rajasthan, and Girnār and Palithan in Kathiawar (Gujarat) are notable examples of this art. The superb architecture of Jaina temples at Mount Abu (Dilwāṛā) in Rajasthan fairly testifies to the perfection attained by the Jaina artists in the field of temple architecture.

The Jaina paintings find reflection in the mini-portraits of *tīrthaṁkara*s and other reputed monks painted with golden and bright colour with profuse illustration in their manuscripts.

There are sufficient evidences to show the contributions of the Buddhist artists in the realm of architecture, sculpture, and painting. The *stūpa*s built at Sāñcī, Bharhut and Amarāvatī, the stone pillars and the cave temples of Kānheri (Mumbai), Kārle (Poona) and Nasik are considered to be the best specimens of the Buddhist art. The *stūpa*s are well known for their gateways and railings richly carved with sculpture depicting scene from the Buddha's life. The *vihāra*s (abodes of the monks) were built in several parts of the country. The *vihāra*s, *stūpa*s, temples and other monuments were elaborately carved and ornamented. The paintings in Ajantā caves depicting scenes from the life of Buddha and his previous existence testify to the great skill of the artists in the field of painting.

The Indian art reached its zenith of progress during the Gupta period (CE 320–550). Many Hindu temples dedicated to Śiva, Viṣṇu, Pārvatī, etc. were built in different parts of the country. The Daśāvatāra temple at Deogaṛh (Jhansi district), a brick temple at Bhītargāon (Kanpur district) and many other temples are good specimens of the temple architecture. The Nāgara and Drāviḍa styles of temple architecture evolved during this period. The pyramidal curvilinear tower constitutes the distinctive feature of the former style, and the upper storey placed over the sanctum, the division of wall by pilasters and niches and the use of the roll-cornice carved with well-shaped arches of the latter. The rock-cut architecture was also revived. The rock-cut caves at Ajantā and Ellorā are famous for their unique beauty and workmanship. The sculpture in the temples at Ellorā and Elephaṇṭā presents a high standard of this art. Many statues of Buddha and Hindu gods have been discovered especially from the excavations at Sārnāth and Nālandā which reveal the high degree of excellence that sculpture had attained. Of these the seated Buddha's image in the museum of Sārnāth is remarkably beautiful. In the temple there are many images of Hindu gods. The stone images with reliefs executed at Aihoḷe, Bādāmī, Kānheri, Ajantā, etc. are also specimens of the sculptural art. The artists of Mathurā produced Brāhmanical, Buddhist and Jaina images made of red stone with white spots. The Mathurā school of art was in a flourishing condition during this period. The mural paintings of Ajantā caves, most of which were done in the Gupta period, are of very high merit and great beauty. They are of all kinds: human beings, animals, birds, plants, etc.

The Indian art reached the height of glory during the Pallava and Coḷa periods. The Pallavas made substantial contribution to the evolution of art in ancient India. Their temple architecture can be divided into two categories, viz. rock-cut and structural. Rock-cut temples can further be subdivided into two groups: pillared halls and monolithic shrines known as *rathas*. Mahendravarman I (CE 600-30) is credited with having laid the foundation stone of art at Mahābalipuram by starting the technique of building stone temples out of solid rocks. He also introduced the new style of cave temple. The Pallavas' metropolis, Mahābalipuram, was made by him "the birthplace of south Indian architecture and sculpture." During the time of Narasiṁhavarman I (CE 630-68) a new style of cut-in cave temples and cut-out shrines was followed. The carvings in stone of shrines or *rathas* were done. A number of cave temples were built at Mahābalipuram between CE 625 and 674. They are named after the Trimūrti, Varāha, Durgā and five Pāṇḍavas. The five *rathas* or monolithic shrines are named after the five Pāṇḍavas. The cave depicting the scene of the descent of the Ganges is a unique masterpiece of Pallava art. There are altogether ten *maṇḍapas* (the larger halls with pillars) bearing beautiful carvings. During the reign of Narasiṁhavarman II (CE 695–722) six temples including the structural temples at Kāñcī and the shore temple at Mahābalipuram were built. The famous Kailāsanātha temple at Kāñcī is the largest among the Pallava temples. Its main features are the pyramidal tower, the flat-roofed pillared hall or *maṇḍapam*, surrounded by a series of cells, resembling *rathas*. There is striking parallelism between the Buddhist rock-cut cave temples and the Pallava temples built in the Draviḍian style.

The Coḷas not only developed the Draviḍian style but also perfected it. Their temple architecture has been appreciated for the purity of its artistic traditions. In the words of Fergusson "the Coḷa artists conceived like giants and finished like jewellers." A new development was the addition of a huge gateway called *gopuram* to the enclosure of temple. The temple built by Rājarāja the Great at Tanjore some time between CE 1003 and 1010 is one of the splendid monuments of Tamil architecture. According to Percy Brown it is a "touchstone of Indian architecture as a whole." Another magnificent temple of great artistic significance was built by Rājendra Coḷa in CE 1025 in his new capital city of Gaṅgaikoṇḍacoḷapuram. The influence of Coḷa art on other countries especially Indo-China and Far-East through trade is a well-acknowledged fact.

Sculpture was generally subsidiary to architecture. The Coḷas employed it as decoration on the walls, pillars, plinths, roofs and other convenient spots in temples. Portraits, icons and decorative sculptures are the main classes of Coḷa sculpture. Among the icons Śaiva figures are predominately very important as the Coḷas were the votaries of Śiva. However, there are some Vaiṣṇava and Jaina images also. The Naṭarāja image made of bronze in its various forms holds important place among the pieces of sculptural art.

The Coḷa painting was a continuation and development of Pallava-Pāṇḍya work in the field. The fragmentary Pallava paintings still traceable in the cave temples of Tirumayam and Memandur and in the temples of Panamalasi and Kāñcī are datable to the seventh and eighth centuries. Of the paintings the most important are those in the *pradakṣiṇā* passage round the sanctum of the Tanjore temple belonging to the time of Rājarāja and Rājendra. On the top of panel on the west wall is the Kailāsa scene with Śiva seated in *yogāsana* on a tiger skin with the Nandī (bull) in front and a group of *ṛṣi*s with a couple of *apsaras* maidens dancing at the opposite end. Śiva is painted red and one of the *ṛṣi*s blue. The scene depicting the journey of two friends to Kailāsa on the invitation of Śiva is very attractive. The whole scene is a superb piece of Coḷa painting. The panel on the north wall of the temple has a battle scene with Śiva standing on the deck of the chariot, etc. There are other beautiful specimens of their painting.

The Hindus, Jains and Buddhists by maintaining equally rich artistic traditions provided cultural unity to India.

7

Sources of the History of Uttar Pradesh
(Ancient Period)*

THE ancient history of Uttar Pradesh, like that of many other oriental countries, is shrouded in mystery. The sources of the early history of this state are not only meagre and confused but rather replete with traditional, mythological and legendary accounts which sometimes contain conflicting and contradictory statements. And thus we are beset with baffling problems while attempting to draw a demarcation line between facts and fictions, and historical and quasi-historical materials. The difficulty is enhanced by the absence of a definite chronology. However, these difficulties and problems may be largely overcome if we study our material with the spirit of a judge.[1]

---

* From *Sources of the History of India*, vol. II, ed. by S.P. Sen (Calcutta, 1979), pp. 289-98.

1. The ideal expressed in the words of Goethe, befitting the occasion and context, is worth quoting :

"The historian's duty is to separate the true from the false, the certain from the uncertain and the doubtful from that which cannot be accepted. . . . Every investigator must before all things look upon himself as one who is summoned to serve on a jury. He has only to consider how far the statement of the case is complete and clearly set forth by the evidence. Then he draws the conclusion and gives his vote whether it be that his opinion coincides with that of the foreman or not."

"The Maxims and Reflections of Goethe" nos. 453, 543, quoted in V.A. Smith, *The Early History of India*, p. 4.

The sources may be arranged in the following order: (1) Literary and traditional accounts; (2) Foreign accounts; (3) Archaeological materials; and (4) Contemporary chronicles or Literary texts.

Literary and Traditional Accounts

The antiquity of Uttar Pradesh can only be determined by looking into ancient texts handed down to us from time immemorial together with the traditions chiefly recorded therein. In the first place the *Śatapatha Brāhmaṇa,* the most important Brāhmanical literature belonging to the later Vedic age, deserves mention because it furnishes both the historical and cultural data relating to the early kings, their kingdoms, dynasties, etc. of the state. Another important source is provided by the famous Sanskrit Epics, the *Rāmāyaṇa* and the *Mahābhārata.* The *Rāmāyaṇa* copiously deals with different aspects of the different parts of ancient Uttar Pradesh. The Ayodhyā Kāṇḍa (LIV, XC, CXV, L, LV, LXXXIII, CXXVII, XXXII, LXVIII, XVI), Bāla Kāṇḍa or Ādi Kāṇḍa (XXXIV, LXIX, LXVIII, XXXII, VII, V, VIII, XIII, XIV, XV, XVI) and Kiṣkindhā Kāṇḍa throw a good deal of light on the ancient kingdom of Ayodhyā, capital of Kosala or Uttara Kosala, a prosperous and well-built city ruled by the clan of Ikṣvākus, the relations of the rulers with other contemporary powers, exchange of cultural teams between Ayodhyā and Mithilā, cultural fellowship between the Ayodhyā rulers and non-Aryan or Niṣāda chiefs, development of art and architecture, literary and cultural activities of the women of Ayodhyā, social customs, religious rites and rituals and so on. Information is also obtained from this epic about Kauśāmbī (founded by Kuśāmba), Prayāga and Kāśī along with their boundaries and their ancient rulers. It is to be noted here that the statements recorded in the *Rāmāyaṇa* should be judged with great caution and they require further confirmation and corroboration from other works either of early or late origin. No less important is the *Mahābhārata*. The Sabhā Parva[2] of this epic mentions about Bhīmasena's conquest of Ayodhyā and Kāśī, the defeat of Kāśīrāja at the hands of Rājā Kumāradeśa, Paraśurāma's attacks on Kāśī and Kosala, ancient city of Dvārikāpurī and its buildings and gateways, etc. Vana Parva[3] also mentions Ayodhyā and Prayāga, and Bhīṣma Parva[4] refers to the ancient kingdom of Kāśī. Udyoga Parva[5] gives a brief description of Rājā Divodāsa, the ruler of Kāśī.

Equally important are the Purāṇas compiled roughly between 200 BCE and CE 600. Out of the 18 Mahāpurāṇas, the *Vāyu Purāṇa*,[6] *Skanda Purāṇa*,[7] *Brahma Purāṇa*,[8] *Viṣṇu Purāṇa*[9] *Mārkaṇḍeya Purāṇa*,[10] *Brahmāṇḍa*,[11] *Matsya*,[12] *Bhaviṣya*,[13] *Liṅga*,[14] *Bhāgavata*,[15] *Agni*,[16] and *Harivaṁśa*[17] Purāṇas provide an elaborate account of genealogies of royal dynasties and supply most reliable information about the ancient kingdom of

2. "Digvijaya Parva", Ch. 30, vv. 2, 6; Ch. 38.
3. Ch. 85.
4. Ch. 9.
5. Ch. 117.
6. Pargiter, *Ancient Indian Historical Tradition*, Ch. VII, pp. 85, 89, 101.
7. "Purvārdha Khaṇḍa" (Kāśī Khaṇḍa), pp. 79-80.
8. Pt. 36, Pargiter, op. cit., pp. 85, 90, 101.
9. Wilson, *Viṣṇu Purāṇa*, pp. 288-89, 305-07, 325-29.
10. Pt. 16 and 20.
11. III, 48, 29-47, cf. Pargiter, op. cit., p. 269.
12. 12-57, cf. Pargiter, op. cit., p. 89.
13. 88-213, cf. Pargiter, op. cit., p. 89.
14. 1, 56, 66, 43, cf. Pargiter, op. cit., pp. 85, 89.
15. Pargiter, op. cit., pp. 85, 89, 90, 101.
16. Ibid.
17. Ibid.

Ayodhyā and its ruler Ikṣvāku of the Solar race and his descendants, Pratiṣṭhāna or Prayāga ruled by Aiḷa or Aryan race, Kāśī and its rulers of Lunar race 1366 years before the Christian era and their dynasty, and Kauśāmbī ruled by Kuru King Nicakṣu, fifth in descent from Parīkṣit. The Purāṇic accounts also help us to know about the glorious rule of Divodāsa, his conquests of other countries, his republican system of government, socio-cultural conditions, educational progress, religious conditions and role of women in the field of artistic and cultural development in ancient Kāśī. We also get information about the victory of Kāśī Nareśa of Kāśya dynasty over Rājā Alarka (son of Rītidhvaja and Madālasā, Rānī of Gandharva) and his attack on frontier states, conquest of Ayodhyā by foreign tribes and their settlement, the struggle of Ayodhyā rulers with the Tālajaṅgha-Haihayas and other important chiefs.

Notwithstanding the fact that some of the Purāṇic accounts are intermixed with myths and legends and are full of interpolations, they are worthy of credence especially about royal genealogies, ancient kings, kingdoms and dynasties. "They form sheet anchors in the troubled sea of Indian chronology." Yet their credibility must be tested and corroborated by other contemporary and collateral evidences and the combined testimony is sure to yield better results.

The next important sources are the works of Pāṇini and Patañjali, Smṛti texts and some other semi-historical works. *Pāṇini* (IV.I.171) mentions Kāśī, and Patañjali refers to Sāketa and the attack on it by the Yavanas.[18] The last-mentioned statement may be corroborated by the evidence recorded in "Yuga Purāṇa" section of the *Gārgī Saṁhitā*.[19] The Greek raid upon

18. B.N. Puri, *India in the Time of Patañjali*, p. 75.

19. Ibid., pp. 28-29.

Sāketa has been mentioned in many standard historical works during the last year of the reign of Puṣyamitra, about 150 BCE.

The *Bṛhatsaṁhitā* of Varāhamihira ascribed to about the sixth century CE refers to Sāketa, Mathuraka and Śūrasenas belonging to Madhyadeśa.[20] In the *Manusmṛti* Śūrasena (Mathurā) has been referred to as Brahmarṣi-deśa.[21] The *Atharva Pariśiṣṭa*[22] also mentions Sāketa and Mathurā in the north and the *Śaktisaṅgama Tantra* refers to the genealogies of the early rulers of Ayodhyā and their descendants, rivalry between Kāśī and Ayodhyā, and the history of Gorakhpur.[23]

Light on the early history of Uttar Pradesh is also thrown by the dramas, plays, poems, court-epics and other literatures of great historical value. The *Meghadūta* and the *Raghuvaṁśa* of Kālidāsa, relatively free from the laxity of the Purāṇas and extravagant overtones of the late poems, give brief but graphic descriptions of Ayodhyā and Kauśāmbī. The *Meghadūta*[24] very clearly mentions about ancient Kauśāmbī, the modern Kośam, as capital of the Vatsa country ruled by Udayana, a prince of the Lunar race and son of Sahasranīka, also called as Vatsa-rāja. The *Raghuvaṁśa*[25] refers to Sāketa of Ayodhyā. *Vikramorvaśī* (III, 15) by the same author also mentions about the independent kingdom of Kāśī.[26]

20. Kern, *Bṛhatsaṁhitā*, Ch. XIV, v. 3 and p. 87. Also see Fleet's *The Topographical List of the Bṛhatsaṁhitā*, ed. Kalyan Kumar Dasgupta (Calcutta, 1973), S.V. Ch-IV, Verse-26, Ch. XV Verse-17 and p. 88.
21. *Manusmṛti*, Ch. II, v. 19, p. 41.
22. Ed. G.M. Boiling and J. Von Negele. Also H.C. Chakladar, *The Geography of Kālidāsa*, pp. 34-35.
23. Cf. Montgomery Martin, *Eastern India*, II, pp. 325-38.
24. *Meghadūta*, English tr. with Sanskrit text by late M.R. Kale, *Purvamegha*, v. 31, p. 57.
25. XIII-61, XIII-79, XIV. 29, XV. 60, XVI. 13, XVII. 36; also cf. H.C. Chakladar, op. cit., p. 33.
26. H.C. Chakladar, op. cit., p. 40.

The *Bṛhatkathāmañjarī* of Kṣemendra (1020-40), a Sanskrit rendering of Guṇādhya's Prākṛt work *Bṛhatkathā*, and the *Kathāsaritsāgara* (Taraṅgas 11-16) by Somadeva (1063-81) also refer to Udayana, a prince of Kauśāmbī.[27] It has also been referred to by Bhāsa in his play *Svapnavāsavadattā* which throws light on the matrimonial and cultural relations between king Udayana of Kauśāmbī and Aṅga and Magadha.

The *Ratnāvalī* of Harṣa and *Lalitavistara* are also very valuable sources for confirming the statements of Kālidāsa and other writers about Udayana, king of Kauśāmbī with its capital Vatsapattana.[28] The *Sāṅkhyāyana Śrautasūtra* also transmits information about the kings of Kāśī.[29]

Some of the Buddhist texts, like the *Mahāvagga* and the Jātakas, and sacred texts of the Jainas are also valuable mines of information for our purpose. Several Jātakas like the *Guṭṭila Jātaka, Sambhava Jātaka, Sarabha-Miga Jātaka, Bhaddaśāla Jātaka, Dhonasakhā Jātaka, Kośāmba Jātaka, Kuṇāla Jātaka, Assaka Jātaka,* and *Sona-Nanda Jātaka* and the *Mahāvagga* mention especially about the rivalry between Kāśī, Kosala, Aṅga and Magadha, the prosperous city of Kāśī, the revival of Brāhmanical culture and annexation of the kingdom of Kosala by the king of Kāśī. Rhys Davids also refers to Sāketa and Ayodhyā as two adjoining cities like London and Westminster.[30] He further mentions that Kāśī was incorporated in Kosala.[31] Another Buddhist book — *Historic Bouddhisme dans Inde par*, H. Kern, tr. G. Huel, p. 23[32] — is also an important source for getting

27. Cf. *Meghadūta*, v. 31, p. 57.
28. Vide A. Cunningham, *Ancient Geography of India*, p. 331.
29. Macdonell and Keith, *Vedic Index*, I, pp. 153-54.
30. *Buddhist India*, p. 39.
31. Ibid., p. 24.
32. H.C. Chakladar, op. cit., p. 33.

the relevant information about the ancient kingdoms of Sāketa, Kauśāmbī, Kāśī, etc.

The tradition recorded by Montgomery Martin in his *Survey Report*[33] also helps us to know about the facts that Kāśīrāja was attacked and expelled by a class of people called Gurkhā (Śiviras), which is further confirmed by a small quadrangle pyramid attributed to Śivirāja near Banaras, and that the Cheros attacked and destroyed the kingdom of the Solar race in Ayodhyā. In the absence of corroborative evidence it is not possible to accept this tradition with certainty.

Foreign Accounts

(A) TRAVELS OF CHINESE PILGRIMS

The accounts left behind by Chinese Buddhist pilgrims, Fa-hien[34] (339–414) and Hiuen-Tsang[35] (635–637), serve as a treasure house of satisfactory and elaborate information about different aspects of history. These accounts throw a good deal of light on the ancient kingdoms like Mathurā (*Mg-tu-lo*), Ayodhyā (*Q-yu-to*) or modern Ayodhyā near Faizabad, Prayāga-Kāśī (*Po-lo-ni-se*), Kauśāmbī (*Kiau-shang-mi*), Saṅkāsya (*Sen-ka-she*), *A-ye mu-ka* or country probably corresponding to Pratāpgaṛh and Rae-Bareilly district, as well as on their contemporary, socio-political and religious life, cultural and literary progress, administrative systems, prevalent customs, monuments and other remains.[36]

33. *Eastern India*, II, pp. 341-71.
34. James Legge, *The Travels of Fa-hien* or *A Record of Buddhistic Kingdoms*, pp. 42-60.
35. Shaman Hwui Li and Samuel Beal, *The Life of Hiuen-Tsian*, Book II, Chap. III, pp. 77, 79, 85, 90, 91; Book III, pp. 98-99. T. Watters, *On Yuan Chwang's Travels in India*, I, pp. 312-13, 332, 335, 361, 366.
36. For proper identifications of the names and places Cunningham's *Ancient Geography of India* has been helpful for our purpose. See, for instance, pp. 293, 295-96, 315, 370.

(B) CLASSICAL ACCOUNTS

The writings of the Greeks also furnish a good deal of information about different parts of ancient U.P. Of them Ptolemy refers to Kassida or Kassidia corresponding to Kāśī. He describes Modera (Mathurā) as "the city of gods." Besides Ptolemy, Magasthenes, Arrian and Pliny also mention about Modoura or Methora as the capital of Saurasenoi.[37]

(C) PERSIAN CHRONICLES

Some Persian chronicles like *Āin-ī-Akbarī* of Abul Fazl (tr. Gladwin, 1800, London, giving the name *Ayeem Akbari)* and *Jamiut-Tawārīkh* of Rashid-ud-din also refer to the old city of Ayodhyā, religious practices at Prayāga, Varanasi, etc. which help us in getting a glimpse into the age-old Indian traditions.

Archaeological Evidence

(A) INSCRIPTIONS

Epigraphic records are indisputably the most important source for getting the nearly accurate knowledge of various stages of long-forgotten past. Inscriptions are of many kinds and in the present context they include, *inter alia,* the inscription taken from the gateway of the fort of Khara dated Saṁvat 1092 (CE 1035),[38] an inscribed brick found at Mora, seven miles west of Mathurā, the Pābhosā inscription,[39] the inscription of the stone pillar of Aśoka[40] set up about 235 BCE at Prayāga, and an

37. For Ptolemy's Geography, see *Ancient India as described by Ptolemy* (Eng. tr. J.W. McCrindle); for Megasthenes and Arrian, see *The Ancient India as Described by Megasthenes and Arrian,* also by J.W. McCrindle. R.C. Majumdar has compiled the classical accounts bearing on Indian History and Culture in his *Classical Accounts of India.*

38. M.R. Kale, op. cit., v. 31, p. 57.

39. B.N. Puri, op. cit., pp. 50-51.

40. A. Cunningham, op. cit., p. 328.

inscribed pillar found at Mathurā (famed as the Mathurā Lion capital inscription),[41] a Kosam inscription of first century CE and an inscription of the Kuṣāṇa monarch found near Kosam,[42] which help us to ascertain the antiquity of the kingdoms and names of their rulers, their military activities, inter-state relations, etc.

(B) COINS

Coins hailing from U.P. may be broadly classified into the following groups : (i) Kauśāmbī coins, (ii) Mathurā coins, (iii) Ayodhyā coins, (iv) Baran (Bulandshahr) coins, (v) Almoṛā coins, and (vi) Coins of Pañcāla (Bareilly, Ramnagar). The large cast coins of Kauśāmbī or Vatsapattana (an ancient city in the Allahabad district) of a period between the third century BCE and the first century BCE bear the names of a number of ancient rulers.[43] The ancient cast coins found in the neighbourhood of Mathurā bearing the inscription and the coins of the Satraps of Mathurā bring to light some Hindu princes of Mathurā who ruled from the third century BCE to the middle of the first century BCE, and Śaka rulers bearing the title Kṣatrapa probably of the second half of the first century BCE.[44] The oldest cast coins and the square inscribed cast pieces of Ayodhyā belonging to the second century BCE clearly show that rulers of two different dynasties ruled here.[45] According to D.C.

41. *Epigraphia Indica*, IX. pp. 141 ff and Sten Konow, *Corpus Inscriptionum Indicarum*, II, pp. 48 ff. Also B.N. Puri, op. cit., p. 53.
42. *A.S.R.* 1911-12, p. 50, cf. D.C. Sircar in *The Age of Imperial Unity* (ed. R.C. Majumdar), p. 175.
43. For these coins, see J. Allan, *Catalogue of Coins in the British Museum, Ancient India.*
44. Rapson, *Indian Coins*, pp. 8-9, 13; Cunningham, *Coins of Ancient India*, pp. 85, 87, 88; *Journal of the Royal Asiatic Society*, 1894, pp. 541, 552 ff ; *Journal of the Asiatic Society of Bengal*, 1854, p. 679; 1897, p. 9.
45. Rapson, op. cit., p. 44. (Pl. IV, 2, 3, 4).

Sircar, the second class coins "belong to later groups of rulers who flourished at the end of the Kuṣāṇa period in the Eastern U.P."[46] The coins of Baran (ancient name of Bulandshahr) bearing the legend *Gomitasa Baranaya* is also important to ascertain the name of an ancient ruler.[47] The three specimens appearing to be of some alloy of silver and heavier than any other Indian coins found near Almoṛā, probably of a date between the first century and the second century CE, provide the names of ancient rulers.[48] The Pañcāla coins of the second century BCE show the connection between its rulers and the dynasty ruling in the south of Allahabad and help us to know the history of Bareilly district and the kingdom of Ahicchatra.[49]

(C) ANCIENT REMAINS OR MONUMENTS

Uttar Pradesh is rich in old remains. They include, *inter alia*, the old ruined town between Hardwar and Kankhal called Māyāpur; the old fort of Rājā Ben covered with broken bricks and ruined mound and *kilāh* or fort of Sītā Rāmjī of Saron between Bareilly and Mathurā; the old fort of Rājā Kaṁsa, remains of extensive buildings, a number of statues and Buddhist monasteries in Mathurā area; old ruined mounds of Kakupur, twenty miles to the north-west of Kanpur, of more than 1000 years ago; the remains of the temple of Prayāga situated inside the fort of Allahabad; cave *stūpa*s and ramparts of Kauśāmbī, modern Kosam; ruins of Ayodhyā; extensive mass of ruins of more than 2000 years old at Baranas; old remains at Gazipur; ruins of the old fort of Saṅkisa or Saṅkāsya of the *Rāmāyaṇa;* monuments in Gorakhpur; and various other Hindu temples, cult-images of deities, Buddhist and Jaina

---

46. In *The Age of Imperial Unity*, pp. 173-74.
47. Rapson, op. cit., 45, p. 11.
48. Rapson, op. cit., 40.
49. The *Imperial Gazetteer of India*, VII, p. 3.

stūpas, *caityas* and other statues, carved pillars and other monuments of architectural pattern in the vicinity of Mathurā, especially the temple railings, pillars, *toraṇas*, apsidal temple of the pre-Christian and early Christian centuries, seals and coins of both Mauryan and Kuṣāṇa periods unearthed as a result of recent archaeological excavation at Soṅkh, near Mathurā, undertaken by a team of archaeologists from Berlin University under the stewardship of H. Haertal, and some other pieces of art from Ayodhyā, Vārāṇasī and other places.[50] They bear witness to the artistic and cultural progress of a very high order, right from the first century CE to the twelfth century CE in an unbroken order, and testify to the co-existence of three principal religions — Brāhmaṇism, Buddhism and Jainism — and their generally amicable relations.

The aforesaid sources have proved to be of substantial help in reconstructing the history of ancient U.P., dealing with social, political, religious, cultural and other aspects of the early people of the region.

50. A. Cunningham, *The Ancient Geography of India*, pp. 293, 295, 297, 306-08, 315, 325-26, 327, 332, 342, 367 and 370; Martin, *Eastern India*, II, 335-39, 346, 348, 350, 368, 371, etc.

8

The Dionysiaka
A Classical (Greek) Source of History of Ancient India*

THE *Dionysiaka*, a Greek epic poem in hexametre verse, is one of the very important classical sources of history of ancient India. It was composed by Nonnos who flourished about the beginning of the fifth century CE or a century later. The poem is divided into forty-eight books of which the first twenty-five are of limited importance as they partly deal with India. Moreover, the accounts furnished therein are more mythological than historical. It is only the Twenty-sixth Book which contains valuable historical data about India. The work as a whole is very useful for supplementing the Greek and Roman accounts of ancient India with regard to its ethnography, socio-economic and political history, towns and cities, subjection to the foreign rule, etc. Besides, the work also abounds in some historico-geographical information about India which are of considerable importance. It is complementary to the *Bassarika* of Dionysios Periegetes of Samos who flourished probably towards the end of the third century CE so far as the study of the above-noted aspects of history of India is concerned.

"The Indians," according to Nonnos, "had extended their empire westwards as far as the shores of the Mediterranean

---

* From *Shodhak : A Journal of Historical Research*, vol. XXVIII, pt. A. Sr. 82, 1999, pp. 1-3.

and the Red Sea. . . ."[1] The details thereof are wanting. However, it is valuable information indicating the extension of political and cultural influence of India to the far distant countries in the west in the pre- and post-Christian era.

Nonnos' work contains allusions to various primitive tribes and races, towns and cities, etc.[2] The "Ariainoi" were evidently the people of Ariana which denotes the land between India and Persia. Strabo[3] and plinty[4] also refer to them. They have been identified with the Aryans. The "term Arya designated in common the Iranians and the Indians of the North."[5] The Ariana in the widest application of the term comprised Aria (Herat), Arachosia (Kandahar), Paropanisadae (Kabul Valley), and Gedrosia (Baluchistan). The "Arachotes," as mentioned by Nonnos, were the inhabitants of Arachosia, a province of Persia, bordered on the north by part of the Paropanisos chain (the Hindukuśa range in the north of Afghanistan), on the east by the Indus and on the west by the Drangians (the people of Drangiana, now Seistan). It was a rich and populous province, and acquired early importance as one ot the main routes from India to Persia. The people of the maritime region immediately to the west of the Indus have been referred to as the Arabians who have been identified

1. J.W. McCrindle, *Ancient India as Described in Classical Literature,* Westminster, 1901, rpt. Delhi 1984, p. 196.
2. *Dionysiaka,* Eng. tr. Osmond De Beauvoir Priaulx, Paris, 1874, Bk. XXVI, pp. 206-9; McCrindle, op. cit., pp. 197-200; also *Dionysiaka,* XXVI, pp. 165f. cf. M.A. Stein, *Memoir on Maps Illustrating the Ancient Geography of Kasmir,* Calcutta, 1899, rpt. Patna 1977, p. 77.
3. *Geog.* XV. II, 1 cf. McCrindle, op. cit., pp. 80-82.
4. *Natural History,* New York, 1962, VI. 23.
5. McCrindle, op. cit., p. 80, notes 1 & 2; H.H. Wilson, *Ariana Antiqua,* Delhi, 1971, pp. 119-22; See also G.P. Singh, "India from Afiana to the Gaṅgā Valley," *Adhyayan* — Journal of the Bhāratiya Itihāsa Adhyayana Sansthan, vol. II, no. 2, Allahabad, 1992, pp. 1-21.

the Arbitai or the Arabics.[6] They were subdued by Alexander the Great in course of his invasion of north-western India. The "Goryandos" belonged to Goryaia! the territory traversed by the River of Ghor, an affluent of the Kabul River. Alexander on his march to India passed through this territory.

Nonnos also makes mention of the "Bolingians," "Prasian," "Cirradioi," "Sabaroi," "Dosareans," "Caspeiri," "Arsanians," "Sibai," "Dardae," "Asene," etc. The "Bolingians" may be identified with Bholingai of Pliny mentioned in his long list Indian races,[7] and Bhūliṅga of Pāṇini.[8] Their seats lay near the Arāvalī range slopes westward towards the Indus. They were one of the branches of the great tribe of the Salvas who were located near Matsya region with its capital at Virāṭa (Vairatnagar near Jaipur). According to *Kāśikā*, a commentary on the *Aṣṭādhyāyī* of Pāṇini (IV.1.173), they were one of the six member states organised in the Salvavayava federacy.[9] They were one of the popular races in the times of Pāṇini (*c.* 550 BCE) and Sandrocottus or Candragupta Maurya (fourth to third centuries BCE). According to Priaulx, Nonnos has taken their name of their leader from the *Bassarika* of Dionysios Periegetes. The Prasian or Prasii were the inhabitants of Prasiake (Prācya region) the capital of which was Pālibothra (modern Patna) on the Ganges. The Cirradioi were the Kirātas,[10] a race spread along the shores of Bengal to eastward of the mouths of the Ganges as far as Arākān. The Sabaroi were located in Dosarene near Sambhalpur, famous for producing the finest of diamonds.

---

6. For details see A. Cunningham, *The Ancient Geography of India*, Varanasi, 1979, pp. 257-59.
7. Op. cit.
8. V.S. Agrawala, *India as known to Pāṇini*, Vararasi, 1963, p. 59.
9. Ibid., p. 57.
10. For details see G.P. Singh, *The Kiratas in Ancient India*, Delhi, 1990, pp. 59ff.

They were a wild race living in the forests without any fixed habitation. The Dosareans may be identified with the Daśārṇas mentioned in the Purāṇas. They inhabited the region to the south-east of the Madhya-deśa (the Midlands) in juxtaposition to the Śabaras or Śaurs Caspeiri (or Kaspeira) denotes Kashmir whose people have been mentioned along with other Indian tribes. The Arsarians were settled in a territory called Arsa lying between the Indus and the Hydaspes (Jhelum). The Sibai (or Śibis) inhabited a district between the Hydaspes and the Indus. They represented one of the aboriginal tribes of the regions of the Indus. They had their capital at Śibipur in the Śorkoṭ region of Punjab. They were one of the republican tribes of Alexander's time. The Dardae were the people of Dardistan, the mountainous region situated to the north of the upper course of the Indus which produced the gold. The Asene (or Asini) were settled within the dominion of Porus. According to Pliny,[11] Nicaea the chief of three cities, belonged to them. This was the city built by Alexander on the battlefield on which he defeated Porus.

From the account of Nonnos it distinctly appears that the women in the tribal society occupied very honourable position. They enjoyed full freedom. They shared the responsibilities of menfolk in dealing with socio-economic and political matters. They were wonderfully expert in the art of writing.

Nonnos' incidental notice of the Greek rule in Bactria in the third and second centuries BCE is also worthy of our attention. He speaks of Euthydemos (*c.* 220–190 BCE), who was the founder of the greatness of the Bactrian kingdom. This kingdom rapidly grew in power under him. He appears to have subjugated a large part of Afghanistan. He held eastern Punjab with its capital at Sagala (Sakala of Sanskrit writers)

11. Op. cit., VI, 20.

which was situated to the west of the Hydraotes (Rāvī) at a distance of about sixty miles from Lahore. The city having been destroyed was rebuilt by his son, Demetrios, in whose dominions it was included, and by whom in honour of his father it was renamed Euthydemia, called "Euthydimeia" by Nonnos.

9

Colonial and Cultural Expansion of the Aryans Outside India
as Gleaned from the Vedic Literature*

THE settlements of the Aryans and the expansion of their culture in different parts of India have been extensively discussed by the oriental scholars of both the East and the West, but the subject alluding to their colonial and cultural expansion outside India is still wrapped in a great degree of obscurity. Hence there is need for making a fresh historical investigation into this subject. The study of the subject under review is primarily based on the information contained in the Vedic texts comprising both the Saṁhitās and the Brāhmaṇas. But at the same time an attempt as far as practicable has also been made to supplement it by the accounts of some of the noted authorities on the Vedic literature as well as by other collateral sources.

The dispersion of the Vedic Aryans from their original homeland Sapta-Sindhu-deśa (corresponding to the land of seven rivers *par excellence*, the Sindhu or Indus and its five tributaries of the west or the five rivers of the Punjab — Vitastā or Jhelum, Asiknī or Cenāba, Paruṣṇī later Irāvatī or Rāvī, Vipāśā or Beas and Śatudri or Sutlej — and Sarasvatī in the east), both as colonizers and traders into the northern Arctic region, northern and southern Europe, central and western

---

* From *Journal of the Department of History*, Manipur University Imphal, vol. II, 1987, pp. 16-29.

Asia, northern and central Africa and Asia Minor for perpetuating their role, establishing their colonies and expanding their culture and civilization, finds some reflection in the Vedic literature. F. Max Müller[1] has also admitted that one of the primary missions of Aryan nations including India was to link all parts of the world together by the chains of civilization, commerce and religion.

It will be profitable if it is made clear at the very outset that the frontiers of the Āryadeśa extended up to Gandhāra in the north-west or Uttarāpatha, Bāhlīka or Bactriana region adjacent to the Oxus or Vaṁkṣu river and Airyana Vaejo in the north, on the one hand, and, on the other, up to Sarasvatī and upper Gangetic Valley in the east, Gaṅgā–Yamunā doab, and Punjab and Kashmir in the north. This was the geographical limit of the contemporary Āryadeśa within which the indigenous Aryans were living and where some of the oldest Vedic hymns were composed and the Aryans culture flourished. This was the real cradle of the Aryan race. This was the centre from where the expansion of the Aryan culture began and the colonization process set in. This was also one of the earliest centres of human habitation in the world.[2]

1. *The Vedas* (Varanasi, 1969), p. 2; *A History of Ancient Sanskrit Literature* (London, 1859, rpt. Varanasi 1968), p. 13.

2. The accuracy of the theories propounded by the scholars about the original cradle of the Aryans have not yet been properly tested. The hypothesis of the central Asiatic home of the Vedic Aryans as suggested by a number of foreign and Indian scholars can be outrightly rejected. Because neither in the Vedic literature nor in the post-Vedic classical literature we find any evidence which refers to the immigration of the Aryans into Sapta-Sindhu from outside. The conspicuous absence of details in the *Ṛgveda* about the coming of the Aryans from outside and their later settlements in the Sapta-Sindhu confirms our belief that they were original inhabitants of the Sapta-Sindhu. The evidence furnished in the *Ṛgveda* (5.4.53.9) clearly show that Rasā, Anitamā →

Actually, this region was the hive of many Aryan and non-Aryan races during the Vedic period. The internal conflicts among the Aryans as well as the occasional eruption of hostilities between the Aryans and non-Aryans were very responsible factors for their dispersion form this zone into different directions which resulted in both geographical and historical changes in the early period. Over and above, being actuated by the desire and animated by the passion to disseminate their culture far and wide through commercial intercourse with the outside world and to establish their

---

→ and Kubhā (Kabul) lying between the Indus and Sarayū were the few places where the Ṛgvedic Aryans had originally settled. A.C. Das (*Ṛgvedic India: Cultural History of India as Depicted in the Ṛgveda*, Calcutta, 1920, Delhi, 1980, vol. I. pp. 32-67, 122f; vol. II, pp. 353f, 370-71, 574-90) after having made a comparative study of the early civilizations of ancient Aryana or Ariana, Babylonia, Assyria, Phoenicia, Asia Minor, Egypt and prehistoric Europe in the light of the results obtained form geological, archaeological and ethnological investigations has conclusively proved that the Aryans had settled in their original home — Sapta-Sindhu — about 25,000 years ago. In support of his contention he has given arguments which are quite logical. In the Ṛgvedic age, there was a large Asiatic Mediterranean sea extending from below ancient Bactrian to the Black sea covering an immense area. The existence of seas (represented in early historic times by the Black sea, the Caspian sea, the Sea of Aral and the Baltic sea) at a time when the Ṛgvedic hymns were composed in the Punjab precludes the possibility of Europe or Central Asia having ever been the cradle of Aryans. Thus the dispersion of the Aryans from their original cradle Sapta-Sindhu in different parts of Asia, Europe and Africa appears to be worthy of credence.

J.A. Ragozin (*Vedic India*, London, 1895, rpt. Delhi 1984, pp. 63f), Muir (*Original Sanskrit Texts*, 1871, vol. II, pp. 322f, 387f), Curzon (*Journal of the Royal Asiatic Society* (hereafter *JRAS*) London, 1854, vol. XVI, pt. II, pp. 187-200), E. Pococke (*India in Greece*, London, 1856, pp. 12f) and some other German and French Scholars (see *La Bible Dans L'Indie* 1870, pref., pp. vii-ix) have also admitted →

supremacy by colonizing the foreign lands, the Aryans sometimes had to go out of their original homeland.

The frequent allusions to the seas in all the four sides (the east, the west, the north and the south) of the Sapta-Sindhu

→ that the Aryans did not come to India from the West, rather they were living originally in India from where their dispersal waves after waves started which resulted in their colonization of different parts of Asia and Europe and extension of their civilization. (See also R.C. Majumdar, ed., *The Vedic Age,* Bombay, 1965, pp. 220-21 for different other theories advocated by Ganganath Jha, *Ācārya Pushpanjali, D.R. Bhandarkar Commemoration Volume,* pp. 1-2; D.S. Triveda, *The Annals of Bhandarkar Oriental Research Institute,* XX, 48ff and other scholars in support of the indigenous origin of the Aryans). The view expressed by Prof. Sayce (*Principles of Philology,* 1874, pp. 101f; *Science of Language,* 1885, vol. II, p. 123), that the primeval Aryan community were living in the highlands of Middle Asia or in Bactriana near the sources of the Oxus (Sanskrit = Vaṁkṣu) and Xartes, is not tenable. Many scholars like him have placed the Aryans on the other side of the river Oxus in a deliberate attempt to prove them of Central Asiatic origin. In fact, the Vedic Aryans of the Bāhlīka region (later called by the Greeks Bactria or Bactriana) south of the river Vaṁkṣu (Oxus of the Greeks) in northern part of Afghanistan (forming part of ancient Bhāratavarṣa) were autochthones like the Aryans of Sapta-Sindhu region. Yāska (*Nirukta,* Pūrvakhaṇḍa, 6.26) has called the Aryans the son of God. Had the Aryans migrated from Europe, Central Asia, or Arctic region towards Sapta-Sindhu they would not have called the Himalayas as Uttaragiri (*Śatapatha Brāhmnaṇa,* 1.2.1.5).

The use of an appellation for a particular group of people in ancient times was determined more by the grade of culture which they represented than by the race which they belonged to. As a matter of fact, from the time of Veda Vyāsa to Manu the distinction between the Aryans and non-Aryans was made more on cultural ground than on ethnic ground. Further, the race has been connected with the language which has made the confusion worse confounded. Romila Thapar (*Ancient Indian Social History,* Hyderabad, 1984, p. 152) has also pointed out that by identifying →

region (*samudrāeva sindhavaḥ*), the sea voyages of the Aryan traders and their sailing across the seas by ships for both commerce and conquest, the sea borne trade and its gain, the praying to the sea for acquiring wealth before undertaking a voyage, the invocation to Indra for exterminating the hostile forces in all the four sides, the "Satari-tra-nau," a sea-going

---

→ language with race all speakers of Sanskrit have been described as members of "that nineteenth-century myth, the Aryan race."

Some Western scholars have committed a mistake by describing that the ancestors of the Indians, Persians, Greeks, Romans, Germans, Slavonians and Celts belonged to the same stock (Aryan) and were living together originally in a common place (Central Asia) before their dispersal towards Sapta-Sindhu. The real mystery behind such proposition made on philological ground has not been unravelled at a large scale. The similarity between Sanskrit and European languages was first emphasized by Filippo Sassetti, an Italian trader of the sixteenth century, who had lived in Goa for five years (1583-88). Two centuries later, Sir William Jones, an oriental scholar (president of the Asiatic Society of Bengal, Calcutta), made a pronouncement in the year 1786 that Sanskrit, Greek, Latin, Zend, Gothic, Slavonia and Celtic belonged to one family of speech (Indo-European family of languages) and sprang from one common source (Sanskrit) which Hegel later called the discovery of a new world. Franz Bopp, the founder of the Science of Comparative Philology, harped on the same tune by publishing his works in 1816 and then in 1833-35 on comparative Grammar. Since then the members of the so-called Indo-European family of languages have been described as descendants of the common ancestor on the Philological ground. The equation of seven European groups of languages — the Hellenic, Italic, Celtic, Teutonic, Slavonic, Lithuanic or Lettic and Albanian (see Isaac Taylor, *The Origin of the Aryans*, London, 1889, pp. 2, 12, 30-31) gave birth to a theory of Central Asiatic home of the Aryans. Without examining the credibility of an evidence of linguistic *palaeontology* this theory was blindly supported. Prof. Max Müller (*Lectures on the Science of Language*, 1861, vol. II, pp. 445-46; *History of Ancient Sanskrit Literature*, →

vessel of hundred oars (allied to rudder), the journey of Indra across the sea for bringing back the Yadus and Turvasus to the Sapta-Sindhu region, the combined sea-voyage of Vasiṣṭha

---

→ pp. 11-13; *The Vedas*, pp. 1-2) on the basis of comparative philology concluded that the Aryans before migrating across the snow of the Himalaya southward towards the Sapta-Sindhu were inhabiting north-western Asia and Europe. But in 1887 (*Biographies of Words and the Home of the Aryas*, London, 1887, rpt. 1912, pp. 93-94, 100) he changed his earlier statement and put forth a new proposition that the ancestors of the Aryans were dwelling "somewhere in Asia" before their separation. These are all speculations which cannot be substantiated either by literary evidence or by an archaeological proof.

Actually, the racial concept of the Aryans put forward by Edward Thomas at a closed door meeting of the Royal Asiatic Society, London, 9 April, 1866 (see Minutes, *JRAS*, New Series, V, p. 420, fn.) as a part of conspiracy to prove the Aryans as a foreign race became the root cause of the whole confusion in modern times. (See also E.J. Thomas' article, "The so-called Indo-Aryan Invasion," *Indian Historical Quarterly*, 1929, pp. 248-53). This myth can be now easily exploded. By no stretch of imagination it can be accepted that the Aryans were a foreign race and Central Asia was their original home.

While determining the origin, identity, antiquity, location and ethnology of any Aryan or non-Aryan group of peoples of ancient times, top priority is to be given to the study of contemporary geographical setting without which justice cannot be done to the task nor can we get an accurate picture of the subject.

There are several theories regarding the origin of the Vedic Aryans, but here I refrain myself from going into further details because it does not fall directly within the scope of the subject. After having thoroughly examined the views of several scholars on the basis of their study of comparative philology, comparative religion and comparative culture, taken into account the testimony of archaeology and ethnology and gone through some works on ancient geography and histories of Near East, Western Asia,

→

and Varuṇa, etc. in the Vedic Saṁhitās[3] and the brāhmaṇas[4] fairly attest to the external commercial contacts of the Vedic Aryans with the outside world as well as their expansion beyond India during the Vedic age. The mention of words — *nau* (boat) *nāvāja* (sailor), *aritri* (oarsman), *navi* (navy or fleet), *san-yatra*, voyage to a foreign land, *paṇi* (trader), etc. — in the

---

→ Egypt, Babylonia and prehistoric European races, I find that the Aryans did not come from Europe (either Russia or Hungary or Austria or Bohemia), Central Asia or Arctic region (Tilak, *The Arctic Home in the Vedas*, pp. 58ff) rather they went outside form their original home — Sapta-Sindhu — for their colonial and cultural expansion.

3. *Ṛgveda* (hereafter *ṚV*) 1.25.7; 1.35.4; 1.46.2; 1.46.8; 1.47.6; 1.48.3; 1.54.4; 1.56.2; 1.112.6; 1.131.2; 1.143.5; 1.136.5; 1.169.3; 1.171.7; 1182.5-6; 1.190.7; 2.39.4; 3.36.7; 3.35.1; 3.118.3; 4.30.17; 4.55.6; 4.80.5; 5.45.10; 5.85.6; 6.20.12; 6.62.2-7; 6.61.9; 7.49.4; 7.55.7; 7.88.3-5; 7.87.6; 8.6.4; 8.92.22; 8.19.14; 9.33.6; 10.47.2; 10.53.10; 10.72.7; 10.131.1; 10.136.5; 10.143.5; 10.55.3; H.H. Wilson (tr.), *Ṛgveda* (London, 1850-54), vol. 1, pref. xii, I, 281f; vol. II, pp. 148f. 310; Max Müller (ed.), *Ṛgveda Saṁhitā*, the sacred songs of the brāhmaṇas together with the commentary of Sāyaṇācārya (1st. edn. 1849-56, 2nd edn. 1890-92), vol. I, pp. 855f; vol. II, pp. 298f, 612f; *Atharvaveda*, 3.15.4; 3.15.6; 2.36.5; 4.7.6; 5.19.8; 6.1.3.1 (Seven seas); 9.2.6; *The Kauśika Sūtra*, the Atharvan school, lays down the rules for performance of rites for securing safety in boats and ships during the sea voyage; *Vājasaneyī Saṁhitā*, 21.7; *Taittirīya Saṁhitā*, 2.4.8.2; see also, John Wilson, *The Social State of the Aryas on the Banks of the Indus in the Times of the Vedas* (Bombay, 1858), pp. 38ff; for the confirmation of the data provided in the *ṚV* about the geographical position and location of the seas in all the four sides of the Sapta-Sindhu as well as for their identification see H.F. Blamford, *Quarterly Journal of the Geological Society*, 1875, vol. XXXI, pp. 524-41; *Encyclopaedia Britannica*, vol. XXIII (9th edn.), pp. 634-38; *Imperial Gazetteer of Indian Empire*, 1907, vol. 1, pp. 53f; H.G. Wells, *The Outlines of History*, pp. 39 and 45.

4. *Aitareya Brāhmaṇa*, 3.39.7; *Śatapatha Brāhmaṇa*, 1.6.3.11; 2.3.3.5; 2.3.3.15.

Ṛgveda also provides some clues to us regarding the trade and commerce of the early Vedic Aryans. Actually, the commerce was the suitable means for the Vedic Aryans for achieving their end, that was to establish the Aryan colonies and to spread the Aryan culture outside India.

The incident relating to the ship wreckage (ship with hundred oars) of prince Bhujyu in the wake of his attempt to conquer an island and his deliverance form the danger by the two Aśvins as narrated in the *Ṛgveda*[5] also confirms the commercial enterprise of the early Vedic Aryans. While corroborating the Vedic account, Bühler has stated that this incident is an indication of the voyage undertaken by Bhujyu in the Indian Ocean.[6] This illustration also goes to prove the dispersal of the Aryans form the Sapta-Sindhu region in all directions to occupy islands of the sea as well as to establish their colonies.

The commercial contacts of Aryans with Babul or Babylonia during the later Vedic age is confirmed by the use of the words *taimat, āliṅgī-vilgi, tābūna, tastūva,* etc. in the *Atharvaveda,*[7] which have been derived from the Babuli language. The external trade relations of the Aryans of Sindh and Baluchistan with Egypt, Babylonia and Assyria can very well be proved by the export of cotton fabrics from Sindh to these countries by the sea routes. This cotton cloth or muslin manufactured in Sindh became popularly known as "Sindhu" in all these three countries. But in Greece this cloth was called as "Sindon" as pointed out by Herodotus himself. According to him, this cloth was very popular particularly in Egypt and Babul. In fact, there was a trade emporium on the bank of the Indus

5. *ṚV*, 1.112.6; 1.116.3-5.
6. Cf. A.A. Macdonell and A.B. Keith, *Vedic Index of Names and Subjects* (hereafter *VI*), London, 1912, vol. 2, pp. 107-08.
7. 5.3.13.6-11.

wherefrom the several merchandize and the commodities were exported to foreign countries in the Vedic period. The seaborne trade in cotton cloth continued up to third or second millennium BCE. The high degree of excellence attained by the manufacturers of the Sindh area in the field of making cotton cloths during the Vedic period has also been accepted by the Vedic scholars and others.[8] But some have taken this account as unworthy of credence.[9] However, the discovery of a few pieces of cotton cloth form Moheṅjo-Dāṛo leaves no doubt in our mind that "Sindhu" was a kind of cotton cloth manufactured in the Indus area and exported to Babylonia and other countries through sea.

The Paṇis, a despised class of Aryans living on the bank of the sea on the eastern side of the Sapta-Sindhu, played a notable role in the expansion of Aryan culture outside India during the Ṛgvedic age both as traders and colonists. They were merchants and traded both by land and the sea routes. They were experts in the art of shipbuilding and sea voyages. They were excellent mariners, probably the earliest, that history knows of. They established their colonies on both the western and southern sea coasts for carrying on their seaborne trade with the outside world. From some of the available indications it can be deduced that they were one of the builders of the urban culture of the Indus Valley. Their contribution to the dissemination of the Indus culture outside the Sapta-Sindhu cannot be belittled. They may be also connected with the traders of Baluchistan and builders of Haṛappan culture. In all probability, it is they who have been described as traders in the Vedas. The archaeological discovery of conch in the

---

8. J.A. Ragozin, *Vedic India* (1895), p. 306; Sayce, *Hibbert Lectures* (London 1887), pp. 138f.
9. For the views of Kennedy and other scholars see *JRAS*, 1898, 252-53.

Indus Valley confirms their sea-borne trade. Despite being Aryans, they did not follow the Vedic religion as a result of which they incurred the displeasure of the Aryans. From the Vedic hymns it distinctly appears that they were by and large greedy and avaricious moneylenders. They were bent upon amassing wealth by hook or by crook. Some of them were hostile to the Aryans, that is why they were contemptuously looked down upon by the latter. And a civilized group among them were later absorbed in the Aryan community. That is why a controversy has arisen among scholars as to whether they were Aryan or non-Aryan traders. Some scholars have surmised that they were non-Aryans. But in the real sense of the term they were Aryan traders as the intensive study of the original Vedic sources as well as the writings of some competent Vedic scholars show.

From the Vedic literature it is quite evident that the Paṇis were accustomed to undertake sea voyages as traders.[10] Yāska has also identified the Ṛgvedic *paṇi* with trader.[11] The name of *bṛbu* appears in the *Ṛgveda*[12] as the most prominent among those Paṇis who were famous for their sea-borne trade.

---

10. For details see *ṚV*. 1.33.3; 4.28.7; 5.34.5-7; 5.45.6; 5.61.8; 6.20.4; 6.31.1; 6.45.31-33; 6.61.1-3; 7.6.3; 8.64.2; 8.6610; 10.10 8; *Atharvaveda*, 5.11.6-7; 20.128.4; *Śatapatha Brāhmaṇa*, III. 2.1.23; see also Hillebrandt, *Vedische Mythologie*, 1.83, 89,92, no.3; 3, 268 (he has identified the Paṇis with Parnians or Parnoi of Strabo); Oldenberg, *Ṛgveda-Noten*, 1, 364; Zimmer, *Altindische Lebe*, p. 257; Geldner, *Ṛgveda-Glosser*, p. 103; Ludwig (tr.) : *Ṛgveda*, 3, 213, 215; Bergaigne, *Religion Vedique*, 2, 3; Muir *Sanskrit Texts*, 22, 114; Eggeling, *Sacred Books of the East* (SBE), 26.31, no. 3; Max Müller, *SBE*, 32, 361 quoted in VI, vol. I, pp. 471-73; *Vedic India* (Classical India, vol. 3), by Louis Renou (tr. from the French by Philip Spratt, Varanasi 1971), pp. 76, 127, 132.
11. *Nirukta*, II, 17; VI, 26-27.
12. 6.45.31.33.

Some of the Paṇis because of being non-Vedic from the standpoint of religion were persecuted by the Vedic Aryans so much so that they were compelled to leave the Sapta-Sindhu in their ships for other countries where they settled as traders and spread the Aryan culture. Others embraced the Vedic faith willy or nilly and continued to live in Sapta-Sindhu. They set out on voyages from the shores of Sapta-Sindhu. They must have settled first on the coasts of Gujarat and afterwards on the Malabar and the Coromondal coasts of the southern Peninsula. From these sea coasts the Paṇis accompanied by the Aryanized Coḷas settled in Chaldea and subsequently established a flourishing colony in Mesopotamia and laid the foundation of the great Babylonian Empire. Others accompanied by the Aryanized Pāṇḍyas voyaged in caravans along the coasts of Persia and Arabia and settled in Egypt. Some of the Paṇis settled in Syria and in the eastern coasts of the Mediterranean sea and founded a colony named Phoenicia after them. Some of them settled on the northern sea coasts of Africa. In pursuance of their propensity to go on sea voyages they carried on their trading activities from the sea coasts of Great Britain and Norway. In all likelihood, they might have set up colonies on the western sea coasts of the Sapta-Sindhu and afterwards might have colonized the southern part of Persia or Iran, eastern part of the Arab, Iraq, Syrla and other countries. Stating the matter precisely it can be asserted that the Paṇis of Sapta-Sindhu established their colonies in Mesopotamia, Babylonia (Babul) Egypt, Syria, Phoenicia, Southern Europe, Northern Africa, Persia, Arabia and Asia Minor and expanded Aryan culture which they carried along with them as reminiscences of their past life among the inhabitants of the sea coasts and of those countries with whom they maintained commercial contacts to a considerable degree. They lighted the torch of Aryan civilization from one corner of Western Asia to other corners of north-western and southern Europe. They left behind an indelible stamp of their commerce and culture on Semitic, Egyptian and Greek civilizations.[13] Herodotus has also revealed the truth that Phoenicians first settled on the coast of Erthyrean Sea (Arabian Sea) and therefrom they spread towards Syria and finally established themselves on the Mediterranean sea coast. The Ṛgvedic Paṇis were not the original inhabitants of Phoenicia as mistakenly supposed by some scholars; rather they were the progenitors of Phoenicians. In order to establish their primeval (Vedic) antiquity they claim that their history is roughly ten-thousand years old. They are known to history as the Punic race.

The above description undoubtedly proves the acquaintance of Vedic Aryans with the art of navigation in ancient times. The facts relating to the ship voyages of two noted Aryans, Bhujyu and Bṛbu, further prove the credibility of Vedic accounts. The sea borne trade carried between southern Baluchistan and Sumeria in the third millennium BCE and the discovery of two different designs of erstwhile boats from Moheñjo-Dāṛo testify to the knowledge of the Indus Valley people including the Aryans about the seaborne trade. In the light of the above facts, this impression, that during he Vedic period there was no commercial intercourse between India and the outside world, can be dispelled. It will not be correct to say that "navigation of the Vedic people confined to the streams of the Punjab could not be very important. . . ."[14] Notwithstanding it cannot be denied that in spite of being gifted with commercial instincts and enterprising spirits and

13. See A.C. Das, op. cit., vol. I, pp. 188-206; vol. II, pp. 586-87; VI, pp. 471- 72; A.K. Mazumdar, *Early Hindu India* (Dacca, 1920, Delhi 1981), p. 342.

14. *Life in Ancient India* (*Studies in Ṛgvedic India*, by Adolf Kaegi, tr. From the German by R. Arrowsmith, Calcutta, 1950), p. 24.

equipped with good vessels, the Ṛgvedic Aryans could not take an active part in the commercial and cultural intercourse with the Western world. Neither any Indian tradition nor any foreign account supports it. The absence of an archaeological evidence also sometimes creates doubts in our minds about the historicity of details furnished in our Vedic literature. But on the whole it must be admitted that the process of dispersal of Aryans from the Sapta-Sindhu and the expansion of their culture had already begun in the Ṛgvedic age itself. During the Sūtra period the practice of going on sea-voyages little declined because of rigidity in caste system and Brāhmanical orthodoxy. From the *Baudhāyana Dharmasūtra* (1.1.24) it appears that it was confined to only certain section of brāhmaṇas.

The possibility of the dispersion of one branch of Aryans from the Sapta-Sindhu towards the northern Arctic region and others towards Persia, Western and Central Asia and Europe and the establishment of colonies and expansion of Aryan culture therein cannot be precluded.

In the last quarter of Erinozoic (Hozoic) or before the dawn of Pleistocene age, the Aryans after crossing the narrow passes of Hindukuśa mountain or the Himalayas reached Central Asia (Jambūdvīpa) and subsequently moving beyond this region they went to northern Arctic region where they established their colonies. During the period concerned this region had congenial climate for human habitation.[15] Likewise, the Aryans of Persia had also settled in the Arctic region. The Vendidad section of the *Zend-Avesta* of the Persians also bears

15. For Geographical situation of the Arctic region see *ṚV*, 1.113. 10-13; 2.27.74; 3.55.6; 5.54.5; 10.138.3; *Taittirīya Saṁhitā*, 3.11.2; *Śatapatha Brāhmaṇa*, II.6.3.8; VI.2.1.8; see also Dana's *Manual of Geology*, pp. 206, 224-25 for the high antiquity of Aryan civilization and Arctic region.

witness to the fact that an early branch of the Aryans under the leadership of Yima emigrated to the Arctic region probably in an interglacial epoch after Airyana Vaejo had been destroyed by ice. The evidence furnished in the *Zend-Avesta* of Aryan immigration to the Arctic region in early times does not prove that this region was their original cradle or Airyana Vaejo was situated therein.[16] But at the commencement of the post-glacial epoch large number of so-called Indo-Aryans returned back to the Sapta-Sindhu through the northern Himalayas and another group of Aryans again moved towards Persia or Iran and some of them dispersed in different directions and settled in some parts of Europe including north western Russia after the Arctic Region had become uninhabitable because of excessive ice. Some of them were probably the ancestors of the Lithuanians and the Slavas.

The theory propounded by B.G. Tilak on the basis of asttonomical calculation regarding the Arctic home of the Vedic Aryans can be fairly disputed. His view, that the dispersion of the Aryans first started from the Arctic region (North Polar regions) which was their original cradle,[17] is not very convincing. C.V. Vaidya, while strongly defending Tilak, has also suggested that the ancestors of the Vedic Aryans lived somewhere in the higher latitudes of the temperate zone or lower latitudes of the Arctic region which was a cold region. It was the region form which they emigrated towards Punjab.[18] But the *Zend-Avesta* does not prove that the original cradle of the Aryans was situated in the Arctic region. Actually, the

16. A.C. Das, op. cit., vol. II, pp. 574, 588-90.

17. *The Arctic Home in the Vedas*, pp. 58-66, 74-88, 90-100, 138-39, 145-48, 387, 420, 434-35; see also his *ORION* (*Researches into the Antiquities of the Vedas*, 1893), pp. 200-06.

18. "Indo-Aryan Invasion of India not a Myth", *IHQ*, 1929, pp. 253-60.

expansion of the Vedic Aryans started form the Sapta-Sindhu which included even Airyana Vaejo in ancient times.[19]

One group of the Aryans because of their internal conflict left the Sapta-Sindhu, reached Persia by land route through the north-west and established a new colony named Airyana Vaejo which was later identified with Iran. The Airyana Vaejo of *Zend-Avesta* roughly corresponds to the Sanskrit Aryanam Vijam (beginning or source of the Aryans).[20] Some of the places connected with Airyana Vaejo are believed to have been situated in or about Central Asia whose greater portion was included in ancient Bhāratavarṣa. The land between the west of the Indus and Iran (including Bahlika, Balkh or Bactria) called Ariana by the classical geographers and historians[21] was very much within the geographical limits of Bhāratavarṣa. This region formerly occupied by the Aryans became eastern Iran of later times particularly after the Persian conquest of the north-western region. The Sanskrit Arya became equivalent to Avestan Airya (Ariya in ancient Persian Tablets and Arriya in Scythian Tablets).

---

19. A.C. Das, (op. cit., vol. II, pp. 372-574) after having thoroughly examined Tilak's theory of the Arctic home of the Aryans based on the data supplied in the *Zend-Avesta* has drawn a positive conclusion that the Arctic region was colonized by the Vedic Aryans after their dispersion from their original cradle — Sapta-Sindhu.

20. J.D. Nadirshah in his article "Airyana Vaejo, the Cradle of the Aryans" (*Proceedings and Transactions of First Oriental Congress* 1920, pp. 84-94) has proved that Airyana Vaejo inhabited by primitive Aryans was lying to the south-eastern foot of the Caucasus which was part of Bhāratavarṣa in ancient times.

21. For details see J.W. McCrindle, *Ancient India as Described in Classical Literature* (Delhi, 1984), pp. 80, n. 1, 81, n. 1; H.H. Wilson, *Ariana Antigua* (Delhi, 1971), ch. III, pp. 120ff.

The old name of the Medes (modern Iran) was Arioi (Aryas) of the classical writers.[22] The description provided in the *Zend-Avesta* (4.46.1.2) of the wanderings of Zoroaster (660–583 BCE), Zarathushtra or Jarshasta associated with Magi brāhmaṇas of *Bhaviṣya Purāṇa* with his followers in search of shelter in a country also indicates the possibility of the dispersion of the ancestors of the Aryans of Iran from Indian borderland. Some of them embraced the new religion Ahur-Mazda. There are some similarities between the Sanskrit and the Zend. The Arya, Sapta-Sindhu, Asuras, Aryamana and Soma in the *Ṛgveda* are identical with Airya, Hapta-Hindu, Ahura, Airyiman and Homa in the *Avesta* respectively. There are many such linguistic similarities. In the days when the Indians and Iranians lived together they had a common pantheon of gods. The Iranians, the ancestors of the Pārsīs, were pure Aryans and originally inhabitated Sapta-Sindhu. They share all the material culture of the Vedic Aryans and were, like them, highly civilized speaking the same language, worshipping many of the gods mentioned in the *Ṛgveda,* specially Fire, and the Sun under the name of Mithra, performing the same sacrifice and observing many social customs that were followed by the Vedic Aryans also. Their separation took place after much bloodshed in a war called in Vedic and Purāṇic literature *Devāsura-Saṅgrāma,* the *deva* representing the Vedic Aryans, and the Asura the Iranians. They were the last to be expelled from Sapta-Sindhu. After their expulsion they roamed about in various regions outside Sapta-Sindhu and at last settled down in Bahlika (Bactriana)

22. McCrindle, op. cit., p. 80, n. 2; also E.B. Cowell, "The Brāhmanical Tribes and the Aborigines", *Ancient India* (Delhi, 1983), p. 63, n. 2.

and Airyana Vaejo which they called their original home. Later, they became followers of Ahur-Mazda.[23]

It is said that the region of Western Asia (lying between India and the Aegean and Mediterranean Seas) comprising "the modern countries of Afghanistan, Baluchistan, Persia, and the northern provinces of Turkey in Asia (Armenia, Asia Minor, Mesopotamia and Syria) is the site of many of the most advanced civilizations of antiquity."[24]

We learn from the Cuneiform inscriptions that the kings of Mitanni, a branch of the Hittites established themselves in the district of Malatia in Asia Minor, and that not only did the kings of Mitanni in the fifteenth and fourteenth centuries BCE bear Aryan names, but also they worshipped the deities of the *Ṛgveda* — Indra, Varuṇa, Mitra, and the Aśvins under their Vedic title Nāsatya. The kings of Mitanni and the Aryans of the *Ṛgveda* were connected in ancient times. The former, no doubt, felt the impact of Aryan culture. In the Boghaz-Koi inscriptions and the famous letters from Tel-el-Amarna occur references to the people of Mitanni in north-west Mesopotamia whose princes bear names like Artatama, Suttarna and Tusratta which seem unmistakenly Aryan in form. The Sanskritized names of the Kassites (from the neighbourhood of Media) who ruled over the whole of Babul or Babylonia between *c.* 1746 and 1180 BCE also bear the stamp of Aryan influence. The Vedic gods, Indra (Ahihan = Ana, Bala and Anu), Agni (Fire), Vina (Vena of 10th Maṇḍala of *Ṛgveda*), Maruta (Matu

23. A.C. Das, op. cit., vol. I, pp. 173ff; vol. II, pp. 360, 588-89; Hang's *Parsi Religion, Essay,* III (1862), pp. 145-59, 163-68, 204-05; *JRAS*, 1854, vol. XVI, pt. II, pp. 187-200; N.M. Chapekar, *Ancient India and Iran* (Delhi, 1982), pp. 18ff; E.J. Rapson (ed.), *The Cambridge History of India,* vol. I, *Ancient India* (Delhi, 1962), pp. 65-66, 68.

24. E.J. Rapson, *Ancient India from the Earliest Times to the First Century* CE (Varanasi, 1981), p. 42.

or Mrtu) and Sūrya (Dianisu = Dineśa), were also worshipped there. The names of princes and the deities they worshipped seem Aryan. Names like Shurias and Marytas seem identical with the Sanskrit Sūrya (Sun) and Marutas (the wind gods).[25]

The expansion of Aryan culture in Babylonia was rendered possible through commercial contacts with the Sapta-Sindhu. The Aryans of Sapta-Sindhu expanded Aryan culture in Sumeria and Chaldea also. In some of the Sumerian seals, purohit Vargu (Bhr̥gu) and a brāhmaṇa (baram) named Kaṇva have also been found.

The words, Papharri and Tupharri used in the *R̥gveda* (10.106.6) are supposed to have been derivatives of Chaldean language.[26]

The expansion of Aryan culture in Mesopotamia, Babylonia, Assyria, Sumeria, Egypt, Chaldea and Western Asia can be proved both from colonial and cultural points of view.[27]

While pushing further towards the west, one branch of the Aryans marched towards Europe. The successive waves of Aryan immigration from Sapta-Sindhu continued till late after R̥gvedic times. Some of them had settlements in northern and western Europe. They could not maintain purity of blood and got themselves mixed with Turanians and Mongol herds. The Aryan speech remained predominant there. The Celts, the Slavas, the Lithuanians, the Hellenes and the Latins came within the pale of Aryans both linguistically and culturally. Schrader, a strong champion of the European cradle of the

---

25. Rapson, *Ancient India from the Earliest Times to the First Century* CE, pp. 42-43; Rapson (ed.), *The Cambridge History of India,* vol. 1, p. 67.
26. C.V. Vaidya, *History of the Vedic Literature,* vol. I, pp. 35, 37.
27. A.C. Das, op. cit., vol. 1, pp. 208f, 250f, 298f; see also *Historians' History of the World,* vol. I, pp. 108-09; Isaac Taylor, *The Origin of the Aryans,* pp. 197-212.

Aryans, also thinks that as a result of the Aryan expansion from the east India, the Iranians, the Kurds, the Kossaeans, the Mitannians, the Hittites, the Phrygians, the Lydians, the Armenians and Phoenicians all of them spoke an Aryan dialect in ancient times.[28] The impact of Vedic culture on different parts of Europe was of far reaching importance. The Vedic tradition in Europe has not yet completely died out.

From the foregoing description it can be plausibly concluded that the Aryans of the Sapta-Sindhu dispersed both by land and sea routes in different parts of Asia, Europe and Africa, set-up their colonies and spread Aryan culture. The impact of Aryan culture on Semitic, Egyptian and Greek civilizations and on the ancient civilizations of Mesopotamia, Babylonia, Assyria, Persia and Asia Minor is discernible in their identical religious and cultural traditions.

---

28. A.C. Das, op. cit., vol. II, pp. 318-20, 341-52 (for Aryan colonization of different parts of Asia, Europe and Africa); see also E. Pococke, *India in Greece*, pp. 12-19, 410; K. Taylor, *Nations of Antiquity*, pp. 11-12.

10

Antiquity of Ayodhyā and Historicity of Rāma

Literary, Archaeological and Scientific Perspectives*

AYODHYĀ, situated on the banks of the sacred river Sarayū at a distance of about 8 km from Faizabad in Uttar Pradesh, was the earliest capital of the Kosala kingdom. It has had a chequered history. It has been in existence since the Vedic age which can fairly be substantiated by the evidence furnished in the Vedic literature. The earliest allusion to it as a city which had eight *cakra* (circles) and nine gateways occurs in the *Atharvaveda*.[1] The description of the city in the *Taittirīya Āraṇyaka*[2] of the *Kṛṣṇa-Yajurveda* is exactly similar to that in the said Vedic text. It has been described in one of the Purāṇas as one of the seven sacred ancient cities of India, the other six being Kāśī, Mathurā, Avantikā (Ujjayinī), Māyā (Hardwar), Kāñcī and Dvārāvatī (Dvārakā).[3] It has been assigned the first place in the order of the seven cities.

---

* From *Krishna-abhinandan (B. Krishna Shastri Felicitation Volume): History, Culture and Archaeological Studies*, ed. P. Chenna Reddy, Delhi, 2008.

1. Ed. with Hindi tr. Rama Sharma Ācārya (Bareilly, 1973-75), X. 2, 31.
2. Ed. H.N. Apte (Poona, 1898), I, 27, 2,3.
3. *Brahmāṇḍa* (Veṅkateśvara Press, Bombay, 1913), IV, 40, 91; also R.P. Sharma, *Paurāṇic Kośa* (hereinafter *PK*) (Varanasi, VS 2028), p. 29.

According to the *Vālmīki-Rāmāyaṇa*, the city of Ayodhyā was founded by the primaeval king Vaivasvata Manu. This gorgeous city was twelve *yojana*s (12 × 4 = 48 *kosa* = 96 miles) in length and three *yojana*s (3 × 4 = 12 *kosa* = 24 miles) in breadth.[4] It is described in some of the Purāṇas as a great city with an extent of ten *yojana*s and a circumference of three *yojana*s.[5] According to the Jaina Purāṇas, it was twelve *yojana*s in length, nine *yojana*s in breadth and thirty-eight *yojana*s in circumference.[6] Its geographical transformation in medieval period with the separation of some of its integral parts and their evolution as separate towns or principalities bearing different names and maintaining independent existence resulted in change in its original size and extent as happened in cases of some other ancient cities of India. However, its geographical identity and hoary antiquity cannot be doubted or disputed.

Ayodhyā, an imperial city, reached a high watermark of its grandeur during the time of one of its powerful sovereigns, Daśaratha (the father of Rāma). The city retained its originality in terms of its length and breadth described in the *Vālmīki-Rāmāyaṇa*. We are told that during his time it was a large, densely populated and well-decorated city. It was a well-planned and fortified city adorned with magnificent buildings, ornamental arches and gateways, splendid pillars and towers, beautiful gardens and markets and well equipped with arms

4. Bāla Kāṇḍa, ed. with Hindi tr. of Yudhishṭhira Mimāṁsaka by Akhilananda (Amritsar, vs. 2025), 5, 6-8.

5. *Vāyu*, text with Hindi tr. of R.P. Tripathi Shastri (Prayāga, 1987), 1, 8, 100-107; *Viṣṇudharmottara* (Venkateśvara Press, Bombay, 1912), 1, 13, 1-12.

6. *Ādi Purāṇa* of Jinasena III, ed. Pannālāl Jaina (Kāśī, 1951), 7, 41; *Uttara Purāṇa* of Guṇabhadra, ed. Pannālāl Jaina (Kāśī 1952) 71, 416; *Padma Purāṇa* of Ravisena, ed. Pannālāl Jaina (Kāśī 1958-59), 3, 169-72; 81, 120; *Harivaṁśa Purāṇa* of Jinasena II, ed. Pannālāl Jaina (Kāśī, 1962), 10, 163.

and weapons. It was full of artisans, traders, merchants, craftsmen and various other professional and occupational groups. It had all the paraphernalia of sovereignty and pride and pomp of royalty.[7] In one of the Purāṇas also, it is described as an opulent and prosperous city.[8] In the time of Rāma, it was popularly known as Rāmanagar (city of Rāma).[9] From demographic, economic, political, religious and cultural points of view Ayodhyā may undoubtedly be reckoned as a classic example of an early urbanism in India.

Manu's son, Ikṣvāku, of the Sūryavaṁśa (Solar dynasty) was the first ruler of Ayodhyā which can be confirmed by the evidence adduced in the *Vālmīki-Rāmāyaṇa,*[10] the *Mahābhārata,*[11] and the Purāṇas.[12] In the *Rāmāyaṇa* of Vālmīki as well as in the Purāṇas, the royal family of Ayodhyā is well represented as being descended from a king named Ikṣvāku. The earliest reference to him occurs in the *Ṛgveda.*[13] Pāṇini (fifth century BCE) in his *Aṣṭādhyāyī* (*Sūtra* VI, 1, 171; VI, 4, 174),[14] Patañjali (second century BCE) in his *Mahābhāṣya* (IV, 2, 104)[15] and

---

7. Bāla Kāṇḍa, 5, 8-23; 6, 5-28; Ayodhyā Kāṇḍa ed. and tr. Akhilānanda (Amritsar, vs. 2019) 51, 21-23; S.C. De, *Historicity of Rāmāyaṇa and the Indo-Aryan Society in India and Ceylon* (Delhi, 1976), pp. 157-58.
8. *Padma,* ed V.N. Mandalika (Poona, 1893-94), *Uttarakhaṇḍa,* 242, 41-42.
9. *Brahmāṇḍa Purāṇa,* III, 37, 33; III, 47, 75; III, 48,1.
10. Bāla Kāṇḍa, 70, 21-22; also Ayodhyā Kāṇḍa, 49, 13.
11. Sabḥā Parva, ed. with Hindi tr. by S.D Satavalekar (Paradi, 1982) 13. 3-6.
12. *Brahmāṇḍa,* III, 60, 20; *Matsya,* text with Hindi tr. (Gorakhpur, 1985), 12, 19; *Brahma,* text with Hindi tr. of T. Jha (Prayāga, 1976), 7, 20; *PK,* pp. 52-53.
13. Ed. with Hindi tr. by Rama Sharma Acharya (Bareilly, 1974-75), X, 60, 4.
14. V.S. Agrawala, *India as known to Pāṇini* (Varanasi, 1963), p. 61.
15. B.N. Puri, *India in the Time of Patañjali* (Mumbai, 1968), p. 74.

Kālidāsa (first century BCE) in his *Raghuvaṁśa*[16] also refer to Ikṣvāku (a famous ancestor of Rāma) of Kosala. Kālidāsa in particular in his said work mentions some kings and princes of Ayodhyā, including Aja, Dilīpa, Raghu, Sagara, Daśaratha, Rāma and his two sons Kuśa and Lava, who were all descendants of Ikṣvāku.

Of the sixty-four kings of Ikṣvāku dynasty who ruled the kingdom of Kosala with its capital at Ayodhyā in pre-Rāma period, Māndhātā and his three sons Purukutsa, Ambarīṣa and Mucukunda, Sagara, Dilīpa and Daśaratha were the most prominent. Rāma was evidently the sixty-fifth king. His period constituted a watershed in the politico-cultural history of Ayodhyā. His period indeed witnessed all-round progress and prosperity of Ayodhyā. In the post-Rāma period too, the kings of the same dynasty ruled Ayodhyā. The last king of this dynasty to rule Ayodhyā was Bṛhadbala, who fought on behalf of the Kauravas against the Pāṇḍavas in the great battle of Kurukṣetra and was ultimately killed by Abhimanyu (the son of Arjuna). On the basis of the Purāṇic ganealogies of Ikṣvāku family of both pre- and post-Rāma period that ruled Ayodhyā and other parts of the Kosala kingdom, ninety-eight generations can be computed from the time of primaeval king Manu down to Bṛhadbala of Bhārata war period.[17]

---

16. Ed. J. Vidyāsāgara (Calcutta, 1902), VI, 71; XIII, 61, 70; XIV, 55; XV, 44.

17. *Vāyu*, 88, 3-212; *Matsya*, 12, 25-57; *Brahmāṇḍa*, III, 63, 115-90; *Brahma*, 8, 28-51; *Viṣṇu*, text with Hindi tr. of Muni Lal Gupta (Gorakhpur, vs. 2041), IV, 2, 63-66; IV, 3, 40-49; IV, 4, 100-12; *Viṣṇu*, Eng. tr. H.H. Wilson (Calcutta, 1961), pp. 289, 299-308; F.E. Pargiter, *Ancient Indian Historical Tradition* (Delhi, 1972), pp. 90-94, 145-49; S.N. Pradhan, *Chronology of Ancient India* (Varanasi, 1979), pp. 118, 145; For details see G.P. Singh, *Early Indian Historical Tradition and Archaeology* (Delhi, 1994), pp. 38-45.

On the basis of the evidence available in Sanskrit, Buddhist and Jaina literature, and some other reliable sources the identity of Ayodhyā and Sāketa can easily be established.

In the Purāṇas, it is Ayodhyā which figures prominently but in one of them in particular[18] it has been referred to also as Sāketa. Patañjali in his *Mahābhāṣya* (III, 2, 111)[19] has used Sāketa in place of Ayodhyā. Kālidāsa regards both Ayodhyā[20] and Sāketa[21] the same capital city of the Ikṣvāku kings of Kosala.

In Buddhist literature too, both Ayodhyā and Sāketa appear to be the same. It is Ayodhyā which has been described therein as Sāketa. In some of the Pāli canonical texts, Ayojjha (Ayodhyā) has been distinctly referred to as an important city.[22] In one of the texts, it is said to have been situated on the banks of the Gaṅgā (the Sarayū of *Vālmīki-Rāmāyaṇa*). It is further stated therein that the Buddha had resided these for some time.[23] In the time of the Buddha (*c.* 563–483 BCE), Sāketa was regarded as one of the six chief cities of India, the other five being Campā, Rājagaha (Rājagṛha), Sāvatthi (Śrāvastī), Vārāṇasī and Kauśāmbī.[24] In one of the Jātakas, Sāketa

18. *Brahmāṇḍa*, III, 54.

19. Puri, op. cit., pp. 10, 11, 29.

20. *Raghuvaṁśa*, XI, 93; XIII, 61; XIV, 29; XV, 38, 60, 98; XVI, 25; XVII, 36.

21. Ibid., V, 31; XIII, 79; XIV, 13; XVIII, 36.

22. *Aṅguttara Nikāya*, ed. R. Morris and E. Hardy, Pāli Text Society (hereinafter PTS) (London, 1885-1900), III, p. 169; *Saṁyutta Nikāya* ed. M.L. Feer and Mrs. Rhys Davids, PTS (London, 1884-1904), III, p. 140; IV, p. 179.

23. *Saṁyutta Nikāya*, III, p. 140; IV, p. 179; see also B.B. Lal, "Ayodhyā of the *Vālmīki-Rāmāyaṇa;* An Enjoying Debate on its Identification", *Purātattva*, no. 16, 1985-86, pp. 79-84.

24. *Dīgha Nikāya*, ed. T.W. Rhys Davids and J.E. Carpenter, PTS (London, 1890-1911, rpt. 1974-60), II, p. 146.

(Ayodhyā) has been referred to as an ancient capital of Kosala.[25] In Buddha's time (sixth and fifth centuries BCE), Sāketa seems to have gained prominence over Ayodhyā. The importance of Sāketa as a city and frequent visits of the Buddha and other Buddhist monks to it have also been highlighted in some of the Pāli texts.[26] In one of the Sanskrit Buddhist texts, *Mahāvastu-avadāna*, we read that Sujāta, one of the descendants of Māndhātā in the line of Ikṣvāku, became king in the great city of Sāketa (Ayodhyā).[27] In another Sanskrit Buddhist text, the city is described to have been adorned with domes.[28] It has been observed that in Buddha's time Ayodhyā sank to the level of an unimportant city but Sāketa and Śrāvastī were two of the six important cities of India.[29]

In the epic and Purāṇic tradition, Ayodhyā seems to have been the earliest capital of the Kosala kingdom, and in the Buddhist tradition Sāketa the next. But the fact remains that Sāketa as a capital was no other than Ayodhyā. Here it must be made clear that in pre-Bhārata war period, from Ikṣvāku down to Rāma, Ayodhyā called Sāketa constantly remained

---

25. *Jātaka*, ed. V. Fausböll (London, 1877-97), III, p. 270.
26. *Aṅguttara Nikāya*, II, p. 24; *Saṁyutta Nikāya*, I, p. 54; IV, p. 73; V, pp. 174, 219; *Vinaya Piṭaka*, ed. H. Oldenberg (London, 1879-83), I, pp. 270, 289; IV, pp. 65, 228; *Jātaka*, tr. various scholars under the editorship of E.B. Cowell (Cambridge, 1895–1913), I (*Sāketa Jātaka*), p. 166; II, p. 162.
27. *Mahāvastu*, ed. E. Senart (Paris, 1882-97), I, p. 348; see also B.C. Law, *Geographical Essays* (Delhi, 1976), p. 23, note.
28. *Bodhisattvāvadāna Kalpalatā*, 3rd Pallava, p. 2.
29. B.C. Law, "Countries and Peoples of India ('Epic and Purāṇic Sources')", *Annals of the Bhandarkar Oriental Research Institute*, Poona (hereinafter *ABORI*), vol. XVII, pt. III, 1935-36, pp. 225f; *Geographical Essays*, p. 130; *Geography of Early Buddhism* (Varanasi, 1973), p. 5; "The Kosalas in Ancient India", *Indian Historical Quarterly* (hereinafter *IHQ*), vol. I, nos. 1-2 (Delhi, 1979) pp. 139-65; see also his article on Ayodhyā in *Journal of Ganganath Jha Research Institute*, Allahabad, vol. I, pp. 423-43.

the capital of the said kingdom, and after the division of the kingdom into two parts — northern and southern — the former's capital was at Śrāvastī and the latter's at Kuśāvatī which have been discussed here in detail later. In the post-Bhārata war period, the rulers of Ikṣvāku dynasty ruled the kingdom of Kosala with its capital at Śrāvastī alone till the fifth century BCE.

In one of the Ceylonese chronicles of the late fourth or early fifth century CE, Ayodhyā is stated to have been the capital of south Kosala[30] which is based on facts. After Rāma's death, south Kosala was really governed from the metropolis Ayodhyā as Kuśāvatī was no longer its capital.

Hemacandra (a Jaina scholar of the twelfth century CE) refers to Ayodhyā and Sāketa as the same city.[31] In one of the Jaina non-canonical texts, *Vividhatīrthakalpa* of Jinaprabhasūri, it is clearly stated that Ayodhyā was also known as Ikṣvākubhūmi (the land of Ikṣvāku), Rāmapurī (the city of Rāma) and Sāketa. In the Jaina canonical tradition, in place of Ayodhyā, Sāketa has been mentioned as the capital of the Kosala Kingdom.[32]

Ayodhyā was a place of veneration for not only the Hindus and the Buddhists but also for the Jains. It was visited frequently by Gautama Buddha and Jaina *tīrthaṁkaras*, Pārśvanātha and Mahāvīra. In Ayodhyā, after sixth century BCE Buddhism and Jainism flourished side by side with Hinduism. And there was no dominance of any religion.

Sageda (Sāketa) of Ptolemy (a Greek geographer of the second century CE) or[33] Sha-chi or Sha-ki (Sāketa) of Fa-hian

30. *Dipavaṁsa*, ed. and tr. H. Oldenberg (London, 1879, rpt. Delhi 1982), III, p. 15.
31. *Abhidhānacintāmaṇi* (Ahmedabad, vs 2013), p. 222.
32. J.C. Jain, *Life in Ancient India as depicted in Jaina Canon and Commentaries* (Delhi, 1984), p. 337.
33. J.W. McCrindle, *Ancient India as described by Ptolemy* (London, 1885), VII, 1, 71 and VII, 2, pp. 164-66, 228-29.

(the Chinese traveller of the fifth century CE[34] has also been identified with Ayodhyā.

F.E. Pargiter,[35] A. Cunningham[36] and Csoma de Koros[37] have also described Ayodhyā and Sāketa as identical. The site of Sāketa has been identified with Sujānkoṭ on the river Sai in the Unnao district.[38] In fact, Ayodhyā and Sāketa like Kāśī-Vārāṇasī and Pratiṣṭhānapura-Prayāga were the twin cities. That is why T.W. Rhys Davids, while describing both as the same, observed that ". . . They were possibly adjoining cities like London and Westminster."[39]

It is worthy of note that the place called Ayodhyā in the Vedic and epic age was associated with Sāketa for the first time in the age of the Buddha. From the sixth century BCE down to the fifth century CE Ayodhyā and Sāketa were regarded as the same city. In post-Gupta times, the city was known more popularly as Ayodhyā than as Sāketa.

Ayodhyā also attracted the notice of famous Maurya ruler Aśoka (*c.* 273–232 BCE). He got one huge *stūpa* erected there in the complex of a monastery on the bank of Sarayū, north of the city, exactly at a place where Buddha used to preach his

34. H.A. Giles (tr.), *A Record of the Buddhistic Kingdoms* (an Account of the Travels of Fa-hsien) (Cambridge, 1923, rpt. Varanasi, 1972), pp. 29-30; T. Watters, *On Yuan Chwang's Travels in India* (Delhi, 1973), I. pp. 354-55.

35. *The Purāṇa Text of the Dynasties of the Kali Age* (hereafter *PDK*) (Oxford, 1913, rpt. Varanasi, 1962), p. 53.

36. *The Ancient Geography of India* (hereafter *AGI*) (Delhi, 1979), p. 341; *Archaeological Survey of India, Reports* (hereinafter *CASK*), vol. I (Shimla, 1871), p. 318.

37. *Asiatic Researches*, vol. XX, p. 442.

38. A Fuhrer, *The Monumental Antiquities and Inscriptions in the North-Western Provinces and Oudh* (Allahabad, 1891), p. 275.

39. *Buddhist India* (Delhi, 1971), p. 39.

doctrine during his stay there as appears from Hiuen Tsang's account of Ayodhyā.[40]

In the post-Maurya period, the historic city of Ayodhyā once again rose into prominence. The period extending from the second century BCE to the second century CE witnessed several vicissitudes in its political fortunes.

The dominions of Puṣyamitra Śuṅga, who had ruled the kingdom of Magadha with its capital at Pāṭaliputra from 184 to 148 BCE, included also the city of Ayodhyā. The evidence of Yavana's invasion of Sāketa (Ayodhyā) during his time is recorded in the *Mahābhāṣya* (III, 2, 111) of Patañjali (who was not only his contemporary but also enjoyed his patronage) and in the *Yuga Purāṇa* (11, 22-26, 94-95 BCE) of the *Garga Saṁhitā* (composed in about 144 BCE). The said Yavana is none other than the Indo-Greek ruler Menander (165–145 BCE) who had invaded and occupied Sāketa and other towns of the Gaṅgā–Yamunā doab towards the end of the reign of Puṣyamitra Śuṅga. The prosperity and fame of Sāketa or Ayodhyā had excited the cupidity of the Greek invader. The city, no doubt, suffered a great blow because of the said invasion. It was Puṣyamitra who got it palisaded on the model of Pāṭaliputra for the sake of its future defence. He, thus, restored its fallen fortunes and pristine glory.

Ayodhyā passed under the sway of the Śuṅgas and their successors which can be confirmed by the epigraphic and numismatic evidence.

Dhanadeva governed Kosala as a viceroy of Puṣyamitra Śuṅga which can be confirmed by his inscription discovered at Ayodhyā in which he has been referred to as *Kosalādhipa* (ruler of Kosala). The inscription also records the erection of a sepulchral monument by him in memory of his father, king

40. T. Watters, op. cit., I. pp. 354-55.

Phalgudeva.[41] The coins of Dhanadeva have also been found at Ayodhyā. Mūladeva (Mitradeva) after having assassinated the Śuṅga monarch Vasumitra (*c.* 141–131 BCE), the son of Agnimitra,[42] some time towards the end of his reign declared himself independent of the Śuṅgas, and in 130 BCE established his hold over Ayodhyā. The coins of Mūladeva along with those of his successors have been found at Ayodhyā.[43] Besides Mūladeva, others whose coins have been found include Vāyudeva, Viśākhadeva and Śivadatta. The next class of coins found there are those of Satyamitra, Āryamitra, Siṁhamitra, Vijayamitra, Devamitra and others. They formed a new line of kings. They had no link with the Śuṅga or any other dynasty. They were actually local rulers of Ayodhyā. They preceded the Kuṣāṇa hold over this region as is evident from the Sahet-Mahet inscription of Kaniṣka.[44] The reigns of Mūladeva and his successors, and the Mitra rulers covered the period from 130 BCE to about CE 158. The inscribed coins bearing names ending in "Mitra" found at Ayodhyā also figure in the work of E.J. Rapson.[45] The inscribed copper coins obtained at the neighbouring town of Faizabad datable to *c.* 150 BCE – CE 100, according to V.A. Smith, belonged to the contemporary rulers

41. Dayaram Sahani, "A Śuṅga Inscription from Ayodhyā", *Epigraphia Indica* (hereinafter *Ep. Ind.*) vol. XX, 1929-30, pp. 54-58; *Journal of the Bihar and Orissa Research Society*, Patna, vol. X, 1924, p. 203; vol. XIII, 1927, facing page 247; *IHQ*, 1929, pp. 602f.

42. *Harṣacarita* of Bāṇa, ed. K.P. Parab (Bombay, 1912), p. 199; tr. E.B. Cowell and F.W. Thomas (London, 1897), p. 192.

43. J. Allan, *A Catalogue of the Indian Coins in the British Museum, Ancient India* (London, 1936), p. 1XXXVIII.

44. *Ep. Ind.*, vol. VIII, pp. 180f.

45. *Indian Coins* (Varanasi, 1969), p. 11 and pl. IV, 2, 3 and 4; also V.A. Smith, *Journal of the Royal Asiatic Society*, London (hereinafter *JRAS*), 1889, p. 51.

of Ayodhyā.[46] According to A. Cunningham, these coins are not older than the second century BCE. Inscribed punch-marked coins and other cast pieces may be older.[47]

It was traditionally believed by the people of Ayodhyā but not yet historically proved that after the death of Bṛhadbala their city remained deserted until the time of Vikramāditya of Ujjain (first century BCE) who came in search of the holy city, erected a fort called Rāmagaḍh, and constructed 360 temples on the spots hallowed by its association with the extraordinary events of Rāma's life. This local tradition was recorded by Francis Buchanam in his Survey Report of Ayodhyā which he visited in about 1810. He has not given his credence to this tradition.[48] I am still on the lookout for an authentic source to examine the credibility of the said tradition. Until I get access to that source, I can neither confirm nor deny it.

There are some epigraphic evidence to prove that the Kuṣāṇa ruler Kaniṣka attacked Sāketa (Ayodhyā), entered into conflict with their rulers and after having defeated them established his hold over there.[49]

According to Purāṇic evidence, the Guptas set up their rule over Sāketa (Ayodhyā), Anugaṅgā (the middle Gangetic

46. *Catalogue of the Coins in the Indian Museum*, Calcutta, *Coins of Ancient India* (hereinafter *CCIM*), vol. I (Oxford, 1906, rpt. Varanasi, 1972), pp. 144, 148-51.

47. *Coins of Ancient India* (London, 1891, rpt. Varanasi, 1971), p. 90 and *PI*, IX, 1-3, 7-11; *PI*, XIX, 13; *JRAS*, 1903, p. 287; *Journal of the Asiatic Society of Bengal*, Calcutta, vol. XLIX, pt. I, 1880, p. 27 and pi. XVI, 1.

48. Cf. Montgomery Martin, *The History, Antiquities Topography and Statistics of Eastern India* (London, 1838), vol. II, pp. 333-36.

49. Sten Konow, *Corpus Inscriptionum Indicarum*, vol. II, pt. I (Delhi, 1929), pp. 72 and 75; *Ep. Ind.*, vol. XIV, 1917-18, p. 142; *IHQ*, 1927, p. 85; also *Indian Antiquary (Journal of Oriental Research)*, Bombay, 1903, p. 382.

basin), Prayāga and Magadha.[50] This is regarding the earliest phase of the Gupta rule (CE 275–300). This shows the extent of the Gupta dominions of pre-Candragupta period and not of his time (CE 319-35) as held by Pargiter.[51]

Gayā copper-plate inscriptions of the famous Gupta emperor, Samudragupta (CE 335-75), bear eloquent testimony to the fact that he had extended his political sway to Ayodhyā. He had his military camp there. During his time it was a seat of *jaya-skandhāvara* or "camp of victory."[52] From an inscription dated Gupta Era 117 = CE 436 of the reign of Kumāragupta I (CE 414-55) discovered at Bharāṭhidiha near Karamaḍāṇḍā in Faizabad district of Uttar Pradesh it appears that during his time Ayodhyā was not only an important city but also a centre of learning.[53] The coins of Puragupta or Purugupta (CE 467-72), brother of Skandagupta, do confirm that he was a monarch of Ayodhyā, which was in all probability the capital during his time. He was patron of Buddhism. During his time Buddhism was in a thriving state there.[54] It has been pointed out by H.C. Raychaudhuri that ". . . the immediate successors of Skandagupta had a capital at Ayodhyā probably till the rise of the Maukharis (of Kannauj)."[55] V.A. Smith observes: "There is a reason to believe that in the 5th century CE Ayodhyā rather than Pāṭaliputra was the premier city of Gupta empire."[56]

---

50. *Vāyu*, 99, 383; *Viṣṇu*, IV, 24, 63; see also D.R. Patil, "Gupta Inscriptions and Purāṇic Tradition", *Bulletin of the Deccan College Research Institute*, vol. II, pp. 2-58; V.A. Smith's View, *Ind. Ant.*, 1902, p. 258, note.
51. *PDK*, introd. xii and pp. 20, 53-54.
52. *Ep. Ind.*, vol. XXXIII, 1959-60, pp. 103-16.
53. *Ep. Ind.*, vol. X, 1909-10, pp. 70-72.
54. See also H.C. Raychaudhuri, *Political History of Ancient India*, 6th edn. (Calcutta, 1953), pp. 586-87.
55. Op. cit., p. 587.
56. *The Early History of India*, revd. by S.M. Edwards, 4th edn. (London, 1967), p. 310.

In the Gupta age, Ayodhyā had no doubt reached the pinnacle of its glory.

H.D. Sankalia had anticipated as far back as 1975 that "Ayodhyā when excavated should give us thick deposits and the earliest should go back to at least 2500 BCE."[57] But this has not yet come true. He was of the view that the antiquity of the places occurring in the *Mahābhārata* and Purāṇas can be proved with the help of archaeology. He felt that "A similar attempt should now be made to test the principal places associated with Rāma — such as Ayodhyā if the story is correct, many of the places which Rāma visited during his fourteen years' exile were in a forest, or such sparsely inhabited localities. So our efforts to be successful should be directed to Rāma's capital, and its vicinity, the Sarayū Valley, or the ancient Kosala. The region to the south called south (Dakṣiṇa) Kosala might yield equally old but different cultural relics."[58] Attempts have, of course, been made by some archaeologists in this direction, but it has not yet been possible for them to find out the habitation layer of the period to which Rāma belonged. Until and unless this layer is found in the course of archaeological excavations at Ayodhyā and the C-14 dates on the basis of the testing of some samples of that period are obtained, no definite date of its antiquity or of the period of Rāma can be suggested. We have no C-14 dates for the earliest period of settlements at Ayodhyā. In fact, it has been found difficult to determine the exact antiquity of the towns and cities described in the *Rāmāyaṇa* of Vālmīki, *Mahābhārata* and the Purāṇas. Generally, they are found to have existed much earlier to the dates suggested by

57. "Prehistoric Colonization in India: Archaeological and Literary Evidence", in *Aspects of Indian History and Archaeology* (*AIHA*), ed. S.P. Gupta and K.S. Ramachandran (Delhi, 1977), p. 304.

58. "Archaeology and Tradition", in *AIHA*, p. 278.

archaeologists. The dates suggested by historians and archaeologists as to the events, towns and cities or kings and rulers of so-called proto-historic period are generally found at variance with each other. The hypothesis of Rāma living in Ayodhyā some time early in the first millennium BCE cannot be accepted. According to H.D. Sankalia, his period falls in between *c.* 2350–1950 BCE.[59] It is worthy of remark that all the dates in ancient Indian history before 326 BCE are tentative and not conclusive. No dates before this can be fixed with absolute certainty.

There have been no systematic and extensive archaeological excavations in and around Ayodhyā till today. However, some scrappy excavations were carried out at Ayodhyā in the late 1960s and 1970s. Archaeological explorations have also been undertaken here from time to time. The archaeological evidence we have about Ayodhyā covers the period from the first millennium BCE to the fifth century CE (PGW Phase–Gupta period).

H.D. Sankalia holds that Ayodhyā of the *Rāmāyaṇa* in a true historical perspective was a city of primaeval antiquity. As a well fortified city it may be ascribed to *c.* 1000–800 BCE. In 1967, in course of his archaeological exploration there he discovered sherds of Painted Grey Ware (PGW).[60] The city had all the characteristic features of urbanism in the late Northern Black Polished Ware (NBPW) phase. The excavation at the site in 1969-70 showed that it was occupied in NBPW times (fifth–second centuries BCE). The upper level of this phase brought to light six terracotta human figurines, two Ayodhyā coins, some iron objects, etc.[61] There is an unmistakable proof of town planning in the late NBPW phase which is confirmed

59. *AIHA*, p. 304.

60. *ABORI*, vols. LVIII-LIX, 1977-78, pp. 893-919.

61. *Indian Archaeology — A Review*, New Delhi, 1969-70, p. 41.

by the discovery of structures of baked bricks, ring wells, etc. in 1979-80.[62] M. Wheeler has also included Ayodhyā in the list of cities of the Gaṅgā–Yamunā doab representing NBPW phase of cultures.[63] K.D. Bajpai has opined that Kosala with its capitals at Ayodhyā and Śrāvastī might have represented an advanced phase of material culture about *c.* 600 BCE.[64] B.B. Lal (former Director-General, Archaeological Survey of India) undertook an excavation work at Ayodhyā in March-April 1975. On the basis of his archaeological findings he has stated that the layout of the city might have begun in early historical period (*c.* 250 BCE – CE 350).[65] The baked brick wall of the Śuṅga period and house complex of Gupta times have also been discovered in the scrappy excavations at the site. Between 1975 and 1980 as many as fourteen different places in Ayodhyā including those three in the vicinity of so-called Rāmajanmabhūmi were excavated under the direction of B.B. Lal which were a part of his large project called "Archaeology of the Rāmāyaṇa sites." The remains of NBPW and other objects discovered by him have been dated *c.* 800–700 BCE with the help of two different methods, C-14 test and thermoluminescence test, conducted in Physical Research Laboratory at Ahmedabad. According to him, the first phase of settlements at the site adjoining Rāmajanmabhūmi started some time between the ninth and seventh centuries BCE.[66] According to Sher Singh, the oldest object from Ayodhyā — a charcoal sample-dates back to *c.* 470 BCE according to C-14 test and after applying the MASCA correction factor it goes to *c.* 520 BCE.[67] But this cannot

62. Ibid., 1979-80, p. 77.
63. *Early India and Pakistan to Ashoka* (London, 1968), pp. 30f.
64. *ABORI*, LVIII-LIX, pp. 434-37.
65. Ibid., pp. 893-919.
66. *Indian Archaeology — A Review*, 1976-77 and 1979-80.
67. "Archaeologists Not Sole Arbiters", *The Statesman*, 2 April 1991.

be taken as a date of earliest settlement at Ayodhyā. R.C. Singh, a Former Director of the Archaeology Department of Uttar Pradesh, recently explored as many as seventeen sites in Ayodhyā but excavated only two of them known as Ṛṇamocanaghāṭ and Guptarghāṭ. On the basis of his archaeological explorations and excavations he has come out with the statement that at most places signs of habitation are not anterior to the second century BCE; only at two places, Maniparvat and Sugrīvaparvat, they could be pushed back to Maurya times. The archaeological evidence available to us shows that there were different phases of settlements at Ayodhyā which, besides PGW period, broadly covers the Maurya, Śuṅga, Kuṣāṇa and Gupta periods.

Fa-hien visited the city of Sāketa (Ayodhyā) some time between CE 400 and 414. He found it in excellent state of preservation. The brāhmaṇas and Buddhists were among the inhabitants of the city. He saw them living harmoniously.[68] Hiuen Tsang visited the city called by him A-yu-te-ye (Ayodhyā) some time between CE 630 and 645. According to him, it was above twenty *li* (or upwards of 3 miles) in circuit. There were 100 Buddhist monasteries where three thousand Buddhist monks, both Hīnayānists and Mahāyānists, used to reside, and 10 Hindu temples. The non-Buddhists were few in number.[69] From the eyewitness accounts of these two Chinese travellers it appears that at Ayodhyā during their times Brāhmaṇism co-existed side by side with Buddhism. In a Purāṇa text of the eighth or ninth century CE we are told

---

68. H.A. Giles, op. cit., pp. 29-30; also J. Legge (tr.), *A Record of the Buddhistic Kingdoms* (*an Account of the Travels of Fa-hien*) (Oxford, 1886, rpt. Delhi, 1972), pp. 54-55.

69. S. Beal, *Buddhist Records of the Western World*, Eng. tr. of *Si-yu-Ki* of Hiuen Tsang (Delhi, 1969), vol. I, pp. 224-25; T. Watters, op. cit., I, 354-55.

that Ayodhyā was adorned with *caitya, devagṛhas, prāsāda, gopura*, etc.[70] It further continued to flourish as a city and as a centre of political, religious and cultural activities.

The ancient city of Ayodhyā partly decayed after 1722 — the year in which the materials including bricks were taken from there by the Muhammedans following their withdrawal from the city for building a new town in its neighbourhood called Faizabad. In fact, the areas now covered by this town, and the adjoining places formed parts of Ayodhyā in the age of *Rāmāyaṇa*. Ayodhyā city in the age of Rāma was as large as Dvārakā in the time of Kṛṣṇa.

V.A. Smith has correctly stated that "the ancient city of Ayodhyā famous as the capital of Rāma was replaced by the modern city of Faizabad. The latter was built in no small degree from the materials of Rāma's capital."[71] Cunningham's description in this regard is very graphic and elaborate. He visited Ayodhyā and the neighbouring town of Faizabad some time between 1862 and 1865. He observes:

> The present city of Ayodhyā, which is confined to the north-east corner of the old site is just two miles in length by about three quarters of a mile in breadth; but not one half of this extent is occupied by buildings, and the whole place wears a look of decay. There are no high mounds of ruins, covered with broken statues and sculptured pillars, such as mark the sites of other ancient cities, but only a low irregular mass of rubbish heaps from which all the bricks have been excavated for the houses of the neighbouring city of Faizabad. This Muhammedan city, which is two miles and a half in length by one mile in breadth, is built chiefly of materials extracted from the ruins of Ayodhyā. The two cities together occupy an area of nearly six square miles, or just

70. *Bhāgavata*, IX, 11, 24-31.
71. *CCIM*, vol. I, p. 144, see also pp. 148-51.

> about one-half of the probable size of the ancient capital of Rāma.[72]

There are some positive evidence to prove the historicity of Rāma. The earliest reference to him as a king occurs in the *Ṛgveda* (X,93,14). This reference is obviously a later addition. On the testimony of *Skanda Purāṇa*[73] it can be proved without an iota of doubt that Ayodhyā was the birth place of Rāma, one of the lineal descendants of Ikṣvāku of Sūryavaṁśa.

The genealogies of the kings of Ikṣvāku dynasty who ruled the kingdom of Kosala with its capital at Ayodhyā constitute a substantial evidence to prove that Rāma was a historical figure. In the genealogical order of the descendants of Ikṣvāku shown in the Purāṇa records, Rāma distinctly figures as the sixty-fifth king of Ayodhyā, as noted before. The historical credibility of the Purāṇic dynastic genealogies can hardly be doubted.

The genealogy provided in the *Vālmīki-Rāmāyaṇa* contains a list of thirty-five kings (of Ikṣvāku lineage) of Ayodhyā down to Rāma.[74] It is, no doubt, a truncated genealogy. But it does prove the historicity of Rāma. The Purāṇic genealogy in comparison to that in the *Rāmāyaṇa* is, of course, more perfect and authentic. However, the reliability of the *Rāmāyaṇa* genealogy cannot be doubted.

The traditional genealogies preserved in the *Rāmāyaṇa* and the Purāṇas including those of ruling Ikṣvāku family of Ayodhyā are "rarely faithful records of times past."[75]

---

72. *AGI*, p. 342; also *CASR*, vol. I, p. 321.
73. Ed. Vasudeva Shastri, Anandasrama Sanskrit Series (Poona, 1893), Vaiṣṇava Khaṇḍa, *Ayodhyā-Māhātmya*, Chs. 1 and 10.
74. *Bāla Kāṇḍa*, 70, 21-44.
75. See Romila Thapar "Genealogy as a source of Social History", in her *Ancient Indian Social History* (Hyderabad, 1984), pp. 326f.

The available literary and archaeological evidence regarding the rule of Rāma's two sons, Kuśa and Lava, over the south Kosala with its capital at Kuśāvatī and the north Kosala with its capital at Śrāvastī respectively following the territorial divisions of the kingdom of Kosala into two parts — Dakṣiṇa Kosala and Uttara Kosala — also go to prove the historicity of their father.

According to both *Vālmīki-Rāmāyaṇa*[76] and the Purāṇas,[77] Kuśa, the eldest son of Rāma, was the ruler of south Kosala with its capital at Kuśāvatī (also called Kuśasthalī), situated at the foot of the Vindhya mountain. There is a perfect harmony between the epic and Purāṇic evidence regarding this aspect of the subject. Kālidāsa also mentions Kuśa[78] and his capital Kuśāvatī.[79] The *Kuśa Jātaka* in place of Kuśa refers to Okkaku (Ikṣvāku) as a king of Kuśāvatī.[80]

The ancient Kuśāvatī, Kuśapura (Kia-she-pu-lo of Hiuen Tsang) or Kuśabhavanapura, according to Cunningham, was named after Rāma's son Kuśa. He says: "The site of Kuśapura was, no doubt, selected by its founder (Rāma, according to *Vālmīki-Rāmāyaṇa*) as a good military position on account of its being surrounded on three sides by the river Gomatī."[81] He found the place utterly desolate. He identifies it with an old town of Sultanpur on the Gomatī at a distance of 28 or 30

76. Ed. D.R. Mankad (Baroda, 1965), Uttara Kāṇḍa, 107, 17; 108, 4; also R.K. Rai, *Vālmīki-Rāmāyaṇa Kośa* (Varanasi, 1965), p. 73.
77. *Vāyu*, 88, 198-200; *Matsya*, 12, 40-44; *Brahmāṇḍa*, III, 63, 188-91; *Viṣṇu*, IV, 4, 104; *Viṣṇu*, tr. H.H. Wilson, p. 308; *Padma*, VI, 208, 46-47; VI, 271, 10-12; also *Pk*, pp. 121, 133.
78. *Raghuvaṁśa*, XV, 32, 63, 97; XVI, 14, 72, 81, 88; XVII, 4; XVIII, 4.
79. Ibid., XV, 97; XVI, 25; also S.C. Banerji, *Kālidāsa-Kośa* (Varanasi, 1968), p. 28.
80. Cf. G.P. Malalasekera, *Dictionary of Pāli Proper Names* (London, 1937, 38, rpt. Delhi, 1983), vol. I, p. 653
81. *AGI*, p. 337.

miles from the present city of Ayodhyā in the north which is just 6 mile in excess of the distance given by Hiuen Tsang. He further adds that "The ruined fort of Sultānpur now forms a large mound, 750 ft square, with brick towers at the four corners. On all sides it is surrounded by the huts of the ruined town, the whole together covering a space of about half a mile square, or about two miles in circuit. This estimate of the size of Sultanpur agrees very closely with that of Kuśapura given by Hiuen Tsang, who describes the place as being 10 *li* or 1⅓ miles, in circuit."[82] V.A. Smith has located Kuśapura in Unnāo district.[83]

After the death of his father Rāma, Kuśa shifted his capital from Kuśāvatī to Ayodhyā from where south Kosala was governed by him and his successors who were sixteen in number. That Rāma installed his son Lava as the ruler of the kingdom of Uttara Kosala with its capital at Śrāvastī, can be proved by the evidence furnished in *Vālmīki-Rāmāyaṇa*,[84] Purāṇas[85] and the *Raghuvaṁśa*[86] of Kālidāsa. In the line of Lava, there were fifteen kings after him down to Bṛhadbala in pre-Bhārata war period.

The epic and Purāṇic tradition regarding the two great divisions of the Kosala Kingdom — north and south Kosala — can be supported by the Buddhist tradition recorded in the *Avadānaśataka*.[87]

---

82. Ibid.

83. Cf. T. Watters, op. cit., II, p. 339.

84. Uttara Kāṇḍa, 107, 5, 17.

85. *Vāyu*, 88, 199-200; *Viṣṇu*, IV, 4, 104-5; see also T. Watters. op. cit., II, pp. 200-201.

86. XV, 32, 63, 97; see also Banerji, op. cit., p. 30.

87. Cf. R.L. Mitra, *Sanskrit Buddhist Literature of Nepal* (Calcutta, 1882), p. 20.

According to Purāṇic evidence, the city of Śrāvastī, situated on the right bank of the Acirāvatī (modern Rāptī), was originally founded in pre-Rāma period by a king named Śrāvasta, the son of Yuvanāsva I, one of the descendants of Ikṣvāku.[88] Cunningham, while supporting the Purāṇic evidence, ascribes the foundation of the celebrated capital city, Śrāvastī (northward of Sāketa or Ayodhyā), to Śrāvasta who ascended the throne of Ayodhyā anterior to Rāma. He also admits that during the early period it formed the part of the kingdom of Ayodhyā. He has identified it with the ruined city of Sahet-Mahet on the south bank of the Rāptī, situated between Akaona and Balrāmpur, at 5 miles from the former and 12 miles from the latter, and at nearly equal distance from Bahraich and Gonda. The exact distance of this ruined city from Ayodhyā, according to him, is 58 miles.[89] In Buddha's time, Śrāvastī was six leagues (about forty-five miles) north of Sāketa as appears from Buddhist literature. V.A. Smith has placed the ruins of Śrāvsatī on the upper course of the Rāptī in Nepalese territory near the point where the river emerges from the hills.[90] The kingdom of Kosala approximately coinciding with the Sarayū-Rāptī doab contained three principal cities — Ayodhyā, Sāketa and Śrāvastī.

Archaeologically, the existence of Śrāvastī was proved as far back as 1907-8 in the course of the excavations carried out thereunder the guidance of Sir John Marshall and Daya Ram Sahani.[91]

---

88. *Vāyu*, 88, 24-27; *Matsya*, 12, 29-30; *Viṣṇu*, IV, 2, 36-37; see also B.C. Law, "Śrāvastī in Ancient Indian Literature", *Memoirs of the Archaeological Survey of India*, no. 50 (Delhi, 1935), pp. 9f.
89. *AGI*, pp. 343-46; *CASK*, I, p. 331.
90. Cf. T. Watters, op. cit., II p. 339.
91. *Archaeological Survey of India, Annual Report*, 1907-08, p. 84.

Śrāvastī was visited by Fa-hien in CE 400.[92] Hiuen Tsang visited this capital city (called by him Shih-lo-fa-si-ti) in CE 632. He found it almost deserted. He says that the old foundations of the palace city were above 20 *li* in circuit. In Buddha's time it was the seat of government of Prasenajīt. He also saw the foundations of the city of his time.[93]

The Purāṇa records bear eloquent testimony to the fact that Gautama Buddha, the son of Śuddhodana of the Śākya family of Kosala, was descendant of the ruler of the same Ikṣvāku dynasty to which Rāma himself belonged. In the Purāṇic genealogical list of thirty kings of the said dynasty who ruled Kosala with its capital at Śrāvastī from the time the Great Bhārata war came to an end to the fifth century BCE, the pedigree and progeny of Buddha are given. He himself figures in the list as the twenty-fourth king. His grandfather, Śākya (the twenty-second king in the list), became the ruler of the north-western portion of Kosala kingdom (after its disintegration) with its capital at Kapilavastu. In the same genealogical list, Prasenajīt, the famous ruler of Kosala and a contemporary of Buddha, figures as the twenty-sixth king.[94] The historicity of Buddha and Prasenajīt and some other rulers of the said dynasty have so far not been doubted by any scholar. But why the historicity of Rāma who also belonged to the same dynasty is often doubted by some historians of ancient India, we fail to understand. We see no reason to doubt his historicity.

The historicity of Rāma can be proved also with the help of the evidence recorded in some Buddhist works. Aśvaghoṣa,

---

92. Giles, op. cit., pp. 30-31.
93. T. Watters, op. cit., I, p. 377.
94. *Vāyu, 99,* 280-93; *Matsya,* 271, 4-18; 273, 52-53; *Viṣṇu,* IV, 22, 1-13; *Viṣṇu,* tr. H.H. Wilson, pp. 369-70; *Brahmāṇḍa,* III, 74, 104-10; *PDK,* 66-67; For details see G.P. Singh, op. cit., pp. 146-48.

a native of Sāketa (Ayodhyā) and a celebrated Buddhist scholar who adorned the court of Kaniṣka (CE 78–125), in his two famous works, *Buddhacarita* (a biography of the Buddha) and *Saundarānanda* (a *kāvya*), has depicted Rāma as a historical personage. In his former work (I, 1), he has mentioned him as a king of Ayodhyā. He has unequivocally stated in his latter work (I, 24) that Rāma and Buddha belonged to the same Ikṣvāku dynasty, which goes well in accord with Purāṇic evidence. He has also narrated the stories connected with the lives and activities of Rāma's two sons, Kuśa and Lava, in his works, *Buddhacarita* (I, 43) and *Saundarānanda* (I, 26).

There is also an epigraphic evidence to testify the existence of Rāma. In the Nasik inscription of a Sātavāhana king Vāsiṣṭhiputra Pulumāvi (CE 131-59), Rāma finds mention along with other kings — Nābhāga, Nahuṣa, Yayāti and Sagara.

Some attempts have also been made by space scientists to prove the existence of Rāma on this earth.

> The clinching evidence about the reality of Śrī Rāma's existence was provided by the Indian Satellite IRS-IA in 1962 which gave to the world the first photograph taken from space showing the remnants of the Stone Bridge (*Setu*) that Rāma had built on the sea to take his army to Rāvaṇa's Laṅkā. It had appeared as a streak connecting Dhanuṣkoṭi (India) witth Talaimannar (Laṅkā). However, when on 14.9.1966 the Gemini-XI satellite went into space, the U.S. Astronauts brought back vastly clear and vivid photographs of the remnants of that *Setu*."[95]

That photograph has been published by the National Geographical Society.[96]

---

95. Cf. *The Challenge of Truth* (pub. by Shri Ramjanmabhoomi Nyasa, Delhi, 2001), p. 4.
96. See Ibid., the back cover page.

N.S. Rajaram, a scientist and historian, seems to be in favour of the view that Ayodhyā was the birthplace of Rāma.[97]

It is striking to note that the historicity of Kṛṣṇa described in the *Mahābhārata* and Purāṇas was also doubted by some historians of ancient India until the archaeological rediscovery of some of the remains of his sunken Dvārakā city from below the surface of the water of Arabian sea in Gujarat by a distinguished marine archaeologist S.R. Rao some time between November 1987 and February 1988. But now his historicity cannot be questioned by any historian. Likewise, the historicity of Rāma described in the *Rāmāyaṇa* and Purāṇas can now be proved beyond doubt with the help of available literary, archaeological and scientific evidence.

In the light of the evidence adduced above about the antiquity of Ayodhyā and historicity of Rāma, the observations made by some historians in recent past, that Ayodhyā of *Vālmīki-Rāmāyaṇa* is not identical with the present one; the birthplace of Rāma in Ayodhyā cannot be identified; Rāma was a mythical and not a historical figure; and Sāketa of pre-Gupta age was given the name of Ayodhyā for the first time in the Gupta period, can be dismissed as unfounded.

97. "Distortions of Indian History from Haṛappā to Ayodhyā", *The Astrological Magazine*, Bangalore, vol. 87., no. 1, January 1998, p. 76.

11

Veda Vyāsa, Manu and Kauṭilya

A Comparative Study of their National Philosophy in Historical Perspective*

MAHARṢI Veda Vyāsa, Manu and Kauṭilya constitute the three bright jewels in the necklace of Mother India. They were the apostles of a strong and prosperous nation which was emerging in ancient India. The former two viewed the nation in a cultural perspective, while the latter viewed it purely in a political perspective, the differentiation in their concepts virtually affected by the contemporary geo-political and cultural situation prevailing in ancient Bhāratavarṣa. That is why they have used the appellation *rāṣṭra* in their respective works both in the context of a state and a nation. However, their political philosophy can easily be distinguished from that of the national philosophy after having a deeper insight in their thoughts and ideas. Their progressive ideas relating to nation, which was in the making in ancient times, have not yet attracted the serious attention of classical Indian historians and other oriental scholars. The reasons are not far to seek. The hitherto prevalent view, that the concept of nationalism emerged in the modern period and ancient India had nothing to contribute to its growth, can be falsified after carrying out an intensive research in the contemporary ancient Indian and foreign (Graeco-Roman) accounts. The treatment of the subject under

---

* From *Journal of the Department of History*, Manipur University, Imphal, vol. 1, 1986, pp. 14-18.

review has been made on the basis of both primary and secondary sources.

Veda Vyāsa had visualized the concept of national unity in a broader framework in the Vedas and the *Mahābhārata*. From the Vedic literature[1] it transpires that he had dreamt of a nation which should hold its head high in the world, whose name and fame should spread far and wide and whose potentates and populace including men and women be effulgent and chivalrous so as to guard it against all possible external aggression and maintain its unity.

His ideal concept of national politics finds more clear reflection in his *Mahābhārata*. There is striking similarity between his philosophical national concepts and that of Manu. Both were against the despotic nation. According to him, a nation without a powerful ruler is dead. He wanted the rulers to acknowledge their allegiance and loyalty to the nation Bhārata. He had postulated that in order to promote the welfare of people a strong nation is indispensable. A song composed by him in praise of a nation fairly attests to his patriotism as well as his intense feelings for keeping the country bound together. The sense underlying the early Vedic hymns finds its echo in his song recorded in the epic.[2] The

1. *Ṛgveda*, 4.42. 1, 5.66.6, 10.173. 1-5, 10, 1.74; *Yajurveda* (*Vājasaneyī Saṁhitā*), 22.22; *Atharvaveda*, 12.1.1-60 (original Sanskrit texts with tr. by Pt. Shree Ram Sharma Acharya Bareilly, 1973-75); see also Pt. Viseshwar Nath Reu, *Ṛgveda par ek Itihāsik Dṛṣṭi* (Delhi, 1967), pp. 209f; P.V. Kane, *Dharmaśāstra kā Itihāsa* (Lucknow, 1982), vol. 2, pp. 637-42 and Acharya Priyavarta Vedavachaspati, *A Study in Vedic Polity* (Meerut, 1983), pp. 18-21, 656-59.

2. See Bhīṣma-Parva (tr. and ed. Shree Pada Damadar Satvalekar and Shree Shruti Shila Sharma with original text, Paradi, 1972) IX. 5-9; Vana Parva, 313, 84; Śānti Parva, 16-17, 56, 11, 63, 28-29. Also Vasudeva Sharan Agrawala, *Itihāsa Darśana*, (Varanasi, 1978) pp. 100-01.

definition of a *rāṣṭra* and the duties of a king and a kṣatriya as suggested by him were more or less repeated by Kālidāsa in our so-called golden age.

Umasankar Diksit,[3] a noted authority on Veda Vyāsa, has also affirmed that he wanted to tie up the Aryans, non-Aryans, Vedic and non-Vedic people and others representing different societies, different castes and different ideologies in a single thread of national unity. He was a milestone towards the long journey of cultural unification of India.

Manu epitomized the nation, Bhāratavarṣa. He was against despotism and anarchy. He had advocated the formation of a national culture to be enriched by the wisdom of kings and application of law. The *rāṣṭra* or a nation comprising several countries and the duties and responsibilities of a king to protect the unity of the country also find reflection in the *Mānavadharmaśāstra*.[4]

The national outlook of Kauṭilya was far more broader than that of his two worthy predecessors. He was not only a political philosopher and diplomat but also a great nationalist. His name goes down in the annals of ancient India as the first builder of the nation. During his time a great danger of Macedonian invasion of India under Alexander was looming large on the political horizon of north-western region. On the other hand, the rulers of the Nanda dynasty were increasingly becoming despotic and voluptuous. The unity and integrity of India was a matter of prime concern for him. At the time of

---

3. *Maharṣi Veda Vyāsa: A Historical and Cultural Biography* (Varanasi, 1968), p. 4.
4. See *Manusmṛti* (original Sanskrit text tr. and annotated by H.G. Sastri and ed. Gopala Sastri Mene, Varanasi, 1970), IX, 251; also V.S. Agrawala, *India as described by Manu* (Varanasi, 1970), pp. 46, 47.

Alexander's invasion of India he was in Taxila. His anxieties knew no bounds, because he wanted that India stretching from the Himalayas in the north to Cape Comorin in the south should remain intact and it should not fall prey to foreign rule. In order to liberate the country from the foreign yoke and to take it out of political morass at the critical juncture he was in search of a man who could transform his dream into reality and preside over the destiny of a nation. This he found in Candragupta Maurya. Like Vyāsa, Vālmīki and Manu, he realized the political needs of the country and gave a new explanation to the concept of a nation. The idea of a despotic nation was repugnant to him also. The existence of several fragmented monarchical and oligarchical *janapada*s in the north-west frontier region was posing a threat to the unity of the country, because Alexander's victory over some of them had given him an easy access and passage to India and heightened his political ambition more and more. Keeping in view the political instability of the country he inspired Candragupta to expel the foreign invaders from his motherland. He isolated somehow the emerging united forces of Parvataka and Alexander. He magnified the picture about the military strength of the Magadha king which terrified Alexander and his army who started retracing their steps. Even after withdrawal of Alexander from India and liberation of north-west frontier belt he could not remain at peace because he had a firm conviction that taking advantage of the political instability of the country the foreign invader may make it again the target of attack. Hence he undertook the responsibility of organizing the whole nation along a new line. The combined forces of Parvataka and Candragupta attacked Pāṭaliputra (the capital of the rulers of Nanda dynasty) at his instance. Nanda dynasty saw its exit about 326 BCE and the supremacy of Candragupta was proclaimed by 325 BCE. It will be out of place to mention the subsequent events.

It will suffice to say that Kauṭilya completely changed the geographical and political map of India not only through his diplomacy but his reasonings and political idealism. One of the memorable features of his national philosophy is that he did everything for the unity of the country and nothing for his self-aggrandisement. His contribution as a philosopher to the building up of a nation will always be remembered. The role which he played in the life of a nation has been highly applauded by other scholars.

His *Arthaśāstra*[5] is also a testimony to his political and national philosophy. Even Viśākhadatta,[6] who flourished seven hundred years posterior to Candragupta has bestowed his praise on his qualities as a guide of the national politics of the country and as a defender of its Integrity.

> The concept of an Indian Empire extending from Sea to Sea and embracing almost the whole of India and Afghanistan was formed and carried into effect by Candragupta and his minister (Kauṭilya or Cāṇakya) in the brief span of twenty-four years. History can show few greater political achievements.[7]

After making a comparative study of the ideas and thoughts of these three ancient Indian national philosophers, we can plausibly conclude that all of them had developed their own concept of nation. But Vyāsa and Manu like Vālmīki were visionaries, whereas Kauṭilya was a practical realist. In the

---

5. Original text, tr. Vachaspati Gairola (Varanasi, 1984). *Prakaraṇa*, 135-36, Ch. I, Sl. 3, pp. 590-91. Kauṭilya's concept of whole country from Himalayas in the north to the south as one nation is very distinct.
6. The *Mudrārākṣasa* (Text with tr S. Singh, Varanasi, 1973), Act I to V, See also 17-18, 30.
7. V.A. Smith, *Aśoka*, p. 104.

real sense of the term he was the builder of the nation in ancient times. The nation carved out by him was not produced again for another several centuries. However, all the three looked upon their motherland as one nation which further inspired the Indians. The country actually benefited much from the national ideals of Kauṭilya.

In the light of the literary evidence it can be, unhesitatingly, pointed out that the very concept of national unity had germinated in ancient India of pre-Christian era and the national consciousness was conspicuous by its presence among the ancient Indians.

12

The Concepts of Varṇa and Jāti in the Jaina and Buddhist Traditions*

THE Jaina and Buddhist concepts of *varṇa* (class) and *jāti* (caste) were almost identical with that of the Brāhmaṇist of the later Vedic period both in theory and practice. The term *varṇa* was used not only in the social order and status group, and *jāti* in that of distinctive mode of birth, pedigree or relationship and caste. Both the terms were, in fact, used in a comprehensive sense in the sociocultural milieu.

The Jains and Buddhists made persistent attempts to counteract the rapidly increasing Brāhmanical tendency to give a hereditary character to occupational distinctions by birth-right, which had earlier resulted in the formation of castes and castes within castes, but did not achieve any spectacular success. They, of course, did not maintain such distinctions on the basis of birth, but could not check the formation of classes and castes, and the basic structure of their society remained unaltered. The trends of social formation in this respect remained almost the same in both the Jaina and Buddhist traditions with some variations.

The fourfold division of early Jaina and Buddhist society represented by the khattiya (Kṣatriya), brāhmaṇa, vaissa or vessā (vaiśya) and suddā (śūdra) can by testified to by the

---

* From *Adhyayana, Journal of the Bhāratiya Itihāsa Adhyayan Saṁsthāna*, vol. VII, nos. 1 & 2, 1997, pp. 45-57.

evidences furnished in the Jaina canon[1] and Purāṇas[2] and Pāli canon.[3] The order of the four "vannas" or *varṇas*, as arranged in both the traditions gives us an impression that the traditional order of the first two *varṇas* was reversed by the Jaina and Buddhist scholars with the result that the kṣatriyas came to be placed first and the brāhmaṇas just next to them from the point of view of social grades. This was obviously an attempt in the direction of changing the existing social order. As regards the remaining two *varṇas* the order was left undisturbed. From the early Buddhist texts and the Jaina canonical and Purāṇic literature it appears that the Jains and Buddhists always stood for the social superiority of the kṣatriyas over the brāhmaṇas. According to both the traditions, the kṣatriyas enjoyed the higher status than the brāhmaṇas in the contemporary society.

The divisions of Jaina and Buddhist society into four *varṇas* were more or less based on the Brāhmanical concept of *varṇa*

---

1. *Uttarādhyayana Sūtra*, ed. J. Charpentier (Uppasala, 1922) and tr. H. Jacobi, SBE, XLV (Oxford, 1895), 25, 31-33; *Ācārāṅga Niryukti*, Bhadrabahu, tr. H. Jacobi, SBE, XXII (Oxford 1884) 19, 27.

2. *Ādi Purāṇa*, ed. and tr. Pannalal Jain (Kāśī, 1951), 1, 16, 243-46, also 183-86; II, 38, 46; *Padma Purāṇa*. ed. Pannalal Jain, 3 vols. (Kāśī, 1958-59), 5, 194; also 3, 256-58; 11, 201-2; *Harivaṁśa Purāṇa* ed. Pannalal Jain (Kāśī, 1962), 9, 39; see also "Account of the Jains", in *As. Res.* IX, (Delhi, 1979), pp. 247ff.

3. *Aṅguttara Nikāya*, ed. R. Morris and E. Hardy, 5 vols, Pāli Text Society (PTS), London, 1885-1900, III, p. 214; *Sutta-Nipāta*, part of the *Khuddaka Nikāya*, ed. Rahul Sankrityayana (Rangoon, 1937) and tr. V. Fausböll, see, X (Oxford, 1898), 1, 7; III, 9; see also T.W. Rhys Davids, *Buddhist India* (hereinafter *BI*, Delhi, 1971), pp. 53-54; B.C. Law, *History of Pāli Literature* (*HPL*), 2 vols., Delhi, 1983, vol. 1. pp. 87-88; *India as Described in Early Texts of Buddhism and Jainism* (hereinafter *IETBJ*), Delhi, 1980, pp. 139-40.

organization. The impact of Brāhmanic tradition on the social organization of the Jaina and Buddhists is clearly discernible. Like the later Vedic society the *varṇa* distinction was maintained to a considerable extent in their society too. Each of the four *varṇa*s was assigned the similar duties, which characterized the Brāhmanical social order. But one noticeable change, which took place was that the Buddhists — mainly the three upper classes, relatively — enjoyed greater amount of freedom than the Jains in the spheres of choosing and changing their respective professions and occupations, which was rendered possible because of the flexibility in the *varṇa* rules.

While drawing a comparative picture of the subject with regard to the social status of each of the four *varṇa*s, we shall here first recount that of the brāhmaṇas. The brāhmaṇas, who occupied the highest position in Hindu society before the advent of Jainism and Buddhism in the sixth century BCE, were put into lower grade than the kṣatriyas in Jaina and Buddhist society. As a result of the reversal of the order of the first two *varṇa*s the brāhmaṇas, called bambhanas in the Jaina tradition, were contemptuously looked down upon. The term *dhijjai* (*dhik-jāti*) or condemned caste has been frequently used for them in the Jaina canon, particularly the Sūtras.[4] Their former position which they held in the Indo-Aryan society was actually restored in the early medieval period, as it appears from the Jaina Purāṇas. The Purāṇic evidence fairly attests to their supremacy during the period concerned.[5]

4. J.C. Jain, *Life in Ancient India as Depicted in Jaina Canon and Commentaries* (hereinafter *LAIJC*), Delhi, 1984, 187; see also his, *Jaina Āgama Sāhitya men Bhāratiya Samāj* (Varanasi, 1965), pp. 224-25.
5. *Ādi Purāṇa*, II, 39, 130-32; II, 40, 182-84.

The privileges enjoyed by the brāhmaṇas like immunity from taxes and rents insofar as the land endowments were concerned are, of course, elucidated in the Brāhmaṇa and Jaina texts, but the Pāli texts do not bear testimony to any privileged position enjoyed by them in the eyes of the law. The Pāli canon[6] provides unmistakable evidence of the execution of criminal brāhmaṇas.

The study and teaching of the Vedas and Śāstras, the priestly duties in connection with all socio-religious ceremonies, acceptance of gifts, etc. constituted their monopoly, as it appears from both the Jain[7] and Buddhist[8] sources.

It is worthy of note that the Jaina writers, like the Buddhists, laid stress on judging the brāhmaṇahood of the people on the basis of their deeds and not birth.[9] It is clearly stated in the Jaina Purāṇas that those brāhmaṇas who did not follow the Vedic tradition, did not perform the prescribed duties or became degenerated on account of their gradual deviations from the ancient path of purity, were deprived of their brāhmaṇahood and were not considered ideally perfect brāhmaṇas.[10] In one of the Purāṇas, a brāhmaṇa named Pravarak has been referred to as an agriculturist, who used to earn his livelihood through plough cultivation.[11]

---

6. *Majjhima-Nikāya*. ed. V. Trenckner and R. Chalmers, 3 vols., PTS (London, 1888-99), II (Madhura Sutta), pp. 83f; *Jātaka* (ed. V. FausbÖll, London, 1877-97), 1, p. 439.
7. *Niśītha Bhāṣya*, Jinadāsagaṇi Mahattara, ed. Upadhyaya Kavi Amar Muni and Muni Kanhaiyalal (Agra, 1957-60), 13, 4423; *Ādi Purāṇa*, I, 16, 246.
8. B.C. Law, *IETBJ*, p. 1545.
9. *Uttarādhyayana*, 25, 29 ff.
10. *Ādi*, II, 38, 43, 47; II, 41, 46-53; II, 42, 179-92; *Padma*, 4, 115-20; 11.201; 109, 80-82.
11. *Harivaṁśa*, 43, 116.

There were various classes of brāhmaṇas including those who were the *purohitas* (the rich and powerful class because of receiving land grants and endowments and other royal grants), those who followed the pursuits of agriculturists, craftsmen, tradesmen and soldiers, those who were employed by the king, as councillors, ministers and ambassadors, those who acted like servants, those who adopted the profession of low-caste-hunters, etc. as recorded in the Buddhist tradition.[12]

In contrast to the Brāhmanical works emphasizing the social superiority of the brāhmaṇas, the Jaina and Buddhist writers repeatedly point to the higher social rank of the kṣatriyas than the brāhmaṇas. According to both the traditions, the kṣatriyas represented the ruling class. They were also the warriors *par excellence*. The Jaina Purāṇas[13] record that their primary duties were to maintain internal order and peace, protect their territories against the external enemies and save the weaker sections of the society from being exploited by the powerful class. There are some instances from the Pāli canon[14] and commentary[15] to show that a kṣatriya prince

---

12. *Dīgha Nikāya*. ed. T.W. Rhys Davids and J.E. Carpenter, 3 vols., PTS (London, 1890-1911), I. pp. 4f; II p. 236; *Saṁyutta Nikāya*, ed. M.L. Fer and Mrs. Rhys Davids, 5 vols., PTS (London, 1884-1904), I, pp. 171 f; *Aṅguttara Nik.* III, pp. 223 f; *Sutta-Nipāta*, pp. 12-16, 122; *Paramatthajotika* (a common *Sutta-Nipāta* by Buddhaghoṣa, who flourished in the fifth century CE), ed. H. Smith, 4 vols. in 2, (London, 1916-18), II, p. 313; *Jātaka*, I, 356, 439; II, 15, 165, 187, 200, 272, 376; III, 162, 219, 513; IV, 15, 207, 270, 276; V, 22, 127, 471; VI, 170 f; R. Fick, *The Social Organisation in North-East India in Buddha's Time* (Calcutta, 1920), pp. 164 f, 221f, 244f, 247; T.W. and C.A.F. Rhys Davids (tr.), *Dialogues of the Buddha* (London, 1959), 1, pp. 6f; B.C. Law, *IETBJ*, pp. 150-63.

13. *Ādi*. I, 16, 184; II 42, 4, 13; II, 44, 30; *Padma*, 3, 56, 246; 11, 202; 78, 12; *Harivaṁśa*, 9, 38.

14. *Jātaka*, II, 5, 290; IV, 84, 169.

15. *Peta-Vatthu Commentary* (by Dhammapala, ascribed to the fifth century CE), ed. E. Hardy, PTS, London, 1901, pp. 111f.

adopted the occupations of a trader, a potter and basket maker without any dishonour or penalty of losing his caste.

The vaiśyas (vaissas of the Jains and vessās of the Buddhists) formed the third grade of the Indo-Aryan society with trade and commerce, agriculture and farming as their distinctive occupations.

They basically belonged to the mercantile class.[16] In the Jaina Purāṇas they have been mentioned as Seṭha, Vaṇika, Śreṣṭhi, Sārthavāha, etc.[17] They, of course, kept themselves engaged in agricultural work and cattle rearing for some time,[18] but later abandoned them because of fear of violence in such activities.[19] In the early medieval age the śūdra took the place of vaiśya as an agriculturist.[20] The term Gāhāva as used in the Jaina sources[21] or Gahapati as referred to in the canonical Pāli texts[22] corresponds to the Seṭṭhis, who were the business magnates in the urban centres. The Jātaka[23] bears an eloquent testimony to the fact that a Seṭṭhi also worked as a tailor and as a potter retaining the respect of his community.

The analysis of the data contained in early Buddhist literature leads us to warrant the belief that the advent of

16. *Padma Purāṇa*, 55, 61; 83, 80; *Harivaṁśa Purāṇa*, 21, 78-80; *Utara Purāṇa*, ed. Pannalal Jain (Kāśī, 1954), 70, 150.

17. *Ādi*, II, 47.215.

18. *Padma*, 3, 256-7; 4, 202; *Harivaṁsam*, 9, 39; *Ādi*, 1, 16, 184.

19. K.C. Jain, *Prācīna Bhāratīya Sāmājika evam Ārthika Saṁsthāyeṅ* (Bhopal, 1971), p. 41.

20. See R.S. Sharma, *Social Changes in Early Medieval India* (First Devraj Chanana Memorial Lecture, 1969), pp. 11-12.

21. J.C. Jain, *LAIJC*, pp. 190-91.

22. *Saṁyutta Nik.*, 1, p. 71; *Cullaniddesa* (Part of the *Khuddaka Nik.*) sec. 135; *Cullavagga* (part of the *Vinaya*), Nālandā, 1956, VI, 4.1: *Aṅguttara Nik.*, IV, 282.

23. *Jātaka*, VI.372.

Buddhism, which brought about a great change in early Indian social system, provided greater amount of laxity to the three upper social grades in respect of change of their vocations. They did not strictly adhere to their respective hereditary occupations to which they were attached in the pre-Buddhist period. The occupational distinction was hardly maintained. The changes concerned also set in motion the process of social transformation.

The śūdras (known as suddās in both the traditions), who belonged to the servile class and low caste, were recognized as the fourth social order. They constituted the lowest strata of early Jaina and Buddhist society like that of the Hindu society. According to the Jaina Purāṇas, they had a degraded position in the society and were not allowed to have access to the Śāstras.[24] They were engaged in the service of upper classes.[25] They have been referred to as dāsasudda in both the Jain[26] and Buddhist sources,[27] who were no other than the slaves devoid of any legal status or legitimate rights. In the Jaina Mahāpurāṇa they have been divided into two groups: (1) kāru śūdra, who had twofold divisions: (a) touchables, e.g. barbers, potters, washermen, etc. and (b) untouchables, e.g. cāṇḍālas, and (2) akāru śūdra comprising the others.[28] There is also an evidence to show that they were not allowed to wear the sacred thread on account of their low birth.[29] The śūdras not only belonged to Aryan social group, but also included the bulk of the people of non-Aryan descent who

24. *Padma*, 3, 28; *Harivaṁśa*, 9, 39.
25. *Ādi*, 1, 16, 185.
26. *Padma*, 8, 258.
27. *Dīgha Nik.*, 1, 104.
28. *Ādi*, 1, 16, 185-88.
29. Ibid., 11.40. 170-1.

were darker in colour.[30] In the commentarial tradition of the Jainas (*Uttarādhyayana* commentary)[31] as well as in the Jātakas[32] we find an illustration of their exploitation by the high caste people. It is worthy of remark that in spite of the preachings of the doctrines of Jainism and Buddhism, their social position did not improve. As a matter of fact, nothing substantial was done to ameliorate their condition.

The prevalence of the system of intermarriage (connubium) among the members of two upper classes, the brāhmaṇas and kṣatriyas, in both the Jaina and Buddhist society resulted in the formation of mixed castes. In violation of the rules of endogamy they resorted to the practice of exogamy. They enjoyed the privileges of marrying the girls from the vaiśya and śūdra families, but on the other hand, the vaiśyas, śūdras and outcastes could not aspire to marry the girls from the families of upper classes. The members of two lower grades married within their own class (*samānajāti* and *samānagotta*). They followed the custom of endogamy. The authenticity of the facts stated above can be examined in the light of the evidences produced in the Jain[33] and Buddhist sources.[34] N. Wagle's view that endogamy, one of the chief characteristics of the caste system, was not practised in early Indian society at the time of Buddha,[35] is not tenable.

30. *BI*, p. 54.
31. *Uttarādhyayana Ṭīkā* (comm. Nemicandra, Bombay, 1937), 13, p. 185 a.
32. *Citta-Sambhūta Jāt.*, no. 498.
33. *LAIJC*, pp. 206-7; *Ādi*, 1, 16, 247-87.
34. *Dhammapada-aṭṭhakathā* (comm. Buddhaghoṣa), ed. H.C. Norman and L.S. Tailang, 5 vols., PTS (London, 1906-15); I. 390; II. 218: *Therigāthā-aṭṭhakathā* (comm. Dhammapāla), ed. E. Mullar, PTS (London, 1893), p. 260; *Jāt.*, 1257f, 477f; B.C. Law, *IETBJ*, pp. 166-67, 174-75, 180.
35. *Society in the Time of the Buddha* (Bombay, 1966), pp. 132-3.

It is significant to note that the Jainas did not strictly follow the *varṇa* rules until the dawn of the seventh century CE. Their social system in its initial phase was fundamentally based on the law of *karma* and not rules of *varṇa, jāti,* caste or birth.[36] The Vedic concept of four *varṇa*s was conspicuous by its absence in Jaina society in its early phase, but, subsequently, during the compositional period of Jaina Purāṇas (seventh to ninth century CE) it received a wide social recognition. The Jaina *ācārya*s actually felt the need of bringing the society within the bounds of the four *varṇa*s for maintaining the social order. Ravisena in his *Padma Purāṇa* (*c.* CE 677), Jinasena II in his *Harivaṁśa Purāṇa* (*c.* CE 783) and Jinasena III in his *Ādi Purāṇa,* which constitutes the first part of the *Mahā-Purāṇa* (*c.* CE 840) upheld the validity of the fourfold divisions of society of the Vedic times, further codified the rules of *varṇa* and thereby paved the way for the perpetuation of the *varṇa* system in Jaina society. Thus, the Jaina *purāṇakāra*s of the early medieval period became instrumental in persuading the people to strictly follow the *varṇa* rules, which had taken a distinct shape in the pre-Purāṇic period, as evidenced by the facts stated in Jaina canonical texts and commentaries. By the ninth century CE the *varṇa* rules of the Vedic times received the stamp of Jainism from Jinasena, which can fairly be substantiated by the evidences adduced by him in his own work.[37] He clearly states that each of the four *varṇa*s had to remain within the limits of their respective duties.[38] According to him, the laws were framed by the state to punish those who violated the established rules of *varṇa* organization.[39] Restrictions were also imposed on the people in regard to the performance of

36. *Padma,* 11, 195-203.
37. *Ādi.,* II, 38, 45.
38. Ibid., 1, 16, 187.
39. Ibid., 1, 16, 248, 251-53.

marriage within the limits of *varṇa*, so as to perpetuate the *varṇa* system and maintain the social balance.[40]

It is also striking to note that in order to lessen the scope of class struggle and professional competition, the Jaina scholars in the ninth century CE propounded a new theory of division of labour, which was based on the *varṇa* system. According to this theory, the people had to choose their occupations remaining within the limits of their respective *varṇa*s, so that they would be able to achieve competency and proficiency in their fields.[41] The other motto behind such a proposition was to check the tendency of the people to abandon their own hereditary professions and adopt those of others.

Guṇabhadra in his *Uttara Purāṇa* (the latter part of the *Mahā-Purāṇa*, composed towards the close of the ninth century CE (*c.* CE 898), enounced the social distinction on the basis of birth or caste,[42] but it had no lasting effect. The social changes concerned marked the departure from the original teachings of Jainism. The followers of Jainism, who originally raised the voice of protest against the *varṇa* system of the Vedic times could not keep themselves away from the undercurrents of the time. This is what Somadeva in his *Yaśastilaka* (*c.* CE 959)[43] has also touched upon.

The fourfold divisions of Buddhist society, on the other hand, was constantly based on the theoretical concept. The *varṇa* distinction was not strictly followed in the Buddhist

---

40. Ibid., 1, 16, 247.

41. Ibid., 1, 16, 187; II, 29.

42. *Uttara Purāṇa*, 74, 492.

43. G.C. Jain, *Yaśastilaka kā Sāṁskṛtika Adhyayana* (Amritsar, 1967), pp. 59, 68-70.

tradition. This can also be corroborated by the statement of Mrs C.A.F. Rhys Davids.[44]

The existence of many despised classes, untouchables and low-caste professional groups below the aforesaid four recognized social grades in Jaina and Buddhist society can also be proved on the basis of evidences recorded in the relevant sources.

In Jaina canon and commentaries we come across a long list of despised castes. The pānas or cāṇḍālas (who were living outside a village and used to carry corpses), the ḍombas, the morattiyas and the mātaṅgas were treated as condemned castes (*jātidugunciya*).[45] The Jaina *Maha-Purāṇa* specifically refers to the cāṇḍālas.[46] The professional group of low caste included cobblers (*padakāra*), barbers (*nhāvita*), etc.[47]

In contradistinction to the upper grades the canonical Pāli texts enumerate the five *hīna jāti*s (despised castes) as the cāṇḍālas (corpse thrower), vena (worker in bamboo), niṣāda (hunter), cammakāra (worker in leather) and pukkusa.[48]

The heterogeneous structure of the society and the multiplication and proliferation of castes accentuated the social differentiation. The social distinctions were maintained in

44. "Economic Condition According to Early Buddhist Literature", in E.J. Rapson (ed.), *The Cambridge Hist. of India* (hereinafter *CHI*), vol. 1, *Ancient India* (Delhi, 1962), p. 186.

45. *Niśīthacūrṇi* (Agra, 1957-60), 4, 1618; *Uttarādhyayana Ṭīkā*. 13, 186; *Vyavahāra Bhāṣya*, comm. Malayagiri (Bhavnagar, 1926), 2, 37; *Antagadadaso*, comm. Abhayadeva, ed. M.C. Modi, (Ahmedabad, 1932), 4, 22; H. Jacobi (tr.), *Jaina Sūtras*, SBE, XLV, 301.

46. *Ādi*, II, 42, 342.

47. *Niśītha Bhāṣya*, II, 3708; 4.1618; *Vyavahāra Bhāṣya*, 3.94.

48. *Aṅguttara Nik.*, I, pp. 107, 162; II, p. 85; III, p. 214; also *Mātaṅga Jāt.*, no. 497; *Ambā Jāt.*, no. 474; *BI*, p. 55.

some form or the other, whether it be on the basis of occupations, social position, status, birth or lineage. Both Mahāvīra and Buddha as true champions of social equality denounced the caste system, but they also could not do away with the age-old restrictions of caste. At the time of the rise of Jainism and Buddhism the social scenario was somewhat different and there was nothing like rigorous caste system in India. The caste as such had not assumed the character of an established social institution. The age of Buddha (*c.* 563–483 BCE) in particular, marked the fundamental departure from the Vedic tradition in respect of the caste system. The caste structure during their times was, no doubt, flexible, but gradually became rigid. On the basis of the comparative analysis of the data available in early Jaina and Buddhist texts we find that a clear-cut line of distinction was drawn by the Jains between upper (*jāti-ārya*) and low caste (*jāti-juṅgiya*) and by the Buddhists between the upper and lower classes (*ukkatthajāti* and *hīna jāti* respectively).

From the Jaina canonical texts (the Sūtras)[49] it appears that the Jains initially opposed the caste system. But during the early medieval age they became strong supporters of caste system, which can irrefutably be proved by the testimony of the *Mahā-Purāṇa* of the ninth century CE.[50] The system further received support from the Jaina writers of the later period.[51] This was one of the factors responsible for the decline of Jainism.

The Pāli canon (the Vāsettha Sutta of the *Sutta-Nipāta*, one of the 15 books of *Khuddaka Nikāya*) also confirms that the Buddha opposed the caste system.[52] In fact, the Buddhist

49. *Uttarādhyayana*, 12, 37; also 25, 29; *Ācārāṅga*, 2 (3), 49.

50. *Ādi*, II, 38, 47; *Uttara*, 74, 491-93.

51. Phulchandra, *Varṇa, Jāti aur Dharma* (Kāśī, 1963), pp. 159-64.

52. B.C. Law, *HPL;* vol. I, p. 88.

tradition theoretically upheld the concept of equality of khattiya, brāhmaṇa, vessā, suddā, cāṇḍāla and pukkasa, as recorded in the *Sutta-Nipāta*[53] and supported by R. Pick.[54] But in practice the social equality was not fully maintained. There are some instances to show that the brāhmaṇas were punished for committing the offence of eating together with the cāṇḍālas.[55] Because of certain restrictions imposed as to commensality, the former were not allowed to take anything used by the latter.

Rhys Davids has differentiated between *varṇa* and *jāti*. The former, according to him, stands for colours and not castes and the latter for birth, which had nothing to do with the building up of caste prejudices.[56] But in Pāli and other contemporary Indian texts these two terms occur as synonyms.[57] The *varṇa* and *jāti*, no doubt, formed the basis of social distinctions. *Jāti* was one of the factors for determining the social status of the people.[58] N. Wagle's view that *varṇa* was order and not caste or class[59] is partly correct. But he also admits that *varṇa* and *jāti* denoted status in the time of Buddha. Rhys Davids' statement that at the Buddha's time in India the caste system was not in existence,[60] seems to be absolutely

53. Ibid., I, 7; III, 9.
54. Op. cit., p. 29.
55. *Jāt*, II, 82; IV, 388; *Dialogues of the Buddha*, 1, 120.
56. *BI*, p. 62.
57. B.C. Law, *Concepts of Buddhism*, p. 11, cf. *IETBJ*, p. 143.
58. *Dīgha Nik.*, pp. 99; *Dhammapada-aṭṭhakathā*, II, p. 218.
59. Op. cit., pp. 122f, 131; See also R.S. Sharma, "Problems of Social Formation in Early India", General President's Address, *Indian History Congress*, 36th Session, Aligarh, 1975; *Material Culture and Social Formations in Ancient India* (Delhi, 1983), for class and caste.
60. *BI*, p. 62.

correct. But his view that "the caste system in any proper or exact use of the term did not exist till long afterwards,"[61] is not tenable. On the combined testimony of E.W. Hopkins,[62] D.D. Kosambi[63] and Romila Thapar[64] it can be proved that in the Buddhist society the caste system existed for some time in spite of their protest, but social distinctions were throughout maintained. Whatever may be the fact, it cannot be denied that the early Indian society of the Jains and Buddhists was free from the rigidity of caste distinctions and restrictions which were prevalent in pre-Buddhist India.

---

61. Ibid.; *Dialogues of the Buddha*, 1.95-107.
62. *CHI*, vol. 1, p. 198
63. *The Culture and Civilization of Ancient India in Historical Outline* (Delhi, 1972), p. 113; see also his "Early Stages of the Caste System in Northern India", in *JABBRAS*, new series, XXII (1946), p. 38.
64. "Society and Law in the Hindu and Buddhist Traditions", in *Ancient Indian Social History* (Hyderabad, 1984), p. 32.

13

The Role of the Brāhmaṇas in Anti-Alexander Movement in North-West India*

THE present paper aims at highlighting the role played by the brāhmaṇas of the southern Punjab and the whole Indus Valley (modern Sindh) in the anti-Alexander movement (which was more or less a resistance movement) between 326 and 325 BCE. The data available in the classical (Greek and Roman) sources alluding to the subject have not yet been properly analysed, harmonized and explained. We, therefore, find a fair scope to deal with the subject afresh on the basis of the data concerned. The paper is primarily based on the accounts of Arrian (*c.* CE 130-80), Curtius (*c.* CE 41-54), Diodorus (*c.* 80–28 BCE), Justin (second century CE), Plutarch (c. CE 45–125), the five well-known historians of Alexander, Nearchos (who accompanied Alexander as an admiral of the fleet), Strabo, a Greek geographer (c. 64 BCE – CE 21) and Julius Valerius (Alexandrian writer of the fourth century CE).

The "brachmans" (brāhmaṇas) of the southern Punjab and the Indus Valley were well aware of the political situation prevailing in north-west India at the time of Alexander's invasion. They were politically very active at that time. Their active participation in the political affairs of the state in the contemporary age can be fairly attested to by the statement

---

* From *Studies in History and Culture*, vol. III. no. 1, 1995, pp. 1-7.

of Nearchos recorded in his *Journal of Voyage*.[1] From Arrian's account of the subject they appear to have possessed separate villages and towns as early as the time of Alexander; to have already assumed the military character on occasions and to have defended themselves with great valour.[2] Their military traditions, no doubt, continued up to the time of Alexander whose invasions they resisted with patriotic heroism. They were, in fact, the leaders of the movement for freedom from the Greek rule in north-west India. Their perfect sense of independence, warlike character, patriotic feelings and loyality to the nation during the period concerned cannot be doubted. M. Elphinstone has observed that they, "defended themselves with that fury and desperation which sometimes still characterizes Hindus."[3]

The brāhmaṇas of the southern Punjab were the first to bear the brunt of attack in the wake of stubborn resistance they offered to Alexander and his army. From the classical accounts of the subject it distinctly appears that the Mallois of Mālawās (who were, by and large, the Brāhmanical tribe) after being defeated by Alexander's army on the right bank of the lower Hydraotes (Rāvī) in November 326 BCE fled to one of their towns on the other side of the river for better security. This town called a city of the brachmans or brāhmaṇas was not only thickly populated but also strongly fortified. Alexander and his troops hotly pursuing them reached the

---

1. Strabo, *Geog.* XV, 1.66. in J.W. McCrindle, *Ancient India as Described in Classical Literature* (hereinafter *AIDCL)*, (Westminster, 1901, rpt. Delhi 1984), 72.
2. Arrian, *Anabasis* (or *Expeditions of Alexander)*, VI, 7, cf. J.W. McCrindle, *Invasion of India by Alexander the Great* (hereinafter *IIA)*, (1st edn. Westminster, 1892), 141-44.
3. E.B. Cowell, (ed.), "The Greek Accounts of India", in *The History of India* (9th edn. London, 1911), rpt. in *Ancient India* (Delhi, 1983), 20.

said town or city and besieged it. According to Arrian, about 5,000 brāhmaṇas left the pen for the sword and defended their city to the last drop of their blood. They displayed exemplary courage but ultimately fell or died fighting during the siege, and a few were taken prisoners or came alive into the enemy's hands. Some abandoned the city and fled to the castle, which being stormed they set fire to their houses, and perished in the flames.[4] The fortified city proved to be a bulwark for many brāhmaṇas. Curtius[5] and Diodorus[6] have also dealt with the subject, but the latter author specifically points out that there were 20,000 defenders of the city of whom 3,000 only escaped by taking refuge in the citadel, where they capitulated or surrendered on certain stipulated conditions. Curtius adds that Alexander after having won the laurel of victory garrisoned the citadel of the brachmans.[7] It is very difficult to ascertain the exact number of casualties because of contradictions and ambiguities in classical accounts of the subject. However, Lassen also confirms that a city of the brāhmaṇas existed in this part of the country where few priests had established themselves for their better protection.[8] The brāhmaṇas commanded great respect in their city. The name of their city is not mentioned by any classical writer. Nor do we know any place of considerable antiquity in this direction with which its identification can be established. However, A.

---

4. Arrian, op. cit., 6-7; *IIA*, 140-44; see also Julius Valerius, *The Itinerary of Alexander the Great*, 115; *AIDCL*, 154-5; J.W. McCrindle, *Ancient India as Described by Megasthenes and Arrian* (2nd edn. Calcutta, 1960), 196; B.C. Sinha, *Studies in Alexander's Campaigns*, (Varanasi, 1973), 51-52.
5. Curtius, *History of Alexander the Great*, IX, 4, 10; *IIA*, 232f.
6. Diodorus, *Bibliotheca Historica* (or *Universal History)*, vol. XVII, 52.
7. Curtius, op. cit., 4.
8. Cf. *IIA*, n. 1, 143.

Cunningham has identified it with the old ruined town and fort of Aṭārī, which is situated about 20 miles to the south-west of Tulamba and on the high road to Multan (Mūlasthāna of ancient times) or about 34 miles to the north-east of the latter.[9] He affirms that "the ruined mound of Aṭārī has a very good claim to be identified with the strong city of the brāhmaṇas which made so stout a defence against Alexander."[10]

The territorial state of the brāhmaṇas, which included a large part of the Indus Valley (or modern Sindh), has been designated by the Greek historians as "Brachmanoi."[11] "This exactly corresponds to Brāhmaṇaka of Pāṇini (*Sūtra,* V.2.71)[12] and Patañjali (*Mahābhāṣya,* IV.2. 104).[13] The latter writer calls it a *janapada.* The *Kāśikā* (a commentary on the former) also describes it as the land of brāhmaṇas, who were, according to him, *āyudhajīvin*s or followers of military art.[14] They had here more effective ascendancy.

The brāhmaṇas inhabiting the upper, middle and lower valley of the Indus were held in high esteem. They played a conspicuous role in the revolt against the Macedonian invader. They kindled the spark of patriotism in the hearts of their contemporary rulers of both upper and middle Sindh and in collaboration with them played an active part in the resistance movement some time between 326 and 325 BCE. They chalked

9. A. Cunningham, *The Ancient Geography of India* (Varanasi, 1979), 192, 199.

10. Ibid., p. 193.

11. Arrian, op. cit., 16; *IIA,* 158-9; Diodorus, op. cit., 102-3; *IIA,* 293-94, 296.

12. V.S. Agarwala, *India as Known to Pāṇini* (Varanasi, 1963), 51.

13. B.N. Puri, *India in the Time of Patañjali* (Bombay, 1968), 74.

14. V.S. Agarwala, op. cit., 51.

out a common strategy to inflict a crushing defeat on the foreign invader. They exercised their influence not only on Musikanus (Mucukarṇa) whose dominions embraced "not only the upper Sindh but the whole of the valley of the Indus down the head of the Delta (Pattalene)" with capital Alor in the Sukkur district,[15] but also on Oxykanos, a ruler of upper Sindh. These two kings after having submitted to Alexander were denounced as traitors by the brāhmaṇas who urged them and their citizens to oppose foreign invaders as part of their *dharma* or duty and to defend their religion and culture. The kings following their advice revoked their submission and fought but were put to sword along with the brāhmaṇas. In course of Alexander's military operations a large number of brāhmaṇas situated within the territory of the former were killed. This phase of the Brāhmanical movement is of greater historical importance.

From the narrative of Arrian we learn that Alexander on leaving the confluence of the Punjab rivers sailed down the Indus and came to the realm of Musikanus. The king tendered his submission without any resistance and was allowed to retain his sovereignty. But the brāhmaṇas prevailed on him and instigated to raise the banner of revolt to throw off the shackles of foreign thraldom. The king after being inspired by them revolted and was at last captured and crucified along with as many of the brāhmaṇas as had instigated him to revolt.[16] It is said that Alexander's army fell heavily upon the brāhmaṇas taking them as their worst enemies. They were mercilessly put to death: "their bodies too were hung up for

---

15. Strabo, op. cit., 1, 21, 33, *AIDCL*, 26, 40.

16. Arrian, op. cit., 15, *IIA*, 157-8, and n. 395; also E.J. Chinnock, *Anabasis*, Eng. tr. (London, 1893), 319; also Curtius, op. cit., 8; *IIA*, 256f.

the kites and vultures by the roads. . . ."[17] The defeat of the brāhmaṇas at the hands of Alexander's army in this campaign, however, did not break the backbone of their resistance.

The King Sambus (Śambhu) of middle Sindh, which had its metropolis at Sindomana or Sehwan on the Indus adjoining the kingdom of Musikanus, was also encouraged by the brāhmaṇas of his territory to resist the attempts of Alexander to conquer Sindh. The interference of the brāhmaṇas in the state politics is exhibited by their influence which they exerted on Musikaṇus to break the peace he had concluded with the conqueror, and on Sambus for not submitting before Alexander. In course of Alexander's operations against Sambus a large number of brāhmaṇas were killed near Sindomana.[18] It is said that "a city of the brāhmaṇas"[19] had to be stormed whilst the operations against Sambus were going on.[20] From the statement of Arrian it is quite evident that after the capitulation of the city Sindomana, Alexander "attacked and won a city which had revolted from him," and seized some of the brāhmaṇas whom he suspected of having instigated the temporary defection of Sambus. He wreaked his vengeance by putting to death "as many of the brāhmaṇas as fell into his hands, having charged them with being the authors of the rebellion."[21] This goes well in accord with the statement of

17. E.R. Sevan, "Alexander the Great", in E.J. Rapson (ed.), *The Cambridge History of India* (hereinafter *CHI*), vol. I (Delhi, 1962), 339.

18. *Arrian,* op. cit., 16; *IIA,* 158-9; Justin, *Historiae Phitippioae,* XII, 10, *IIA,* 325-6; Plutarch, *Life of Alexander* (*as told by Alexander in his Letters*), Ch. 64; *IIA,* 313f.

19. Diodorus, op. cit., 103; *IIA,* 296 f.

20. Arrian, op. cit., 5, 16; *IIA,* 158-59.

21. Ibid.; W. Vincent, *The Voyage of Nearchus,* Eng. tr. (Oxford, 1809), 136; J.T. Wheeler, "Greek and Roman India", in his *The History of India from the Earliest Ages* (1st edn. London, 1881), rpt. in *Ancient India* (Delhi, 1983), 106; B.C. Sinha, op. cit., 53.

Diodorus, who mentions that Alexander "was satisfied with punishing those who advised the resistance, and pardoned all the others."[22]

As indicated by the classical authors, the city taken by Alexander was near Sindomana. In that case it may be identified with Amree, eighteen miles below Sindomana or Sehwan, which although now an insignificant village is said to have been once a large city.[23] It may have been probably one of the towns of the brāhmaṇas in that locality. However, this identification seems to be of little dubious nature.

The city captured by Alexander, in fact, belonged to the brāhmaṇas of the lower Indus Valley. The latter resisted every attempt of the former to conquer their city, but they could not meet with desired success, and, eventually, lost their city, which according to Diodorus was the "last town of Brachmanoi being situated at the extremity of the Brachman country on the river Indus." He has mentioned it as *Harmatelia*[24] which tolerably agrees with *Brahamathala* or *Brāhmaṇa-sthala.*[25] The capital city of the brāhmaṇas called by Alexander's historians *Brāhmaṇa* corresponds both in name and position with *Brāhmaṇavāha* (abode of brāhmaṇas) of Rajaśekhara (ninth century CE),[26] Bahmanābād of the Muslim geographers, *Brāhmaṇabād* of the Muhammedan historians, Bamiwan of the Sindhians or Bahmanava, which Cunningham has identified with the ruins situated near an old bed of the Indus at the distance of about 47 miles to the north-east of Hyderabad. It was situated, according to him, on the eastern bank of the

22. *History Univers,* XVII. 569 f.; A. Cunningham, op. cit., 226-7.

23. H.H. Wilson, *Ariana Antiqua* (Delhi, 1971), 205.

24. Diodorus, op. cit., 102; *IIA*, 294-5; *History Univers, XVII,* 56; cf. A. Cunningham, op. cit., 226.

25. A. Cunningham, op. cit., 226.

26. G.S. Rai (ed.), *Kāvyamīmāṁsā* (Varanasi, 1964), 236.

Indus and was one mile in length and the same in breadth and just four miles in circuit.[27] It is said to be one of the oldest sites in Sindh.[28] This city was actually situated in close proximity to ancient city of Pattala in lower Sindh. It had, no doubt, an honorific denomination.

The brāhmaṇas appear to have instigated the potentates and populace of the whole Indus Valley to rise in open revolt against Alexander[29] and consequently, many of them were slaughtered or massacred by his troops. They offered the stoutest resistance to the foreign invader. They, indisputably, played an effective role in the anti-Alexander revolt. As a matter of fact, they were both instigators and fighters.

Arrian while assessing their role in the anti-Alexander movement categorically remarks that "Brāhmaṇa philosophers were the leaders of the patriotic movement in lower Sindh. They were hanged on a gibbet by Alexander, whose task was becoming more and more arduous on account of the patriotic movement inspired by them."[30] This can be further corroborated and also supplemented by the account of Plutarch. He expressly states that the entire responsibility for political awakening of the people of the Indus Valley to shake off the yoke of servitude of Macedonians from their necks was heaped on the brāhmaṇas by Alexander himself. In the context of the brāhmaṇas dwelling in the city he observes:

> These philosophers were specially marked down for revenge by Alexander as they gave him no less trouble than the mercenaries, they reviled the princes who declared for

---

27. G.S. Rai, op. cit., 228-31; *IIA*, Index note T, 355-56.

28. A. Cunningham, *Coins of the Indo-Scythians, Sakas and Kushans*, (London, 1888, rpt. Varanasi, 1971), 37.

29. *IIA*. Intro., 4.

30 Arrian, op. cit., 16; 77.4. 159-60.

> him and encouraged the free states to revolt against his authority. On this account he hanged many of them.[31]

He further adds that the heads of a number of brāhmaṇas were chopped off. One of the revolutionary brāhmaṇas, when taken prisoner and condemned to death was asked just before his execution as to why he had incited the kings and the people of different kingdoms to revolt. He boldly replied, "Because I wished them to live with honour or to die with honour.[32]

The Brāhmanic opposition to a foreign invader in Punjab and Sindh in the fourth century BCE has its own importance in the political history of ancient India. E.R. Bevan deriving his authority from Plutarch, whom I have quoted above, observes that

> . . . the Europeans in this region had more implacable enemies than the native princes. The power behind the throne was the Brahman community, and here for the first time we come upon an opposition inspired by the conception of a national religion, the only germ to be found in ancient times of the idea of Indian nationality. It was the philosophers (i.e. the brāhmaṇas) who denounced the princes, if they submitted to the foreigner, and goaded the free tribes into revolt.[33]

The brāhmaṇas of Punjab and the Indus Valley, no doubt, laid down their lives in defence of freedom, religion and culture, and by their heroic deeds and supreme sacrifices presented one of the earliest examples of patriotism. The suppression of Brāhmanical opposition could not have been an easy task for Alexander, since the brāhmaṇas were respected throughout the land. The taking up of arms by the meek brāhmaṇas must

31. Plutarch, op. cit., Ch. 59; *IIA*, 306.
32. Plutarch, op. cit., 64; *IIA*, 313-14.
33. *CHI*, vol. I, 339.

not be regarded as a strange phenomenon or a mere figment of Greek imagination. The country was menaced with a calamity during the Macedonian avalanche, and so the brāhmaṇas valiantly rose to defend their honour and their earth and home.

14

The Concept of National Integration in Ancient India*

It is really very difficult to justify the application of the term, national integration, as such, in ancient Indian context for manifold reasons. The data available in the sources at our disposal are too meagre to project a distinct picture of the subject under discussion. There is a good deal of controversy among the scholars with regard to the emergence of the concept of national integration in ancient India. The use of the appellation *rāṣṭra* by ancient Indian classical writers in varied contexts further creates confusion and misunder-standing in our minds. However, on the basis of the slender thread of evidence furnished in the literary texts, classical treatises on India, the general historical records, and other contemporary sources, we can prove it with certain amount of confidence that the said concept was not totally absent in ancient India and there were few attempts at the political unification of the country.

The modern concept of national integration finds expression in the form of national consciousness, which was conspicuously present among the Vedic Aryans. This can be amply substantiated through the impartial examination of the ideas contained in the hymns of the Vedas. From the Vedic

---

* From *Dimensions of National Integration: The Experiences and Lessons of Indian History*, ed. N.R. Ray (Calcutta, 1993), pp. 121-30.

literature, the *Yajurveda* (*Vājsaneyī Saṁhitā*),[1] the *Ṛgveda*[2] and the *Atharvaveda*[3] it transpires that the concept of one nation had emerged among the indigenous Aryans of Bhāratavarṣa. This finds confirmation in their invocations to gods for the unity, stability and prosperity of a nation, and solicitation to their kings to guard the nation against aggressors, hostile forces and so on. They were also familiar with the concept of "Swarājya," which they wanted to maintain at every cost. The Brāhmanical lirerature (*Tattirīya Saṁhitā*, 7.5.18 and *Tattirīya Brāhmaṇa*, 3.8.13) also provide some references to the national awakening in contemporary India. But the authenticity of this particular evidence furnished in the brāhmaṇas is not beyond question.

The *rāṣṭra* or nation comprising several countries and the duties and responsibilities of a king to defend the integrity and maintain the unity of the country also find little reflection in the secular literature, i.e. the Smṛtis and the Dharmasūtras. The *Manusmṛti*,[4] the *Yājñavalkya Smṛti* (1.321), *Viṣṇu Dharmasūtra*

---

1. Original Sanskrit Text with parallel Hindi tr. Pt. Shree Ram Sharma Acharya (Bareilly, 1974), 22. 22; see also Vasudeva Sharana Agrawala, *Itihasa-Darsana* (Varanasi, 1978), pp. 101-2.
2. Shree Ram Sharma Acharya (tr., Bareilly, 1974-75), vol. 2, 4. 42.1; 5. 66. 6; vol. IV, 10. 173. 1 & 5; 10.174. 2; see also Pt. Viseshwar Nath Reu, *Ṛgveda Par Ek Itihāsik Dṛṣṭi*. (Delhi, 1967), p. 209.
3. Shree Ram Sharma Acharya (tr., Bareilly 1973), vol. 2, 12.1. 8.12.1.14; see also P.V. Kane, *Dharmaśāstra kā Itihāsa*, (Lucknow, 1982), vol. 2, pp. 639-42 and Acharya Priyavarta Vedavachaspati, *A Study in Vedic Polity* (Meerut, 1983), pp. 18-21, 656-59 (for study of *Bhūmi Sūkta* of Maṇḍala 12).
4. Original Sanskrit Text tr. and annotated by H.G. Sastri and ed. Gopala Sastri Nene (Varanasi, 1970), IX. 251; see also V.S. Agrawala, *India as Described by Manu* (Varanasi, 1970), pp. 45-47.

(3.4.5) and *Kāmandakīya Dharmasūtra* (4.50-56)[5] have slightly touched on the ideas connected with the ways and means of making the Indian Nation strong and prosperous in ancient times.

The loyalty of ancient Indian rulers to the nation, called Bhārata and their patriotism as reflected in the Bhīṣma Parva[6] of the *Mahābhārata* fairly attest to their intense feelings for keeping the country bound together. The sense underlying the early Vedic hymns in this regard finds its echo in this epic. The ancient Indian historical traditions also confirm the truth that the ideas connected with the oneness of the country were visualized both by the potentates and populace of early India. Actually, they had a well-established tradition of looking upon their mother land as one nation, which further inspired the Indians. Thus in the twilight of the literary evidence it can be established that the very concept of national unity had germinated in the ancient India of pre-Christian era.

Here we must take note of the fact that prior to Persian and Macedonian invasions of India no such event took place, which might have posed a threat to the unity and integrity of the country. Hence there never arose any necessity for the ancient Indians to think in terms of integrity of nation to that extent, which we do today. In spite of diversity of race, language, religion and culture the country remained united till the beginning of the sixth century BCE without losing any of its parts and retaining the age-old geographical identity and political boundary. The country in the real sense of the term was never found on the verge of disintegration. Therefore, the said concept of national integration made slow progress. In view of the facts stated above we don't find a

5. Quoted in P.V. Kane, op. cit., p. 639.

6. Tr. and ed. Shree Pada Damodar Satvalekar and Shree Shruti Shila Sharma (Paradi, Gujarat, 1972), IX. 5-9.

fair scope to apply this concept in such a way that it could suitably match the modern one.

In pre-Mauryan Age (650–321 BCE) India had been politically parcelled out into a multitude of petty states (some powerful monarchies and some tribal republics), whose rulers and heads were continuously fighting among themselves for supremacy or building up imperial states and owed no allegiance to any overlord. The political rivalries and wars shattered the unity of the country. Before Alexander's invasion (326 BCE) of India, there was no paramount authority to maintain the unity and integrity of the country, whose geographical boundary extended up to Ariana. Both from the literary and classical (Graeco-Roman) sources it appears that the political conditions of both north-western India and Gangetic valley were not conducive to the growth of the feeling of unity. However with the said invasion, the history of India took a significant turn.

It is worthy of remark that Alexander's invasion proved to be a boon in disguise for India. In fact, it constituted a milestone towards the political unification of India. R.K. Mookerji has correctly stated that

> Alexander's invasion promoted the political unification of the country. Smaller states which handicapped unity were now merged in the larger ones, such as those of Paurava, Abhisara or Taxila. These conditions were favourable for the rise of an Indian Empire to be shortly founded by Candragupta. It swept away internal barriers which prevented the unification of the lands concerned. The confederacies of other tribes which had maintained their proud isolation from other political systems were utterly broken. Smaller principalities were swallowed up in a realm such as those given by Alexander to the Paurava. This no

> doubt made it simpler for the Mauryan king, who few years later took these countries in his great Indian Empire.[7]

H.C. Raychaudhuri has also more or less supported this view. To quote him,

> It helped the cause of Indian unity by destroying the power of the petty states of north-west India, just as the Danish invasion contributed to the union of England under Wessex by destroying the independence of Northumbria and Mercia.[8]

Alexander's creation of vast empire comprising Punjab and Sindh marked the beginning of disintegration in ancient India. The Macedonian occupation of north-western India for about eight years hurled a challenge to the integrity of the country. But fortunately, the political anarchy and convulsions, which ensued following the death of Alexander in 323 BCE, led to the disruption or dismemberment of the empire carved out by Alexander on the north-western frontier. The whole area was the theatre of war and the provinces were about to turn into independent kingdoms. Taking advantage of the emerging situation Candragupta, the first historical founder of the great Mauryan Empire decided to liberate India from foreign yoke, unify it with the help of northern states and thereby restore its fallen glory. He also resolved to restore India to a geographical position held in pre-Alexandrian period extending as far as Ariana. The political unification of the country achieved during his time (321–297 BCE) constitutes a solitary example of an attempt at integration of India in ancient times. Admittedly, it was during this age that the whole of India was politically united for the first time under one head

7. *Hindu Civilization*, pp. 294-5.
8. *Political History of Ancient India* (Calcutta, 1953), p. 263.

and rule. Further the uniform system of administration helped keep the country well-knit together.

Candragupta placed himself at the head of the Indian kings, who were smarting under the frustration caused by the foreign rule, and, after Alexander's departure defeated his generals, exterminated the Macedonian garrisons, drove away the Greeks from Punjab and Sindh and finally consolidated his imperial authority over these provinces by 321 BCE. The classical writers have also acknowledged the importance of the role played by Candragupta in the political unification of India in the fourth century BCE Justin says that he "shook the yoke of servitude from neck of India"[9] and gave liberty to it after Alexander's retreat. But his explanation that he "soon converted the name of liberty into servitude after his success subjugating those, whom he had rescued from foreign dominion, to his own authority"[10] is not a reasonable one. Because, he had to do so for tying them into a single thread of unity. Plutarch's[11] view, that he subdued not only Punjab but the whole of India, is perfectly justified.

The task of integrating the country was accomplished at a much later stage. Seleucus Nikator, one of the ablest generals of Alexander, after having obtained possession of the Asiatic dominions of his master and establishing his supremacy over a large area extending from Western Asia to Afghanistan, proceeded to take possession of Punjab. His ambition was to

---

9. Watson's tr. pp. 142-43, cf. H.C. Raychaudhuri, op. cit., pp. 272-73; See also J. Talboys Wheeler, *India from the Earliest Age* (Delhi, 1973), vol. III, p. 176.

10. Justin, *Hist. Philipp Lib.* XV, Chap. IV. cf. F. Max Müller, *A History of Ancient Sanskrit Literature* (Varanasi, 1968), p. 246.

11. *Life of Alexander*, LXII; See also his *Vita-Alexandri* C-62, Vide, Max Müller, op. cit., p. 248.

carry out the designs of his great commander Alexander but it was never fulfilled. The presence of an overwhelming force, which Candragupta had deployed on North-West Frontier to defend its integrity, was enough to strike terror in the heart of Seleucus. Nevertheless, a conflict took place between Candragupta and Seleucus some time between 305–302 BCE in which the latter was ignominiously defeated. Consequently, the Indians occupied some of the countries situated along the Indus, which formerly belonged to the Persians. They also obtained a larger portion of Ariana, which Alexander deprived of them and established there settlements and provinces. Thus during this period India again obtained possession of eastern Iran, which she had lost a few centuries earlier to it. The country which Seleucus ceded to Candragupta comprised the four Satrapies beyond the Indus called, Aria (Herat), Archosia (Kandhar), Gedrosia (Baluchistan) and Paropanisadae (Kabul).[12] The inclusion of Kabul Valley within the Indian empire can be testified to by Aśoka's inscriptions in Greek and Aramaic found on a rock at Shari-Kuna near Kandhar in Afghanistan, four Edicts found in the vicinity of Shalata and Qargha in province of Laghman in Afghanistan bearing inscriptions in Aramaic and Prākr̥t in Kharoṣṭhi script, etc.

Thus the empire which he established embraced the whole of northern India lying between the Himalaya and Vindhya mountains together with that portion of Afghanistan which

12. Paul Masson-Qursel et. al., *Ancient India and Indian Civilization*, (London, 1934), pp. 36-37; E.J. Rapson, *Ancient India* (Varanasi 1981), p. 53; W.W. Hunter, M. Elphinstone, E.B. Cowel et. al., *Ancient India* (Varanasi, 1983), Ch. IX, p. 90 ; R.G. Bhandarkar, *A Peep into the Early History of India* (Varanasi 1978); Romila Thapar, *A History of India* (Middlesex, 1966), vol. 1, pp. 70 ff; V.A. Smith, *The Oxford History of India* (Delhi. 1981), p. 52; see also W.W. Tarn, *The Greeks in Bactria and India*, Cambridge, 1938. p. 100 and *Ind. Ant.*, vol. VI, pp. 114 f.

lies south of the Hindukuśa, north-western India comprising the trans-Indus regions, western India including Kathiawar and Saraushtra, central India including the regions of north of the Narmadā River, Gangetic Valley and far-south including Tamil land and Mysore. Thus he not only organized his empire in Punjab keeping numerous petty chieftains under his controlling authority, but provided unity to the country stretching from the bank of the Sindhu to the mouth of the Gaṅgā.

As a matter of fact, India emerged for the first time in ancient India as a unified country under the banner of Candragupta Maurya. The analysis of the facts warrants us to admit that the political unification of India was achieved during his time through the establishment of an empire over the whole of Hindustan and the Punjab. The empire was not merely composed of a number of provinces brought together under a single sceptre, it was a real unit based on the principle of uniformity of rule and the welfare of the people, at large. Candragupta had a clear vision of the unity of the country. Historically it will not be fair and accurate to hold the view that his attempt was only at the establishment of an empire and not the integrity of the nation. Actually, the consolidation of the empire was the media for achieving his end that was to provide stability to the country. F.W. Thomas has aptly remarked that "the establishment of a single paramount power in Hindustan embracing a part even of the country south of the Vindhya mountains and standing in relation to the still independent areas, supplies a unity which previously was lacking and which in fact was rarely realised in later ages."[13]

The success or failure achieved in the field of integration of a country should be judged not by applying the modern

13. Quoted in E.J. Rapson (ed.), *The Cambridge History of India*, vol. I, *Ancient India* (Delhi, 1962), p. 420.

concept of national integration but by taking in view the changing concept of unity and integrity in the contemporary situation. Candragupta's concept of national unity after being put on the touchstone of several changes effected in the political system of the country in course of passage of time may, of course, be taken today as a concept of imperial authority, but viewed in the perspective of exigencies of the situation which he faced, the danger of disintegration which he averted, and the success which he achieved in maintaining the unity of the country extending from Afghanistan in the north to far-south, it appears that this concept was basically a concept of unity and integrity.

With the emergence of several poltical regions, kingdoms, empires, etc. in the Indian subcontinent during the period *c.* 200 BCE – CE 300, the process of disintegration started.

The foregoing treatment of the subject gives us the impression that the concept of national integration never remained static. It had to undergo transformation according to needs, changes and situation. From the Vedic Age down to the sixth century BCE the unity and integrity of the Indian nation remained intact because of geographical barriers and other impediments. Moreover, the ancient Indians did not face any problem of disintegration during this period. They had a clear concept of the unity of India. But as a result of the Persian and Macedonian invasions India lost greater parts in the north-western region. But Candragupta during the reign of twenty-four years made every possible effort to unify the country by recovering all the lost possessions. Actually it was he who saved India from disintegration. He restored India to its pristine glory by giving her back, which she lost between sixth and fourth century BCE. His was the first and the last attempt at the political unification of the country in ancient times.

15

North-West India
As Described by the Greek and Assyrian Travellers of the First Century*

APOLLONIUS, the Greek traveller, accompanied by a learned Assyrian called Damis travelled in different parts of north-western India in CE 43-44 for acquiring first-hand knowledge of its history and culture. The former recorded all that he saw and heard in course of his visit to India in his diary or notebook and the latter in his journal. Their works along with other relevant sources were later utilized by one of the early Greek historians called Philostratus the Athenian (*c.* CE 170–245) for writing the biography of Apollonius.

Philostratus, the biographer of Apollonius, was born at Lemnos and studied at Athens but flourished in the reign of the Roman Emperor Severus (*c.* CE 193–230). The Emperor's wife, Julia Domna, who was famous for her patronage of men of learning and genius, handed over the memoirs of Damis (bequeathed to her by his descendants) to Philostratus with a request to write the life of Apollonius on the basis of its contents. But Philostratus not only utilized the memoirs of Damis but also epistles or letters of Apollonius which were then in circulation and an account of his career at Aegae by a Roman historian, Marius Maximus (*c.* CE 165–230), to accomplish his task. The Empress, however, did not live to see the book

* From *Journal of the Asiatic Society of Mumbai* (New Series), vols. 77-78, 2002-03, pp. 171-81.

which saw the light of the day in or some time after CE 217. It was written in Greek language. It is divided into eight books, of which the second and third deal with his Indian travels. According to this biographical work, Apollonius was born about the beginning of the Christian era at Tyana, a city in Cappadocia (Asia Minor). He was a philosopher of the School of Pythagoras. It was his cherished desire to extend the frontiers of his knowledge by travelling into foreign countries. He is said to have travelled extensively. In the earlier part of his life he visited Egypt, Italy and Persia. Later, he turned his attention to the East. He wanted to explore the "wonders of India and make himself acquainted with the learning and wisdom of the brāhmaṇas, the fame of which had been spread in the West by the companions of Alexander." He along with his Assyrian companion from Nineveh reached Babylon where they halted for some time. Therefrom they along with a guide supplied by the Parthian King Bardanes (*c.* CE 42–45) set out to visit India. First, they entered Afghanistan by crossing the Kaukasos (Hindukuśa), north of Kabul. Further, westward of the Indus they crossed the Kophen (the Kabul River) and visited Kabul and the adjoining regions.

After crossing the Indus into the Punjab eastward they made some stay at Taxila (Takṣaśilā). Having passed the Hydraotes (Rāvī) they pursued their way through several "countries" to the Hyphasis (Beas) beyond which they could not travel. On the return journey they visited Sindh as their itinerary shows. From the narratives of their journey it appears that they were provided with different new guides and interpreters proficient in the Greek language at different places in India in the course of their journey. They are believed to have interacted with all classes of population during the journey. Philostratus has furnished an original and authoritative account of their travels in his biography of Apollonius which is based on the information supplied by the travellers themselves in their respective works. It is very useful for throwing light on early history and culture of north-west India to about the middle of the first century CE.

The travellers' accounts of society, economy, polity, religion, philosophy, education, urban life and art and architecture of the people of the north-west and that of the foreign invasions are preserved in the work of Philostratus.[1]

The social structure of the people of the north-west was somewhat different from that of other parts of India. The frequent allusions to the brāhmaṇas called "Sophoi" (Sophists or "Teachers of Wisdom") and philosophers in the accounts of the travellers[2] give us an impression that they occupied the highest position in the society. They were held in high esteem. Their supremacy was well established in the society. They followed a variety of pursuits. Some were engaged in public affairs and attended the king as counsellors. Some of them were advisors of the king in the management of his estates. The others practised religious austerities, performed religious rites and rituals, conducted sacrifices and imparted religious instructions to their respective disciples.[3] They had their own chiefs who were invested with some authority in religious and administrative matters which speaks of their hierarchical

---

1. *The Life of Apollonius of Tyana*, ed. and tr. F.C. Conybeare, 2 vols. (London, 1912, rpt. 1927), Books II and III; tr. E. Berwick (London, 1811), pp. 11ff.
2. Berwick, op. cit., pp. 16f; Conybears, op. cit., II, XXVI-XXVII; III, VI-VIII; Osmond De Beauvoir Priaulx, *The Indian Travels of Apollonius of Tyana* (Paris, 1873) cf. *The Classical Accounts of India* (hereinafter *CAI*), compiled by R.C. Majumdar (Calcutta, 1960, rpt. 1981), pp. 392, 396-9, 405-7, 411.
3. Conybeare, op. cit., II, XXVI-XXVII; *CAI*, pp. 391, 396-7; Berwick, op. cit., pp. 17-29.

system.[4] Except the brāhmaṇas there is no reference to any other upper or lower social class despite the fact that the kṣatriyas had been living in both the Punjab and Sindh and the Sodrai or śūdras in only Sindh since time immemorial along with them. The traditional social system might have possibly undergone some changes by the time of the visit of the travellers. The fourfold division of the society was no longer acceptable to them. The classes and castes as such were conspicuous by their absence in their society at that time. There is no mention of either their social stratification or social distinctions or caste restrictions in the travellers' accounts of the subject.

The north-west Indian society was basically patriarchal. The joint family system was followed. The mode of life was simple. Music, singing and dancing were the three principal means of amusement of the people. The kinship system formed a very important part of their social life. The marriage customs were based on the rules of both endogamy and exogamy. The mutual choice of bride and bridegroom played its own role in the arrangement and performance of the marriages. The dowry system was in vogue. We are told by the travellers that they were informed by the contemporary king (Parthian) at Taxila that his father had "married the daughter of the Hydaspian king (whose kingdom was on the river Jhelum) and received with her seven villages as pin-money."[5] Monogamy was the rule and polygamy the exception. The women did not occupy high position in the society because of the Brāhmanical orthodoxy. They did not enjoy freedom in any walk of life. The incidental notices of slavery have also been made in the

4. Conybeare, op. cit; *CAI*, pp. 399, 405-7; J.W. McCrindle, *Ancient India as Described in Classical Literature* (hereinafter *AICL)* (Westminster, 1901, rpt. Delhi, 1984), p. 193.

5. Conybears, op.cit, II, XXVI; *CAI*, p. 391.

travellers' accounts. In Taxila, the travellers saw some male servants with the king. They were employed for domestic purposes.[6] We do not come across any evidence of women slaves in their accounts. However, slavery was not a recognised social institution.

The travellers have provided a detailed account of the economic activities or material life of the people of north-west India. The most extensive and the most fertile plain in the whole country, irrigated in all directions and well-cultivated, which the travellers speak of[7] is no other than the fertile territory of the Punjab (eastward of the Indus) watered by the Indus and its five tributaries, namely, the Rāvī, the Jhelum, the Cenāb, the Sutlej and the Beas. About the land and its produce they observe:

> The land here is the best in India, black and very productive; its wheat stalks are like reeds, and its beans three times as large as the Egyptian; its sesame (sesamum) and millet are also extraordinarily fine. Here, too, grow those nuts, which for their rarity and size are, as a sort of curiosity, often found in Greek temples. The grapes of the country however are small, like the Lydian and Maeonian. . . .[8]

Like other parts of India, in the north-west too agriculture was the backbone of economy. It was the means of subsistence for the bulk of population. The agricultural production was very high because of fertility of land and facility of irrigation. All kinds of crops were produced. The people had achieved self-sufficiency in food. On the heights they witnessed various kinds of aromatic plants and the cinnamon tree, and in the

6. Conybears, op. cit., II XXVI: *CAI*, pp. 388, 391, 404.
7. *CAI*, pp. 395-6; *AICL*, p. 193.
8. Conybears, op. cit., II, XXVII-XXVIII; *CAI*, p. 395; *AICL*, p. 193.

hollows the pepper plant and frankincense-bearing trees. The pepper was highly valued by the Indians.[9]

The Indus region was also fertile. In the words of the travellers: "The Indus like the Nile overflows the country, and deposits a fertilising mud, which as in Egypt, prepares the land for the husbandman (cultivator)."[10] In the Punjab and Sindh, there were some artisans and craftsmen and other occupational groups engaged in various avocations. Some indigenous industry also flourished along with arts and crafts. There was a class of metalworkers in Taxila. They made several objects of gold, silver, copper, bronze and iron. There were some weavers, leather workers and manufacturers of cotton dress. The paper made from the papyrus plant was used for writing. Taxila continued to be the centre of trade and commerce. The people were engaged in different occupations and professions for the sole purpose of earning their livelihood The travellers inform us that "The people at Taxila wore cotton, the product of the country, and sandals made of the fibre or bark of the papyrus and leather cap when it rained. The better classes were clad in byssus (having a silky appearance). . . . This byssus (a stuff looking like silky bunch of filament or thread used for making dress, etc.) grows on a tree. . . . It is exported into Egypt for sacred uses."[11] The travellers' statements that ". . . The Indian money was of orichalcum and bronze — purely Indian and not stamped like the Roman and Median Coins"[12] throw some light on the coinage system.

The prevailing form of government in some parts of north-western India at the time of the visit of the travellers was monarchy. The city-state of Nysa at the foot of the mountain

9. Conybears, op. cit., *CAI*, pp. 394-5; *AICL*, p. 193.
10. Conybears, op. cit., II, XVI-XVIII; *CAI*, p. 387.
11. Conybears, op. cit., II, XVIII-XX; *CAI*, p. 387.
12. Conybears, op. cit., II, XVI-XVII; ibid., p. 385.

called Meros between the Kabul river and the Indus or in the valleys of Kohimor in the Swāt was "ruled by a king."[13] The city or hill state was one of the famous seats of aristocratic oligarchy at the time of Alexander's invasion and also in the post-Alexandrian period but later it adopted the monarchical form of government, the reason and the exact period of which are still unknown to us.

There was hereditary monarchy in Taxila which can be attested to by what its king himself told the travellers. The relatives of the king sometimes, according to Indian custom, acted as regents. The king was assisted by nobles in running the government. The city was governed by good laws. The king used to transact the business of his kingdom (between the Indus and the Jhelum) and to decide the cases according to the law of the land.[14] The punishments were awarded according to the nature of crimes. Strabo (*c.* 64 BCE – CE 21) also makes a mention of the most excellent laws of Taxila.[15] The king "told his visitors among other things that he paid blackmail to a tribe of barbarians on his borders for the protection of his dominions against the attacks of other barbarous tribes."[16]

Porus the elder also ruled his kingdom between the Jhelum and the Cenāb according to the monarchical constitution. All the sovereigns in the Kabul and the Punjab at that time were independent.

The Indus Region was then Under the Rule of the Satrap[17]

From the accounts of the travellers it distinctly appears that

13. *CAI*, p. 385; *AICL*, p. 192.
14. *CAI*, pp. 391, 393.
15. H.L. Jones, *The Geography of Strabo*, VII (London, 1949), Bk. XV, p. 47.
16. *AICL*, p. 193; see also *CAI*, p. 389.
17. *CAI*, p. 387.

the people in the north-west were by and large followers of the Brāhmanical culture. However, there were Buddhists few and far between. The travellers like the classical historians failed to notice the distinction between Brāhmanism and Buddhism.[18] There were two sects of philosophers, viz. "Brāhmaṇas" and "Sarmanes" (Skt. Śramaṇa and Pāli Sāmana) which correspond to the "Brāhmaṇa" sages or ascetics and the Buddhist monks respectively.

The sun worship was prevalent among the brāhmaṇas.[19] The sacrifices formed an integral part of the religious practices of the people. Where the travellers crossed the Indus the natives told them that "when the season for the rise of the river is at hand, the king sacrifices on its banks black bulls and horses and after the sacrifice throws into the river a gold measure like a corn measure . . . for an abundant harvest, or for such a moderate rise of the river as would benefit the land."[20]

The age-old tradition of receiving education under the care and guidance of the brāhmaṇas continued to exist in the north-west till about the middle of the first century CE. We are informed by the travellers that the "brāhmaṇas" before admitting anybody for educating him used to "inquire into his character and parentage."[21] They, like the sophists of Greece, used to teach various subjects to their pupils. The philosophy was given the highest importance as a subject of study. Besides "astrology and divination," the subjects relating to "those sacrifices and invocations in which the god's delight" were also taught by them.[22]

---

18. See *CAI*, p. 411.
19. Ibid.
20. Ibid., p. 387.
21. Ibid., p. 391.
22. Ibid., pp. 391, 406.

Both the travellers during the three days of their sojourn at Taxila[23] learnt from its king (who possessed the knowledge of Greek language) through the interpreter about its past history and got an opportunity to see with their own eyes the city as well as all the relics and monuments of historical and archaeological importance. Their accounts of the growth of urban culture and art and architecture at Taxila are of exceptional importance. While giving a vivid description of Taxila as a city they observe that it was laid out on a symmetrical plan.

> It was about the size of Nineveh, walled like a Greek city, and was the residence of a sovereign who ruled over what of old was the kingdom of Porus.[24]

> They found the city divided by narrow streets, well-arranged, and reminding them of Athens. From the streets, the houses seemed of only one storey, but they all had an underground floor.[25]

> There were underground rooms equal in length to the chambers above. . . . The archaeological finds have revealed that access to inner chambers was from the upper chamber. The reverse process misled the traveller who could not speculate whether it was a single storied or a double storied building till he (Apollonius) actually went inside to find out the real thing.[26]

---

23. At that time no foreign traveller was allowed to enter Taxila without a permit and to stay there for more than three days as per the law of the land.
24. Conybeare, op. cit., II, XX, XXV; *CAI*, pp. 387-8; *AICL*, p. 192; see also *The New Encyclopaedia Britannica* (hereinafter *EB*), new series, XVII, rpt. (Chicago 1980), p. 1083.
25. *CAI*, p. 388.
26. B.N. Puri, *India as Described by Early Greek Writers* (Varanasi, 1971), pp. 148-9.

The travellers also saw the king's palace, which according to them, was not distinguished by any superior splendour or extraordinary magnificence from the residences of the citizens of the better class. There were no sentinels or bodyguards, but a few attendants or servants. The same simplicity was observable in the courts, halls, waiting and inner rooms; and it pleased Apollonius more than all the pomp of Babylon.[27] According to Philostratus, "It was no less magnificent an architecture and the main chamber and the porticos and the whole of the vestibule was very chaste in style."[28] The city visited by the travellers in CE 43 can undoubtedly be identified with Sirkap and its king called "Phraotes."[29]

The credibility of the information supplied by the travellers regarding Taxila city can be tested by archaeological discoveries

27. *CAI*, pp. 388-9; *AICL*, pp. 192-3.

28. Cf. Conybears, op. cit., II, XX.

29. The three important sites of urban settlements in Taxila have been archaeologically located at Bhir Mound, Sirkap and Sirsukh which are often described as three different cities. But, in fact, they formed parts of Taxila city. They successively saw their rise and fall at three different periods of history. The first remained under the occupation of the Persians in the fifth century BCE and the Indo-Greeks from the third century BCE to the beginning of the second century BCE; the second was under the rule of the Indo-Greeks from the early second century BCE to the early first century BCE, the Scythians or Śakas in the first century BCE and the Parthians in the first half of the first century CE; and the third was occupied by the Kuṣāṇas in the latter half of the first century CE and remained in their possession till the early third century CE. The city remained in existence until it was destroyed by the Hūṇas in the fifth century CE.

    The extensive ruins of Ṭaxila city are lying scattered within a radius of about 3 miles from north to south and 2 miles from east to west in the vicinity of Shāhḍherī at a distance of about one mile north-east of Kāla-kā-Sarāi and about 22 miles north-west of Rawalpindi in Punjab.

at the site. Sir John Marshall, who carried out excavations at the site for over a period of twenty years at regular intervals between 1912 and 1937, has conclusively proved that the city visited by Apollonius of Tyana in "CE 40 or thereabouts" was no other than the city of Sirkap which belonged at that time to the Parthian ruler. His findings at this particular site include the structural remains like the royal palace looking like a glorified private house but with more spacious courts and rooms, blocks of the private dwelling houses of the citizens, large houses belonging to the rich, single-storey structures of one or two rooms, narrow side-streets, small shrines and many other monuments and antiquities.[30] The palace complex was modelled on the same lines as its Assyrian counterpart, had several entrances and outer fortifications. This can also be more or less corroborated by the evidence produced by R.E. Mortimer Wheeler on the basis of his findings in the course of excavations carried out at the same site in 1944-45. The remains of the stone city wall were also discovered.[31]

There is striking similarity between the observations of the travellers and the findings of the archaeologists.

The travellers inform us that just outside the walls of the city was a beautiful temple of shell marble with a shrine and many columns. Round the shrine were hung pictures on copper tablets representing the feats of Alexander and Porus. The various figures including those of elephants, horses, soldiers, and armours were portrayed or carved in a mosaic of orichalcum, silver, gold, and oxidized copper, but the weapons, including the spears, javelins and swords, in iron. The metals were so ingeniously worked into one another that the pictures they formed were comparable to the productions of the most famous Greek artists from the points of view of drawing,

30. *Taxila*, I (Cambridge, 1951), pp. 140-41.

31. *Ancient India*, no. 4 (1948).

vivacity of expression and truthfulness of perspective. We are further told that it was not till after the death of Alexander (*c.* 323 BCE) that Porus placed them (all the above-mentioned pieces of art) in the temple including one which represented "Alexander as a conqueror and himself as conquered and wounded and receiving from Alexander the kingdom of India."[32] This artistic representation constitutes the monumental evidence of Alexander's victory over Porus, the elder of Punjab, and the kingdom which the latter got back from the former (after tendering his submission) in recognition of the valour he displayed and the talent and ability he proved during the war.

Philostratus explicitly mentions that "They saw a temple in front of the wall about 100 ft in length and built of steel-like stone."[33] The temple lay north to the wall and it was not inside the city proper. Some scholars have mistaken this temple for Jandial temple exhumed in the excavations at Sirkap.[34]

The former was obviously built in the time of Porus and the latter in the Scythio-Parthian period.

The travellers saw the famous "Temple of the Sun" inside the city and in it statues of Alexander and Porus, one of gold and the other of bronze, of exquisite beauty which excited their admiration. Its walls were of red marble, but glittering with gold and the image of the god was of pearls.[35] The art of painting was also known to the people of Taxila as mentioned by them.

The travellers' description of Taxila city as a whole shows the perfection the people had attained in all the branches of

32. Conybeare, op. cit., II, XX, XXV; *CAI*, p. 388; *AICL*, p. 192.
33. Cf. Conybears, op. cit., II, XXII.
34. Puri, op. cit., pp. 147-9; *EB*, new series, XVII, p. 1083.
35. *CAI*, p. 388.

art-architecture, sculpture, iconography and painting in the past. The deities and objects contrived reveal the ingenuity of the artists. "They were so garbed in Greek costumes that it was difficult for a visitor to discriminate whether it was a Greek object or an Indian one. The fact that they were found in Indian temples was the only clue for discrimination. This shows the highest achievements of the Indians in the field of art."[36] The antiquity of all the specimens of art preserved inside the temple at Taxila as witnessed by them goes back to the last quarter of the fourth century BCE. All of them remained in excellent state of preservation till the time of their visit. Taxila was no doubt a large, well-planned, magnificent and fortified city. Strabo and Arrian have described it as "the greatest of all the Indian cities between the river Indus and the Hydaspes (Jhelum)" but without giving any details thereof. In fact, among all the classical writers Philostratus is the only one who has provided a picturesque description of the city with all accuracy and precision based on the eyewitness accounts of Apollonius and his fellow-traveller and friend, Damis, which can also be confirmed by archaeological evidence.

There are also some fragmentary but very rare types of evidence of Alexander's invasion (*c.* 326–325 BCE) in the accounts of the travellers. After leaving Taxila they set out on the journey to the Hyphasis or the river Beas and after two days reached the plain where Porus had been defeated by Alexander. There they saw the place adorned with a triumphal arch and a statue of the great conqueror in a four-horse chariot, as he appeared in the battle of Issus. A little farther on they came upon two other arches on one of which was Alexander and on the other Porus — the one saluting, and the other in an attitude of submission. As they approached the Hyphasis, they saw the altars Alexander had built there and also a bronze

36. Puri, op. cit., p. 150.

pillar with the inscription: "Here Alexander halted."[37] Philostratus conjectures that this pillar was raised by the Indians in joy at the return homeward of Alexander. It is a proven fact that he did not cross the Hyphasis to occupy the neighbouring lands. We learn that the land of the brāhmaṇas between the Hyphasis and the Ganges was never invaded by Alexander not out of fear but because of being dissuaded by the appearance of the sacrificial victims.

About the Scythian invasion we have been supplied with only this much information by the travellers that "the Indian people drove back the Scythians who invaded their territories."[38] However, we cannot pass over it in silence. It is also said that many cities were built in the Gangetic region by the people of India the details of which are wanting. There is also a passing reference to the city of Patala in the lower Indus Valley which in the fourth century BCE was famous for its oligarchical constitution. We are told by Apollonius that "He saw too the mouth of the Indus, and Patala, a city built on an island formed by the Indus where Alexander collected his fleet."[39]

There is no difference of opinion among modern scholars about the historical authenticity of the diary of Apollonius of Tyana, but about the value of the journal or memoirs of his learned friend Damis which also formed the basis of the work of Philostratus their views are contradictory.[40] According to A. Cunningham, Philostratus professes to have utilized Damis' narrative of the journey.

---

37. *AICL*, p. 193; *CAI*, pp. 393-4.

38. *CAI*, p. 400.

39. Ibid., p. 408; See also *AICL*, p. 195.

40. Conybears, op. cit., vii.

> His account is manifestly exaggerated in many particulars regarding the acts and sayings of the Philosopher, but the descriptions of places seem to be generally moderate and truthful. If they were not found in the narrative of Damis, they must have been taken from the journals of some of Alexander's followers; and in either case they are valuable, as they supply many little points of information that are wanting in the regular histories.[41]

Professor Brigg, on the other hand, doubts the very existence of the memoirs of Damis. But others admit its existence and hold that it also abounds in some valuable information about India. It is true that there are some errors and discrepancies in his account of the subject but it cannot be dismissed as entirely fanciful. Actually, the facts and fictions have been jumbled up in it. From the style of his presentation one could get an impression that he is a story-teller. While forming an estimate of Damis as a traveller, McCrindle observes:

> His description of the country between the Hyphasis and the Ganges is utterly at variance with all known facts regarding it. As Alexander had not carried his arms into that part of India it had remained quite unknown, and hence for his account of it Damis had to depend entirely on the resources of his own imagination. For the geography, however, of the country between the Indus and the Hyphasis he was not without guidance, for it had been traversed by Alexander and described by his historians. . . . Damis, in fact, tells nothing that is true about India except what had been told by writers before him. . . .[42]

Priaulx (reviewer of the work of Philostratus) is of the view that Damis never accompanied Apollonius in his Indian journey. He rather fabricated the journal Philostratus speaks

41. *The Ancient Geography of India* (Varanasi, 1979), p. 91.
42. *AICL*, p. 195.

of, for it contains some facts, from books written on India which he collected at Alexandria, the great mart for Indian commodities and resort for Indian merchants.[43] His view is no longer tenable. The doubts of both McCrindle and Priaulx about the visit of Apollonius to India can be set at rest on the basis of what he himself says about this visit: ". . . the very journey I have undertaken — and I am the first of my countrymen who have undertaken it," as recorded in his biography by Philostratus. It is a well-proven fact that he along with his Assyrian friend visited north-western India during the reign of the Parthian king, Bardanes (CE 42–45), and kept record of it. He was a great traveller and many of his descriptions embody the results of his personal observation during the travels. There is no valid reason to doubt the visit of either Apollonius or Damis. Their narratives of journey also do not leave room for any doubt about their visit to India. Some of their statements regarding India are consistent with each other.

As a matter of fact, the works of both the travellers have relative value. Their accounts of life and culture of the people of north-west India and that of Alexander's invasion go to supplement the classical accounts of the subject. The early history of north-west India can be reconstructed to a certain extent on the combined testimony of both the travellers.

---

43. Cf. *CAI*, p. 412.

16

Trade and Commerce in Ancient India in the Light of Jaina and Buddhist Traditions Bearing on its Economic and Cultural Contacts with the Asian Countries*

THE Jaina canon, commentaries, non-canonical texts and early Purāṇic records, the canonical and the post-canonical Pāli literature and some Sanskrit Buddhist texts on the whole bear eloquent testimony to the fact that internal and external trade flourished side by side in ancient India between the sixth century BCE and the ninth century CE. The Jaina and Buddhist traditions also fairly attest to the expansion of Indian culture in the neighbouring as well as far-off Asian countries through external trade relations with them. The maritime trade in particular was one of the effective means for establishing economic and cultural contacts with those countries. From remote antiquity India maintained commercial and cultural contacts with the outside world both by land and sea routes. One of the characteristic features of economic life of the ancient Indians was their intense urge to have commercial intercourse with different Asian countries and thereby to diffuse and disseminate Indian culture there as far as possible. The Indian traders and merchants exchanged not only goods but also elements of culture with their Asian counterparts. The respective roles of the Hindu colonists, Buddhist and brāhmaṇa

---

* From *Studies in History and Culture*, IV, 1, 1996, pp. 1-13.

missionaries, kings and rulers in the diffusion of Indian culture in the Asiatic countries at different periods of history have been sufficiently highlighted by a number of Indian and foreign scholars[1] in their respective works. But the substantial contributions of the traders and merchants to the spread of Indian culture in those countries during the period under review as reflected in Jaina and Buddhist literature did not attract their serious attention. Some scholars[2] have of course dilated upon the trade pattern and the role of Indian merchants in the process of Indianization in South-East Asia in general. However, there is fair scope to throw some new light on the subject concerned.

The traders and merchants occupationally attached to their respective guilds (commercial or trading organizations) played significant roles in providing boost to trade and commerce during the period concerned. The freedom of initiative and

1. R.C. Majumdar, *Ancient Indian Colonies in the Far East,* 1, Champa (Lahore, 1927), 22ff; *Suvarnadvipa;* 1 (Dacca, 1936), 37ff; *Kambujadesa* (Madras, 1944), 36ff; *Ancient Indian Colonisation in South-East Asia* (Baroda, 1955), 15ff; *Hindu Colonies in the Far East* (Calcutta, 1944), 5ff; B.R. Chatterji, *Indian Cultural Influence in Cambodia* (Calcutta, 1928), 7ff; R. Le May, *The Culture of South-East Asia* (London, 1964), 74-141; E.G. Reischauer and J.K. Fairbank, *A History of East Asian Civilization,* 1, *East Asia: The Great Tradition* (Harvard 1960), 5ff; H.G.Q. Wales, *The Making of Greater India: A Study in South-East Asian Cultural Change* (London, 1951), 7-65; B. Harrison, *South-East Asia: A Short History* (London, 1954), 8-18; D.G.E. Hall, *A History of South-East Asia* (Oxford, 1960), 20ff; *Burma* (London, 1950), 7-9; *The Making of South-East Asia* by G. Coede's, tr. from French by M. Wright (London, 1966) 27f; P.C. Bagchi, *India and China* (Calcutta, 1927), 15-75; N.P. Chakravarti, *India and Central Asia,* (Calcutta, 1927), 17ff; A. Stein, *Innermost Asia,* 4 vols. (Oxford, 1928).
2. John F. Cady, *South-east Asia: Its Historical Development* (New York, 1964), 21-48; Harrison, op. cit., 12ff.

mobility in trade went a long way in encouraging them to carry on their professions for the economic prosperity of the country as well as the people. The lucrative commerce and economic gains further encouraged them to sail across the Indian Ocean and to go to distant lands. They entered into commercial intercourse with different Asian and European countries. They carried with them the Indian thought and culture. They, professedly, became torchbearers of Indian culture and civilization. They contributed their share to the cultural expansion not only in South, East and South-East Asia but also in other Asiatic countries through the medium of trade.

It is worthy of note that in the times of Mahāvīra and Buddha everybody (irrespective of class, caste, creed or faith) was free to choose his own profession because of removal of social distinction. However, it is a fact to be reckoned with that trade was the distinctive occupation of the *Vessās* (vaiśyas) who formed the third grade of the Indo-Aryan society.

The merchants have been referred to in the Jaina canon[3] as *vaṇi* or *vivaṇi*s and in the Purāṇas[4] as *vaṇika, vaṇija* and vaiśya. In one of the canonical Pāli texts[5] *vanijjā* (trade and commerce) is included in the list of six important professions of the Buddhists.

The agricultural produces and industrial goods were sold in markets, inland and foreign. The inland trade was carried

---

3. *Niśītha Bhāṣya, Cūrṇi,* Jinadāsagaṇi Mahattara, ed. Upadhyaya Kavi Amar Muni and Muni Kanhaiyalal (Agra, 1957–1960) 16, 5750.

4. *Ādi Purāṇa,* 1st part of the *Mahāpurāṇa,* Jinasena III, ed. & tr. Pannalal Jain, Jain Granthmala, nos. 8 & 9, Bharatiya Jnanapitha (Kāśī, 1951), 1,1,68; *Padma Purāṇa,* Ravisena, ed. Pannalal Jain, Bharatiya Jnanapitha (Kāśī, 1958-59), 3, 257, 6, 154; 55, 60.

5. *Majjhimanikāya,* ed. V. Trenckner and R. Chalmers, Pali Text Society (London, 1888-99), I (Mahadukkhakkhandha Suttam), 83-90.

on both by land-routes and water-routes. The traders and merchants following land-routes transported their goods from one place to another by carts or wagons. Those who travelled across the country in a caravan using carts laden with goods were known as the caravan traders. And their leader called *sātthavāha* (or *sārthavāha*) used to lead the caravan. They were guided by a land-pilot (*thalaniyāmaka*) in course of their journey. Those who followed the river-routes transported their merchandize by country boats. Besides, there were other seagoing vessels, which were used for carrying on trade by sea.[6] According to the Pāli canon (second or first century BCE) those merchants and traders who followed land-routes were called *thalapathakammikā*. They were distinguished from *jalapathakammikā* or those who followed water-routes.[7] According to the Jaina canon (fourth or fifth century CE) *thalapattana* stands for those market towns where the goods were supplied by the bullock-carts and *jalapattana*, on the other hand, was the sea-port from where the Indian goods were shipped outside and foreign goods were unloaded.[8]

Campā, Mithilā, Mathurā, Vārāṇasī (Benares), Śrāvastī, Ujjain, Saurāṣṭra, Paiṭhan on the Godāvarī, Dakṣiṇa-Madurā, Gauḍa, Sāgaia or Sākala, Gandhāra and Takṣaśilā were famous

6. *Niśītha Cūrṇi*, 20, 6533; *Padma Purāṇa*, 33,46; 55,61; 83,80; *Harivaṁśa Purāṇa*, ed. Pannalal Jain, Bharatiya Jnanapitha (Kāśī, 1962), 8, 134; *Ācārāṅga Sūtra* tr. H. Jacobi, Sacred Books of the East, XXII, I (Oxford), 1884, rpt. Delhi, 1973), 2, 3, 1, 13-20, 139-41; *Bṛhat-kalpa (Sūtra) Bhāṣya*, ed. Muni Puṇyavijayaji (Varanasi, 1933), 1, 3066, 3078; *Jātaka*, tr. various hands under the editorship of E.B. Cowell, Cambridge, 1895-1913, 1, 107, 194f.

7. *Jātaka*, tr. various hands under the editorship of E.B. Cowell, Cambridge, 1895-1913, I. 121.

8. *Bṛhatkalpasūtra Bhāṣya*, 1, 1090; see also J.C. Jain, *Life of Ancient India as Depicted in the Jaina Canon and Commentaries* (Delhi, 1984), 148.

trade emporiums. The existence of three important port-towns, Bharukaccha (modern Broach in Gujarat), Suppāraka (modern Sopārā in the Thane district to the north of Bombay) and Sovīra (near Saurashtra) on the western sea-coast and that of Tāmalitti or Tāmralipti (modern Tāmaluk in Midnāpur district of West Bengal) not only facilitated the carrying on of internal trade but also promoted the growth of external trade and commerce with the outside world including the Asian countries. The internal trade relations existed between them to a large extent. The principal articles of trade were various kinds of cloth, textile fabrics, gold, ivory, brocades, jewellery, groceries, perfumes, etc. Each commercial centre contained a market complex where commodities were brought for sale.

Campā (situated on the Ganges near modern Bhagalpur) was one of the important centres of trade, both internal and external. As stated in one of the Jaina canonical texts, the sea-faring merchants of this city loaded their ships with various saleable goods such as betel-nuts, sugar, rice, oil, ghee, molasses, vessels, medicines, drugs, cloths, jewels, etc. and sailing across the Indian Ocean proceeded to the port-city of Gambhira. Here they unloaded their goods and loaded the ship with various commodities and returned safely. The traders of Campā used to travel up to the city of Mithilā in connection with their trade.[9] The trade was carried on between Ujjain and Campā through Kauśāmbī and Varanasi.[10]

The merchants from Mathurā used to travel to Dakṣiṇa-Mathurā (Madurā) for trade.[11] Soppāraya (Suppāraka or

9. *Nāyadharmmakahāo*, ed. N.V. Vaidya (Poona, 1940), 8, 97-8; Jaina, op. cit., 149; 369; "Trade and Commerce in Ancient India" ("from less known Jaina Sources"), *Quarterly Review of Historical Studies*, Calcutta, XVII, 1 (1977-78), 48-9.

10. *Āvaśyaka Niryukti*, Bhadrabahu (Ratlam, 1928), 1276f; *Āvaśyaka Cūrṇi*, Jinadāsagaṇi Mahattara (Ratlam, 1928), 448.

11. *Āvaśyaka Cūrṇi*, 472; 709(a); *Bṛhatkalpa Bhāṣya*, 1, 1239.

Sopārā) was another emporium of trade where five hundred trade men used to carry their business.[12] The trade was also carried on between Surattha (Saurāṣṭra) and Pāṇḍumahurā (Dakṣiṇa-Madurā) by sea.[13] The merchants of Uttarāpatha or the frontier countries used to carry gold and ivory to Dakṣiṇāpatha for sale. Cloth was an exchangeable commodity. Mathurā and Vidiśā were manufacturing centres of cloth. Gauḍa was famous for silken garments. From the Jaina canon it appears that Tāmalipti, Sindhu-Sauvīra (Sauvīra adjacent to the river Sindhu) and Nepal were noted for the trade of fine cloths.[14] From the Jaina Purāṇas we gather the information that the merchants used to purchase cotton from Uśirāvatī (near Puṣkalāvatī, the western capital of Gandhāra) and sell in Tāmralipti.[15] The valuable gems were also the items of trade for the traders of the frontier countries.[16] The Indian merchants imported horses from Bāhlīka (modern Balkh in Afghanistan) and Greece.[17]

The early Buddhist literature contains valuable references to the land-routes followed by different traders. One of the important inland land-routes north to south-west was from Sāvatthi (Śrāvastī) to Patitthāna (Pratiṣṭhāna or Paiṭhan on the Godāvarī).[18]

---

12. *Bṛhatkalpa Bhāṣya,* 1, 2056; also *Āvaśyaka Cūrṇi,* 69.
13. *Āvaśyaka Cūrṇi,* 11, 197.
14. *Bṛhatkalpa Bhāṣya,* 1,3912.
15. *Ādi,* ll, 46, 145; *Harivaṁśa,* 21, 75-16.
16. *Ādi,* II, 32, 70.
17. *Uttarapurāṇa,* 2nd part of the *Mahāpurāṇa,* Guṇabhadra, ed. Pannalal Jain, 1st edn. Bharatiya Jnanapitha (Kāśī, 1954), 68, 562.
18. *Sutta Nipāta,* ed. Rahul Sāṅkṛtyāyana (Rangoon, 1937), vv. 976-7 and 1011-13; tr. V. Fausböll, *Sacred Books of the East,* X, 1 (Oxford, 1881, rpt. Delhi, 1973), 184, 188; also T.W. Rhys Davids, *Buddhist India* (Delhi, 1971), 103.

Another route north to south-east was from Sāvatthi to Rajāgaha (Rajagṛha) and back and also towards borders, i.e. Gandhāra.[19] The north-western route extended from Sāvatthi and Kauśāmbī to Takkhasilā or Takkasilā (Takṣaśilā the eastern capital of Gandhāra). Further westward the journey was performed over land to Sind (from where horses were imported) and to Sauvīra and its ports.[20] Northward the trade route connected India with Central and Western Asia by way of Takṣaśilā and Sāgala in north Punjab. The Pāli canon (the Jātaka records)[21] and commentary[22] are littered with references to various land-routes. It is evident from the Pāli text that from east to west the trade was carried on largely by rivers by means of country boats. Upwards the rivers were used along the Ganges as far west as Sahajāti, along the Yamunā as far as Kauśāmbī, and downwards along the Ganges as far as Campā and Tāmralipti. Downwards the boats were also taken either across or along the coast to Burma.[23]

The Jātakas testify to the existence of trade relations between Varanasi and Ujjain, Videha and Kashmir, Gandhāra and Varanasi and Sāvatthi.[24] The other Pāli texts refer to such

19. *Jātaka,* tr. various hands under the editorship of E.B. Cowell, Cambridge, 1895-1913. I, 92; 348, 377f; *Vinayapiṭaka,* ed. H. Oldenberg (London, 1879- 83), 1, 81.

20. *Jātaka,* tr. various hands under the editorship of E.B. Cowell, Cambridge, 1895, 1, 124, 178, 181; II, 31, 287; *Vimānavatthu-aṭṭhakathā* (Comm.), 336; Hopkins, *Journal of the American Oriental Society,* New York, XIII, 257, 372.

21. *Jātaka,* tr. various hands under the editorship of E.B. Cowell, Cambridge, 1895. I, 196, 201; II, 12, 70, 423, 434; III, 152.

22. *Dhammapada-aṭṭhakathā,* ed. H.C. Norman, Pali Text Society (London, 1906-14). II, 31.

23. *Vinaya Texts,* 3, 382; 3, 401, cf. B 1, 103-4.

24. *Jālaka,* tr. various hands under the editorship of E.B. Cowell, Cambridge, 1895, II, 248, 294; III, 363, 365, 369.

relations between Rājagaha and Sāvatthi and between Rājagaha and Vesālī.[25] Further, we are told of traders going from Videha to Gandhāra,[26] from Magadha to Sovīra,[27] from Bharukaccha round the coast to Burma,[28] from Varanasi down the river to its mouth and thence on to Burma[29] and from Campā to the same direction.[30]

In the age of Buddha the traders of Campā (the capital of Aṅga) and Magadha used to visit each other's kingdom for trade purposes.[31] The traders of Aṅga used to travel in a caravan with their merchandize to Sindhu-Sauvīradeśa for trade.[32]

Benares was the centre of both internal and external trade. The traders of this city were well known for dealing in cotton, silk and woollen clothes, and also muslin. The weavers of this place produced soft and beautiful garments. It had direct trade relations with Gandhāra and Takṣaśilā. Rich merchants of Benares used to cross over high seas with ships laden with merchandize. They also traded with Burma. The commercial importance of the city for the Buddhist traders has been

25. *Sutta Nipāta*, vv. 1012-13; *Vinaya Texts*, tr. Rhys Davids and Oldenberg, Sacred Book of the East, XVII, II (Oxford, 1882, rpt., Delhi, 1974), *The Mahāvagga*, VIII, 1, 2, 171.

26. *Jātaka*. tr. various hands under the editorship of E.B. Cowell, Cambridge, 1895. III, 365.

27. *Vimānavatthu-aṭṭhakathā*, 336, 370.

28. *Jātaka*, tr. various hands under the editorship of E.B. Cowell, Cambridge, 1895. III, 188.

29. Ibid., IV, 15-17.

30. Ibid., VI, 32-35.

31. Ibid., II, 148, *Vinaya Mahāvagga Cullavagga*, 337.

32. *Vimānavatthu-aṭṭhakathā, 332.*

highlighted not only in the Pāli texts[33] and commentaries[34] but also in some of the Sanskrit Buddhist texts.[35] Gandhāra was also a trading centre. Its red blankets also formed part of the trade.[36] Śrāvastī was another famous trade emporium. The traders from this place travelled up to Campā in Bihar and Tāmralipti in Bengal in the wake of their trade and commerce.[37] The city of Mithilā is said to have contained several market complexes.[38]

The market economy was well controlled and well regulated. Within the country all kinds of produce were brought to markets for sale. There were *āpanas* or shops where various commodities including textile fabrics, groceries, oil, grain, perfumes, articles of gold and jewellery, etc. were brought for sale. Coins made of gold, silver and copper of different denominations served as standard currency and were

---

33. *Jātaka,* tr. various hands under the editorship of E.B. Cowell, Cambridge, 1895, I, 124, 178, 181; II, 31, 122, 287; III, 286; IV, 405, 445; VI, 47, 77, 144, 154; *Vinaya Mahāvagga,* VIII, 2; VIII, 3. 1, cf. Sacred Book of the East, Oxford, XVII, II, 195-96; *Mahāparinibbāna Suttam,* text with Hindi tr. and ed. S.G. Prajnananda (Lucknow, 1981), 5, 16.
34. *Sumaṅgalavilāsinī,* commentary on the *Dīgha Nikāya,* ed. Rhys Davids, PTS (London, 1886-1932), II, 563; also B.C. Law, *History of Pāli Literature* (Delhi, 1983), II, 435; *Dhammapada-aṭṭhakathā,* I, 123.
35. *Divyāvadāna,* ed. E.B. Cowell and R.A. Neil (Cambridge, 1886), 22, 510; *Mahāvastu* ed. E. Senart (Paris, 1882-97), II, 166-7; III, 268.
36. *Sumaṅgalavilāsinī,* II, 389; Law, op. cit., 434; *Jātaka;* VI 47; *Vinaya Mahāvagga,* 8, 1, 36.
37. Rahul Sankrityayana, *Purātattva Nibandhdāvalī* (Allahabad, 1939), 33-35.
38. *Jātaka,* tr. various hands under the editoriship of E.B. Cowell, (Cambridge, 1895–1913); VI, 330.

used as chief medium of exchange or for transacting the business.[39]

The foreign trade was carried on largely by sea-routes and partly by land-routes. The ambitious Hindu, Jaina and Buddhist merchants not only followed land-routes but also undertook the sea-voyages in the ships laden with merchandize and sailed across the seas for carrying on trade with the Asian countries. They generally reached Malay Peninsula, the Indonesian islands and Indo-China (Campā or south Annam = modern Vietnam, and Kambuja, called by the Chinese Funan, or modern Cambodia) beyond it by crossing the Bay of Bengal.[40] Their trade relation with another South-East Asian country, Burma (Brahmadeśa), was established both by land and sea-routes. They followed the sea-route through the Bay of Bengal and land-routes through Manipur to Upper Burma and through Arākān to Lower Burma.

They entered into trade relations with Ceylon (neighbouring South Asian country) only by sea-route. The so-called Greater or Further India and Indian or Indo-Malay Archipelago were colonized by the Hindu and Buddhist merchants in a very remote age.[41] Regarding the routes

39. For details see, *Life of Ancient India as Depicted in the Jaina Canon and Commentaries,* 158-61; *Jātaka,* tr. by various hands under the editorship of E.B. Cowell, Cambridge, 1895-1913, I, 111, 290, 404, 411, 425; II, 267; IV, 82, 228, 488; VI, 29, 336; *Vinaya,* IV, 248-50; *Cullavagga,* V, X, 10, 4; *Majjhima Nikāya,* ed. V. Trenckner and R. Chalmers, Pali Text Society (London, 1888-89), I, 359, 447; *BI,* 100; *Cambridge History of India,* 1, ed. E.J. Rapson (Delhi, 1962), 194; *Journal of the Royal Asiatic Society of Great Britain and Ireland,* London (1901), 874-82.

40. See May, op. cit., 224f (for map of Asia showing sea-routes between India and the South-East Asia, and between India and the Indo-Chinese Peninsula).

41. *Journal of the Greater India Society,* Calcutta, DC, 62ff.

followed by the traders for establishing trade relations with Central, East and South-West Asia it may further be added that the overland route passed through Khyber to the Upper Kabul Valley and then across the Hindukuśa to Balkh in Afghanistan. There were several routes from Balkh towards Central Asia and China on the east and to the Mediterranean and Black Sea on the west. The route from the Vaṁkṣu (Gk. Oxus) River leading towards the Caspian Sea was also in use. The land-route between China and India passed through Balkh and Kashagar in Central Asia. The sea-borne trade was also carried on between India and China.[42] The land-route between India and South-West Asia (Persia) passed through Afghanistan. The enterprising Indian merchants sailed from different ports on the sea coast and settled down not only in the countries and islands of South-East Asia but also in other Asian countries and left behind an indelible imprint on their life and culture. They profoundly influenced and greatly modified their religion, language, art and culture. The maritime trade carried on in early centuries of the Christian era led to the diffusion of Indian culture in different countries of the Far-East including those on the mainland of Indo-China to a great extent which further gave fillip to India's politico-cultural contacts with those countries. The commercial and cultural intercourse of India with the Asian countries had virtually commenced three or four centuries before the dawn of the Christian era and further continued till the end of the ninth century CE and even beyond that. The Indian merchants also established commercial contacts with some European and African countries.

The Indian traders frequently visited Suvarṇadvīpa (Malay Peninsula, Java, Sumatra, Bali, Borneo, and other islands of

---

42. See Bagchi, op. cit., 60-63.

the East Indies),[43] which was famous for trade in gold and spices, and Suvarṇabhūmi, which is generally applied to the vast region stretching from Burma to Indonesia, but actually it is identical with Lower Burma[44] (Pegu and Moulmein districts). The latter region has also been identified with "Sudhammanagore,"[45] i.e. Thaton (the Gold Coast) at the mouth of the Sittaung River. It was formally styled as Sonaparanta (Golden Frontier), the possessor of mines of gold, silver, rubies, amber, etc. The desire to acquire immense gold and other minerals provided stimulus to the traders to sail to these regions of South-East Asia. The aborigines of the regions came into contact with the Indian merchants and learnt the first lesson of culture from them. Such economic and cultural fellowship gradually led to the fusion of the two distinct races and cultures.

From a non-canonical Prākṛt Jaina work composed by Saṅghadāsagaṇi Vācaka probably in the latter half of the sixth century CE, it distinctly appears that some traders proceeded from Campā with cotton yarn and reached Tāmralipti and therefrom they set out on sail in the ships laden with merchandize for different other countries. In course of the journey they visited Suavarṇabhūmi or Suvarṇadvīpa, Kamalapura (Kambuja on the mainland of Indo-China), Yavanadvīpa (the island of Java in Indonesia), Siṁhaladeśa (Ceylon), Barbara and Yavana.[46] Barbara may undoubtedly

43. Majumdar, *Suvarṇadvīpa*, I, 37.

44. Ibid., 56f.

45. *Śāsanavaṁśa*, 10, 12 cf. Law, *Geography of Early Buddhism* (Varanasi, 1973), 70; *BI*, 104, note 1.

46. *Vāsudevahiṇḍi*, tr. B.L. Sandesaria (Bhavnagar, 1946), 187-92; see also Motichandra, *Sārthavāha* (Patna, 1966), 166-68; *Quarterly Review of Historical Studies*, Calcutta, XVII 1, 47.

be identified with Barbarei of Ptolemy[47] and Barbaricum of the *Periplus*.[48] The name is evidently the Hellenized form of the Hindu word Bahardipur. It was situated on the middle mouth of the Indus. It was a maritime port and a great emporium of coral trade. It was not very far from the modern Karachi. The place stretched up to the Arabian Sea. Yavana was Alasanda (*dvīpa*) or the island town on the Indus, which was also called Alakanda (Alexandria), famous for corals.[49]

The non-canonical Jaina text by Udyotana Sūri (CE 778) provides an interesting account of the trading merchants who flocked to the city of Vijaya (one of the three cities of Annam along the eastern coast of Indo-China).[50]

The Jaina canon[51] and commentary[52] also testify to the trade relations between India and Pārasakūla (Persia) by land-routes. The articles in which they traded include *śaṅkha* (conch), *popphala* (nuts), *candana* (sandalwood), *aguru* (aloe), *mañjittha* (madder), gems, silver, gold, pearls and corals. There was regular trade between India and Persia during the Gupta period.

From the Jaina sources we further learn that the Indian merchants entered into trade relations also with Central Asia, China, Joniya (Greece) and Arabaka (Arabia).

---

47. *McCrindle's Ancient India as Described by Ptolemy* (London 1885) VII. 1, 60, 148; also 370-1, notes.

48. *The Periplus of the Erythraean Sea*, tr. from the Greek and annotated by W.H. Schoff (London, 1912), 38, 165, also 270.

49. *McCrindle's Ancient India as Described by Ptolemy*, 370-1, notes; Law, *History of Pāli Literature*, II, 367.

50. *Kuvalayāmala*, cf. *Quarterly Review of Historical Studies*, Calcutta, XVII, 1, 49.

51. *Āvaśyaka Cūrṇi*, 448, 507.

52. *Uttarādhyayana Ṭīkā* (Bombay, 1937), 3, 64; see also Motichandra, op. cit., 168-69.

The Buddhist literature abounds in references to sea voyages undertaken by the Indian merchants in connection with their trade and commerce with the Asian and other countries. It is clearly stated in the *Suppāraka Jātaka* that a merchant ship carrying six hundred passengers from the port town of Bharukaccha sailed across the six seas for about four months.[53] The destination not being indicated in the text it has been conjectured that they following the sea-routes from Broach to Mediterranean might have visited south-east Arabian and African countries.[54] The *Śaṅkha Jātaka* furnishes us with an account of the wreck of a ship of a brāhmaṇa merchant of Benares who was on his way to Suvarṇabhūmi.[55] The *Mahājanaka Jātaka* illustrates the truth concerning visit of prince Mahājanaka of Videha to Suvarṇabhūmi in a ship with seven hundred passengers.[56] The *Valāhassa Jātaka* relates the story of the arrival of five hundred shipwrecked merchants from Benares at the town of Sirisavatthu in *Tambaparṇidīpa* (Tāmraparṇī or Ceylon, one of the Purāṇic nine divisions of Greater India).[57] The *Silānisamsa Jātaka*[58] and the *Samuddavānija Jātaka*[59] also contain valuable references to the sea voyages. The *Baveru Jātaka* speaks of India's maritime trade with Baveru (Babylonia)[60] through the Arabian Sea and Persian Gulf. The

53. *Jātaka,* tr. various hands under the editorship of E.B. Cowell, Cambridge, 1895–1913, IV, 138-42.
54. For details see *Journal of the Bihar and Orissa Research Society,* Patna, VI, 195.
55. *Jātaka,* tr. various hands under the editorship of E.B. Cowell, Cambridge, 1895–1913, IV, 10, 15-17.
56. Ibid., VI, 34-36.
57. Ibid., II, 127f.
58. Ibid., II, 112f.
59. Ibid., IV, 65-67.
60. Ibid., III, 1267.

Vinaya narrates the story of how Mahinda travelled by water routes from Pāṭaliputra to Tāmralipti and therefrom further to Ceylon.[61] The Pāli Nikāyas mention long voyages lasting even for six months.[62] The Sanskrit Buddhist texts also contain some incidental allusions to India's sea-borne trade in early times.[63] The course of the ships was steered by the *Niyyāmaka* (*niryāmaka* or water-pilot).[64]

Rhys Davids further observes that

> . . . later texts of about the third century BCE speak of voyages down the Ganges from Benares to the mouth of the river and thence across the Indian Ocean to the opposite coast of Burma; and even from Bharukaccha round Cape Comorin to the same destination.[65]

The Jātaka records testify to the trade relations between Bharukaccha, Benares and Campā on the one hand and Suvarṇabhūmi (Burma) on the other. According to the *Manorathapūraṇī* (commentary on the *Aṅguttara Nikāya*) and *Apadāna*

---

61. *Vinaya*, III, 338.

62. *Dīgha Nikāya*, ed. T.W. Rhys Davids and J.E. Carpenter, PTS (London, 1890-1911), 1, 222; tr. T.W. Rhys Davids and C.A.F. Rhys Davids in *Dialogues of the Buddha*, Pali Text Society, (London, 1899-1921), 1, 283; *Aṅguttara Nikāya*, ed. R. Morris and E. Hardy, Pali Text Society (London, 1885-1900), III, 368; IV, 127; *Saṁyutta Nikāya*, ed. M.L. Peer and Mrs. Rhys Davids, Pali Text Society (London, 1884-1904), III, 155; V, 51.

63. *Divyāvadāna*, 4f, 26f, 40f, 112f, 229-32, 376f; *Avadānaśataka*, ed. J.S. Speyer (St. Petersburg, 1906), I, 129; II, 476.

64. *Jātaka*, tr. various hands under the editorship of E.B. Cowell, Cambridge, 1895–1913, IV, 137-8; see also *Jātaka*, tr. various hands under the editorship of E.B. Cowell, Cambridge, 1895-1913, III, 267; *Journal of the Royal Asiatic Society of Great Britain and Ireland*, London, 1899, 432.

65. *BI*, 96.

(canonical Pāli text) there was regular trade between Bharukaccha, Suppāraka and Suvarṇabhūmi.[67]

The *Apadāna* explicitly mentions the visit of traders and merchants from Sonnabhūmi (Suvarṇabhūmi), Malaya (Malay peninsula) and the distant land of Cina or Cinarattha (China) to India.[68] Another Pāli canon, *Niddesa*, speaks of India's commerce by sea with Yona (Ionia, i.e. Greece) and Paramayona (which may be "located either in western Asia or identified with some Greek island in the Mediterranean, if not with Ionia proper"). The text further mentions that the Indian sea-going merchants visited twenty-four countries, notably Kālamukha, Suvarṇabhūmi, Tambaparṇī, Java, Vesuṅga, Verāpatha, Tamali and Takkola towards the east, and followed ten difficult land-routes after reaching the harbour.[69] Of the places mentioned, Kālamukha may be identified with the Arākān coast and Suvarṇabhūmi may be located in Lower Burma (the "Gold country"). Tambaparṇī and Java are no other than Ceylon and the Island of Java respectively. Vesuṅga and Verapatha nearly correspond to Ptolemy's Besyngeitai (a mart) and Berabai (a city or port-town)[70] which have been placed by G.E. Gerini in Burma.[71] Tamali is identical with Tāmraliṅga in Malay

66. *Jātaka*, tr. various hands under the editorship of E.B. Cowell, Cambridge, 1895-1913, III, 188; IV, 15-17; VI, 34.

67. Cf. G.P. Malalasekara, *Dictionary of Pāli Proper Names* (London, 1960), II, 1223; also *Avadāna*, II, 476 vr. 13ff.

68. *Apadāna*, 1,2; II, 357f; cf. Law, *India as Described in Early Texts of Buddhism and Jainism* (Delhi, 1980), 177-8,188.

69. *Mahāniddesa*, ed. L.D. La, V. Poussin and E.J. Thomas, 1,154-55; II, 414-15; also Law, op. cit., 187-8 Indi.

70. *McCrindle's Ancient India as Described by Ptolemy*, VII, 2, 4, 196-7.

71. *Researches on Ptolemy's Geography of Eastern Asia* (London, 1909, rpt. Delhi, 1974), 64-84.

peninsula (known to Ptolemy as the Golden Khersonese).[72] On the combined testimony of Ptolemy,[73] Gerini,[74] and some authorities on the history and culture for South-East Asia,[75] Takkola (a mart or port town) can be easily identified with modern Takūa-Pa on the west coast of the Isthmus of Kra in Malay Peninsula. It may perhaps be modern port or Trang. It was the first landing stage of the Indian traders and colonists. On the weight of the evidence B.C. Law's identification of Takkola with "an ancient seaport near Thaton in Lower Burma"[76] can be disposed of. Some other scholars have also mistakenly identified Takkola with Rangoon, Burman Talaing Taikkula, etc.[77] It is striking to note that "a fourth-century CE pillar inscription of the Buddhist Sea Captain, Mahānāvika Buddhagupta of Raktamṛttikā (modern Rangamati in Murshidabad district, Bengal) has been discovered in the Wellesley district of the Malay peninsula."[78] The post-canonical Pāli text not only makes mention of some important trading centres like Bharukaccha, Madhurā (Mathurā), Sāgala Sovīra. Surattho (seaport town, identical with modern Surat), Varanasi

---

72. May, op. cit., 74-76; Sylvain Levi, *E'tude Asiatique*, II (Paris, 1925), 40-55.

73. *McCrindle 's Ancient India as Described* by Ptolemy, VII, 2, 5, 197-99.

74. *Gerini*, op. cit., 85-87.

75. May, op. cit., 76; Cady, op. cit., 30, note 17; see also Wales "Archaelogical Researches on Ancient Indian Colonisation in Malaya", *Journal of the Royal Asiatic Society*, Malayan Branch, Singapore, XVIII (1940), 5-40.

76. *History of Pāli Literataure*, II, 369.

77. See *McCrindle's Ancient India as Described by Ptolemy*, 198 and note 27, 449, Appendix 7.

78. Kern's *Verspreide Geschriften*, III (1915), 255, quoted in McCrindle's *Ancient Indian as Described by Ptolemy*, 389 notes.

and Alasanda (the island town of Alexandria on the Indus) but also points to India's commercial intercourse with Suvarṇabhūmi, Cina (China) and Takkola.[79] The text also refers to the visit of traders and merchants from various countries to India.[80]

The items which were generally exported from India to foreign countries include cotton cloths, ivory and ivory work, conch, diamonds, corals, etc. There is recorded evidence to show that various kinds of plain and dyed cloths, cotton and silk cloths and muslin were exported from Varanasi, Bengal and other places.[81] The best quality of sandalwood was imported from Malaya (Malaysia) by the sea-faring Indian merchants.[82] Different kinds of precious gems, etc. were imported from Siṁhaladeśa (Ceylon) and other countries.[83] In course of the sea-borne trade the Indian merchants obtained "perfumed wood, gold, precious stones, spices and other condiments from South-East Asia" which in return got "high quality cotton textiles from India."[84] Silk cloth was generally imported from China. Woollen cloths, different varieties of blankets, etc. were imported from Central Asia. The Indian merchants learnt the art of growing silk from China and that of growing betel leaves from Indonesia. Similarly the method of growing cotton spread from India to China and Central Asia. In the age of the Kuṣāṇas the Buddhist traders had maintained their trade relation with the Roman Empire.

79. *Milindapañha*, ed. V. Trenckner (London, 1880), 359, also 327f; also tr. T.W. Rhys Davids, Sacred Books of the East, Oxford, XXXVI, II, 269; Law, op. cit., 367-69.

80. *Milindapañha*, 331.

81. *Mahāvastu*, 1, 235-6.

82. *Vinayavastu*, Gilgit Manuscript, III, II (Srinagar, 1942), 64.

83. *Cullavagga*, 9, 1, 3.

84. Cady, op. cit., 21f.

Trade was no doubt one of the channels for radiation of Indian culture in different Asian countries. The Hindu, Jaina and Buddhist merchants of the pre- and post-Christian era contributed not only to the material prosperity of the country but also to the evolution of Indian culture in the Asiatic countries. They also made some contributions to the spread of Indian culture in South, South-East, Central, East and South-West Asia through external trade relations with them. Some sections of the traders set-up their colonies particularly in the countries of South-East Asia and introduced Indian manners and customs, religion and philosophy, script and language, art and other elements of culture. Hinduism and Buddhism spread there side by side. Sanskrit inscriptions have been discovered in Burma, Malay Peninsula, Cambodia, Annam, Java, Sumatra, Borneo and Campā. The Pāli, a derivative from Sanskrit, was adopted in a large part of Indo-China. The Hindu and Buddhist styles of architectural and sculptural art also flourished there.[85] John F. Cady has correctly observed that, "trade was a perennial influence in the historical development of South-East Asia."[86] However, it will not be fair to say that the culture that flourished in South-East Asia was the legacy or heritage of India. The countries in South-East Asia had their own cultural tradition. They evolved their own traditional or indigenous culture by assimilating the Indian elements. The same applies to other neighbouring Asian countries. Buddhism spread in Ceylon (South Asia), China (East Asia) and Persia (South-West Asia) also through trade. The Brāhmanical religion, Buddhism, Sanskrit and Pāli languages, Brāhmī and Kharoṣṭhī scripts, etc. spread in Central Asia also through contacts with the Indian traders. They no

85. For details see Cady, op. cit., 27-48; Harrison, op. cit., 12, 15; Hall, Burma, 7f.

86. Cady, op. cit., 21.

doubt culturally influenced those who came into contact with them. But it can hardly be denied that they also learnt some arts and crafts from their Asian counterparts. This shows intra-Asian influences through economic and cultural interactions.

17

Politico-Cultural Relations of Tibet and Burma with Bihar and their Impact

Ancient and Early Medieval Period*

This paper aims at providing a systematic and graphic account of politico-cultural relations of Tibet and Burma with Bihar and their impact during the period under notice. The subject has not yet received the treatment it deserves. Some of its important aspects are still shrouded in obscurity. There is a fair scope to make a fresh historical disquisition into the subject. It is worthwhile to mention here that the preponderant influence of Bihar which invariably extended in ancient and medieval period far to the sub-Himalayan and Himalayan regions — an undeniable fact to be reckoned with — has not yet received the serious attention of historians. An attempt can be made to trace its early relations with other states and kingdoms or the relations of its ancient rulers with contemporary powers. It is significant to note that the relations of Bihar with Tibet and Burma left indelible imprints on their language, literature and cultural pattern. We have both historical and traditional accounts of the subject.

The history and traditions of Bihar go back to the earliest dawn. In the days of greatness of Magadha, Mithilā, the Licchavis of Vaiśālī, Gautama Buddha and Mahāvīra, it was indeed the central point of the culture and activities of most

---

* From *The Thinker*, IX, 4, 1981, pp. 26-35.

of the Indian peninsula. The remains of splendid cities, ancient monasteries, universities, temples, shrines and places hallowed by association with the great religious leaders, the figures of mythology and other relics and remnants are fine reminiscent pieces constituting the monumental evidence to its past glory and grandeur.

The relations of Tibet with Bihar as amply testified to by literary and other evidences can be traced back to time immemorial. Our Epics — the *Rāmāyaṇa* and the *Mahābhārata* — the Purāṇas, *Alberuni's India* (CE 1030), Abul Fazal's *Āin-i-Akbarī* and even Herodotus (fifth century BCE) refer to Tibet by applying various appellations. However, the earliest known name of Tibet was Tribistap and of Burma Brahmadeśa.

In the absence of any trustworthy document as evidence it is very difficult to say when the foundation of this relation was laid but on the authority of Tibetan scholar Tsepon D. Shakabpa[1] it can be definitely asserted that there was a close relationship between Tibet and Bihar which is noticeable in various perspectives. In ancient times, the royal family of Magadha, whose history, the history of India, began at least 2500 years ago, had already established its link with Tibet. Even the Tibetan kings traced their ancestry to the son of a noble family of Magadha in Bihar. This son of Magadha, while in Tibet, was taken care of by Mak Gyapa and when he grew up, he wandered in various places of Tibet and ultimately reached Yalung where he was greeted by the people who were adherents of Bon-religion in prehistoric times. The boy was placed on a wooden sedan chair by the people who accepted him as their leader and gave the name Kyatr: Tsenpo, meaning "Neck-enthroned king." Until the coming of this boy from Magadha, the Tibetans lived in caves in the Palaeolithic Age.

1. *Tibet — A Political History* (based on 57 Original Tibetan Sources) (London, 1973), pp. 23ff.

He is believed to have built the first house there known as "Yumbulagang" which is still present in central Tibet. Certain sections of the Tibetan people are considered to be the direct descendants of the royal family of Magadha. Besides, the various paṇḍits of ancient monasteries of Bihar, who visited Tibet at different periods of history, played a notable role in discovering many secret proofs showing the Tibetans' origin. The tradition, hitherto popular in Tibet, also confirms this truth. Atīśa Dīpāṅkara, the paṇḍit of Vikramsila University of Bihar, who visited Tibet in the eleventh century, discovered a document in a pillar of the Jokhang or Central Temple in Lhasa that was written during the reign of Songtsen Gampo in the seventh century CE, which shows that they are descended from monkeys as the caves of their ancestors can still be seen near the mountains called Gongpori behind Tsethang. Another paṇḍit, Śaṅkarapati (Dele Dakpo) wrote a letter about one hundred years after the death of Buddha in which he unravelled the mystery that majority of Tibetans are descendants of Rupati, Military Commander of Kaurava army who fled to Tibet with his followers following the defeat in the Bhārata War, whose exact date cannot be determined with absolute amount of certainty.

The established relations took different turns at different periods of history. It is a strange irony of fate and coincidence of history that Tibet established its relations with Tirhut or northern Bihar (which in the days of Upaniṣads, perhaps 2600 years ago, was the centre of learning and religion), by maintaining its political hegemony over it for nearly half a century. One strange episode occurred in Tirhut soon after the death of Harṣa of Kannauj who died at the close of CE 646 or beginning of CE 647: a Chinese envoy was attacked by the troops of Arjuna of Tirhut, a former minister of Harṣa and usurper to the throne. The famous Srong T-san Gampo of Tibet with combined forces of Tibetans and Nepalese invaded Tirhut, utterly defeated the opposing army, took the usurper prisoner and sent him to China, Tirhut or northern Bihar accordingly passed under the sovereignty of Tibet.[2] The duration of Tibetan rule in Tirhut has not been hitherto known. Tibetan rule in Tirhut lasted only for about half a century (CE 647 or 648 to 703), the date when Nepal recovered its independence as determined by E.H. Parker, a competent authority on the history of Thang Dynasty of China. Sylvain Levy conjectured that CE 879 epoch of the Nepalese era might possibly mark the time when Nepal threw off its allegiance to Tibet. In the year 703, it is recorded that Tirhut or northern Bihar also threw off Tibetan suzerainty like that of Nepal. Waddele had also printed the narratives in 1910 in *Asiatic Quarterly Review* according to which both Nepal and Tirhut became independent of Tibet in CE 703. Parker's important article entitled "China, Nepal, Bhutan and Sikkim and their mutual relations" as set forth in Chinese official documents, appeared in the first number of *Journal of Manchester Oriental Society* (1911, pp. 129-152).[3]

After CE 778 when Trisong Detsen sent men to Magadha in Bihar to obtain one relic of the Lord Buddha for great *chorten* (*stūpa*) of Samye Basalnang, the minister who had visited southern Bihar and Nepal in earlier times, wrote that two large bodies of cavalry were sent to Magadha. It is said that when a *mahārājā* who then ruled a territory north of the Ganges saw the Tibetan cavalry bearing down upon his city, mistook it for the vanguard of an army, and assuming that it would be followed immediately by foot soldiers and elephants, surrendered, but it was a religious mission, not sent to make territorial conquest. The Tibetan army crossed the Ganges and arrived at Magadha in Bihar. The ruler of Magadha and

2. *JBORS* (*Journal of the Bihar and Orissa Research Society*), Dec. 1917, Vol. III, Pt. IV, pp. 555-56; Sir John Houlton, *Bihar — The Heart of India* (Calcutta, 1949), p. 101.

3. *JBORS*, Dec. 1917, vol. III, Pt. IV, pp. 555-56.

his followers knowing that the Tibetans would not attack the monastery of Odantapurī deposited most of the possessions there and moved eastward; however the Tibetans continued on to Bodh-Gayā. There they made offering to the sacred *bodhi* tree, obtained the desired relic and then turned back towards Tibet. They erected an iron pillar on the banks of Gayā to mark the site of their crossing. The Great Pagoḍā at Gyantse in Tibet is also said to have been modelled on the Bodh-Gayā Temple. About the importance of *bodhi* tree and its worship and Bodh-Gayā as a sacred place, Hiuen-Tsang has given a very authentic and detailed account in his annals of travels.[4]

Equally great and interesting like the political relation is the cultural relation between the two. The three ancient renowned universities of Bihar — Nālandā (founded in 414–455 by Kumāragupta I), Odantapurī or Uddaṇḍapura both near modern town Bihar (Vihāra) from which the town and province took their name and further sacked by Bakhtiyar Khalji in CE 1197 and Vikramśilā (near modern Bhagalpur bearing the old name Campā, believed to have been founded by Dharmapāla) and other *mahāvihāra*s were the great centres of cultural contacts between Tibetan monks and accomplished scholars popularly known as paṇḍits of these universities during the period ranging from the latter half of the eighth century (not ninth century or CE 1000 as wrongly supposed by some eminent historians) to the middle of the seventeenth century. Especially during the time of Pāla kingdom the exchange of cultural teams between the two was the order of the day which subsequently shaped the religious and literary structures of Tibet.

On the invitation from Tibetan kings the *vihāra*s used to send forth from time to time pre-eminent scholars to the Land of Snow on the mission of preaching Buddhism or reforming

---

4. S. Beal, *The Life of Hiuen Tsang* (London, 1884), pp. 103-04.

the religion. After the translation of Buddhist works from Sanskrit into Tibetan began by monks, the nucleus of Tibetan Buddhist literature began to take shape. Tibetans began to study Sanskrit under Indian monks both in Tibet and in southern Bihar. Influx of Tibetan monks in these universities started to learn Sanskrit. The great *ācārya*s like Śāntarakṣita and Guru Padmasambhava of Nalanda University and Atīśa Dīpāṅkara of Vikramsila University and host of other paṇḍits and teachers and a band of scholars from these universities went to Tibet, preached Buddhism and translated several Sanskrit, Pāli and other works into Tibetan. Various other paṇḍits like Śailendra Bodhi, Dānaśīla and Jinamitra came from these universities to central Tibet and translated the Buddhist texts. The Tibetan Buddhism became a queer admixture of Tantrism or Śāktism and the the pre-historic Bon *dharma*.[5] This truth can be further corroborated from other sources. B.C. Law[6] also holds the view that the students from Tibet frequently visited Vikramsila University. Placing his reliance on Tibetan works, he points out that Atīśa Dīpāṅkara, a native of Bengal, who was at the head of this university from CE 1034-38, was induced to go to Tibet and re-establish the Buddhist religion there.

The first authentic evidence of cultural contact can be noticed during the reign of a king named Tho-tho-ri Nyantsen born in CE 173 (twenty-eighth king), eighteen generations after Pode Kungyal, who received a book of Buddhist scripture in Sanskrit through a paṇḍit of one of these universities, which was called by King Kyenpo-Sangua the secret which marked the initial introduction of Buddhism into Tibet. The most cardinal feature to be noted here is this that during the reign of Songtsen-Gampo (CE 617), Thon-Mi-Sambhota along with

5. K.C. Bhanja, *Mystic Tibet and the Himalayas*, (Darjeeling), 1st edn, June, 1948), p. 55.

6. *The Magadha in Ancient India*, (Delhi, 1976), pp. 43f.

other 16 companions were sent to these universities to learn Sanskrit and when they returned, they used their knowledge of Brāhmī and Gupta scripts to devise a Tibetan script. Thus it is quite obvious that the current Tibetan script was derived from the Brāhmī and the Buddhist script which was in Nālandā and Magadha as early as CE 350, when King Song-tsen-Gampo (629-49) sent his minister and other students to Magadha to study the script of Gupta. The amazing similarities of the Tibetan script with that of Brāhmī-Gupta script can be seen in *Buhler Indische Palaeographic* Plate-IV, Col. I-VII. I am here prone to observe that this fact has not been given its due importance by Suniti Kumar Chatterji, as a result of which his analysis of the Tibetan linguistic structure seems to be completely wrong and thus untenable.

Another king during the latter half of the eighth century, Ti-Song-De-Tseo invited the Tāntric Buddhist teacher and preacher of mysticism, popularly known as Guru Padmasambhava who hailed from the ancient Nalanda University to preach the doctrine of Lord Buddha. He was well versed in magical arts associated with Tāntric form of Buddhism acceptable to Tibetan people. He preached in Tibet the Buddhism which is nothing but mystical aspects of Hinduism which relates to charms, miracles and occultism. Padmasambhava seems to be more honoured in Tibet than Lord Buddha himself. In hundreds of monasteries the priest image occupies central position, while that of Lord Buddha always represented by a much smaller image is assigned a less conspicuous place. To quote Charles Bell: "For, the people say that Buddha would be helpless without the priests, who spread the doctrines and the books in which these doctrines were expounded." Padmasambhava, great Tāntric teacher is called Gandhi-Maharaja by Tibetans and according to their mythology Mahatma Gandhi was the incarnation of this man Śāntirakṣita, another paṇḍit of Nālandā, also visited Tibet and preached Buddhism. The first monastery was built in Tibet in CE 835.

Another Tibetan king, Chang-Chhup-od sent Nagtso with gold and a letter to invite the great *ācārya* or *mahārāṇā* Paṇḍit Atīśa Dīpāṅkara (982–1054), the rector of Vikramsila University seat of Buddhist learning, to come to Tibet for removing the doctrinal differences between Hīnayāna and Mahāyāna schools. Atīśa with twenty-four of his disciples went to Tibet in CE 1042, stayed there for several months, made corrections and revisions of the Tibetan translation of Buddhist texts by clearing up many contradictory points and at Toling wrote a Sanskrit work called *Bodha Pāṭha Pradīpa* which is called *Changchup Latngye Domme* in Tibet meaning "the Lamp that shows the Path of Enlightenment." Drom Tonpa and many Tibetans became his disciples. In CE 1044, he visited Kailāsa-Mānasa and spent a week in a cave on the shore of the lake below the present Gossul Gompa where are his footprints. During this period many Tibetans went to Vikramsila University and became students there. He also removed the conflicts between Buddhism and Bon-Religion (pre-Buddhist religion). He died there in CE 1054 and his remains are preserved in *chorten* (*stūpa*) at Ney thang. From another source[7] also we come to know that during the reign of Srong-san Gampo, a great Buddhist philosopher named Kamalaśīla (who defeated the Chinese pilgrim, Hiuen-Tsang in intellectual disputation) was brought to Tibet from Magadha and was placed at the head of the metaphysical branch of the Buddhist Church in Tibet. Tāranātha[8] also supports the view that Neyapāla, king of Magadha had with him Jo-Adisha who propagated Buddhism in Tibet P. Banerjee[9] on the authority

7. *Bengal, Past and Present*, Jan–June, 1917, Vol. XIV, pp. 88-89.
8. *Indian Antiquary*, 1875, vol. IV, p. 366.
9. *Journal of the Asiatic Society Letters*, 1953, vol. XIX, no. I, p. 107.

of Bhandarkar's *List of Northern Indian Inscriptions* has also observed that Buddhists from different parts of the world visited Bihar.

The relations between Burma and Bihar is testified to by epigraphic, literary and other sources. Burma maintained a direct cultural link with Magadha right from the seventh century to CE 1492. It was the Burmese practice to send Mission to Bodh-Gayā which was revived by various Burmese kings. Burmese pilgrims used to visit Bodh-Gayā, one of the holiest places in the world and the most sacred of all places to Buddhists, and paid reverence to the famous *bodhi* tree under which Gautama Buddha attained enlightenment (*mahānirvāṇa*). A Mon inscription at Shwehsandaw Pagoḍā at Prom as it runs "Many persons from all the provinces came into his presence to attend him" bears an eloquent testimony to the fact that Burmese pilgrims used to go on religious mission to Bodh-Gayā during the time of Buddha. During Pagan period (CE 1044–1287), Kyan Zitthaw was the king of Burma who undertook the restoration of the Mahā-Bodhi temple at Bodh-Gayā. Dammazedi (1472-92), the greatest of the rulers of Wareru's line (the Mon Hegemony) maintained friendly intercourse with Magadhan rulers by reviving the practice of sending mission to Bodh-Gayā. The fact that when this famous temple was sacked during the first Muhammedan invasion at the end of twelfth century, a king of Burma expressed his desire and obtained the permission of government in 1876 to restore it, though he could not, greatly reflects its old cultural ties between the two places. The Pagan Buddhism, as a result of the friendly intercourse, became a strange mixture of Hindu Brāhmanic cults — Vaiṣṇavism in particular — Mahāyānism and Tantrism in general. Bodh-Gayā as the homeland of Buddha has been mentioned in Burmese antiquities and scriptures as the Holy Land.

This cultural contact had its impact upon Burmese language and literature, which accidentally, no doubt, help us in ascertaining their real origin. Pāli became the language of their Buddhist scriptures. Burmese vernacular literature was no doubt the product of the monastic schools of Bihar. Even Pagan culture had its roots in the study of Pāli literature. The earliest law book in Burma known as *Dhammathat* which consists of law ascribed to ancient Indian sage Manu brought into Burma by Hindu colonists is the Pāli version of the Laws of Manu. The Burmese got their alphabet from here and their medieval chronicles bear witness to the fact that their clan descended from Buddhists and their court terminology is akin to what was prevalent in Magadha region in the remote period. Even Burmese Chronicle of 850 BCE shows that Burmese stories have been taken from Sanskrit and original texts. The earliest record in the third century Buddhist inscription found at the Annam coast is in Sanskrit language used both by Burmese and Siamese. In spite of the fact that Burmese is a monosyllabic tonal language closely akin to Tibetan in general and blend of four main types — Mon (Tai alphabet tinged with Indian culture, the language akin to that of Khmer (Cambodian), Shan language and the Arakanese of the coastal strip with an admixture of Indian blood — almost all technical, classical and many other terms have been derived from Pāli language which was the most popular language between present Nālandā and Bodh-Gayā regions of Bihar. As a matter of fact, by CE 50 many Buddhists from Magadha regions had permanently settled in Burma. According to local chronicles Candra dynasty founded in the middle of the fourth century CE ruled in Arākān with Vaiśālī as their capital, the ruins of which now called Vethali, 8 miles north-west of Mrohaung testifies to its former greatness. It is true that Hindu dynasty ruled in Burma for a long time especially in Arākān from CE 600–1000, whose record is called Śrī Dharma-rājanya-vaṁśa. Hindus colonized even upper Burma and a number of inscriptions have been found written both in Sanskrit and Pyu (the earliest Chinese inhabitants of Burma) languages. Hiuen Tsang also refers to several Hinduized kingdoms in Indo-China with Śrīkṣetra as its capital at Prome (Lower Burma) wrongly identified by some with Tripura. The Mon country of lower Burma was under the name of Ramannades. Thirteen dyṇasties of Dharmavijaya of pure kṣatriya lineage ruled there. The Mongoloid stock of Indo-Chinese peninsula and those Burmese who entered Burma during ninth century and eleventh century from their earliest recorded home, Kansu, north-west of China between Gobi Desert and north-east of Tibet which they left in Neolithic times, got absorbed in and mixed with the earlier inhabitants of the place in such a vigorous way that they certainly seem to be strange mixture of the overflowing from the two great neighbouring countries, the Chinese element being by far the preponderating factor. Though ethnically and culturally the people of Burma are indeed Indo-Chinese, again here it can be noted that the Indo-Chinese Peninsula was a battleground between the Aryans and non-Aryans, or between the Indian and Chinese civilizations for a longer period, but Indian culture triumphed everywhere save in Annarn and Tonkins.

The foregoing arguments in general and their ethnic and linguistic features in particular, though not enough here, lead me to warrant the belief that Tibeto-Burman people have all the clear traces of mixture. Many people who now inhabit Burma and Tibet are undisputably descendants of the Aryan inhabitants who were there in the earliest days of the kingdoms. Tibetans belong to Aryan stock including the royal family of Magadha and Kosala, Lichchavis of Nepal and non-Aryan stock including Mongoloid of Indo-Chinese stocks with admixture of Indian blood and Turko-Mongoloid stock. Burmese also belonged to both Aryan and non-Aryan stock. Thus it seems to me that simply by calling them as Indo-

Mongoloids, multitude of scholars including S. Sanang Setzen, the Mongolian chronicler, the author of *Mongol Kbadum Tog-Budji*, who traces the Mongol royal lineage to that of Tibetans, devoid of elaborate and satisfactory explanations, have palpably travestied the truth and crucified the historical facts. S.K. Chatterji's arguments about the term Indo-Mongoloid advanced in his monograph[10] heavily weighted with fantastic descriptions, blindly supported by many other scholars, which deplorably lack an appreciable degree of distinctness, the classifications of Indo-Mongoloid race by leading Anthropologists which hardly fit in with the fair historical process of justification and the analysis of their linguistic structures by Grierson in the Linguistic Survey of India and T.C. Hodson[11] and others which are based on mere assumptions, are neither convincing nor appealing to me and apparently look inconclusive. Space does not permit me to throw much light on the subject in support of my arguments, but discussion is not closed here. Suffice to say that what percentage of Aryan and non-Aryan blood cowed through the vein of the people between the Vedic age and CE 1000 especially in South-East Asian belt who commingled and migrated in different directions, perhaps nobody can say.

To sum up, it is quite heartening to note that the celebrated paṇḍits, distinguished brāhmaṇas and other accomplished scholars of the three said monastic universities of Bihar — Nālandā, Odantapurī and Vikramśilā — once a cultural cynosure played unquestionably notable role in shaping the politico-religio-literary structure of Tibet and Burma in the wake of their friendly intercourse and cultural fellowship which, as a whole, is a great episode of pan-Indian significance and comparable to other distinctive hallmarks in the cultural history of mankind.

---

10. *Kirata-Jana-Kriti*, A.S.B. 1974, pp. 20, 22, 26, 44, 45.
11. *JRAS*, 1913, pp. 315-22.

18

Kālidāsa's Description of Raghu's Conquest of Prāgjyotiṣa

Historical Interpretations*

THE description provided by Kālidāsa (generally placed between the period ranging from the first century BCE to the fifth century CE) of Raghu's conquest of Prāgjyotiṣa or Kāmarūpa in his famous work *Raghuvaṁśa* offers little scope for its historical interpretations. The description is, of course, poetical but the theme is evidently historical. He is one of those ancient Indian writers (either as a classical poet or a dramatist) whose portrayal of contemporary historical events as well as geographical settings is, no doubt, worthy of our attention to a considerable extent. He appears to have possessed considerable knowledge of some important countries adjoining India's border in the north, east and the west. We also find evidence in the text of his knowledge of the people inhabiting the different places conquered by Raghu.

Here it must be made clear at the very outset that Kālidāsa intended to apply the name Kāmarūpa[1] to the old province of

---

* From *Proceedings of North-East India History Association*, Xth Session (Shillong, 1989), pp. 62-67.

1. *Raghuvaṁśa* (ed. M.R. Kale with the commentary *Sañjīvanī* of Mallinātha, and with a literal Eng. tr. and copious notes, Delhi, 1972), Canto IV, vv. 83-84.

Assam and the name Prāgjyotiṣa[2] to its capital town (Pura = a Prāgjyotiṣapur), situated on the bank of river Lauhitya or Brahmaputra which is also identified with the modern town of Gauhati.

Raghu was the mightiest and the most illustrious of Ikṣvāku kings of the Solar dynasty, that ruled at the city of Ayodhyā in the aorthen Ganges valley in the pre-Rāmāyaṇic age. After being installed on the throne as king by his father Dilīpa, he set out on his *digvijaya* or conquest in all four directions, viz. the east, west, north and south with the ulterior motive to conquer the populace and potentates of the regions concerned and to compel them to acknowledge him as the sovereign ruler of India.

After having subdued the Parasikas (the ancient Persians or inhabitants of that part of Persia, which was lying adjacent to the Indus), the Yavanas, the Hūṇas and the Kāmbojas in the north-west and the tribal people of northern Himalayan region, he descended to the plains, crossed the Lauhitya and

---

2. Ibid., Canto IV, v. 81; B.C. Law (*Geographical Aspect of Kālidāsa's Works*, hereafter *GAKW*, Varanasi, 1976, p. 15) also holds that "according to Kālidāsa the people of Kāmarūpa and Prāgjyotiṣa are two different nations." In another source (*Annals of the Bhandarkar Oriental Research Institute*, vol. XVII, pt. III, 1936, p. 241) he has pointed out that according to *Raghuvaṁśa* the Prāgjyotiṣa country lay evidently to the north of the Brahmaputra River. Pargiter's statement (of his English translation of the *Mārkaṇḍeya Purāṇa*, Bibliotheca Indica Series ASB, Calcutta 1904, vol. II, Pt. II, p. 328, note) that the "*Raghuvaṁśa* places it beyond the Brahmaputra" runs contrary to the truth. There is no such information in the text. Therefore, his view seems to be entirely based on assumption. It is not possible to think that the poet was ignorant of the location of this country. Whether it is Prāgjyotiṣa or Kāmarūpa (interchangeable in ancient Indian literature and inscriptions) the fact remains that its king, during whose time the said ancient kingdom extended up to the Himalaya on the north and the borders of China on the east, surendered at the feet of Raghu.

finally reached the kingdom of Prāgjyotiṣa or Kāmarūpa in the valley of Brahmaputra.[3]

We are further told that as soon as he along with his army crossed the river Lauhitya, the lord of Prāgjyotiṣa began to tremble out of fear. Raghu's very name struck terror into the heart of the king of Kāmarūpa, but he later somehow was able to please the conqueror, who was advancing towards his kingdom, by paying him homage in the form of presenting some of his excellent war-elephants with which he generally used to encounter other conquerors. It is also stated that he worshipped the shadow of his (Raghu's) feet (the orb of the splendour or lustre) with the offering of flowers in the form of precious gems in the same manner as the presiding deity of Hemapīṭha (corresponding to Svarṇapīṭha, one of the four divisions of Kāmarūpa as stated in "Haragaurī-Saṁvāda," and extending up to Puṣpikā River) was worshipped. This is clear indication of the fact that the king of this land surrendered at the feet of Raghu. The following verses from the text will bear an eloquent testimony to the facts as stated above:

चकम्पे तीर्णलौहित्ये तस्मिन्प्राग्ज्योतिषेश्वरः।
तद्गजालानतां प्राप्तैः सह कालागुरुद्रुमैः॥

न प्रसेहे स रुद्धार्कमधारावर्षदुर्दिनम्।
रथवर्त्मरजोऽप्यस्य कुत एव पताकिनीम्॥

तमीशः कामरुपाणमात्याखण्डलविक्रमम्।
भेजे भिन्नकटैर्नागैरन्यानुपरूरोध यैः॥

---

3. *Raghuvaṁśa* (ed. M.R. Kale), Canto IV, vv. 60-81, also tr. pp. 31-33, Notes, pp. 111-18 ; *Raghuvaṁśa* (ed. with tr. by Brahma Shankar Mishra, Vāranasi, 1956), Canto IV, pp. 115-18. See also Bhagavat Sharan Upadhyaya, *India in Kālidāsa* (hereafter *IK*) (Delhi, 1968), ch. 111, pp. 62-63. H.C. Chakladar, *The Geography of Kālidāsa* (Indian Studies, Past & Present, Calcutta, 1963), pp. 24-25 and D. Sarma (ed.), *Kāmarūpa Śāsanāvalī* (originally by P. Bhattacharyya Vidyavinoda, 1868-1938), Gauhati, 1981, pp. 136-38, 153.

कामरूपेश्वरस्तस्य हेमपीठाधिदेवताम्।
रत्नपुष्पोपहारेण च्छायामानर्च पादयोः।।

cakampe tīrṇalauhitye tasminprāgjyotiṣeśvaraḥ,
tadgajālānataṁ prāpteḥ saha kālāgurudrumeḥ ॥

na prasehe sa ruddhakarmadhārāvarṣadurdinam ।
rathavatmarrjoapyasya kuta eva patakinima ॥

tamīśaḥ kāmarūpāṇamātyā-khaṇḍalavikramam ।
bheje bhinnakaṭenārgeraṇyānuparūrodha yeḥ ॥

kāmarūpesvarastasya hemapīṭhādhidevatām ।
ratnapuṣpopahāreṇa cchāyāmānarca pādayoḥ ॥

— Raghuvaṁśa, IV, 81-84.

All the kings (including that of Kāmarūpa) conquered by Raghu became destitute of their white umbrellas (an emblem of royalty and independence) and banners and eventually became his vassals. Having thus conquered all the quarters the conqueror performed the Viśvajit sacrifice at the end of which he, assisted by his ministers of state, allayed the wounded feelings of the defeated kings by honouring them with marks of great respect and restored them to their respective thrones in their capitals with their banners, swords and royal umbrellas.[4] However, the reference to the undisputed universal sovereignty is an indirect poetic expression of an unqualified glorification of Raghu, who out of lust for power led his armies into battles.

The poet, unfortunately, does not provide any indication either about that particular king of Prāgjyotiṣa or Kāmarūpa, who was brought to subjection by Raghu or about the period during which the incident might have occurred, which, undoubtedly, mark the desideratum of the narratives.[5] The

---

4. *Raghuvaṁśa*, IV, 81-84.

5. Ibid., IV, 85-88.

evidence furnished in the text is undeniably too vague to project a clear picture of the subject concerned. In this connection we should not forget that, after all, it is a poetic description. However, the modern researches on the works of Kālidāsa, as well as the interpretations of the data contained in the text by different annotators lend support to the subjugation of the king of Prāgjyotiṣa or Kāmarūpa by Raghu. Moveover, there are some other evidences with the help of which we can prove the historicity and determine the antiquity of the episode.[6]

Raghu's conquest of Prāgjyotiṣa or Kāmarūpa is supported by Mallinātha's (ascribed to the later half of the fourteenth century, approximately it falls sometime between *c.* CE 1325–1425) commentary (*Saṅjīvanī*) on the text, as well as by the statements of M.R. Kale,[7] Bhagavat Sharan Upadhyaya,[8] H.C. Chakladar[9] and S.C. Banerjee.[10] R.G. Basak has categorically stated that "Kālidāsa's poetical description (of Raghu's victory over the king of Prāgjyotiṣa) was, undoubtedly influenced by the actual historical occurrences of his time."[11] Walter Ruben has also admitted that Raghu as a valiant warrior achieved remarkable success in his expeditions launched out against India in all four directions. He won laurels of victories over his opponents and thereby brought the whole of India under his political sway.[12] Mark Collins also refers to

6. See ibid. (ed. M.R. Kale), pp. 87-88.
7. Ibid. Intr. xvii & xxxix, also tr. text, p. 33 and notes, pp. 1.7-19.
8. *IK*, pp. 63-64.
9. Op. cit., pp. 23-25.
10. *Kālidāsa-Kośa* (Varanasi, 1968), p. 29.
11. *The History of North-Eastern India* (extending from the foundation of the Gupta Empire to the rise of the Pāla dynasty of Bengal, *c.* CE 320–760), Calcutta, 1967, p. 266.
12. *Kālidāsa — The Human Meaning of his Works* (Berlin, 1957), p. 42.

the ancient kingdom of Prāgjyotiṣa along with other principal kingdoms of India which were subjugated by Raghu.[13] Regarding the historical validity of Kālidāsa's statements S.P. Pandit has observed that ". . . he (Kālidāsa) . . . cannot be supposed to have brought down the history of the most celebrated ancient Indian kings to such a sorry end."[14]

The similarity found between the relation of the famous Raghu with the lord of Prāgjyotiṣa (against whom the former launched military expeditions) and that of the Gupta monarch Samudragupta (*c.* CE 335-80) with the king of Kāmarūpa[15] can no doubt be held justified, to some extent. Because, Kāmarūpa during both the periods maintained its autonomy and was not included in either's empire. But its ruler acknowledged the allegiance to both. However, the former event was just a passing phase in the political history of ancient Assam, and the latter reduced the status of the kingdom to a subordinate state.

Whatever the facts may be, it is very hard to confirm the views held by some scholars that as Kālidāsa belonged to the fifth century CE, his description of Raghu's *digvijaya* is nothing but a reflection of the victories of the Gupta kings (either Samudragupta or Candragupta II Vikrāmaditya, *c.* CE 380–412 or both) or the defeat of Kāmarūpa ruler at the hands of Raghu stands for the defeat at the hands of Samudragupta.[16]

---

13. *The Geographical Data of the Raghuvaṁśa and Daśakumāracarita* (Leipzig, 1907), pp. 10-17.

14. Quoted by M.R. Kale, op. cit., Intr. xxx.

15. R.G. Basak, "Historical basis and Model for Kālidāsa's Description of Raghu's Conquest", *Proceedings and Transactions of the Second Oriental Conference*, 1922, pp. 333-34.

16. See M. Collins, op. cit., p. 48 and fn.; Walter Ruben. op. cit., p. 42; S.K. Bhuyan, *Indian Historical Quarterly*, vol. V.

Actually, we do not find any clue in the text, which associates the event concerned with the Gupta kings or which shows that the poet ever attempted to delineate the war exploits of Raghu in honour of any Gupta king. As a matter of fact, no Gupta king figures in the text by name.[17] Moreover, latest researches have demolished the hitherto prevalent view that the poet belonged to the fifth century CE. Thus it will not be reasonable to connect the event concerned to the Gupta period. Nor do we find it possible to endorse fully the view of Walter Ruben that it was "sequel to the artistic inscriptions in honour of similar victories of earlier rulers and a sequel to the tradition of world conquerors, for this ideal of conquest had been held up to every Indian prince for a thousand years."[18] This statement, in fact, questions the authenticity of Kālidāsa's statements about Raghu's conquest. Judging by the data available in the text we do not find it relevant. The actual period during which Raghu undertook his campaign against the king of Prāgjyotiṣa has been discussed in the para following the next.

The present writer does not agree with B.C. Law and Ajay Mitra Sastri[19] who have suggested that Raghu met the Kirātas in the eastern valley of Brahmaputra. It is also said that they either fled away after Raghu approached towards them or were defeated in a battle with him. They no doubt had their settlements in the Brahmaputra Valley as evidenced by a number of literary sources, but the Kirātas whom Kālidāsa refer to were one of those seven tribes, who were vanquished by the mighty conqueror in the mountain regions of the northern Himalaya (comprising Kashmir and Ladakh) and in

17. Op. cit., p. 42.

18. *GAKW*, p 23.

19. Cf. *India as Seen in the Bṛhat Saṁhitā of Varāhamihira* (Varanasi 1969), pp. 82-83.

the Tibet region. Moreover, after defeating them he came down to the plains and then proceeded towards the Brahmaputra Valley. Therefore, we do not find any basis to support the view that Raghu also conquered the Kirātas of Prāgjyotiṣa. The above statements can be amply substantiated by the evidences furnished by the author of the text[20] himself, as well as by D.C. Sircar[21] and B.S. Upadhyaya.[22]

On the basis of genealogical charts of Ikṣvāku kings of Ayodhyā in general and the lineage of Raghu[23] in particular, the antiquity of the episode concerned may fairly be pushed back to the pre-Rāmāyaṇic age, when Prāgjyotiṣa was known as a *mleccha* and an *asura* kingdom. The king conquered by Raghu possibly might have been a tribal belonging to this dynasty and having his settlement along with his followers in the hill region in the vicinity of Kāmākhyā or Gauhati with which sometimes Prāgjyotiṣa as a capital town is also identified. Kālidāsa no doubt sometimes touches upon the epic and Purāṇic details but Raghu's conquest was definitely undertaken during the period preceding the epic and Purāṇic ages because he flourished before the dawn of the age of *Rāmāyaṇa*.

To conclude, Raghu entered the kingdom of Prāgjyotiṣa or Kāmarūpa from the Himalayan region in the north in the pre-epic age and conquered it, but did not annex to his kingdom. The king was subsequently allowed to maintain his independent status within his own kingdom.

---

20. *Raghuvaṁśa*, IV, 76-80.
21. *Studies in the Geography of Ancient and Medieval India* (Delhi 1971), p. 200.
22. *IK*, pp. 62-63.
23. For details see the genealogical chart inserted in *Vālmīki-Rāmāyaṇa Kośa* (R.K. Rai, Varanasi, 1965, p. 136) in which Raghu figures as 21st in descent in direct line from Ikṣvāku, the first king of Ayodhyā.

19

Historicity of Bilhaṇa's Account of Vikramāditya's Invasion of Kāmarūpa*

THE historicity of Bilhaṇa's account of a western Cāḷukya ruler Vikramāditya's invasion of Kāmarūpa as provided in his *Vikramāṅkadevacarita*[1] can be examined in the light of the facts stated in the contemporary epigraphic records, standard historical books on ancient Indian history and other relevant sources.

Vikramāditya VI Tribhuvanamalla, the most striking personality among the rulers of the Cāḷukya dynasty and a valiant warrior, after having overrun Mithilā, Magadha, Aṅga and Vaṅga, vanquished his two contemporary rulers of the Pāla dynasty, Ratnapāla (*c.* CE 1030-53) of Kāmarūpa and Nāyapāla (*c.* CE 1041-72) of Gauḍa in course of his northern campaigns some time between CE 1050-53. Actually, this campaign was undertaken by him during the time of his father, Someśvara I (*c.* CE 1042-68), which coincides with Ratnapāla's time. Vikramāditya VI met with feeble opposition from the decadent Pāla monarchy. But, he along with his army was ultimately beaten back by Ratnapāla of Kāmarūpa. Consequently, they retreated and returned home by way of

---

* From *Shodhak*, vol. XXVI, pt. A, Sr. no. 76, 1997, pp. 3-5.

1. *Vikramāṅkadevacarita* ed. G. Bühler with Introduction (Bombay Sanskrit Series 1875, No. 14), Ch. III, v. 74 and Intro. pp. 23, 31; also ed. Pt. Ramavatar Sharma (2nd edn., Kāśī, 1927), Ch. III, vv. 73-75.

southern Kosala. This invasion, however, did not result in the loss of Kāmarūpa's territory. It was only the Cāḷukya's influences which was felt in remote parts of India. As a matter of fact, Vikramāditya VI after having accomplished his task as assigned to him by his father ascended the throne of Kalyāṇa (the ancient Cāḷukya capital in Kanarese district of Karnataka in the Dekkan or Dakṣiṇāpatha (established by his father in CE 1053) in CE 1076 and ruled up to CE 1126. The facts stated above can be confirmed by the statements of R.S. Tripathi,[2] R.G. Bhandarkar[3] and Bühler.[4]

S.L. Katare, while identifying Bilhaṇa's Vikramāditya with Vikramāditya VI, a Cāḷukya ruler of Kalyāṇa, supports this view that he was defeated by Ratnapāla of Kāmarūpa.[5]

The Baṛgāon copper-plate grant[6] and Sualkuchi copper-plate grant of Ratnapāla[7] bear an eloquent testimony to the fact that the master of the Dekkan sustained discomfiture at the hands of Ratnapāla. H.C. Ray identifying the lord of the Dekkan as mentioned in the above grants with Cāḷukya

2. R.S. Tripathi, *History of Ancient India* (Delhi, 1985), pp. 361, 421-23.

3. R.G. Bhandarkar, *Early History of the Dekkan* (2nd edn., Delhi, 1979), p. 83.

4. Bühler, *Indian Antiquary* (hereinafter *Ind. Ant.*), vol. V, pp. 317, 324; vol. X, pp. 316-18. See also J.F. Fleet, *Ind. Ant.*, vol. VIII, p. 105 for reign periods of Someśvara I and Vikramāditya.

5. "The Cāḷukyas of Kalyāṇī" in *Indian Historical Quarterly*, vol. XVIII, 1941, pp. 11-34 and in *Indian Culture*, vol. IV, no. 1, pp. 43-52.

6. M.M. Sharma, *Inscriptions of Ancient Assam* (Gauhati, 1978), text, lines 34-35, p. 157; tr., p. 163, notes, p. 169; *Kāmarūpaśāsanāvalī* (first compiled and ed. by Padmanath Bhattacharya Vidyavinoda, 1868–1938, some 12 grants from Bhāskaravarman to Dharmapāla), tr. P.D. Chowdhury, R.K. Deva Sharma and D. Sharma and ed. D. Sharma (Gauhati, 1981), p. 83 (text); Hoernle, *JASB*, vol. LXVII, 1898, pt. I, no. 1, pp. 99-105.

7. Hoernle, *JASB*, LXVII, 1898, I, pp. 120-25, lines 11-12.

Vikramāditya VI (*c.* CE 1076–1126) corroborate epigraphic evidence that his invasion of Kāmarūpa took place during Ratnapāla's reign.[8] Hoernle also admits that Ratnapāla entered into with all those powers, who find mention in his grants. But he identifies the Gurjara king with the western Cāḷukya Jayasiṁha I Someśvara I. He has ascribed Ratnapāla to CE 1010–1050,[9] which is not acceptable. His statement, that his Baṛgāon was recorded during the 25th year of his reign, i.e. CE 1035,[10] also runs contrary to truth.

N.N. Vasu is perfectly correct in holding the view that Kāmarūpa was invaded by the ruler of Dekkan during the time of Ratnapāla; it eventually ended in fiasco.[11]

Since Bilhaṇa, a Kaśmīrī chronicler, flourished in the court Cāḷukya king Vikramāditya VI and enjoyed his patronage, he attempted to immortalize the exploits of his master by showing in the text victory over Ratnapāla, which has been contradicted by Bühler[12] himself.

Some scholars like K.L. Barua[13] and P.C. Choudhury[14] while

---

8. H.C. Ray, *Dynastic History of Northern India* (Calcutta, 1931), vol. I, pp. 250-51.
9. *JASB*, XVII, 1, p. 105.
10. Ibid., p. 102.
11. N.N. Vasu, *Social History of Kāmarūpa* (Calcutta, 1922), vol. I, p. 167.
12. *Vikramāṅkadevacarita*, Intro., 1 p. 23, 31.
13. K.L. Barua, Early *History of Kāmarūpa* (Shillong, 1933), p. 142. He wrongly places his between CE 1000–30 (Ibid., p. 149).
14. P.C. Choudhary, *The History of Civilization of the People of Assam to the Twelfth Century* CE), (Gauhati, 1959), pp. 253-54. The date, CE 1010-40 as suggested by him for Ratnapāla is not correct at all (Ibid., p. 251). In *Inscriptions of Ancient Assam* as referred to above Ratnapāla has been tentatively ascribed to the eleventh century CE (p. 35). In *Kāmarūpaśāsanāvalī* (p. 97) Ratnapāla has been placed between CE 930–80 which is totally wrong.

taking into account Vikramāditya's invasion of Kāmarūpa during his father's time (between CE 1050-53) before his accession (in CE 1076) as simply being guided by the actual period of his reign (CE 1076–1126) and the tentative chronology of Pāla rulers, which does not fit in the accepted chronology in ancient Indian context, have mistakenly synchronized the event concerned with the time of Harṣapāla (CE 1080-95). They are of the opinion that he was the contemporary of Cāḷukya ruler Vikramāditya VI of Kalyāṇa, as referred to by Bilhaṇa, and not Ratnapāla, which, on the weight of evidence, can fairly be disputed.

20

Indian Society and Culture During Medieval Period*

DURING the Sultanate period (CE 1206–1526) the Turks and Afghans virtually formed the ruling class or represented the nobility. These foreigners constituted an exclusive ruling oligarchy or aristocracy. Throughout the thirteenth century the Turks monopolized power and played the role of the leader of the Muslim community in Asia. The Indian Musalmans were excluded not only from a share in the power but also from the state service. As a result of the Turkish monopoly of authority, towards the end of the thirteenth century a large number of Muslim refugees entered India from the Central Asian countries and swelled the rank of the ruling class. This led to the fusion of the Muslims of different races and nationalities. Inter-marriages proved to be one of the contributory factors in the process of their fusion and commingling. The converted Muslim population gradually began to increase with the expansion of the Turkish dominion and authority. It consisted mostly of Hindus of low castes who for various reasons had abandoned religion of their forefathers and turned Muslims. The Indian Muslims were neither admitted into the aristocracy of the conquerors or ruling class nor were given a share of their social and economic privileges. No Indian Musalman was appointed to a high post throughout the so-called Slave period. However, with the

---

* From *An Introduction to General Foundation Course* (Manipur University, Imphal), 1999, pp. 52-68.

advent of the rule of the Khaljis the whole socio-political scenario underwent tremendous changes. The Turks began to loose their monopoly of power and a new chapter was opened in the medieval history of India by adopting the policy of associating Indian converts with the administration. The credit for this goes to Alauddin Khalji (1296–1316). As a matter of fact, it was he who introduced the policy of appointing Indian Musalmans to some of the important posts. In the time of Feroz Tughluq (1351-88) Khwaja Jahan, a brāhmaṇa converted to Islam, became prime minister. From the middle of the fourteenth century the Indian Muslims began to have a share in the state service to some extent.

During the period concerned the Muslim population was divided into two categories, namely men of the sword and men of the pen. Those who belonged to the former category were soldiers and were mostly of foreign origin. They were graded into *khān, malik, amīr, sipahsālār,* etc. This was a descending hierarchy in which the Khan occupied the highest place. Those who belonged to the latter category were mostly non-Turk, foreigners or their descendants. The most important section in this group was that of the ecclesiastics or theologians who were styled as the Ulema. They were a highly influential class and were consulted by the Sultan and his ministers not only on important points of law but also on matters of state policy. They exercised preponderant influence on the government and the rank and file of the Muslim society. Alauddin Khalji was the first Sultan to carry out the administrative policy in disregard of their advice. He had scant regard for the spirit of the Islamic law. But his successors blindly followed their advice on all political and administrative matters which sometimes proved to be detrimental to the interest of other religious groups.

The lowest strata of the Muslim society during the said period was composed mainly of the artisan, the shopkeeper, the clerk and the petty trader. The slaves may also be included in this group. Every king or noble and every well-to-do men owned slaves who were employed in household work and in other work.

The Hindus formed the vast majority of the population. Before the advent of the Turks they were rulers and in possession of the entire country. Even during the Sultanate period the departments of revenue and finance were manned by them. The *khuls, chaudharīs* and *muqaddams* were all Hindus. During the Turko-Afghan rule of about three-and-a-half centuries a considerable number of the upper and middle class Hindus were deprived of employment in state service, civil and military. Socially, politically and religiously the Hindus had to suffer during this period. They were not only deprived of their position as rulers, ministers, governors and commanders of troops, but were also treated contemptuously. The Turkish Sultans and their principal followers created havoc by compelling the proud chiefs of the Hindu families to give their daughters in marriage to them and by forcibly converting them to Islam. The perpetual humiliation and the religious persecution of the Hindus greatly affected their social position and family honour.

The Hindu society during the period concerned was basically caste-ridden. The Hindus were actually compelled under the Turkish rule to make their caste rules more rigorous and rigid. The child marriage became common owing to continuous practice of the Turkish Sultans to marry Hindu girls. Seclusion of women became a general practice in the upper and middle class Hindu families. Widow remarriage was unthinkable in those days except among low caste people. The condition of the Hindus in general and the women in particular during the Turkish rule was not good. The annals of the period are replete with instances of ill-treatment, religious persecution and social exploitation of the Hindus at the hands of Turko-Afghan rulers.

During the Mughal rule (1526–1761) the population also was not homogeneous. The Hindus, who formed the great majority, were divided into classes and castes. The upper classes of them belonged mostly to the Rājpūt, brāhmaṇa, kāyastha and vaiśya castes. They did not inter-dine or intermarry among themselves. The Rājpūts as a rule belonged to a class of warriors. They held high ranks as *mansabdār*s in the imperial service. The brāhmaṇas were engaged in priestly profession and some of them like Gujarātī Nāgars took to the study of Persian and were employed as officers. Under the later Mughals a few members of the class were appointed even as governors of provinces. The kāyasthas were engaged largely as clerks, secretaries (*munśī*s) and revenue officers. The vaiśyas formed the mercantile community. Some of the lower caste Hindus in Bengal and certain other parts had been converted into Islam and some high caste Hindus in the Punjab and Kashmir had been compelled almost in the same manner to abandon their ancestral religion. Several new sub-castes had come into existence during this period, such as the Kāzī, the Toshkhānī and Āghā among the brāhmaṇas of Kashmir, *munśī*s among those of Gujarat, Qanungo and Raizādā among the Kāyasthas, and Bakhśīs and Mehtās among the first three higher castes in several parts of the country. The caste system among the Hindus was as much rigorous and rigid during this period as it was during ancient periods. The Jaina and Buddhist societies were also not free from the social distinction. However, the rigidity of the caste system of the Hindus was conspicuous by its absence among them.

The Mohammedans were divided into two sections, viz. those who had come from Arabia, Persia and other countries for employment or trade, and those who were converts from the indigenous Hindu population or descendants of early converts. The number of the latter class was fairly large. Besides the Arabs, the Persians, the Turks, the Mongolians and the Uzbeks, there were some Abyssinians and Armenians. All the Muslims, whether Indian or foreign, were divided into two sects, the Sunnis and the Shias. They formed a great majority of the Muslim population. Among the Indian Muslims many still retained their class affinities with the corresponding groups in Hinduism from which they had sprung.

Although there were several other religious communities, such as the Parsis in Gujarat and Bombay, Christians on the west coast, especially in Cochin-Travancore and the foreign European trading community in several parts of the country, the subcontinent was mainly peopled by the indigenous Hindus and Indian and foreign Muslims, who were found living side by side and working together at the Mughal court. However, the antagonism between the two major communities (Hindus and Muslims) continued to exist throughout the Mughal period. The religious toleration granted by Akbar the Great to the Hindus was stubbornly opposed by the rank and file of the Muslim population. The Muslims conscious of their dominant position were generally arrogant and hostile to the Hindu religious beliefs and way of life. However, during the tolerant reigns of Akbar and Jehangir the Hindus enjoyed complete religious freedom and some temples dedicated to their deities were also built. The Muslims though opposed to idolatry worshipped the local Hindu deities in the rural areas.

The slavery continued to exist. Eunuchs were freely bought and sold, and although Akbar had prohibited it, the prisoners of war were similarly converted into slaves and compelled to embrace Islam.

Unlike in the ancient period the women of the Mughal age did not enjoy a respectable position in society. *Purdāh* system and child marriage had become common on account of the influence of Islam and conduct of Muslim rulers and nobles. Except those of the lower classes, Hindu women did not move out of their houses. The Muslims observed *purdāh* much more strictly than the Hindus. On account of early marriage there were many widows in our society and they were not allowed to remarry. Polygamy was common among Musalmans. Although Hinduism did not prohibit polygamy, monogamy was by and large prevalent as a rule among the Hindus. Only the Hindu ruling classes were exception to this practice. There were many Hindu women of outstanding ability and exceptional calibre during this period, notably Rānī Durgāvatī of Goṇḍwānā (a brave soldier and a capable administrator), Rānī Karṇāvatī, Mīrābāī, Tārā Bāī, etc. Among the Muslims Nūr Jahān, Mumtāz Mahal, Cānd Bībī, Jahānārā, Rauśanārā, etc. played an important part in the affairs of that time.

Agriculture provided the means of livelihood to a vast majority of the people. Besides the agriculturists who were the producers, there were industrial workers and traders, the nobles and officers of the civil and military departments, professional and religious classes, servants, slaves and beggars. The middle-class people consisting of professional classes and ordinary state employees were fairly well off. The upper and middle-class merchants were also economically prosperous. Skilled workers earned sufficient to lead a decent life, but the condition of the unskilled workers, menial servants and low shop-keepers deteriorated from the time of Akbar to that of Aurangzeb, and worsened further indeed during the days of the later Mughal emperors. During the reign of Aurangzeb agriculture, industry, and trade were badly affected because of his incessant wars and the inefficiency of the administration.

The *bhakti* movement was a watershed in the religio-cultural history of the Sultanate period. *Bhakti* means worship of a personal god through love and devotion. Its doctrine is very old among the Hindus. It is well expounded in the *Bhagavad-Gītā* and the Upaniṣads. But this movement was revived with considerable force during this period. The movement practically began in the twelfth century but gained momentum during the fifteenth and sixteenth centuries. The religious leaders or reformers belonged to southern, northern, western and eastern India. One of their primary objectives was to reform Hinduism. They raised their voice against distinctions of caste by birth, idol-worship, untouchability, elaborate rituals, useless religious ceremonies and paraphernalia, and many other evil practices that had crept into Hinduism. Their another equally important object was to bring about reconciliation between Hinduism and Islam and to foster friendly relation between the followers of the two religions. They preached the unity or oneness of God and equality or brotherhood of man and regarded God as very loving and merciful. They (the *bhakta*s or devotees of a personal god) strongly advocated the worship of a personal god by dances, music and religious songs and emphasized that the *bhakti* or true devotion and complete surrender to God alone lead to salvation.

The earliest exponent of the doctrine of *bhakti* was Rāmānuja (1060–1118). He was born in a brāhmaṇa family in a village in the vicinity of Madras and spent his youth at Kañjīvaram which was a great centre of Vaiṣṇava worship. In the early years of the twelfth century he preached Vaiṣṇavism, i.e. devotion to Lord Viṣṇu, and laid emphasis on *bhakti* as the sole means of salvation. He treated all human beings as equal. Nimbārka, who was a contemporary of Rāmānuja, belonged to the south but passed most of his times in Brajabhūmi (Mathurā) in the north. His preached the worship of Kṛṣṇa and Rādhā. Madhva (1199–1278) who was born at Kalyāṇapur in the Udipī district of South Kanara, was a devotee of Viṣṇu. He rejected the qualified monism of Rāmānuja. His ideals were based on the *Bhāgavata Purāṇa.* Many other Vaiṣṇava teachers spread the *bhakti* cult among the people in the south.

Another celebrated reformer was Rāmānanda. He was born in a Kanyākubja brāhmaṇa family of Allahabad. He flourished in the last quarter of the fourteenth or the first half of the fifteenth century. He mostly lived in Benares. It was through him that the *bhakti* movement spread far and wide in north India and became very popular. He was the first Hindu reformer to preach in the language of the people, i.e. Hindustānī. He regarded God as a loving father and worshipped Him under the name of Rāma. He was opposed to caste distinctions. He preached the doctrine of *bhakti* to the people of all castes. He had twelve principal disciples one of the whom was Kabīra, a weaver by profession. He had a large number of followers who belonged to his school. Vallabhācārya, a Telugu brāhmaṇa of southern India, was a renowned Vaiṣṇava saint. He was born in 1479 near Benares where his parents had settled in course of their pilgrimage to northern India. He was a distinguished exponent of the Kṛṣṇa cult.

One of the notable exponents of *bhakti* cult was Kabīra, who flourished towards the close of the fifteenth century. He was the most famous disciple of Rāmānanda. His early life is shrouded in mystery. There are different stories about his origin. Whatever may be the fact, it is almost certain that he spent most of his life at Benares. He stood for a compromise or harmony between Hinduism and Islam. He preached the unity and brotherhood of the Hindus and the Muslims. He raised a voice of protest against the distinctions of caste, idol-worship, rites and ceremonies, hypocrisy, brāhmaṇa supremacy, etc. His preachings had far-reaching effects on both the Hindus and Muslims of northern India.

Guru Nānak, the founder of the Sikh religion, was born of Khatrī parents in 1469 at the village of Talwaṇḍī (modern Nankānā Sāhib) at a distance of about 35 miles to the south-west of Lahore (west Punjab). At the age of thirty, he became a saint and travelled almost all over the country preaching his cult of *bhakti*. He like Kabīra preached harmony between Hinduism and Islam. He preached the gospel of universal toleration. He vehemently opposed the caste system, idolatry and untouchability. He also denounced the evil customs, superstition, external formalities, religious fanaticism, dogmatism, etc. of both the Hindus and Muslims. He laid emphasis on the unity of God. He stood for devotion to one single God. He was the reviver of the pure monotheistic doctrine of the Upaniṣads. He had both Hindu and Muslim disciples. During the closing years of his life he setted at Kartārpur (Ḍerā Bābā Nānak) in the Jalandhar Doab where he died in 1538.

Another preacher or leader of the *bhakti* movement was Nāmadeva of Maharashtra. He flourished in the first half of the fifteenth century. Like other reformers of the age, he preached the unity of God and opposed image-worship and priestly ritualism. He believed that one could attain salvation only through love of God. His followers belonged to all castes and classes, including a few Muslim converts to Hinduism.

Caitanya or Gauraṅg Mahāprabhu was the greatest Vaiṣṇava saint and reformer. He was born in 1485 at Nāḍiā (Bengal) in a learned brāhmaṇa family. At the age of twenty-four he renounced the world, became a saṁnyāsī and spent the rest of his life in preaching the doctrine of love and devotion to Kṛṣṇa. He sang songs in praise of God and held *kīrtana*s. He believed that "through love and devotion, song and dance, a state of ecstasy could be produced in which the personal presence of God would be realized." He spent eighteen years in Orissa and six years in Vṛndāvana, Gaur and other places. His disciples came from all castes. One of them was a Muslim. He left behind an indelible imprint of his personality on the masses of both eastern and northern India. The Caitanya cult of Vaiṣṇavism became very popular. His name is still very popular in Bengal and millions of people worship him as an incarnation or *avtāra* of Śrī Kṛṣṇa. He died in 1533 at the age of forty-eight.

The *bhakti* movement spread in different parts of the country. Its effects were of far-reaching importance. It reduced the distinctions of caste and birth. The low caste people began to have a feeling of self-respect. The supremacy of brāhmaṇas and domination of priests were weakened. The reformers preached in the local language which gave a great impetus to the development of vernaculars. The conversions to Islam declined. The leaders of this movement succeeded in achieving their first objective which was to bring about the simplification of worship and liberalization of the traditional caste rule, but failed to realize the second objective which was the Hindu-Muslim unity. Neither the Turko-Afghan rulers nor the Muslim community accepted their creed. However, it cannot be denied that the bitterness of relations between the Hindus and the Muslims was reduced to a considerable extent through this movement and both began to live amicably, though it was a transitional phase.

The medieval age witnessed spectacular progress in the field of art. The Turkish Sultans adopted both Central Asian and indigenous (Indian) styles of architecture. The distinctive features of the former were the domes, lofty towers or minarets, the arches, etc. and that of the latter flat roofs, open courts, columns, shafts and pillars, decorative elements, carvings, etc. It is worthy to note that early conquerors almost invariably built their mosques, palaces and even tombs out of the materials of Hindu and Jaina temples which they had callously destroyed. The Sultans sometimes converted the Hindu and Jaina temples into mosques by demolishing their flat-roofs and providing domes and minarets in their places. One feature common to Hindu and Islamic arts with reference to temple and mosques was the open court encompassed by chambers or colonnades.

The first architectural monument erected by Qutab-ud-din Aibak (1192–1210) was the well-known Quwat-ul-Islam mosque (or Qutub mosque) at Delhi which was begun in 1195 and finished in 1199. It was built on the plinth of a Hindu temple and out of the materials of many Hindu shrines. Most of the columns, shafts and capitals of this mosque were originally parts of Hindu temples and were hurriedly adapted to the needs of a Muslim mosque. The images and carvings on the columns, shafts and capitals were defaced to suppress the fact. The next mosque built by him at Ajmer is known as Aḍhāī (or Ḍhāī) Din kā Jhoṅpaṛā. The building was originally a Sanskrit college and temple built by a great emperor, Vigraharāja Viśāladeva. The upper parts of it were demolished and domes and arches were erected. One can notice countless human figures on the pillars with defaced faces and hands and feet. The construction of famous Qutub Mīnār at Delhi was begun by him and completed by Iltutmish (1211–1236). It is essentially Islamic in form or design. Balban (1265–1287) built his palace known as the Red palace. His tomb at Delhi is purely Muslim in execution. The arch at the entrance of the tomb is the best so far erected by the Turks in the country. Alauddin Khaljī (1296–1316) was a great builder and erected many buildings. Two of his buildings known as Jamāit Khānā Masjid at the shrine of Niẓāmuddīn Auliyā and the famous Alāī Darwāẓā at the Qutub Mīnār are notable. Both these show a preponderance of Muslim architectural ideas. The buildings of the Tughluq period do not possess that splendour which characterized those of the so-called Slave and Khaljī dynasties. They are simple, formal, prosaic and even austere. The important specimens of the Tughluq architecture are the tomb of Tughluq Shah, the city of Tughluqabad and Feroz-Shah. The Sayyids and the Lodis tried to revive the splendour and the grace of the Khaljī period but they attained only qualified success. The best of the Paṭhān Building is the Moṭh kī Masjid built by the minister of Sikandar Lodi (1488–1517). This is considered to be the finest specimen of the architecture of the Lodis.

In the field of architecture each province evolved a distinctive style of its own. The buildings erected by the Sultans are characterized by a synthesis of Hindu and Muslim architectural ideas. The shrine namely the tomb of Rukn-i-Ālam built by Ghiyās-ud-dīn Tughluq at Multan some time between 1320 and 1324 is considered as "one of the most splendid memorials ever erected in the honour of the dead." The artists of Bengal possessed inborn sense of art. The architecture was characterized by the pointed arches on short pillars and the Muslim adaptation of the traditional Hindu temple style of curvilinear cornices and of beautifully carved Hindu symbolic decorative designs like the lotus. The ruins of these buildings are found at Gaur or Lakhanauti, Tribeni and Pandua. The earliest specimens of Bengal style of architecture are the tomb and mosque of Zafar Khan Ghazi which were built mostly out of the materials from the Hindu temples. The capital city of Ahmedabad founded by Ahmad Shah was enriched by a number of lofty buildings which were built largely out of the materials of the old temples and buildings. One of the best examples of the Gujarat style is the well-known Jami Masjid at Ahmedabad and erected by Ahmad Shah in 1411. It has fifteen domes which are supported on two pillars. There are two remarkable mosques at Dhār, the ancient capital of the Kingdom of Mālwā, built out of the materials of old Hindu buildings. Both the mosques betray Hindu influence, as pillars of tombs are Hindu in form. But the buildings of Māṇḍu which were established as a capital by the local sultans are peculiarly Muslim in design and execution and bear a close resemblance to those of Delhi. In the valley of Kashmir the local Sultans adopted the old Hindu tradition of stone and wooden architecture. There was a harmonious blending of the Hindu and Muslim architectural styles. Some of the important buildings there belong to the reign of Zain-ul-Abidīn (1420–1470). The Bahamanī Sultans (1347–1526) of the Deccan were patrons of art in general and lovers of architecture in particular. The style of architecture adopted by them was a mixture of Indian, Turkish and Persian elements. The mosques at Gulbarga and Bīdar are beautiful specimens of this art, but the most remarkable Deccan architecture is found at Bījāpur. The magnificent mausoleum of Muhammad Adil Shah at Bījāpur popularly known as Gola Gumbaz betrays the influence of Turkish art.

The art of painting and decoration did not receive much encouragement at the hands of Sultans and the Muslim nobility because of the Quranic prohibition. However, there are some fragmentary evidences about the ornamental designs painted on walls or engraved on furniture, arms and saddles and embroidered on flags and costumes. Besides, ornamental pottery and metal work were well developed. Inlaid metal basins, porcelains and profusely decorated brass and silver pots were in the royal household and also in the houses of the nobles and high officials.

The Hindus had already attained perfection in the fields of architecture and sculpture before the advent of the Turks. The medieval specimens of their art in northern India are found in Rajasthan. Most of the rulers of Mewar were patrons of art and architecture. Rāṇā Kumbhā erected numerous forts and other buildings. The most beautiful and well known among them are the fort of Kumbhalgaṛh and the Kīrti Stambha or Jaya Stambha (pillar of victory). It is built partly of red sand-stone and partly of white marble and is enriched by numerous images of Hindu gods and goddesses with inscriptions engraved at the bottom of each. There is another pillar at Chittor which is embellished with beautiful carving and lattice work. At Amber, near Jaipur, there are ruins of old buildings belonging to this period and also in several other states of

Rajasthan. The rulers of the Vijayanagara empire were celebrated for their patronage of art. They built council chambers, palaces, public offices, temples and other splendid buildings which excited the admiration of foreign travellers. Kṛṣṇadeva Rāya (1509-29), the last great Hindu ruler of southern India, erected many monuments of artistic beauty at Hampī, the capital of the Vijayanagara kingdom. It is striking to note that many buildings, temples, etc. at the capital city are still in excellent state of preservation. Some monuments are, of course, in ruins there as well as in surrounding regions.

The Hindu architecture of the Sultanate period seems to have remained uninfluenced by Islamic ideas. It was only after the advent of the Mughals that the Hindu architects and artists came under the influence of Islamic art.

The Mughals were also great builders. By the time of Babur's invasion of India, the Central Asian architecture with the domes, the lofty minarets, the arches and the vaults, which had been brought to India by the early Turkish invaders, had flourished for over three centuries side by side with the indigenous Hindu architecture which was characterized by roofs, narrow columns, the arches, etc. The buildings of Babur's time include a large mosque in Kābulībāgh at Panipat and Jama Masjid at Sambhal in Ruhelkhaṇḍ, both built in 1526. During his time (1526-30) another mosque was erected by his general, Abul Baqi at Ayodhyā by demolishing a Hindu temple (so-called Rāma temple) which had been in existence there since ancient time. This mosque is now almost in ruins. None of these possess any special architectural significance. Humayun (1530-40 and 1555-56), though equally fond of architecture did not leave a prominent architectural monument to his credit. The two mosques built by him, one at Agra and the other at Fatehabad in Hisar are in ruins and do not show any originality of design or execution. Probably the best example of the Indo-Muslim architecture in the country before the reign of Akbar is the mausoleum of Shershāh (1540-45) which was built by himself at Sahasram in Bihar. The building is Muhammedan in design but its interior is embellished with Hindu corbelling and horizontal architraves. Shershah constructed another important building namely the Purānā Kilā on the site of Humayun's palace at Delhi called Dīn Panāh which he had razed to the ground. Only a part of the Purānā Kila has escaped the ravage of time.

A large number of magnificent monuments, splendid edifices, etc. were erected during the reign of Akbar the great (1556–1605). He extended his patronage to the artists in his court. The style of architecture evolved by him represented a fusion of the Hindu and Muslim styles which may be called the national Indian style of architecture. The fusion of two different styles was rendered possible because of his unflinching faith in the fundamental equality of all religions. The greatness of his personality, broad religious outlook, magnanimity and catholicity find reflection also in the monuments which were erected by his order at Agra, Fatehpur Sikri, Allahabad, Lahore, Attock and other places. The walls of Agra Fort, nearly 70 ft. high, are one-and-a-half miles in circumference, and are entered by two gateways that on the western side being known as the Elephant Gate as its main archway was flanked by two stone statues of elephants and the other, which is smaller, is called Amir Singh Gate. Within the enclosure Akbar erected more than 500 buildings of red sandstone. Many of these were pulled down by Shah Jahan who replaced them by white marble pavilions. The most important buildings of Akbar's time inside the fort are the Akbarī Mahal with the bastion and the Jahāngīrī Mahal intended for the heir apparent and his family. These palaces are made of red sand stone. The Jahāngīrī Mahal is Hindu in design and ornamentation. The greatest architectural achievement of Akbar is his new capital at Fatehpur Sikri crowned with fine buildings, the prominent among which are Dīwān-i-Khās, Dīwān-i-Ām, Panch Mahal, Mariam's palace, Jodhā Bāī's palace and Bīrbal's palace, Ibādat Khānā (house of worship bearing the stamp of the Hindu, Buddhist, Jaina and Muslim style of architecture), etc. Outside the enclosure stands the Jami Mosque with its lofty portal known as the Bulanda Darwāẓā. Inside the enclosure of the mosque lies the tomb of Shaikh Salim Chishti which is built of white marble. Most of these buildings reveal mixed style which is partly Muslim and mainly Hindu in character. It took about eleven years (1569-80) to complete Fatehpur Sikri. The Lahore Fort was constructed at almost the same time as the Agra Fort. The buildings inside were similar to the Jahāngīrī Mahal at Agra. Elephants and lions figure in the brackets and peacock in the friezes from which it may reasonably be inferred that Hindu craftsmanship predominated. The Allahabad Fort was built at a later time and many of its buildings including its inner walls have disappeared. Akbar built several other buildings the notable among which are the fort of Attock, a mosque at Amber and some other places.

The new style of architecture evolved by Akbar produced a profound effect on buildings all over the country including those of the Rājpūt rulers of Rajasthan. The palaces built during the reign of Akbar at Amber, Bikaner, Jodhpur, Orcha and Datic bear unmistakable influence of the Mughal style of architecture. Even Hindu temples could not escape the nationalization effect of Akbar's architecture. Hindu temples at Vṛndāvana show clearly that some of their features were borrowed from the contemporary style of the Mughals.

Jahangir (1605-27) was more devoted to miniature painting than to architecture. Nevertheless, he erected a few buildings which are of exceptional merit. The tomb of Itmād-ud-daulā at Agra built by Nūr Jahān is the most remarkable building of the reign built of white marble. The next notable building is the mausoleum of Akbar at Sikandrā which was erected under Jahangir's supervision between 1605 and 1612. The style of the building bears resemblance to that of the Buddhist *vihāras*.

The Mughal architecture reached the zenith of its excellence in the time of Shah Jahan (1627-58). His reign was the golden age of Mughal architecture. He erected magnificent buildings at Agra, Delhi, Lahore, and several other places. He pulled down many of Akbar's red sandstone structures in Agra and rebuilt them of white marble. Inside the Agra Fort he built Dīwān-i-Ām (the Hall of Public Audience), Dīwān-i-Khās (the Hall of Private Audience), the Khās Mahal, the Śīśa Mahal, the Motī Masjid (Pearl Mosque), etc. The Jama Masjid at Agra is a notable piece of architecture. He also built Mussamman Burja, a beautiful octagonal structure, of marble in the fort of Agra from where he could see the beauty of the Taj. The most famous of his buildings at Agra is Taj Mahal. This marble mausoleum was built by him in memory of his beloved wife, Mumtāẓ Mahal. It took twenty-two years (1631-53) to complete it. Twenty thousand workmen were employed to construct it. It is rightly looked upon as one of the architectural wonders of the world. V.A. Smith's view that it is "the product of a combination of Europe and Asiatic genius" is no longer accepted by historians. Percy Brown observes that "while the structural portions seem to have been principally in the hands of Muhammadans, the decoration was mainly the work of Hindu craftsmen. The building though mainly Persian in design, contains some features of Hindu architecture and decorations." In 1638, Shah Jahan founded a new city of Shahjahanabad (present Delhi) and built therein a palace-fort which is popularly known as the Lāl Qilā or Red Fort. Inside the fort many beautiful structures of white marble were erected which include Dīwān-i-Ām, Dīwān-i-Khās, the Motī Mahal, and Raṅga Mahal. The buildings are surmounted with domes and hanging balconies, and these were ornamented and lavishly decorated with perforated screens and mural paintings. At a little distance from the Red Fort in Delhi he built the famous Jama Masjid. He erected the hall of forty pillars and many other buildings inside the fort at Lahore. He built a magnificent mausoleum over Jahangir's tomb on the right bank of the Rāvī, about four miles from Lahore. After Shah Jahan's death the Mughal architecture began rapidly to degenerate. His successor Aurangzeb (1658–1707) took little interest in the development of this art. The Bādshāhī mosque at Lahore, though of great size, is a poor imitation of the Jami mosque at Delhi. After the emperor's death the style of the art completely deteriorated and the buildings that were erected during the first half of the eighteenth century revealed bankruptcy of taste and poverty of design, finish and decoration.

The Quranic precept of abhoring images of living beings no doubt stood as a barrier in the way of the growth of the art of sculpture. However, Akbar not being an orthodox Musalman encouraged this art. During his time the statues of Jaimal and Fatha, the Rājpūt heroes of Chittor, seated on an elephant, were carved out of stone and placed at the gate of Agra Fort. The elephant gate of Fatehpur Sikri is still guarded by the mutilated figures of two collosal elephants. Jahangir too had the taste for this art. The two life-size marble statues of Rāṇā Amar Singh and his son Karaṇa Singh were made and erected in the palace garden at Agra below the Jharokhā-Darśana. We have no evidence to show that Shah Jahan encouraged this art. Aurangzeb being an orthodox Sunni Musalman was deadliest opposed to this art, and hence ordered the statues at Agra and Delhi to be broken to pieces and stone elephants of Fatehpur Sikri and Agra to be defaced and damaged. The art, therefore, disappeared for want of patronage. The Mughals were lovers of decorative relief carving and embellished their buildings with this art which on account of their patronage reached a high level of excellence. The marble carving on the walls of the uppermost terrace of Akbar's tomb at Sikandrā is of 52 different varieties and of exquisite beauty. Besides, the building is embellished with representation of plants, flowers, etc. and a conventional vase design. Relief carving was supposed to be indispensable in high class Mughal buildings. The marble screen work carved in stone was equally fashionable. The marble screen work at Shaikh Salim Chisti's tomb at Fatehpur Sikri is a notable example of this art.

In spite of the Quranic prohibition, the Mughal emperors loved painting. The fusion of two styles of this art, Indian and Persian, began to take place from the time of Akbar onwards. The most important stage in its evolution was reached between 1569 and 1585 when he got the walls of his palace at Fatehpur Sikri embellished with the masterpieces produced by the joint labours of the Hindu and Persian painters. Thirteen out of seventeen leading artists of Akbar's court were Hindus. Abul Fazl speaks highly of their art. He writes "More than a hundred painters became famous masters of the art, and attained perfection" (*Āin-i-Akbarī,* vol. 1, p. 107). This is specially true of the Hindus. Akbar created separate department of painting with Khwaja Abus Samad as it head. His deep interest led to the creation of a school of painting which may be called the National Indian School of painting. This school of painting continued to flourish in the reign of Jahangir who was well known for his exemplary aesthetic taste. Both Hindu and Muslim painters adorned his court. The Mughal school of miniature painting reached its climax under Jahangir who was the soul and spirit of the art. Shah Jahan continued his ancestral patronage but he did not have the same passion for painting which his father and grandfather had. He was more devoted to architecture than to painting. Therefore, the art of painting fell from the high standard that it had previously attained. The number of court painters was reduced and the quality of their production too suffered. The court painters in the time of Shah Jahan were both Hindus and Muslims. His death struck a blow to the art of painting. Aurangzeb being an orthodox Musalman was opposed to the pictorial art which declined rapidly for lack of court patronage. He defaced the paintings in the palaces at Bījāpur and Golconḍā and white-washed the figures in Akbar's mausoleum at Sikandrā. In Rājpūtānā, however, the art continued to flourish. It became known as the Rājpūt school of painting. Jaipur was one of its chief centres. A new school known as the Kangra School came into existence in the second half of the eighteenth century. The art of these schools is spoken highly of by competent critics.

The classical music and dance were also patronised by the Mughal rulers. Babur was skilled in the art of music and is said to have written a treatise on it. Humayun was equally interested in song. The classical Indian music received tremendous encouragement at the court of Akbar. There were altogether thirty-six musicians at his court, the prominent among whom were Tansen and Baiju Bawra. Jahangir inherited his father's taste for music; he maintained many first-rate musicians at his court and extended to them his royal patronage. There were six musicians at his court, and some dancing girls were also at his service. The two notable musicians at the court of Shah Jahan were Ram Das and Mahapatra. During the first ten years of his reign Aurangzeb like his predecessors extended his patronage to the musicians. He also maintained many good singers at his court. But later he, when advanced in age and began practising self-restraint and abstinence, dismissed the musicians from his court. The banishment of musicians from his court and the withdrawal of the royal patronage caused a great setback to the art. However, the tradition of classical Indian music and dance continued to flourish.

21

Trade and Commerce in Southern India

From the Persian, Arabic, Russian and Italian Travellers' Accounts of 13th to 15th Centuries*

THE present paper aims at providing a brief account of the development of trade and commerce in southern India from the thirteenth century to the beginning of the Portuguese period in the fifteenth century. The study of the subject under review is primarily based on the accounts of Persian, Arabian, Russian and Italian travellers. The voyages and travels to India preceding the Portuguese discovery of the Cape of Good Hope was, no doubt, extremely hazardous, an exceedingly assiduous task and glaringly full of uncertainties. That is why, the picture emerging from the travellers' accounts handed down to us alluding to the subject during the period concerned apparently appear to be very gloomy. Many Indian nomenclatures and appellations have not been properly identified in MS; many ideas are obscure; some explanations and illustrations are very sketchy and scanty and some details are incomplete and largely mixed with fabulous description lacking commendable accuracy. The confusion sometimes becomes worse confounded. Thus in order to overcome this difficulty I have placed my complete reliance on the first authentic classical commercial record popularly known as *The Periplus* of the first century CE which is as valuable a document as the journals of Marco Polo, Columbus and Vespucci. However, the

* From *Shodhak,* vol. XXVI, Pt. B, Sr. no. 77, 1997, pp. 99-104.

trustworthiness of the original accounts presented here can't be wholly denied and its paramount value for the general readers, researchers and scholars, from the point of view of conducting the preliminary investigation into the subject, can't be totally dismissed.

As early as the fifth century BCE Herodotus, a recognized Greek historian had emphatically pronounced that India is "the wealthiest country on the face of earth." The correctness of this assertion finds popular expression in the subsequent history of commerce. The growth of civilization and spread of culture in both the directions, the east and the west paved the way for the organized trading system and commercial intercourse that gradually developed in the succeeding periods. This also afforded an excellent opportunity for the travellers from diverse lands to get acquainted with natural history of and highly-prized luxuriant products and articles of commerce in India as well as to undertake explorations to find the shores and islands of the Indian sea for the purpose of carrying on the trade on a large scale. The growth of Indian ports, harbours and coastlines and the creation of an active merchant marine and trading vessels further facilitated and conditioned the development of trade and commerce. Trade was carried on to distant lands by exchanging the products. The memory of age-long understanding between Egypt, Arab, Persia, Greece, Rome and China on the one hand and India on the other provided further incentives for the opening of fresh avenues for starting extensive trade which was admittedly designed to amass the wealth and the fortunes. The trade was mainly carried on by sea and not over land. The common routes pursued by them were Red Sea, Persian Gulf, Gulf of Aden, eastern coast of Africa, Island of Madagascar, Zanzibar, etc.; especially the Arab traders departed from the Red Sea, then proceeded to Muscat and thence reached the coast of Malabar.

Development of Trade and Commerce

The account of the voyage undertaken by Marco Polo[1] — The father of modern geography and Venetian traveller in the thirteenth century (1271-94) — deserves our first attention here. His account is considered to be the manual of Asiatic geography. He set out on his journey in 1271 and after encountering various dangers and passing Cape Comorin sailed alone the coast of Malabar where he noticed the abundance of pepper, ginger, sapphires, emeralds, precious stones, topaz, the amethyst, etc. and the diamonds of Golcoṇḍā. According to him, the vessels from the coast of Malabar or Coromondel took twenty days in reaching the Islands of Madagascar and Zanguebar (Zanzibar) and three months in returning. Yule[2] further states that Marco Polo also describes the cinnamon (precious bark used for medicine) a valuable product of Malabar which was exported to Roman merchants. In Marco Polo's time one shipload of pepper used to go Alexandria, China and Rome. The pepper was one of the most important articles of lucrative trade and commerce between southern India and Roman Empire or between Venetian merchants and Indian merchants. Marco Polo further refers to the trade of Malabar in pearls, gold, silver, precious stones with Persian Gulf, "Irak," Khurasan and Rome. The ships from Malabar used to carry the local products to the Gulf of Aden and Egypt. The trade contact was both regular and intimate. "The commerce of India," Marco Polo found

1. Cf. *India in the Fifteenth Century being a Collection of Narratives of Voyages to India* (tr. into English and ed. R.H. Major, First published by the Hakluyt Society London, 1857, rpt. Delhi, 1974), pp. Introduction, 56, 315, 333.

2. *The Travels of Marco Polo*, II, pp. 49, 56, 315, 333, 3S9; III, XXV, Ref. to W.H. Schoff. *The Periplus of the Erythraean Sea* (hereafter as *The Periplus*), (London, 1912), pp. 84, 214, 227, 249; see also M. Edwardes, *A History of India* (Bombay, 1961), p. 93.

"stretching like one immense chain from the territories of Kublai Khan to the shores of the Persian Gulf and Red Sea." This is really one of the notable facts.

Marco Polo's statement can be further confirmed by the account of Ibn Battuta,[3] a celebrated Arabian traveller and indefatigable explorer, who visited India about the middle of the fourteenth century. He started in AH 725 = CE 1324 from his native land Tangier, reached Hindustan during the time of Muhammad Tughlak (1325-51) and left behind a very reliable account about his experience. He reached the distant ports of Calicut where he found Chinese junks (a flat-bottomed ship of large dimension used in China and Japan) awaiting. He also mentions Malabar's natural products, i.e. pepper, ginger and spices. The Chinese vessels brought costly gifts at Calicut and remained there for about three months. He highly speaks of the maritime habit of the people of Malabar coast. They captured all the vessels which attempted to pass their port without paying the toll. Both these accounts are remarkably perspicuous and accurate.

Abd-er-Razzak (1413-82) who set out on his journey as a Persian ambassador from Sultan of Herat to the Kingdom of Vijayanagara in AH 845 = CE 1442[4] further observes that Calicut was the chief and noble emporium in the southern Peninsula which like that of Ormuz (the Mouth of Persian Gulf) invited merchants from every city and every country. He found abundance of precious articles brought there from maritime

3. The account of his travels was translated by Prof. Lee from abridged Arabic manuscript and printed for the Oriental Translation Committee, London, 1829, cf. R.H. Major, op. cit., Introd., liv, lvi, lvii, lviii.

4. Narrative of the voyage of Abd-der-Razzak (AH 845 = CE 1442) was translated from Persian into French by M. Quairerncre. It was rendered into English with notes by R.H. Major, op. cit., pp. 13, 19.

countries, especially Abyssinia or Ethiopia, Zirbad and Zanzibar islands. Time to time ships arrived here from the shore of the House of God (Mecca) and other ports of the Hedjaz. From Calicut vessels laden with pepper continually sailed for Mecca. The inhabitants of Calicut were adventurous sailors. In its harbour all the desired articles of trade could be found.

So is the equally valuable account of the travels of Nicola Conti,[5] another celebrated Venetian traveller, who visited the interiors of India in the early part of the fifteenth century. In the province of Malabar he found ginger called by the natives cobobi, pepper, Brazil, woods, cinnamon known by the name of crassa, a larger kind of lac, etc. He refers to Calicut as a maritime city, eight miles in circumference and chief centre of trade in India.

A. Nikitin,[6] a Russian traveller who left on a long voyage to the kingdoms of the Deccan in the year 1470, elucidates that in the country of Calicut — a port for the whole Indian sea — ginger, colourplants, muscat, cloves, cinnamon, aromatic roots and many other spices can be procured at a very cheaper rate.

The above description of all the articles of trade and commerce as provided by the various travellers needs further verification, corroboration and elaboration. According to the classical source[7] the cinnamon (a precious bark or herb used

---

5. The Travels of Nicolo Conti was translated from the original of Poggio Bracciolini, with Notes, by J. Winter Jones, keeper of the printed books British Museum, cf. R.H. Major, op. cit., pp. 17-20.

6. The Travels of A. Nikitin was translated from the Russian with Notes by count Wiclborsky. It was first published in 1821 under the title of *Sofiyski Premennik* or *Sophian Chronicle*, vol. II, pp. 145-64. Refer to R.H. Major, op. cit., pp. 20f.

7. *The Periplus*, pp. 6, 82.

for medicinal purpose) was a very important article of trade with Roman merchants throughout the Malabar coast. The Egyptian inscription of queen Hatshepsut's expedition of fifteenth century BCE also refers to cinnamon wood as one of the marvels brought back to Egypt. This article further attracted both Greek and Roman merchants.

Watt[8] also refers to the cinnamon of Malabar coast as one of the valuable perennial herb used for medicine purpose. Both Schoff[9] and Watt[10] further elaborate that long pepper (in Sanskrit *pippalī*) which was known in comparatively recent times as black pepper — a perennial herb — was extensively cultivated from very early time in the forests of Travancore and Malabar of southern India. The trade of pepper with Persia, Rome, Egypt and China by sea goes to remote antiquity. The trade in this article was extensively carried on. The sailing of the Chinese junks to the Malabar coast probably began in the second century BCE and continued up to the period under discussion. The trade with Rome and Alexandria also in this article continued up to Marco Polo's time and beyond. Other articles like topaz, sapptives and amethyst (unidentified in MS.) according to *The Periplus*[11] were precious stones of Calicut. *The Periplus*[12] also says that the Dutch who purchased the pepper sold at Calicut in later centuries do not pay in cash for it but exchange for it many kinds of merchandize, such as cotton, opium, vermilion, quick silver, pepper, etc.

The letter from the king Zamorin of Calicut[13] to the king

8. *Commercial Products of India*, p. 313; cf. *The Periplus*, pp. 83-84.
9. *The Periplus*, pp. 194-95, 213-14.
10. Op. cit., p. 891.
11. Ibid., pp. 167. 226.
12. Ibid., p. 215.
13. Refer to *The Perlplus*, p. 227; see also for further reference, M. Edwardes, op. cit., pp. 143-51.

of Portugal carried by Vasco-da-Gama on his return from India bears an authentic testimony to the commercial importance of Calicut in south and its commercial intercourse with Portugal. The letter reads as follows:

> In my kingdom there is abundance of cinnamon, cloves, ginger, pepper and precious stones, what I seek from thy country is gold, silver, coral and scarlet.

Abd-er-Razzak[14] has also revealed this fact that the merchants from the country beyond the Ganges comprising the whole south-east peninsula — Schahrinou (Śivanur in the province of Bījāpur, 50 miles south-east from Dharwar in Karnataka), Bidjanagar (Vijayanagara), Kalbergah (Gulburgā), and Bīdar (Bedor) (both latter grouped in the province of present Karnataka) — used to visit Ormuz (a small island in the Persian Gulf), a vast emporium of whole world and brought here those rare and precious articles which could have been conveniently transported by sea. Traders from these countries already mentioned, frequently resorted to this place in exchange for the commodities which they usually brought. Bargains were made by money on exchange. For all objects, with the exception of gold and silver one tenth of their value was paid by way of duty. The author specifically mentions that the port of Vijayanagara was once the metropolis of a mighty Hindu empire.

A. Nikitin[15] in his account also refers to the trade of Kulburga (Gulbargā and Beuruk (Bīdar).[16] He informs us that particularly in Bīdar there was a trade in horses, goods, stuffs,

14. R.H. Major, op. cit., pp. 5-7; see also M. Edwardes, op. cit., pp. 119-24; Eliot and Dowson's *History of India as Told by its Own Historians*, vol. IV.

15. R.H. Major, op. cit., pp. 12-14.

16. Hamilton (*Description of Hindustan*, p. 105, quoted in R.H. Major, op. cit., p. 14) points out that Bidar was the chief town of the whole of Muhammedan Hindustan. →

silks and all sorts of other merchandize. Here practically all sorts of Indian goods were sold. As many as 20,000 horses were brought from Bīdar to "Shikhbaludin peratyr," a bazaar at Aladinand (20 *kros* distant) for sale. At this place a fair, perhaps the best throughout the land of Hindustan held once a year was largely frequented by traders from all parts of India. This place, "Shikhb-Aladin Peratyr" or bazaar Aladinand has not been clearly identified by the author. Stroef[17] deriving the authority from Ibn Battuta relates that the chief object of the latter in coming to Bengal was to see a great saint named "Shiekh Falal Oddin" who dwelt in the mountains of Karuru (?) adjoining the mountains of Tibet and was held in great veneration at that time. In his memory everything was brought and sold at the Aladinand bazaar. The accounts of the topography given by both Nikitin and Stroef are not only vague but at the same time wrong also. According to some reliable sources,[18] "Shikhbaladin Peratyr" or bazaar Aladinand was not in Bengal, this place was no other than present Malabar coast. The ancient capital of Kerala known as Vanji, or Karuvur or Karouru of Ptolemy or modern Parur or Karur, where Periyar River implies the Cochin backwaters, was a very busy trading centre as well as an important port. The saint of this name might have resided somewhere there or in western Tamil kingdoms in Medieval times.

→ "After the Muhommedan conquest the province of Beder was the Seat of the Bhamener dynasty of Deccan sovereigns whose capital was Kalbergoh (Gulbarga). Beder was formerly noted for works of tutenag inlaid in land with silver. Before the Mohammedan invasion it was the capital of Hindoo sovereignty. Near the ruins of the old Beder Ahmed Shah Bhamenee founded the city Ahmadabad, which he made his capital in place of Kalbergah and this is the modern Bedar."

17. Cf. R.H. Major, op. cit., pp. 12-13.

18. *The Periplus*, pp. 205-08; *Imperial Gazetteer of India*, vols XX, XXI; V.A. Smith, *The Early History of India*, pp. 340-41.

22

Trade and Commerce in Northern and Eastern India
From the Narratives of 16th and 17th Centuries Travellers*

THE present paper deals with the history of the development of both internal and external trade and commerce of northern and eastern India in the sixteenth and seventeenth centuries as described by the Dutch, Portuguese, English, Italian and French travellers. It is indeed a fact that some of the occasional blunders because of the unfamiliarity of the travellers with the Indian nomenclatures and vague topographical details can be noticed in their narratives, but at the same time we find that some of the statistical and historical data furnished in their commercial documents and reports are characterized by great minuteness, precision, accuracy and authenticity. All Indian appellations have been transliterated in such simple, clear and proper style that we hardly find any scope to doubt the credibility of their statements. However, somewhere as necessitated by the occasion and befitting to the context an attempt has been made to corroborate some details by similar references from other dependable contem-porary sources.

Francisco Pcisaert, a noted Dutch Sailor, after having transacted the business of the United East India Company at the Factory in Agra for seven years (1620-27) during the time of Jahangir observed in his most faithful commercial Report[1]

---

* From *Shodhak*, vol. XXVII, pt. A, Sr. no. 79, 1998, pp. 1-7.

(published between 1626 and 1627) based on his actual experiences and personal observations that in Agra there was a Nakhasa, a great market, where in the morning horses, camels, oxen, cotton goods and many other commodities were sold. On the other side of the river Jamunā there was a city named "Sikandrā" through which passed all the merchandize brought from "Purop" (i.e. *pūraba* or the east) and "Benga Ian Purop." The author has used the term to include the Mughal province of Allahabad, Bihar, Orissa and Bengal. The cotton goods from Bengal, raw silk from Patna, spikenard (a valuable medicine or drug), borax (drug), ginger and many other numerous articles of commerce were traded here. The officers of Nūr Jahān Begum, who built a *sarāī* at Agra used to collect the duties on all these goods before they were shipped across the river and also on innumerable kinds of grain, butter and other provisions which were produced in the eastern provinces and imported there. Agra was the chief emporium of India in the sixteenth and seventeenth centuries. The traveller narrates that the commerce flourished here both during the times of Akbar (1556–1605) and Jahangir (1605-27) due to the royal patronage. All goods from Gujarat, Tatta (or Sind), Kabul, Kandhar, Multan and Lahore passing to the Deccan or

1. *The Remonstrantie* (Report), tr. from the Dutch by W.H. Moreland and P. Geyl, London, 1925, pp. 4-7, rpt. in India, CE 1, Oriental Series No. 8 under the title *Jahangir's India,* Delhi, 1972. *The Journal of the Voyage* was published more than once in Holland. Thevenot translated two thirds of the whole in his *Divers Voyages Curieux* (Paris, 1663). John de Lact summarized in his *De Imperio Magnimogolis,* Pub. 1663 vide *Journal of the Royal Asiatic Society,* January 1923, p. 85; see also *Early Voyages to Terra Australis,* Hakluyt Society, London, 1859; Henry Kingsley, *Tales of Old Travels,* London, 1869; *Ongeluckige voyagic Van't Schip Batavia,* rev. edn. Amsterdam 1648; Dr. de Hullus incharge of the colonial records in the Rijksar Chief (Hague) traced the Ms. and Bijlsma, incharge of records and R. Burn supplied further information for all the translators and annotators.

Burhanpur from Bengal and the whole eastern part of the country passed this way. The indescribable quantities of merchandize especially cotton goods were carried through the roads to Agra from all these areas. Jaunpur produced and exported large quantities of cotton goods, such as turbans, girdles, white plain calico-cotton goods, etc. Benares and Oudh also produced girdles, turbans, clothes and other articles for consumption in local markets.

He[2] further states that Patna yielded annually 1000 to 2000 maunds of silk, the best of which was sold at 16 or 17 *mohur*s per maund (of 50 lb.) taking the *mohur* equivalent to Rs. 7 approximately, the price will be Rs. 110 or 120. Most of it was consumed in Gujarat and rest in Agra market. The English letters[3] from Patna show that the silk obtained in Patna came from Bengal. The Muslin (*cassa*) was also exported from Bengal to Patna. All the cotton goods exported from Bengal to Patna were further sold at Agra.

He[4] further refers to the commercial intercourse between eastern India and Portugal. The Portuguese carried an extensive trade with Dacca, Tsettagham (Chittagong), Shabazpur in Backergunj district and Sonārgāon in Bengal and Pipli Bander coast of Orixa (Orissa). The main articles of trade were the fine Muslin (*cassa* and *malmal*s) of Bengal and other cotton goods of Orissa. Dacca Muslim, a product of high reputation once commanded high price both in Roman Empire and medieval Europe and constituted the main source of wealth of India. Pipli Bander — a famous port in Orissa was used for those vessels which were not taken up the Hooghly River. Many Portuguese trading vessels used to come annually

2. Ibid., p. 8.
3. *The English Factories in India*, 1618-21, p. 192; cf. *Remonstrantie*, pp. 7-8; See also *The English Factories in India*, 1622-23, p. 281.
4. *Remonstrantie*, pp. 8-9.

from Malacca, Macao, Java and Sumatra with all spices (cloves, nutmeg, mace), woollen cloth, lead, tin, quicksilver and vermilion and exchanged these articles for the return voyage with Bengal Muslin or loaded their frigates with butter, rice, gingerly seed and such other goods which yielded large profits. All these countries were very fertile and yielded immense quantities of grain, such as wheat, rice, sugar and butter, the large quantities of which were brought up through river Jamunā or carried by oxen overland to the province of Agra. In the other direction vessels used to carry from here much *sāmbhar* salt, opium, printed cloths, large quantities of cotton goods which supported the extensive trade to and from Agra.

According to the Dutch traveller,[5] the Indigo of Agra was the most important article of commerce throughout the whole world. No merchant ever afforded to neglect the importance of Indigo trade, the best quality of which was grown in Agra and its vicinity. The other places like Koil (modern Aligarh) and Gorsa, mentioned frequently in English records as Coria or Curja, identified by W. Foster[6] with Khurja now in Bulandshahr district (U.P.) were also presumably the centre of Indigo trade. Most of the produce were brought by Armenian, Lahore and Kābulī merchants. The Banjana-indigo of Agra was bought by Dutch merchants also. The classical source[7] also mentions that Indigo used in dyeing the clothes at Agra was exported to the coast of Melinde (the Azania of *The Periplus*). It constituted the principal article of trade for the Governor of Mozambique also who sold them to the Kaffirs for carrying up to the country of Abysinia.

5. Ibid., pp. 15-18. See also Shodhak, vol. 23, Pt. C, 1994, pp. 177-84.

6. *Tlie English Factories in India,* 1646-50, p. 56.

7. W.H. Schoff, *The Periplus of the Erythraeun Sea* (hereafter *The Periplus*), (London, 1912), p. 179.

Both eastern and northern India extensively carried on the trade with Gujarat. Agra used to export annually to Ahmedabad large quantities of goods, for example, Patna Silks, Satins, Velvets and various kinds of curious stuffs. Among all the articles imported by Gujarat mention may be made of spikenard, asafoetida, pepper and numerous other drugs, Bengal Muslin and *malmal* (*cassas*) and other cotton goods from Bengal and other eastern provinces.[8]

The traveller[9] exhaustively deals with the trade of northern India conducted with Dutch with great profit and honour. The principal resource of the Dutch at this time before the development of their lucrative trade with China and Japan, was their monopoly of cloves, mace and nutmeg — all spices from East India Islands. The chief Indian market for the species was in the north. Large quantities were brought to Agra by Indian merchants from east coast. Most of the exports were paid in gold and silver. The *pagoḍā* — the gold coins of the coast — may be taken as worth something over Rs. 3 at that time. The following figures indicate the requirements of all the Dutch spices by Agra:

Agra requires —

700 Mds or 35,000 lb. Cloves at Rs. 200 per maund of 50 lb.
600 Mds or 30,000 lb. Nutmeg at Rs. 100 per maund of 50 lb.
30 Sockels Mace at Rs. 300 per maund of 50 lb.
All items from Holland.

The approximate prices —

700 Mds cloves at Rs. 200 per maund of 50 lb.	Rs. 140,000
600 Mds nutmeg at Rs. 100 per maund of 50 lb.	Rs. 60,000
30 Sockels mace estimated per maund of 50 lb.	Rs. 15,000
Total	Rs. 2,15,000

8. *Remonstranite*, p. 19.

9. Ibid., pp. 21-29.

The Dutch accrued large profits on all the goods which were brought to Agra by their ships from Holland. In the competition which ensued between the English and Dutch for the monopoly of trade, the latter surpassed the former by all practical means. The Dutch used to send Agra every year "rarities to the value of 100,000 guilders, (The Dutch guilder of 20 stivers was accounted for in India at this time as 5/6 rupee, the rupee being taken at 24 stivers) consisting of large pearls, large and fine emeralds, sapphires, rubies, gold artware of kinds which can be described better verbally than in writing, for instance, an antique box or casket with various ingenious locks, etc." The following rarities were sent to Agra by ships from the Dutch country —

> "10 small gold chains of the most ingenious work, 20 Sabres costing 10 to 15 guilders each — embellished with some gold work slightly curved. 20 handsome musical barrels wrought with gold. Some sea-horse teeth marbled on the inside with black stripes, much esteemed. 2 or 3 good battle pictures painted by an artist with a pleasing style for the Muslims. One or two maps of the entire world and some decorative pictures with rude figures. 10 large cases in which to keep scissors, mirrors, razors and other implements. 10 to 20 gilt mirrors costing 8 to 10 guilders each. 1 case red woollen cloth costing 15 to 16 guilders each. 10 to 20 pieces tapestry, both silken and woollen from 3 to 8 elbs long. 5 to 10 pieces *cassa* (some textile made in Europe) of bright colours, green, red or variegated. No cloth of gold should be sent, as it is supplied from Persia of good quality and much cheaper. Aftabs used by Moslems, Betel boxes, Fan handles, Handles for fly-switches and dishes and cups with covers. All these goods were sold by local Dutch merchants in the Mughal palace and open market at Agra."

The annual offtake of Dutch commodities in Agra may be estimated as follows —

Quick silver: 50 Maunds or 2500 lb — Rs. 160-180 the maund.

Tin: 30 maunds at Rs. 38 or 40 the maund.

Ivory: 50 maunds, whole pieces sell at Rs. 70-80 the maund and split pieces at Rs. 20-30.

Arms-rings were made from the ivory for Hindu women and worn as ornaments in Multan and the Eastern provinces.

Red woollen cloth at 8 to 10 guilders the ell.

The author uses the word "pice" to denote both the *dām* (price) and the half-*dām* (or *adhelā*). In Akbar's time 40 *dām* or 80 *adhelā* was equivalent to a rupee, but the price of copper rose sharply early in the seventeenth century and therefore rupee was exchanged for 30 *dām* or less. The above statistical data no doubt bear creditable testimony to the fact that Agra was the chief commercial market for the Dutch caravan.

Pelsaert[10] further describes that Agra imported from Lahore ormesines and carpets woven there and many other goods from distant lands such as fruit from Kabul, asafoetida from Kandhar and other commodities obtained from Multan. The exported goods from Agra to Lahore include most of the spices purchased from the Dutch, all kinds of white cotton goods procured both from Bengal and Golcoṇḍā, ivory, quick silver, vermilion, coral, turbans, girdles and all sorts of silk goods obtained from Ahmedabad and Patna, lac, drug, pepper and many other too numerous things to be described. From Agra, Multan also received large quantities of cotton, coarse yarn, Bengal cotton goods, turbans, painted clothes, small quantities of spices, etc. The three rivers — the Rāvī, the Indus or Sindh and Jhelum or Beliat — served here as commercial routes. The goods sent from Agra to Kashmir were coarse

10. Ibid., pp. 31, 35-36.

cotton cloth and yarn for local consumption and also pepper, opium, cloves, mace and nutmeg — all spices, etc. Kashmir also extensively exported to Agra plenty of walnuts, saffron, shawls, woven cloths, etc.

The same Dutch source[11] reveals that the drugs obtained in Agra, Kashmir and Eastern Himalayas — Bhutan — like borax, spikenard, etc. were items of regular trade for the Dutch. The Agra merchants extensively carried on the trade in drugs. They brought to Donga or Dogam (150 *kos* from Agra) once an important centre of trade in Jehangir's time all the drugs, quick silver, brass, copper, etc. Particularly spikenard (very valuable medicine or drugs used particularly for stiffened limbs gold at Agra from Rs. 6 to 7 per maund) was exported from Agra to other places like Tatta (capital of Sind), Multan, Persia, the Deccan or probably the whole world.

Reverend Samuel Purchas (1575–1626),[12] a famous English traveller, in his pilgrimage (Pub. 1626), which is a collection of voyages and travels of master Ralph Fitch (who visited India during Akbar's time, 1585), William Captain Hawkins (who visited India during Jahangir's time in 1608) and Thomas Roe (1615-16). Travellers like Stevens, Coryah, John Fryer (1672-76), Davis Terry, Michel Bourne, Covert, Withington (1614), Raymond and most of others provide a reliable account of the trades of northern and eastern India during the period concerned. All these travellers' accounts, if collectively used will definitely provide better geography of the country than

11. Ibid., pp. 44-45.

12. *Early Travels in India*: *16th and 17th Centuries* (Reprints of Rare and curious narratives of old travellers in India in the sixteenth and seventeenth centuries, ed. J.T. Wheeler, under the title *Purchase Pilgrimage* (the portion dealing with India) and the *Tavels of Van Linscholen.* These originally appeared in Saturday Evening Englishmen Journal, ed. T.O.B. Saunders and later reprinted in a book form from Calcutta, 13 December, 1864, rpt. Delhi, 1975), pp. 13, 59-60.

any other map. According to Purchas, in the ports of Orixa (Orissa) twenty or 30 ships were yearly laden with rice, lacca, long pepper, ginger, mira bolins and the yerua — made of all herbs growing in the wild woods. Side by side the mentions of the products of Satgāon (Chittagong) especially the cotton cloth and silk. From the description of whatsoever is available we can conjecture that both the countries exchanged their products. He further observes that during the time of Master Ralph Fitch (sixteenth entury) and in the seventeenth century four great markets were held at Agra where all things were sold very cheap. There were twelve Indico (Indigo) mills there Coryat[13] informs us that Lahore, one of the fairest and ancient cities of India standing on the Indus was resorted to by the merchants from all ports of India including Agra. John Mildnall[14] in his letter dated, Casbin (Persia), 3 October 1606 testifies to the fact that he had been at Agra and Lahore where he presented to the kings nine horses, jewels, rings and obtained-articles of trading. Master Withington (1614)[15] states that from Agra goods may be conveyed on camels in twenty days to Lowribander Port on Sindh River or Tatta which was the chief centre of trade.

John H.V. Linschoten, a Portuguese traveller, who visited India in 1583[16] says that Bengal merchants resorted to Goa — a metropolitan or chief city of all oriental India, to buy and sell the things. The traders came to Goa to buy wares. All kinds of spices, dried drugs, fine and coverlets, sweet Gummes sold there came from Bengal, Sind, China and Cambodia. All kinds of silks, satins and other cotton goods sold by Hindu merchants at Goa were brought by Portuguese from Bengal.

Father Stephen Cacella and Father John Cabral, Portuguese

---

13. Ibid., p. 63.
14. Ibid., p. 65.
15. Ibid., pp. 69-70
16. Ibid., pp. 165-170, 189.

Jesuit travellers, who visited Assam in the seventeenth century, perhaps between 1626 and 1627[17] bring only this fact to light that the merchants from Patna, Rajmahal and Gaur visited the markets of Koch-Bihar with their local produce. The details are lacking.

Cesare de Federici[18] a Venetian traveller in his description of 1565 observes that at Sandwip island off the coast of Noakhali district Eastern Bengal and Assam 200 ships were laden yearly with salt. Here such was the abundance of materials for shipbuilding that the Sultan of Constantinople found it cheaper to have his vessels built here than at Alexandria. In 1609 this island was captured from the Mohammedans by the Portuguese who had been expelled from Arākān.

J.B. Tavernier, a seventeenth century (1676) French traveller[19] provides a very authentic and eye witness account of the trade and commerce of Eastern India. According to him the merchants from Tipperah (present Tripura) and Patna visited Dacca to buy coral, yellow amber, tortoise shell, bracelets, sea-shells with numerous rounds, toys, and square pieces of the size of coins. The gold and silk from Tripura were sent over land to China in exchange for silver. The abundant gold was brought to different ports of India from Tripura or Tipperah country which was procured chiefly from the river washings in Assam. The French account may be further confirmed by other relevant sources.[20]

---

17. C. Wessels, S.J., *Early Jesuit Travellers in Central Asia* (Pub. 1924) Refer to the *Journal of the Assam Research Society*, October, 1937, vol. V, N. 3, p. 90.
18. B.C. Allen, E.A. Gait, G.H. Allen and H.F. Howard, *Gazetteer of Bengal and North East India* (Delhi, 1979), p. 157.
19. V. Ball, *Travels in India*, (tr. from original French edn. of 1676 and ed. W. Crooke, London, 1925), vol. II, Ch. XVI, pp. 214-15.
20. *The Periplus*, p. 259; *Economic Geology of India*, p. 231; *Alamgirnamah* of Muhammad Kazim, 1663 in the *Indian Antiquary*, July 1887.

23

The Annals of Tribal–Mughal Conflicts in North-East India during the Reign of Jehangir (1605–1627)*

THE beginning of seventeenth century constituted a turning point and heralded the dawn of a new phase — a phase of aggressive imperialism in the arena of Mughal politics and diplomacy in the medieval history of north-east India. The Ahom-Mughal conflicts have been profusely dealt with and prolixly narrated, but no sincere, concerted and painstaking efforts have ever been made to portray the pen picture of the subject under review. The principal object is here to lift up the dark-lengthening curtain befalling the face of the subject and present as far as possible a systematic, graphic and succinct account thereof in a chronological order.

Its Causes

In their determined bid for the territorial expansion of the Empire from the lower Kāmrūpa up to the confines of China or Turkistan beyond the Himalayas via Tibet and in the persuasion of the vigorous and energetic policy for the restoration of imperial prestige, the Mughals by bringing the refractory tribes of Bengal under their control, suppressing the various rebel tribal chiefs and annexing the territories of Kachar, Sylhet, the Jaintia Hills and Hill-Tipperah to the

---

* From *Journal of Indian History*, vol. LIX, Pts. 1-3, 1981, pp. 163-75.

Mughal dominion wanted to unfurl the Timurid banner higher even up to the dome of Peking. William Robinson[1] observes that the "people with whom they will come into conflict are ferocious and would not brook submission to foreign power." The grim determination of the tribal chiefs to maintain their independence by resisting the onrush of the invaders and to extend all their help to Ahom monarchs in the event of any conflict furnished the pretext for the eruption of hostilities during the reign of Jahangir also.

Array of Events — Invasion of Kachar

We shall now refer to the pivotal landmarks round which a set of panormic events of momentous significance revolve. The period concerned is crowded with such significant events. In the first half of the seventeenth century the Mughals made a number of attempts to subjugate the Kachari Tribe. The first abortive invasion as recorded in Persian chronicle[2] occurred in 1608 when Islam Khan was the Governor of Bengal. When Shaykh Kamal and the army came from Sylhet in a very exalted position to conquer the territory of Kachar, some Kachari chiefs despatched regiments to oppose the imperialists. In a sanguinary battle fought at the hill and the fort of Asurainagar the Kacharis fought very bravely and repeatedly made night attacks on Mughal force, but at last, the imperialists defeated the enemy and captured the fort. After continuing the fight for a month with the help of reinforcement sent by Islam Khan, Shaykh Kamal and other imperial officers along with the new regiment attacked the fort of Asurainagar.[3] The hill and the fort of Asurainagar fell in the hands of imperialists. Shaykh

1. Robinson, *Descriptive Account of Assam* (Delhi, 1975), p. 165.
2. Mirja Nathan, *Baharistan-i-Ghaybi* (English tr. Dr. M.I. Borah, — D.H.A.S. (Gauhati, 1936), vol. 1, Bk I, Ch. X, p. 220.
3. The MS. *Baharistan-i-Ghaybi* (vol. 11, note 57, p. 823) spells it as Asurabatgar which has not been properly identified by the author.

Kamal by sending envoys to the Rājā of Kachar made a peace with him. The great imperial officers sent a memorial to Emperor submitting as follows:

> . . . Through the benign influence of the Emperor we have somehow defeated the Raja of Kachar with the purpose that either he should voluntarily surrender or he should be made a prisoner and his dominions should be brought under the rule of Imperial Officer Shaykh Kamal, an officer of Islam Khan made peace with him (Raja) to suit his own purpose and left the expedition where it was. If this work is entrusted to us, then with the favour of the fortune of error, we shall conquer the territory of Kachar within a short time and send the Raja to the Imperial Court.[4]

Now Islam Khan accompanied by Shaykh Kamal, his own officers, Mubariz Khan and other imperialist officers again led an expedition against the Rājā of Kachar, stormed and occupied the fort of Asurainagar and established a *thānā* there. He wanted to advance further but the Kachari Raja sent his envoys and made his submission with great humility.

Shortly after this, the second invasion occurred in 1612 when Qasim Khan, other imperial officers and Mubariz Khan undertook an expedition to Pratāpgaṛh[5] which belonged to the Rājā of Kachar. In a very fierce battle the Kachari force exhibited excellent bravery and killed many Mughal imperial officers and made many of them wounded. But the wheel of fortune turned adversely. The Kachari forts at Asura-tikri and Pratāpgaṛh were captured. The Rājā of Kachar submitted with humiliation, acknowledged their overlordship and made peace by giving forty elephants and Rs. 1 lakh for the Emperor, five

4 Ibid., vol. I, p. 221.

5. Ibid., vol. II, p. 837. Pratāpgaṛh was a Mahal in the *sarkāra* of Sylhet. There is Mauze of this name in the district of Sylhet situated within the Sub-Division of Karimganj bordering on Kachar.

elephants and Rs. 20,000 for the *sūbedāra* and two elephants as well as Rs. 20,000 for Mubariz Khan, *thānedāra* of Bandasal who commanded the invading force.[6]

J.N. Sarkar[7] in his translation of the Persian Annal, *Baharistan-i-Ghaybi*, also clearly mentions about this war. S.K. Chatterjee in his monograph[8] also mentions that Kachari king made peace with the Mughals paying tribute. Besides these reliable and authentic accounts recorded in Persian Annals and other historical works we are also informed that some time before 1627 a Muslim chief Jamal Khan while invading the country of Kachar and erecting a fort at Khaspur was disastrously defeated by Kachari king Bhīmbal Nārāyaṇa but this has not been confirmed by any Muhammedan chronicler. About this conflict K.L. Barua[9] only mentions that after the death of Usman, Bayazid of Sylhet and the Rājā of Kachar submitted without putting much resistance.

Expedition for the Suppression of Anti-Mughal Campaign of Various Hill Chiefs

In between the territories of "Khasta" (Khasia or the Khāsīs-Hill Tribe living at present in the Meghalaya) and Kachar, a group of people not clearly identified played their parts in this conflict very vigorously.

During the reign of Amir Taymur Sahib who advanced up to the extremity and later returned to the capital of Iraq, these people were left to protect the country. This statement has

---

6. Ibid., vol. I, Bk II, Ch. IV, p. 326; E. Gait, *History of Assam*, 2nd edn. (Calcutta, 1926), p. 253.

7. *Journal of the Bihar and Orissa Research Society* (hereafter *JBORS*), March 1921, vol. VII, Pt. I, BAB — II, Dastan-161-l, 253-a, pp. 4-5.

8. *Kirāta-Jana Kṛti* (A.S.B., Calcutta, 1974), p. 125.

9. *The Journal of the Assam Research Society*, October, 1937, vol. V, no. 3, p. 68.

also been confirmed by Edward Gait.[10] According to Mirja Nathan's[11] account Mubariz Khan with the help of imperial force invaded the portion of their territories and brought under his possession some of these people bearing the dreadful appearance who were sent alive to Qasim Khan. After returning to Sylhet he sent Mirak Bahadur Jolair with an army to the newly conquered territories to keep vigilant watch over the surrounding areas. These people were further sent to imperial court. The splendid services rendered by Mubariz Khan and Mirak Bahadur Jolair won for them a great honour and the new territories were assigned to them in lieu of their increased allowances. Here we have got enough reasons to believe that the Khāsīs, the Kacharis and other unknown tribes must have played conspicuous role in resisting the attempts of the imperialist force, but unfortunately neither the tradition nor any local records help us in ascertaining the exact truth.

The most filibustering expedition was launched by Mir Abdur Razzaq against the eighteen Hill *rājā*s mentioned in M.S.[12] as "Hizdah Rājā" and the kingdom of Rānī Maydon.[13]

10. E. Gait, op. cit., p. 253.

11. *Baharistan-i-Ghaybi*, pp. 324-25.

12. Ibid., vol. II, note 6, p. 843, "The Eighteen hill chiefs were ruling over the strip of the level country at the foot of the Himalayas from Darraṅg westward in the direction of Bhutan Duwārs. Out of 18 Duwārs 11 were situated on the border of Bengal and Goalpāṛā and 7 in the north of Kāmarūpa and Darraṅg. The hill chiefs as vassals of Ahom were responsible for keeping the frontier intact." Various authorities mention of these hill chiefs. Montgomery Martin (*The history, Antiquities, Topography and Statistics of Eastern India*, Delhi, rpt. 1976, vol. V, Bk III, Ch. I, pp. 619-22) mentions of ten hill chiefs who ruled over the regions to the south of Brahmaputra, e.g. Barduwār Bholagram, Chhaygaon, Mayapur, Mairapur, Lukiutam Duwār, Bangram, Duwār, Vaga Duwār, Beltola, Dumuria and Rānī Duwār. Some of these Duwārs are also called as *deśa*s, e.g., . . . Deśa Dumuria,

→

After plundering some villages he obtained many slaves and captives. The enemies came from all sides and began to shower arrows on Mughal force. In a skirmish Mir was fatally wounded, many of his followers were killed and large number of them were made captives. After a short interval Mirja Nathan led an expedition against "Hizdah Rājā" and Rānī (the Garo Tribe Chief) for their complete subjugation. All the Eighteen Hill Rājās and Rājā of Rānī (Gāro chief and other frontier chiefs) formed an alliance for making an attack and raised fort at Hatrani. All the eighteen Hill Chiefs attacked on Mirza with the help of twenty-two thousand infantry and fell upon the fort of Pāṇḍu in the last *pahara* of night dividing their army into three divisions. Thus their regiment of the right wing consisting of nine thousand men entered from the Kāmarūpa Duwār. In a skirmish the elephant of Mirza was taken into custody. They set fire to *cabūṭarā* and attacked the

→ Deśa Panbari, Deśa-Beltola and Deśa Rani. He clearly states that Vaga Duwār and Dumuriya both were ruled by the Gāro chiefs. Rānī Duwār or Rājā's residence was at the foot of the Gāro mountain probably at Noghurreah. According to him the Gāros were more warlike than the Assamese. Gait (op. cit., pp. 112, 298, 334) also mentions of these Duwars. In Robinson's (op. cit., pp. 283, 289). Map of Assam "Banksa Duwārs" seems to be corruption of Voga Duwār, a hill tract bordering on Bhutan to the north of Kāmarūpa and Darraṅg. The chief of this Duwār was the Gāro (the tribes living in the Gāro hills). This is the place which has also been referred to in Baharistan. All the authorities differ from each other and consequently no systematic and trustworthy account of these hill chiefs is available. Even Mirja Nathan's list also does not conform to the statements of other authorities.

13. *Baharistan-i-Ghaybi,* vol. II, note, 7, p. 843. Deśa Rāni is situated at a distance of a few miles on the south-west from Gauhati. It was given by Rājā Gadadhar Singh (the Ahom Ruler of Assam) to the Gāro Queen who was descendant of Rājā Arimatta. He named it as Deśa Rānī.

fort from the side where Islam Quil and Mir Bahadur (commander of the fleet) were posted. Khizr Khan and Nazr Muhammad Beg at this critical juncture having recovered two to three fatal wounds fell back inside the fort with their wounded horse. Mirza said:

> It is clear to me that the enemy is making a rush, and if they succeed and enter the fort by making breaches in different places and inflict a heavy defeat upon us, they will kill us one by one with our horse and we have to take our journey to go ten steps in advance and accept martyrdom so that after death every one of us may have some name and fame.[14]

Mirza himself, owing to entry of the second regiment of the enemy consisting of more than seven thousand infantry by the Kāmākhyā Duwār, took a position for battle. In short, the brave warriors and valiant fighters coming from three sides drove away the enemies with their dreadful swords and won laurels of Victory. Mirza himself with a band of his experienced comrades fell upon a second regiment and performed the marvellous feats of action like Rustam. The hill chiefs for some time offered brave resistance and had even hand to hand fight. Casualities were on both sides. The Commander of the Tribal Army named Wakuk Rājā (the Kuki chief. The Kuki tribes were living in Manipur, Kachar, Mizo Hills and Hill Tipperah) was killed by one of the soldiers of Mirja Nathan. The third regiment of the enemy consisted of six thousand infantry. The chiefs or the *rājā*s fighting bravely drove them away out of forts, but many of them sustained injury and many were killed. But by the end of the first *pahara* of the day Mirja Nathan proved himself triumphant blowing the kettle-drum of victory.[15]

---

14. Ibid., p. 415.
15. Ibid., pp. 416-17.

Mirja Nathan in order to inflict a crushing defeat on all the eighteen Hill Chiefs and all the people of hill regions marched towards Ranihat with a fleet and a large number of experienced soldiers. The army brought the boats to the brink of the water below the fort and hill in spite of enemy's attack from above with their large infantry and heavy shower of fire and stones. Many people were wounded and killed. After Suna Ghazi with the help of his men occupied the hillock and garrison, they became intoxicated with the wine of bravery and making no discrimination between hills and dales pursued the fleeing enemy till they reached the interior of the hills where the residence of the Gāro chief was situated. It was plundered and burnt. The villagers who rose in open revolt with the arms against the Mughals were put to death and many of them were made captives. The following day they again plundered fifteen villages of the hill-men. About 500 hill tribes were taken as captives[16] in a fierce battle of great historical importance.

Being undaunted in their courage and spirit, about eighteen thousand hill people with Rājā Baldeva, brother of Rājā Parīkṣit attacked the fort of Pāṇḍu and killed many Muslim soldiers.[17] But soon Mirza Yusuf, Islam Quli Adil Khan, Musa Khan and others in order to wreak the vengeance attacked the enemy and put many of them to death.

When Mirja Nathan was engaged day and night in capturing Prasuram (another rebel leader), the enemies finding the Mughals in few numbers came out of jungles and attacked upon this group. In this encounter seven men were killed in the jungle and some came out half-dead. Fata (the *fauẓdāra* of the Imperial elephant Shah Inayat) obtained martyrdom but no definite trace is found.[18]

16. Ibid.

17. Ibid., vol. 11, Ch. I, Bk III, p. 452.

18. Ibid., vol. 11, Ch. IV, p. 512.

After six days of this incident, Shaykh Ahmed and other officers of Mirza marched against Kaltakary and his son Tahana (two hill chiefs of Rangdan region in the district of Goalpāṛā, the hilly tract lying to the north of Rangjuli hills). They fought gallantly but unfortunately the details of exploits are not available. Neither the local chronicles nor the Persian Annals furnish any reliable evidence. Some turbulent hill chiefs gave protection to Prasuram. All the Mughal regiments marched up to the hills and set the Rangdan ablaze as a result of which the enemy fled away and took shelter in the hills and dense forest. Sadat Khan and his party ultimately became successful in recovering the plundered things from the enemy and put many of them to the sharp edge of dreadful swords.[19]

Sounding the trumpet of victory from Amjunga (the hill fort) Mirja Nathan marched to the foot of the hills of the Gāros (garuan)[20] who were very famous hill tribes of those days. S.N. Bhattacharya[21] is absolutely wrong in stating that "Mirja Nathan marched to the foot of the Karwan Hills." There is no such hill in Assam. The MS. Baharistan[22] giving a clear picture confirms that it was the hill of the Gāros. After Mirja Nathan arrived there and pitched his camp, many of the tribal chiefs came and made their submission. Three of them were given robes of honour. Such a terrible battle was fought that owing to heavy showers of arrows from both sides the birds of air could not fly. Next morning Mustafa Quli Beg with five hundred infantry reached the villages of the hill-men at the outskirts of hills, attacked the three villages, burnt them and brought down about five hundred hill people as captives.

19. Ibid., p. 514.

20. Ibid., vol. 11, note, 10, p. 849

21. S.N. Bhattacharya, *A History of Mughal North East Frontier Policy* (Calcutta, 1929), p. 205.

22. *Baharistan-i-Ghaybi*, vol. II, pp. 528-29.

Muslim Chief named Jamal Khan left no stones unturned to subjugate the hill tribes. One of the rebel chiefs named Jankara[23] was brought alive as captive which created the terror and horror among the hill tribes. Jadu Nayak[24] a son of Chutiya (name of the tribe living at that time in Sadiya region) Rājā fiercely opposed the imperial forces. Those who opposed the imperial forces of Nik Muhammad[25] at the time of their invasion of adjoining villages were put to death.

When Mirja Nathan marched towards the territory of Barduwar[26] and raided, Nik Muhammad with some of the lovers of battle went up to hills with great difficulty. Many brave and ferocious hill-men fought with big knives weighing sixteen Indian seers but at last all were killed and their heads were brought which naturally produced a great panic among the hill men. The *rājā* finding himself unable to resist any longer fled up to Upra-Rājā Khamranga, i.e. the *rājā* of the Upper Hills, and took shelter there. The Mughal army entered the hills, attacked the fort raised by Bamun Rājā and Kanwal Rājā between the hills, raided and destroyed the villages within the hills and captured Rājā Khamranga who later on surrendered at the feet of the Mughal.[27]

23. Ibid., p. 530.

24. G.C. Baruah, *Ahom Buranji* (original text with parallel English tr. Calcutta, 1930), p. 130; Gait, op. cit., p. 110. He observes that Jadu Nayak is mentioned by some writers as chief of the Chutia tribe and by some as the Kachari tribe.

25. *Baharistan-i-Ghaybi,* p. 533.

26. Ibid., p. 850. Barduwār is the name of territory adjacent to the passes of Gāro Hills. Montgomery Martin, op. cit., p. 619. "The Raja is Garo and lives at Bhagpoor two days journey south-west from Gauhati. It is close to the mountains inhabited by independent Garos who consider the Baraduwar Raja as their chief." He also makes a mention of the Gāro chief named Koiram who lived in the area bordering Susang'go.

27. *Baharistan-i-Ghaybi,* pp. 618-19.

Mirja Nathan[28] further states that another two hill chiefs known as Bamun Rājā and Kanwal Rājā of the territories lying adjacent to Barduwar also surrendered to the Mughal. In the absence of any contemporary maps with topographical details it is very difficult to locate exactly the geographical position and the extent of the territories of the *rājā*s. Mirja Nathan wrote to all eighteen Hill Rajas that "If you desire your own welfare you must surrender to me by tying the thread of obedience on your own necks, otherwise you shall have to repent like Rājā Baldev." This was the warning which compelled those aforesaid hill chiefs to surrender. Nay, everyone of them got a robe of honour and returned immediately to their respective places so that other hill tribes might come to submit at the earliest opportunity. The Jaintia (Tribe living in the Jaintia hill) Rājās known as Bhu Singh and Man Singh (grandsons of king Jasamattarai) submitted four thousand paiks (the Garosy) of the country of Lamdani.[29] Half of them were the staunch followers of the eighteen Hill *rājā*s.

The years 1615-19 represent a fateful period as it constituted epoch-making events in the history of north-east India. The events of the period present before us a panorma of internecine conflicts with triumphs and defeats, imperialistic determination to wreak vengeance, seizure of power, etc. The memorable episode of this period was the rebellion of hill *rājā*s of Dakhinkol.[30] At the time of Syad Hakkim and Syad

28. Ibid., p. 566.

29. Ibid., p. 350, Lamdani corresponds to the lower hill region on the southern border of Assam. The higher range of the hill region is called "Upparia" by the author.

30. Shihabuddin Talish, M.S., Faihiyyah-I-Ibriyyah (original Persian Text) p. 26; Sir J.N. Sarkar, *JBORS*, December 1915, vol. 1, Pt. II, verse 51, p. 182. According to him Dakhinkol stretches from the kingdom of the Nak-Kati Rānī to the village of Sadiya; H. Blochmann, *Journal of the Asiatic Society of Bengal* (hereafter *JASB*) →

Abu Bakar's invasions of Ahom Kingdom all the hill chiefs were planning to raise the banner of revolt against the Mughal rule. Sultan Khan, Mast Ali Beg, Mirza Khwaja Ahamed and party in consultation with Khwaja Daodat Khan wrote to Mirza: "It is reported that the hill *rājās* are proposing to become Haram Khwur (disloyal). Now it is the best opportunity to imprison all these big and petty chiefs who are present here and then let us go to the Gāro and stay there free of the trouble of the territory."[31] A week after all the big and petty hill *rājās* abruptly joined together and raised the fort at Ranihat. But soon Mirza despatched a cavalry regiment which attacked this fort and dashed it to ground. S.N. Bhattacharyya[32] also states that since March 1618 Mirja Nathan has been busy in subduing the rebel chiefs of Dakhinkol for the consolidation of imperial authority. All the hill chiefs of Dakhinkol having the indomitable spirit, untiring energy, unflinching faith and doggedness of determination made a bold venture to capture the strategic hill fort of Ranihat. After having failed in the early attempts made in 1619 for the fortification of hill fort they appealed to Ahom King Pratap Singh for help on the plausible ground of community of interest. The Ahom King by giving quick response to the invitation sent a large army to their assistance. He responded to all appeals for men and money made by the turbulent Hill *rājās* of Dakhinkol.[33] After five months of hard

→ 1872, vol. XLI, pt. I, pp. 75-76; Muhammad Qazim, *Ālamgirnāmāh*, Tr. Henery Vansittart, *Asiatic Researches*, 1799, vol. 2, p. 171. His speculation that it "extends from the village Sadiya to Srinagar" seems to be absurd and an astounding statement. He has failed to provide the exact geographical position of the place. Sir J.N. Sarkar, *JBORS*, March 1921, vol. VII, Pt. I, (BAB-II, 267-a.), pp. 4-8. Mirja Nathan informs us that Sahan (Shitab Khan) was sent to conquer whole Dakhinkol.

31. *Baharistan-i-Ghaybi*, vol. II, p. 570.
32. S.N. Bhattacharya, op. cit., pp. 199-209.
33. Ibid., pp. 246 f.

fighting in 1619 the hill chiefs aided by Ahom Force inflicted a crushing defeat on the Mughal force commanded by Mirja Nathan[34] and thus clogged the wheel of his progress towards the kingdom of Assam. It is clearly stated in Assamese chronicles[35] that during Pratap Singh's time (1603-41) various Frontier Rājās, Man Singh, Rup Singh, Laket Dimarua, Garkur Rājā, Bamun Rājā and other chiefs fought with Musalmans. It is also to be noted here that Pratap Singh with the help of various Jaintia and Kachari chiefs attacked and captured the fort of Pāṇḍu. This fact can be further substantiated by other sources.[36]

But this glorious victory soon faded away and turned into a vigorous defeat. After they lost their strategic places, all the eighteen Hill *rājās* tendered their submission to imperial authority within three days one after another. Mirja Nathan placed all the eighteen hill chiefs under surveillance and directed his further efforts to keep watchful eyes on their activities.[37]

The process of reverses soon followed. After this incident occurred, Nik Muhammad while trying to capture Chutiya prince Jadu Nayak reached in the interior of hills, set fire to three places where the rebels had constructed the fort, killed many rebels and inflicted heavy punishment on them. Rājā Nilrangily of upper hill region received a reward of Rs. 300, the Qalicha (carpet) throne and *ṭīkā* of Rājā-ship for handing over Jadu Nayak (the chief of Chutiya tribes) as prisoner to Nik Muhammad Beg.[38] The Kuki tribes also played an

34. *Baharistan-i-Ghaybi*, pp. 571f.
35. G.C. Barua, *Ahom Buranji*, p. 106.
36. Gait, op. cit., p. 109.
37. *Baharistan-i-Ghaybi*, vol. 11, Ch. V, p. 620.
38. Ibid., pp. 683-85.

important role in resisting the Mughal advancement in this region, but ultimately they were also forced to surrender after a force of three thousand cavalry and ten elephants commanded by Sa'adat Khan was despatched against the Kuki *rājā*.[39] Thus the Mughal imperial authority was re-established in the hilly region by January 1620.

Pacification and Submission of the Frontier Tribes to the Mughal Authority

Some of the frontier tribes also raised the banner of revolt against the Mughal rule in north-east India. According to Mirja Nathan[40] "Chatsa Rājā" probably the Bhutia chief named Sat Rājā ruling over the hilly tract on the east of Bhutan Dwārs of Darraṅg[41] (the Koriāpar Duwār) also known as the Mombas and Rupabar, brothers of Akra (the name of the Aka tribe) Rājā along with other frontier chiefs offered brave resistance to the Mughal force at the time of arrival of Sa'adat Khan at the foot of the hills and fought bravely but ultimately all of them were driven away.[42] Mirza sent his force towards "Uttarkol"[43] against the Aka Rājā to raid Lamdani[44] hills of

39. Ibid., p. 569.

40. Ibid.

41. Robinson (op. cit., p. 290) while giving the clear geographical data informs us that "Darrang on the north is bounded by continuous range of mountains inhabited by the Bhutias, Daflas and Akas (all Frontier tribes); Dr. S.K. Bhuyan (*Anglo-Assamese Relations, 1771-1820*, D.H.A.S. Gauhati, 1949, pp. 36-37) also states that the tribes near the Darraṅg Duwārs are known as Paschima Daflas.

42. *Baharistan-i-Ghaybi*, pp. 556f.

43. Gulam Hussain Salim, *Riyazu-s-Salatin* (tr. Abdus Salam, I.A.D. Series, Delhi, 1975), p. 14. In the mountain tract to the east of Assam towards Uttarkol "Mari" and "Majmi" (the present Miris and Mishmis) Tribes are found. Muhammad Qazim, *Alamgirnama*,

→

lower region and upper hills of upper region. The fortune was adverse to them. The Aka Rājā and his brother were brought in chains. This incident ultimately produced consternation among all the eighteen Hill *rājā*s after which many minor and major chiefs submitted one by one except Bhutias who were told by Shitab Khan's messenger that "I will pillage and burn up to Bhutan hills and will not leave

→ tr. Henry Vansittart, *Asiatic Researches*, 1799, vol. 2, p. 171. The author informs us that "Uttarkol begins at Gauhati whose boundary of majesty terminates in mountains inhabited by tribes called Meeri and Mechmi; Shihabuddin Talish (M.S. Fattiyyah-i-Ibriyyah, p. 26) also states that "Uttarkol stretches from Gauhati to the home of Miri and Mishmi tribe." Muhammedan Chroniclers' statemetns can be further corroborated by other sources. Blochmann, *JASB* 1872, vol. XLI, pt. I, pp. 75-76; Sir J.N Sarkar, *JBORS*, 1915, vol. 1, p. 182. In another source Sir J.N. Sarkar (*JBORS*, March 1921, vol. VII, pt. I, Dastan-272, 13 pp. 4-8) further confirms that there was great rising of these frontier tribes against the Mughals.

44. All MSS. speak of Lamdang or Landoh. Sir J.N. Sarkar (*JBORS* March 1921, vol. VII, pt. I, BAB-IT, Dastan, 250-a, pp. 4-8) translates it for Nāga Hills. He further mentions that it is not properly identified. In other source (*JBORS* 1915, vol. 1, (51), p. 182) he identifies it with Aka or Anka or Nagas. In M.S. Fathiyyah-i-Ibriyyah, p. 26, also the word is mentioned but not properly identified by the author. Gait, op. cit., p. 141) also suggests that it may be a mistake for Aka or Anka. Vansittart (*Asiatic Researches*, 1799, vol. 2, p.171) also does not identify it properly. He simply contends that the most famous mountain to the northward of Uttarkol are Duleh and Landah. Blochmann (*JASB* 1872, vol. 41, pt. I, pp. 75-76) says that if the word is correct, it would refer to tribal aborigines not mentioned in our ethnological works. He further quotes Dalton who suggests that "The breadth of Assam from the hills inhabited by Mishmi, Miris, Daflas and Akas to the Nāga Hills, etc. are in proper geographical order. Dr. S.K. Bhuyan (*Deodhai Assam Buranji*, D.H.A.S. Gauhati 1932, p. XXIV) refers it to the Rājā of Jaintiā known as Landha Sultans.

even a bird of your race alive."[45] However after receiving customary gifts from the Mughal the Bhutia tribes also abandoned the planning of attack.

On the basis of all the details furnished in Persian Annals and other relevant sources we have got sufficient evidence to infer that some of the frontier tribes i.e. the Akas, the Mombas, the Miris, the Mishmis, the Daflas (living at present in different hill regions of Arunachal Pradesh) along with other Bhutia brethrens of Bhutan must have displayed excellent bravery in their encounters or conflicts with the Mughals. This will definitely go down in history as supreme example of patriotic instincts and animated spirits of the tribal people of north-east India. The absence of its details in both Persian and Assamese chronicles and other standard historical records can no longer stop us in unveiling this mystery. To allow to lay this fact in obscurity won't be judged as historically fair enough.

It is worthy of remark that J.N. Sarkar's[46] statement leaves no doubt that the Mughals conquered both Uttarkol and Dakhinkol, the different territories of Hill Chiefs including the Jaintiā and entered into endless war with Mongoloid Kingdoms.

Invasion of Hill-Tipperah

The Mughal invasion of Hill-Tipperah under the leadership of Nawab Fateh-Jang in the years 1620 during the reign of Jasadhar Māṇikya (1613-23) not in the year 1625 as mistakenly supposed by Aitchison[47] is also worth mentioning here. In this fierce battle many were killed and wounded on both sides

45. *Baharistan-i-Ghaybi,* p. 677.

46. *JBORS* March 1921, vol. VII, pt. I, pp. 3-8.

47. C.U. Aitchison, *A Collection of Treaties, Engagements and Sanads,* vol. II (Calcutta. 1931 p. 930).

and ultimately the *rājā* along with his wives were made captives and brought to the court of Khan. Mirja Nathan's[48] account is incomplete here. According to other sources[49] Udaipur (the capital of Tipperah during the period concerned) was taken by Nawab Fateh-Jang and the *rājā* was sent to the Emperor at Delhi as a prisoner where he was offered his. throne again on condition of paying annual tribute, but the *rājā* refused to do so and ultimately returned to Vṛndāvana where he died at the age of seventy-two. The Mughals occupied and governed the country in military fashion until after two and half years when they were forced by an epidemic to retire.

Conclusion

The tribal-Mughal conflicts undoubtedly forms an important chapter in the Medieval history of north-east India. It is gratifying to note that the vigorous resistance offered by the tribal populace and potentates of both lower and upper regions of north-east India to the Imperial authority of the Mughals during seventeenth century of pan-Indian character proved to be the most effective in stemming the tide of the progress of the Mughal rule in eastern Bengal and Assam. The chivalrous and glorious role played by them in this conflict despite several reverses proved to be a stumbling block in the way of the execution of the Mughal's ambitious project of extending the political sway from Lower Kāmarūpa up to the confines of China or Turkistan beyond Himalaya via Tibet and unfurling the Timurid banner on the wall of Peking. The saga of their dash, spirit, heroism, patriotism and gallantry, indisputably constitute an addition to the glaring examples set by other tribal brethrens, other mighty heroes, illustrious fighters and victorious monarchs of medieval Hindustan.

---

48. *Bahariatan-i-Ghaybi*, pp. 539, 554f.

49. Report of E.F. Sandys, cf. *Bengal and Assam, Bihar and Orissa*, (London, 1917) p. 466; Aitchison, op. cit., p. 193; W.W. Hunter, *Statistical Account of Bengal*, vol. VI (London, 1876), p. 466.

24

The First Indian War of Independence
1857–1859

THE period 1857–1859 may be regarded as the first phase of the Indian War of Independence.

The year 1857, no doubt, marked the commencement of the War of Indian Independence. The celebration of 150th anniversary of that war in 2007 at national level and commemoration of the historic events of the year of said war is really a matter of gratification for the people of India.

The distortion and falsification of the history of the first Indian War of Independence 1857-59 at the hands of some Indian and British historians have created some vacuums in our knowledge of the subject. Furthermore, the diametrically opposite views expressed by some historians and scholars regarding the anti-British Indian movement of the period under notice, and the succinct and imperfect account and hazy picture of the subject presented in some of the works do not render it possible for many of us to arrive at any definite or plausible conclusion about its real nature and character.

The British historians, who have called 1857 war a mutiny, sepoy war or sepoy revolt, include Charles Ball (*The History of the Indian Mutiny*, 2 vols., London, 1858); T.R.E. Holmes (*A History of the Indian Mutiny and of the Disturbances which Accompanied it Among the Civil Population*, London, 1888; *History of the Indian Mutiny*, London, 1898); J.W. Kaye (*A History of the*

Sepoy War in India, vols I & II, London 1870, vol. III, London 1876); G.B. Malleson (*History of the Indian Mutiny*, 3 vols, London, 1878-80); Kaye and Malleson (*The Indian Mutiny of* 1857, 6 vols, London, 1888, rpt. 1891); G.W. Forrest (*A History of the Indian Mutiny*, 3 vols, London, 1904-12, *Selections from the letters, Despatches and Other State Papers Preserved in the Military Deptt. of the Govt. of India*, 1857-8, 4 vols, Calcutta, 1893–1912); M.L. Innes (*The Sepoy Revolt*, London, 1897); R.G. Wilberforce (*An Unrecorded Chapter of the Indian Mutiny Being the Personal Reminiscences, Compiled from the Diary and Letters Written on the Spot*, London 1894, rpt. Delhi, 1976); P.E. Roberts (*History of British India under the Company and the Crown*, London, 1921, rpt. 1945); Hibert (*The Great Mutiny*, Delhi, 1884); Thompson and Garratt (*Rise and Fulfilment of British Rule in India*, Allahabad, 1973); L.J. Trotter and W.H. Hutton (*History of India from the Earliest Times to the Present Day*, 1st Indian rpt. Delhi, 1975); W.H. Russell (*My Diary in India in the Year 1858-59*, 2 vols., London, 1860); R. Aikes (*Notes on the Revolt in the North-Western Provinces of India*, London, 1858); John Lawrence and John Seeley. Those who called the war of 1857-58 a rebellion include N.A. Chick (*Annals of the Indian Rebellion*, 1857-58, Calcutta, 1859-60); A. Duff (*The Indian Rebellion, its Causes and Results in a Series of Letters*, London, 1858); and J.B. Norton (*The Rebellion in India*, London 1857). They all have admitted that the Indian revolt or rebellion of 1857-58 was directed against British imperialism. Kaye and Mallesson (two of the noted British authorities on the subject) consider it partly a mutiny and partly a war of independence. H.G. Rawlinson (*A Concise History of the Indian People*, London 1938, rpt., 1956) asserts that the "Indian mutiny was not a national movement." A. Llewellyn (*The Siege of Delhi*, London, 1977) also rejects the idea of a nationally organized movement for Independence from the foreign rule.

It is significant to note that while speaking on character of the upheaval in the House of Commons on July 27, 1857, Disraeli declared that the movement was a "national revolt" and not a "military mutiny."

The most prominent among the Indian historians who call the 1857 war a mutiny and a revolt is R.C. Majumdar which is evident from his very work, *The Sepoy Mutiny and the Revolt of* 1857 (Calcutta, 1957). Placing his reliance exclusively on the British records he wrote this work. He is of the view that the feeling of nationalism or patriotism was conspicuous by its absence in 1857. The movement of 1857, according to him, was more a mutiny or revolt than the national war of independence. He, however, considers it as a first step towards national struggle for independence (Ibid., pp. 234-37, 278).

The British General James Outram called it "an organized national movement and war of independence."

Karl Marx was the first scholar to unequivocally call the anti-British Indian movement of 1857-59 the first Indian war of Independence. The work, *The First Indian War of Independence 1857-1859* (Moscow, 1959, 4th rpt., 1975), by Marx and Engels, is based on their articles on "1857-59 national liberation revolt in India" printed in the *New-York Daily Tribune.* The said work is English translation of the Russian edition prepared by the Institute of Marxism-Leninism of the CCCPSU (Cultural Council of the Communist party of Soviet Union) in 1959. It was in use in 1959. The authors refuted the false contention of the British ruling classes that the movement was an armed sepoy mutiny and there was no involvement in it of broad sections of the Indian population. They laid emphasis on the fact that the movement started from the very beginning as a "national revolt — a revolution of the Indian people against British rule." They clearly stated in their articles that the revolt "brought together not only people of different religions

(Hindus and Muslims) and castes (brāhmaṇas, Rājpūts and, in some cases Sikhs) but also of different social standing." Although the British press left no stone unturned to hush up the participation of the Indian people in anti-British revolt, Marx asserted in his early articles that the Indian people not only sympathized with, but also supported, the revolt in every way. In his article "The Indian Revolt" (London, 4 September 1857), Marx proved beyond doubt that broad sections of the people — the peasants most of all — took part in the movement in a direct or indirect way. He categorically stated that the "Liberation struggle of the Indian people was against the domination of foreign colonialists." The colonial exploitation nurtured the Indian Revolt. He wrote, "sepoy regiments have murdered their European officers; Musalmans and Hindus, renouncing their mutual antipathies, have combined against their common masters; "disturbances beginning with the Hindus have actually ended in placing on the throne of Delhi a Mohammedan emperor"; and the mutiny has not been confined to a few localities." ("The Revolt in the Indian Army," *New-York Daily-Tribune,* no. 5065, 15 May 1857).

In his monumental work, *The Indian War of Independence-1857* (London, 1909, immediately proscribed, 1st pub. in India, Bombay, 1947), V.D. Savarkar has conclusively proved that the Indians' fight against the British for the Independence of their country from the foreign rule first commenced in 1857. He says that 1857 movement was nothing but a war of independence (op. cit., pp. 261-62). He has provided a picturesque description of the subject under treatment. His work abounds in valuable information about the heroes and heroines who sacrificed their lives while fighting against the British in the holy war of Independence. The said work is called "the Bible of the Indian Revolutionists." In his rarest of the rare works, *Bhārat Meṅ Angrejī Rāj* (*The British Rule in India,*

3 vols., Allahabad, 1929, immediately banned, 2nd edn., 1938), Sundar lal; in his *Eighteen Fifty Seven,* based on his study and research of nearly two years (with a Foreword by Maulana Abdul Kalam Azad, Delhi, 1957), S.N. Sen; and in his *History of 1857* (based on eye-witness accounts, Delhi, 1934), N.K. Nigam have also pointed out that the movement of 1857 was national in character, and it was no doubt the first battle of independence. S.N. Sen (*eighteen Fifty Seven,* Delhi, 1957, 3rd rpt., 1995, pp. 412-13) categorically states that it would be wrong to dismiss the outbreak of 1857 as a mere military rising. It became a revolt, assumed a political character and ended as a war of independence. Raj Bali Pandey (*Bhāratīya Itihāsa kā Paricaya* — Introduction to Indian History), Varanasi, 1963, calls it "a national uprising" and also "a war of independence." K.M. Panikkar (*Survey of Indian History*) is absolutely correct in stating that it aroused national awakening. All were "united in object — the expulsion of the British and the recovery of national Independence." One of the noted historians of modern India, Bipan Chandra, has also admitted that it was a struggle for freedom. In his *India's Struggle for Independence* 1857–1947 (Delhi, 1989, pp. 31ff, 40), he has asserted that the Revolt of 1857 was a part of Indias struggle for independence. That Revolt, according to him, was "a source of inspiration for the National Liberation Movement."

Tara Chand one of the greatest Indian historians of modern india, emphatically says that the uprising of 1857 was not a mutiny. It was rather a general movement to overthrow the British rule from the country. (For details see his *History of the Freedom Movement in India,* vol. II, ch. II, "The Revolt of 1857", pp. 40ff, 96ff.)

In fact, the anti-British Indian movement of 1857-59 first began as a mutiny as the sepoys (native soldiers to the British service or the men and officers of the native regiments of the

Anglo-Indian army) ignited its spark that blazed up into a conflagration. It soon turned into a revolt or rebellion and gradually assumed the character of a national movement (to a considerable extent) also called the first war of Indian Independence. The war of Independence had virtually commenced in 1857 and continued up to 1859 which can be well substantiated by going deeper and deeper into the entire course of events that took place during the period.

The people of India, including the tribals, started raising the voice against the British from the very beginning of their rule in the country. They wanted to frustrate the attempts of the British to consolidate their imperial authority. They were determined to throw off the yoke of British servitude from the neck of India. The British rulers started receiving blow after blow from 1770 onwards. Not a year passed without armed resistance to British rule in one part of the country or the other. There were, no doubt, several anti-British revolts in India before 1857 like those of Pahāḍiyā tribe of Rajamahal and Bhagalpur (1770-78), Tilaka Manjhi and his followers in Santhal Pargana, Bhagalpur and adjoining regions (1781-84), Mahadeva Koli tribe of Maharashtra (1784-85), Tamad of Chhota Nagpur (1789, 1794-95), Koyas of eastern Godāvarī region in Andhra Pradesh (1803), the tribal people of Chhota Nagpur (1807-08), Bhils of Gujarat (1809-28), tribal peasants of Bihar (1811-20), Bhils of Rajasthan (1812-17), the people of Bareilly (1816), Mahadeva Koli of Maharashtra (1818), Kols of Chhota Nagpur (1831-32), Mahadeva Koli and Bhils of Maharashtra (1830-48), Muṇḍas of Chhota Nagpur (1820, 1832), the tribal people of Orissa (1835-36), the tribals of Bastar, Madhya Pradesh (1842), Bhils of Gujarat (1846), the people of Barsat, Bengal (1831), the people of Faridpur, Bengal (1847), the fanners of Mopala, Kerala (1849, 1851-52, 1855), Kandlia tribe of Orissa under the leadership of Chaka Bishoi (1850), the Khāsī tribe of present Meghalaya (1828-39), the Angam, Nagas of Nagaland (1832, 1844, 1849, 1855), the tribes of North-East Frontier region and Upper Assam (1830-43), Santhal tribe led by four brothers, Sidho, Kanhu, Chanda and Bhairo (1855-56), and Bhils of Madhya Pradesh (1856-57). But the greatest revolt that shook the very foundation of British empire in India occurred in 1857, and for some time at least the fate of Britishers in India was hanging in the balance. The revolt of 1857 that broke out during the time of Lord Canning (1856-58) was an epoch-making event in the history of modern India. The first serious attempt to overthrow the British Raj in India was made in 1857. The year 1857 was the hundredth anniversary of the battle of plassey (1757) and it was prophesied that it would be the end of British rule.

Lord Dalhousie's (1848-56) policy of Doctrine of Lapse, Annexation, and Abolition of Royal Titles, Pensions and Privileges contained the seeds of revolt by the rulers, Nawabs and princes against the British. On the ground of his policy of Doctrine of Lapse, according to which the ruler of a state not having a male issue was not allowed to make his or her adopted son the next successor, and the sovereignty of such state passed back or lapsed to the British paramount power, he annexed a number of Indian states to the British dominion. The states annexed include Satārā (1848), Jaitpur in Bundelkaṇḍ, Sambhalpur in Orissa, Baghat, a petty hill state in the Punjab (1850), Udaipur (1852), Nagpur (1853) and Jhansi (1854). He also annexed Berar in 1853 and Oudh in February 1856 to the British dominion. The Nawab of Oudh, Wajid Ali Shah, was deposed, given a pension of Rs. 12 lakh and deported to Calcutta. The annexation of Oudh deeply offended the Muslims of northern India. It also created a feeling of anger and despair in the minds of the disbanded 60,000 soldiers of Oudh. In pursuance of his imperialistic policy, Dalhousie also abolished the titles and pensions of some native rulers. Nānā Sāhib, the adopted son of the last Peśwā Bājī Rāo II, was not allowed the pension of his adoptive father nor was he permitted to use the title of Peśwā. After the death of the titular Nawab of the Carnatic and the *rājā* of Tanjore in 1855, their titles and pensions were abolished. The *jāgīra* of the latter were also confiscated. The last Mughal Emperor of India, Bahadur Shah Zafar, was deprived of all privileges enjoyed by him earlier. It was also decided that on his death his family would have to vacate the ancestral palace and the fort at Delhi. This shocked the Muslims in general. The rulers who were dispossessed of their states and the Nawabs who were deprived of their privileges formed a sort of confederacy to fight against British imperialism. The feeling of hatredness towards the British started growing in the hearts of both Hindu and Muslims rulers.

The anti-British feeling started growing among other sections of the people too. During the time of Lord William Bentinck several rent-free estates in Bengal had been taken over which had caused a great unrest among the dispossessed *zamīndāra*s (landlords). Thousands of *jāgīra*s had been taken over in the Decean in the time of Lord Dalhousie. This was also a rude shock to the landlords. After the annexation of Oudh the *tāluqdār*s (mini-landlords) were deprived of many of their estates and they too were unhappy. Moreover, several thousand people were deprived of their livelihood. And so Oudh became a hotbed of discontent. The followers and dependants of the dispossessed landlords and the Nawab of Oudh were very much discontented. The *tāluqdāra*s and landlords forfeited the right of collecting the land revenue from the cultivators and, hence, they were deprived of their income as well as the status. Under the new land revenue settlement, the British started collecting the land revenue directly from the cultivators. The new land revenue system was too oppressive to be tolerated by the cultivators. The peasants also became the victim of British policy of economic exploitation. The British adopted stringent measures for collecting land revenue from them. The company had dealt a death blow to the indigenous industries with a view to encouraging the use of English goods. This had thrown many workers out of job. Not only the working class, traders and artisans but also the peasants, *tāluqdāras*, landlords and other people decided to join hands with the rebels. Each section of the society had some grievance or the other against the British.

Several restrictions were imposed by the British on the observance of the traditional Indian social customs and religious system, beliefs and practices. The frequent British onslaught on the Hindu religion and culture was greatly resented. The British Government was bent upon converting the Indians to Christianity. And, thus, the cry was raised, "religion and traditions in danger." The Hindus and Muslims rallied round under one banner to fight the British.

The Indian soldiers were very often ill-treated by the English soldiers and officers. They were debarred from holding the higher posts and ranks in the army. They were not adequately paid and there was no avenue of promotion for them, whereas the English soldiers enjoyed all facilities. This discriminatory attitude of the British towards them was not tolerable. As the British empire expanded, the Indian sepoys were required to serve farther and farther away from their homes without any extra allowances. They were even called upon to fight in wars across the seas. This they could not tolerate. The high castle orthodox brāhmaṇas in particular took it a sin to cross the seas. In 1856, the General Service Enlistment Act of Lord Canning was passed by which the sepoys enlisted under this Act could be sent wherever the need arose. The soldiers of the annexed states were deeply offended as they were thrown out of service. The disbanded soldiers of Oudh in particular were rendered idle. All these caused widespread resentment among the Indian soldiers against the British.

The reasons for anti-British fight were, of course, different, but the goal — to liberate the country from the foreign rule — was common.

All sections of the Indian people were seething with discontent. They were suffocating under *pax-Britannica* or British paramountcy. Their fulmination and fermentation knew no bounds. The fire that had been smouldering since long burst out in flames which spread to different parts of the country over a period of time. The spontaneous outburst of accumulated or pent-up anti-British feelings found its reflection in various forms of revolt. India was virtually sitting on the mouth of a volcano that was burning beneath. It did not take much time to erupt and explode.

The planning and preparations began for launching a movement or waging a war against the British for the Independence of the country. Nānā Sāhib, Tāṅtyā Ṭope, Azimulla Khan, Bahadur Shah of Delhi and his Begum (wife) Zīnat Mahal, Rānī Lakṣmī Bāī of Jhansi, Hazrat Mahal, Begum of deposed Nawab of Oudhi Wajid Ali Shah, and Kunwar Singh of Jagdispur (Bihar) were some of the prominent leaders who planned armed revolution against the British with all dexterity and ingenuity. They took up the organization of the movement in their own hands. The people in India and abroad were contacted to garner their support and mobilize public opinion against the British.

Nānā Sāhib sent his able aide or counsellor Azimulla Khan to England to plead or represent his case. He met there Raṅgojī

Bāpū, the leader of Satārā, who had gone to England to regain the state of Satārā from the British. Both made an outline of revolution while they were in London. Raṅgojī Bāpū returned to India. Azimulla decided to tour East Europe and other countries to get help for the Indians in their revolution against the British. He toured Russia, Italy and other European countries and also Egypt and Turkey to fulfil his mission. The history was repeated later by the Indian revolutionaries abroad in the course of their struggle for freedom. In the meantime, Raṅgojī Bāpū established contacts with the Indian princes, sepoys and the people and instigated them to rise in open revolt against the British. After the return of Azimulla Khan to India, Nānā Sāhib started organizing secretly the dissatisfied forces against the British. He started corresponding with the rulers of Delhi, Lucknow and Mysore who had been the victims of British imperialism. Nānā Sāhib accompanied by his brother Bālā Sāhib and Azimulla travelled from Kanpur to Biṭhūr, Delhi, Ambala, Mathurā, Agra, Kalpi, Lucknow and other cities on the excuse of making pilgrimage to places, but, in fact, his real objective of undertaking the tour was to establish contacts with the populace and potentates and to ensure that everything was properly organized. Secret meetings were organized at several places in which several *rājā*s and Nawabs resolved to rise in revolt against the British. Secret meetings were held at Red Fort in Delhi.

Bahadur Shah and his Begum Zīnat Mahal, Begun Hazrat Mahal, Wazir Ali Naqi Khan and others participated in the meetings and chalked out their strategy to fight the British. Correspondence began between the organizers of the movement regarding their planning and preparations. The letters were passed between Bahadur Shah of Delhi, Nānā Sāhib of Kanpur, Begum Hazrat Mahal of Lucknow, Rānī Lakṣmī Bāī of Jhansi, Commander Nabi Baksh of Patna,

Kunwar Singh of Jagdispur and host of other leaders. Maulavi Ahmad Shah of Fyzabad visited Delhi, Agra, Lucknow, Meerut, Patna and even Calcutta preaching holy war against the British. Nabi Baksh Khan of Patna kept up correspondence with all the chiefs for complete revolution. Contacts had been established between Delhi, UP, Bihar, Bengal, Bombay, Satārā and the Punjab. Ali Naqi Khan made an extensive tour of the whole of India in the guise of a hermit to hide his identity and conceal his motive. He instigated the Hindus, the Muslims and the sepoys to rise in revolt against the British. The Hindus and Muslims touching the sacred water of the Ganges and the Holy Quran respectively vowed to fight unitedly against the British Raj in the country. Likewise, Maulavi Alam Shah undertook extensive tours form Lucknow to Agra and instigated the people to start a revolution to oust the British from the country. The *tāluqdāra*s and *zamīndāra*s also contributed their mite to the making of anti-British revolt a success.

The Indian troops serving the British were contacted in almost all the cantonments for seeking their co-operation as the success of the movement greatly depended on[1] their participation. They were ready for the revolution by wide-spread distribution of red lotus flowers which they accepted hoping that "everything will turn red." They were instructed to kill their English officers and then march to Delhi to rally round under the banner of Bahadur Shah of Delhi. The Hindus and Muslims formed a combined front to fight their common enemy, the English, the usurpers of their lands and their kingdoms. *Capātī*s symbolizing the message of revolution were distributed among the common people to awaken them politically. They were asked to keep themselves ready for the revolt. Paṇḍits, sādhus, Maulavis and Bards were employed to carry the message of revolt from door to door and village to village. It was hoped that the year 1857 would mark the end of the British rule in India. Paṇḍits and Maulavis had already prophesied the fall of the British exactly a hundred years after the Battle of Plassey, that is in June 1857. Keeping these prophecies in view, the leaders of the movement had fixed the date 31 May 1857 for a national uprising against the British. But because of the Greased Cartridge incident that triggered the revolt of the sepoys, the anti-British movement began about two months before the said fixed date. The cartridges greased with the fat of the cow and the pig were supplied to the native soldiers asking them to bite their end with their teeth and then to fit them in the new improved (Enfield) rifles with deliberate intention to defile the religion of both the Hindus and Muslims. This news spread like fire among the soldiers of Native Regiments. This was a signal for outbreaks in several cantonments.

The 29 March 1857 was an eventful day in the history of Indian Mutiny. On that very day the soldiers of 34th Regiment of the Native Infantry at Barrackpur (about 30 km north of Calcutta) defied the order of British Army officials to touch the greased cartridges. They revolted against the British under the leadership of their fellow Mangal Pandey. After having shot dead Major Hudson (who had ordered soldiers to arrest him) and injured many other British officers, Mangal Pandey shot at himself and was injured. He was made prisoner, court-martialled and sentenced to death by hanging. He was hanged on 8 April 1857. He was the first to become a martyr in the holy war of 1857. This incident sparked off a series of revolts and rebellions in other parts of the country.

On 24 April 1857, Col. Smith ordered the sepoys of a Native Regiment at Meerut to use greased cartridges. Only five out of ninety sepoys obeyed his order and the rest eighty-five refused to do so. On 9 May all eighty-five soldiers were made prisoner, court-martialled at Meerut and sentenced to ten years' rigorous imprisonment for refusing to touch greased cartridges which added fuel to fire. On 10 May 1857, the soldiers of three Native Regiments at Meerut rose in open revolt. They shot down their English officers, stormed the jail, released the prisoners, set the English bungalows on fire and marched off to Delhi crying out that "the British Raj was ended."

The mutineers of Meerut reached Delhi on 11 May captured the city and put a great many Europeans to death. Then they occupied the Red Fort and palace and proclaimed the last Mughal king, Bahadur Shah, emperor of India. Delhi was declared independent. The independence of Delhi was a great success for the Indian revolutionaries and a major blow to the British rulers. Bahadur Shah declared *Jaṅga-e-Āzadī* (War of Independence). He exhorted the Hindus and Muslims to fight unitedly against the British for the Independence of the country. He issued a *fatwā* (decree) to "drive out the Ferangees (Britishers)" to attain the freedom of the country. The Hindus and Muslims accepted him as their leader, and having the unity of purpose and goal decided to fight shoulder to shoulder against the British. Mutineers from other cantonments in the country also began to pour into Delhi to extend their support to the compatriots. 11 May 1857 was no doubt a historic day. It proved to be a turning point in the history of the first Indian war of Independence.

On 14 September 1857, Delhi was attacked by the British soldiers commanded by General Wilson. The city (Delhi) was sacked and plundered by the Company's troops. Thousands of soldiers on both sides were killed. A large number of rebels and revolutionaries and many innocent people were put to death to strike terror in the hearts of Indians. The atrocities were perpetrated also on the inhabitants of Delhi of which an eye-witness account has been provided by the famous Urdu poet Mirza Ghalib in his book *Dastabu,* diary and letters dealing with Gadar (revolt) of 1857. After the terrible fight lasting for ten days, Nicholson with the help of a large number of British, Gorkha, Sikh, Punjabi and Kashmiri soldiers recaptured Delhi on 24 September 1857, though he himself was killed just at the moment of victory. Mirza Illahi Bux, a relative of Bahadur Shah, betrayed him and gave his secrets to the British. Bahadur Shah was soon made prisoner. Actually, he was captured from the Tomb of Humayun at Delhi. And his two sons and a grandson were executed before his eyes. Bahadur Shah, a sad and broken man, was brought back to Red Fort for his trial which began in January 1858. Delhi then being under the army rule of the Military Governor General Wilson, he was tried in court-martial fashion. He was charged with masterminding the rebellion against the British as is evident from the *Proceedings of the Trial of Bahadur Shah* (Delhi, 1895). The judgement of the military court was pronounced on 29 March 1858. He was sentenced to deportation. Accordingly, in November 1858, he was deported to Rangoon where he died on 7 November 1862, at the ripe old age of 87. His mausoleum, which still exists there, constitutes a monumental evidence to the tragic episode.

The Delhi declaration of war of Independence on 11 May 1857 had a far-reaching impact on the lovers of freedom in the country. The whole of northern India was virtually up in arms against the British rule. Kanpur, Jhansi, Lucknow, Bareilly, Varanasi, Agra and Allahabad in Uttar Pradesh were the main centres of events. In Bihar, Bengal, Orissa, Assam, Rājpūtānā, Gujarat, Maharashtra, Madhya Pradesh (Central India), Punjab (Sialkot, Lahore and adjoining regions) and North-West Frontier region (Peshawar) also some events connected with the anti-British movement took place. Here we shall first provide the details of events that took place in north-east India especially Assam.

The year 1857 was a landmark in the history of north-east India. The flames of the Great Revolt of 1857 also flared in north-eastern part of India touching the borders of Bengal. This revolt reverberated both in the valleys and hills of Assam. During the first fortnight of August 1857, the rebels from Bihar, Bengal, Uttar Pradesh and other parts of India reached Gauhati with the messages of Bir Kunwar Singh of Jadgishpur (Bihar), Nānā Sāhib of Kanpur and other leaders to convey to the people inhabiting both Brahmaputra Valley and upper regions (lower and upper Assam). They disseminated the news of carnage at Meerut, Delhi, Kanpur and other places and appalling cruelty inflicted upon the people there through the whole of north-east India and thereby kindled the spark of patriotism in the hearts of the people. (*Brig. General Shower's Report on the Military Defence of Assam Frontier, Sylhet and Khāsī Hills, vide volume of Letters received from the Govt. dated Headquarters Shimla, 29th October, 1862,* vol. 47 *Oct.-Dec. 1864.*) On 17 August 1857 the news spread about the coming of rebels from different parts of northern India to Gauhati. In September 1857, Maniram, Dewan of Kandarpeśvara, the grandson of Ahom king Purandar Siṁha, raised the banner of revolt against the British rule in Assam. The revolt first began in Brahmaputra Valley. The people inhabiting the valley extended their full support to Maniram. On being inspired by his Dewan Maniram, the prince Kandarpeśvara also joined the revolt. Maniram motivated the prince to overthrow the British Raj for which be appealed to him to instigate the soldiers of Gauhati, Jorhat, Dibrugarh and Golaghat to rise in revolt against the British as is evident from his letters. The soldiers soon rose in revolt but they were overpowered by the British. Kandarpeśvara was arrested at Jorhat and Maniram at

Calcutta. The latter was brought back form Calcutta to Jorhat where he was tried and hanged along with his close associate Piyali Barua on 26 February 1858 (Benudhar Sharma, *The Rebellion of 1857 vis-a-vis Assam*). No doubt, the populace and potentates of Assam directly or indirectly took part in the war of liberation of the country from the British colonial rulers. Some of the hill tribes also descended upon the plains to attack on British Sepoys. *(Vide Letters recd. from the Govt. of Bengal, Foreign Deptt.,* vols. 42 and 43, 1857.)

There were some repercussions of the revolt of 1857 in the Khāsī-Jaintiā Hills and North Cachar Hills of Assam. Exaggerated stories of fall of the British power caused some excitement amongst the Khāsī and Jaintiā tribes. They rose in revolt against the British in September 1857. Some of the Khāsī chiefs and the ex-*rājā* of Jaintiā began to intrigue with a view to recovering their lost possessions.When both Khāsī chiefs and ex-Jaintiā *rājā* became ready to fight, the *rājā* was ordered to live at Sylhet under surveillance and the Khāsī chiefs were pacified by friendly admonitions. (Benudhar Sharma, op. cit.; E. Gait, *A History of Assam,* Calcutta, 1926.) However, some Khāsīs and Jaintiās remained undeterred in their spirit and continued the revolt to drive out the British. The tribes of North Cachar Hills also took active part in anti-British revolt of 1857. Everywhere the revolt was crushed by the British. The Khāsī, Jaintiā and Cachari tribes convicted of mutiny or held guilty of rebellions were tried under Act XIV of 1857, and sentenced to death, deportation or lifelong imprisonment under section III & IV of Act No XVII of 1857 as evidenced by some of the British records (vols. of *Letters recd. from the Govt. of Bengal, Fort William,* vol. 47, 1857, vol. 44, 1858-59.)

The scene of revolt was also witnessed in the Barak Valley (Cachar region) of Assam. The news of mutiny at Meerut spread among the soldiers of 34 Native Infantry at Chittagong (East Bengal). On 18 November 1857, 300 soldiers of that Infantry mutinied against the British Raj. After burning their lines, breaking open the jail and releasing the prisoners and plundering the treasury, the mutineers (including Thangal General of Manipur, according to L.W. Shakespeare, *History of the Assam Rifles,* London, 1929) marching through Tripura and Sylhet reached Cachar where they were supported by three Manipuri princes (names not recorded) who were later arrested for entertaining the hostile design towards the British and sent to Alipur Jail. At Latu in south Cachar, the rebels numbering about 200 came up soon afterward and in fierce fighting that ensued they killed Major Byang of Sylhet Light Infantry. Twenty-six of the rebels were also killed. A few days later, the rebels were attacked by Sylhet Light Infantry under Lt. Ross. They together with some Manipuri princes headed for Manipur.

They were repeatedly attacked by regular troops. Many of the rebel soldiers were killed or arrested. Only three or four escaped death or capture. Thangal General was one of those who escaped and reached Manipur. He later took service in the royal court of Manipur state. (*Proceedings of the Govt. of India, Home and Foreign Deptt, 1857-58 and 1858-59;* vol *of Leltters from the Govt. of Bengal, Fort William, Foreign Deptt, 1857-1859;* also S. Choudhury (ed.), *The Mutiny Period in Cachar,* Silchar, 1981.)

Of all the leaders who played vital roles in the war of Indian Independence, mention may first be made of Nānā Sāhib and the brave brāhmaṇa Marāṭhā commander of his forces, Tāṅtyā Ṭope. Both fought together against the British from June 1857 to December 1857 in Kanpur and adjoining regions. They were directing the operations there. They received public support at Kanpur where Tāṅtyā had killed hundreds of Britishers, and the latter took revenge of this mass killing by hanging hundreds of Indians. The fort of Kanpur was captured by Nānā Sāhib on 26 June 1857. The capitulation and massacre of General Wheeler's force took place on 27 June 1857. Nānā Sāhib resisted the British army bravely and courageously, but he was defeated and General Havelock captured the city on 17 July. The city was recaptured immediately. Tāṅtyā Ṭope was defeated at Kanpur by Havelock on 16 August. He returned to Gwalior and reorganized his army there and captured Kalpi where he was joined by Nānā Sāhib. Their joint army attacked and captured Kanpur. A terrible battle was fought between their joint army and the British army from 1 to 6 December on the plains of Ganges. Thereafter, Tāṅtyā Ṭope returned to Kalpi and Nānā Sāhib fled away towards Nepal and never returned. Kanpur was captured by General Campbell in December 1857. After the conquest of Kanpur, the English wreaked a terrible vengeance upon the people. Tāṅtyā Ṭope, however, continued his struggle against the British with new vigour and valour.

The whole of Oudh soon became free. Only its capital, Lucknow, remained in English hands. At Lucknow, the revolt was headed by the young but very brave Begum Hazrat Mahal (wife of deposed Nawab Wajid Ali Shah). She was soon joined by sixty thousand disbanded soldiers and supported by civil population (Hindus and Muslims), *tāluqdāra*s, *zamīndāra*s and others. Kaye and Malleson (*History of Indian Mutiny*, vol. III, p. 340) have correctly observed that "the struggle of the Oudhians must be characterized as a war of Independence." The struggle for Independence commenced on 30 May 1857 and continued up to 31 March 1858. In the early phase of their struggle, the rebels besieged Sir Henry Lawrence and all other Englishmen and women and some loyal Indian sepoys in the Residency. Lawrence was shortly after killed by a shell but the garrison held out for nearly four months. General Havelock and General Outram came to their rescue. They forced their way into the Residency in September 1857 but were themselves besieged. A fierce fighting took place between the Indian forces and the British army at many places in Lucknow in November 1857. Havelock died fighing on 24 November. A terrible battle was fought at Lucknow between the Indian rebels and the British army in March 1858. Lucknow was finally captured on 31 March 1858 by General Campbell. Begum Hazrat Mahal personally took the field, but was defeated and driven to Nepal where she took refuge. After the conquest of Lucknow, the English forces massacred the inhabitants mercilessly. The scattered revolts in Oudh continued up to April 1859.

The revolt led by a Maulavi named Liyaqat Ali in Allahabad, and the revolt in Benares in June 1857 were mercilessly and ruthlessly suppressed by General Neil. The revolts at Bareilly and other places in Uttar Pradesh were also crushed.

A man who fought against the British undauntedly, indomitably, valiantly and relentlessly at the age of 80 was none other than Bir Kunwar Singh of Bihar. He was the ruler of Jagdishpur state. He was well known for his bravery and boldness. In 1857 itself he organized the Indian rebels in Bihar and eastern Uttar Pradesh and himself took the command to fight the British. All sections of the people rallied round under his banner and put up a valiant fight to achieve their goal. He played a notable role in persuading the Indian people as well as the leaders for driving out the British from the country. As a true patriot he aroused the feeling of nationalism among the Indians. While fighting against the British in his own state, he displayed exemplary courage. He defeated the British at many places. He continued his fight until his death in April 1858. After his death the struggle against the British was continued by his brother Amar Singh but he was defeated by a huge British army in October 1858. The state of Jagdishpur thereafter fell into the hands of the British. In his biography of Kunwar Singh, K.K. Datta, the famous historian, has described him as a freedom fighter.

The rebels in some parts of Uttar Pradesh and central India were led by Rānī Lakṣmī Bāī of Jhansi and Tāṅtyā Ṭope. The Rānī of Jhansi took a prominent role in the anti-British revolt and directed the entire operations herself in the territory from the southern bank of the river Yamunā to the ranges of Vindhyas. In order to suppress the revolt in that territory, Major General Hugh Rose attacked Jhansi on 21 March 1858. A fierce battle was fought between Rose's forces and the troops of Rānī. The battle lasted for eight days. The Rānī resisted the attack with the help of her forces. She showed marvellous feats of valour and fought gallantly, clad in male attire. Many Britishers were killed. In the meantime, Tāṅtyā Ṭope along with his 20,000 men reached there to help the Rānī. However, the British army defeated the Rānī on 1 April, and with all the power in his command Rose attacked the fort of Jhansi on 3 April. The Rānī again showed remarkable courage and bravery and by herself leading her forces defeated the British army and forced them to retreat. The British, however, with the help of some traitors captured Jhansi on 3 April, 1858. In spite of this, Rānī Lakṣmī Bāī did not lose courage and with her adopted son left the fort of Jhansi and advanced towards Koonch Gaon, forty-two miles from Kalpi where she met the leaders like Rāo Sāhib, Tāṅtyā Ṭope, Nawab of Bāndā and the kings of Banpur and Shāhgaṛh. A battle was fought at Koonch Gaon between the forces of the rebels and the forces of Hugh Rose. The British forces won the battle. Hugh Rose attacked

Kalpi on 24 May 1858 and conquered it after a week. Thereafter, the three leaders, the Rānī of Jhansi, Rāo Sāhib and Tāṅtyā Ṭope, made a plan to subdue Gwalior. They along with eleven thousand men and arms and weapons marched towards it in the hope that its Mahārājā (Sindhia) would join them, but the Mahārājā along with his minister Dinkar Rāo opposed them at Morar but were defeated. The army of the Mahārājā, however, joined the rebels. Gwalior was captured by Rānī of Jhansi and Tāṅtyā Ṭope. Meanwhile, On 6 June 1858, Rose left Kalpi and ten days later occupied Morar. The next day he attacked the rebels and defeated them. He attacked Gwalior and surrounded the fort from all sides. He defeated the army led by Tāṅtyā Ṭope. Thereafter, the Rānī of Jhansi assumed the leadership of the army and fought with great courage and bravery. But she could not resist the army for a long time. While she was running away on her horse, she was pursued by the British soldiers. She was overtaken by the British horsemen of the Hussars who fired shot after shot on her and made her thoroughly injured. She wanted to make a jump while she was on her horse but could not. The British horsemen attacked her. Her sword met with many swords but at last one horseman of the foe hit her on the head and then on the chest. She fell down, and ultimately died on 17 June 1858. No doubt, she died fighting against these British soldiers. She never accepted her defeat in the course of fighting the British. She rather went on fighting relentlessly till the end. The example of bravery set by the young Rānī of Jhansi of 22 while fighting against a foreign ruler goes without parallel in the history of the world.

Rānī Lakṣmī Bāī proved herself the best and bravest leader of the rebels. She had achieved her purpose and fulfilled her mission. The flame of patriotism was burning in her heart. Her fight against the British was not only for the defence of her own state but also for the freedom of the country. She was one of the brightest jewels in the necklace of Mother India.

After the death of Rānī Lakṣmī Bāī, Tāṅtyā Ṭope continued the struggle alone. Everywhere he took very active part in the revolt. His sole purpose was to drive out the British from the country for its freedom. He carried on a guerilla campaign against the British in traditional Marāṭhā style. While continuing his struggle for freedom, he crossed the river Narmadā and reached south India in June 1858 and started organizing an army in the name of Peśwā. The British Army pursued him there. In October 1858, he reached Nagpur and instigated the people there to rise in revolt against the British. From there, he reached Baroda. In Udaipur, about 50 miles from Baroda, he was surrounded by the British Army. He again escaped from there and while he was passing through a forest in Alwar (Rajasthan), a traitor named Sardar Man Singh helped the British make him prisoner. Thus the last great leader of the revolt was made prisoner on 9 April 1859, tried and hanged to death on 18 April 1859. He died the martyr's death. He, no doubt, sacrificed his life for a noble cause. With his death, the Indian struggle for Independence came to an end. This struggle began on 29 March 1857 and ended on 18 April 1859.

At all crucial periods of its history — ancient, medieval or modern — India was betrayed by her own sons. During the 1857-59 movement too, some Indian traitors sided with the British instead of extending their help and co-operation to their fellow countrymen. The rulers of Hyderabad, Gwalior, Baroda, Jodhpur, Jaipur, Patiala, Nābhā and Jind states remained more loyal to the British than to the leaders of the movement. The Punjab armies and the Gurkha soldiers also remained loyal to the English. Their loyalty helped the British suppress the movement. South India by and large remained indifferent to the uprising of 1857-59. The date fixed for national uprising was 31 May 1857. The rising, however, began prematurely which upset the whole plan. There was neither any mass movement nor any mass leader. The British Soldiers and Generals were more experienced and trained in the art of war than the Indian soldiers and leaders. Moreover, the British soldiers were better equipped with arms and weapons than their Indian counterparts. That is why they succeeded in crushing the movement. Most of the rebel leaders were killed in battles and wars with the British, imprisoned, hanged, deported or fled away, wandered here and there and lost their lives.

The Indian revolutionary leaders, of course, failed to achieve their goal — to free the country from the foreign rule. But the sacrifices they made, the blood they shed and the examples they set greatly inspired the leaders of Indian Freedom Movement (1885–1947).

The 1857-59 movement, no doubt, helped arouse the feeling of nationalism. It really marked the beginning of Indian National Movement which saw its culmination in the attainment of *Swarāj* on 15 August 1947.

Index